WHAT TO EXPECT WHEN YOU'RE HOMESCHOOLING

WHAT TO EXPECT WHEN YOU'RE HOMESCHOOLING

A MEMOIR

DAVID BATTS
& TERRI BATTS

Tabula Rasa CSG
W Melbourne, FL

To our children without whom this book would not have been possible: We are genuinely proud of each of you and love you with all our hearts.

For every reader who finds a piece of themselves within these chapters, may you find the courage and strength to parent and homeschool well - it is thankless but worth it.

To my mother-in-law who offered me ten thousand dollars to abandon my wife and son - shame on you. I wouldn't have accepted any amount of money to miss this journey.

To the people who intentionally made our life much harder than it had to be - fuck you.

Tabula Rasa CSG
7801 Maplewood DR.
W Melbourne, FL 32904

Publisher's Cataloging-in-Publication
    Names: Batts, David (David Blake), author. | Batts, Terri, author.
    Title: What to expect when you're homeschooling : a memoir / David and
        Terri Batts.
    Description: Melbourne, FL : Tabula Rasa CSG, [2024] | Includes bibli-
        ographical references.
    Identifiers: ISBN: 979-8-9904110-1-2 (hardcover) | 979-8-9904110-
        0-5 (softcover) | 979-8-9904110-2-9 (ebook) | 979-8-9904110-3-6
        (audiobook)
    Subjects: LCSH: Batts, David (David Blake) | Batts, Terri. | Home school-
        ing. | Education--Parent participation. | Alternative lifestyles. |
        LCGFT: Biographies. Classification: LCC: LC40 .B38 2024 | DDC:
        371.042--dc23

TELL US WHAT YOU THINK

Let other readers know what you thought of *What to Expect When You're Homeschooling*. Please write an honest review for this book on your favorite online bookshop.

★ ★ ★ ★ ★

CONTENTS

FOREWORD BY JOSHUA BATTS

When my dad first had the idea to write this book, he'd asked me if I wanted to write a foreword. I'm currently writing this after a fair bit of conversation between the two of us. I wasn't going to write one, but I would rather like to offer a few words.

The first of which is plethora. It means "a lot."

Humor aside, this project has meant a lot to my parents. It's not hard to find people who say they want to do all kinds of lofty things, especially writing a book "someday." That's why this book got written though: it meant a lot. Of course, something being meaningful to someone doesn't immediately make it valuable or useful. There's a reason the saying "the road to hell is paved with good intentions" exists.

If that sounds harsh, that's because it is. We like to think of ourselves as very thoughtful and insightful individuals. There's a million autobiographies out there rotting in landfills, written by people who thought their stories were more interesting or compelling or useful than they really were. Parents especially find it difficult to overcome their bias that sees their children as the tiny, helpless little ones they raised, and fail to recognize their own missteps later on when the children grow up.

The tree remembers, but the axe forgets.

Dear reader, you are the axe.

What convinced me to write this foreword is that much of this book is written from the perspective of the axe, which I believe to be vastly more useful than just another self-help book or success story. Valuable lessons are often bought with pain, while insight might require tragedy. Both have been true in my family. The only way I've found around this is to watch others' mistakes and try my best to learn from them. It sometimes works.

If you intend to homeschool, you have to ask yourself if it means enough to you to truly follow through. Then you have to ask yourself if it means enough to you that you'd look at your good intentions and recognize where you've been the axe. Lastly, you have to ask yourself if it means enough that, when you face difficulty, you're willing to listen to others like your spouse or children and swallow bitter pills.

After all that, could you still face your child when they're grown and listen to them tell you how you've been the axe? Your precious child, now grown and eloquent and intelligent and someone you're deeply proud of, reciting to you the sins you never realized? As you hear them, you understand the depths of what you failed to see and it cuts deeper than words from anyone else ever could.

I can't imagine.

That's why I'm writing this foreword though, because I know the co-author, my dad, does understand this. I put him through that, and this is what he wrote.

I hope it helps.

- Joshua Batts

CHAPTER 1

NOT YOUR PARENTS'
HOMESCHOOLING BOOK

How much does it cost to homeschool?
What's the best curriculum to use?
How do we handle socialization?

If these are the three main questions you have about homeschooling, this is not the book for you. This book is written for homeschoolers and aspiring homeschool parents who either know the answers to those questions or do not see them as the priority (the answers, by the way, are $500 or less per year per child, the best curriculum is whichever your kids use, and home education co-ops are a great place to start teaching your children to socialize).

So, you are beyond the basics. You may already be several years into your homeschool journey. Or perhaps you've known for years that you will one day homeschool your children, and as that day approaches, it's getting scary. Whatever your situation, you are not entirely new to this. And that means the questions you have are much harder to answer—questions such as the following:

- *How do you nurture the family dynamic and integrate homeschooling into parenting?*

- *How can homeschoolers provide their special needs children the unique care and education they need, if they can at all?*
- *How do we prepare our children to enter the hypercompetitive global job (and dating!) markets?*
- *Am I qualified to homeschool my children?*

If that's more where your head is, then this is the book for you.

You already know the reasons *to* homeschool and the basics of *how*. You're already looking for education options beyond the public school system and expensive traditional private schools. And you already have or know school-aged children you wish to insulate from an increasingly tumultuous public school environment, or you have children who have special needs that must be met. Furthermore, you probably already have all the motivation you need to avoid the public school system. The statistics are neither hard to find, nor surprising.

In the United States today, 80 percent of public high school graduates do not read, write, or perform math at more than a grade school level. Low reading scores show that the majority of US children are not prepared for future success.[1] Seventy percent of prison inmates did not graduate high school or are said to have low literacy. If your children cannot read proficiently by the fourth grade, they have a much higher chance of living a low-income life, being in the welfare system, going to prison, or living a drug-influenced lifestyle. Reading proficiency alone can determine a child's future success in society. It is a statistically common trait among successful people that they can read at a proficient level. The United States ranks 125th out of 194 other countries in literacy rate.[2]

If that's not enough, daily articles run across media outlets reporting school violence and bullying, educators being sexual predators, and of course—-school shootings. We see parents' rights being stripped away by teachers and school boards, who are not only supposed to educate children, but also protect the students under their care. The school system has begun to have a distinct feel of political weaponization against kids

---

1 - Annie E. Casey Foundation, "State of Literacy in America," AECF.org.

2 - James Burton, "List of Countries by Literacy Rate," World Atlas, August 12, 2020, https://www.worldatlas.com/articles/the-highest-literacy-rates-in-the-world.html.

and parents. No matter what political leaning one may have, any fight that uses children as leverage is not on the side of good, and it's not beneficial for the children they purport to be so concerned about.

As easy as it is to cast our public school system in the painful light of reality, we have not written a book to highlight the numerous and extensive ongoing issues with our public schools. This book is not meant to be anti-public school—we respect people's decision to send their children to public school if they choose (although we do not, nor should you, expect the same courtesy in return).

We are speaking to those parents and guardians who want and demand something different, something better for their children than what the government-run public school system, or even what expensive private schools can offer. If you already know that homeschooling is the best of all choices for your family, then the question is no longer one of *why*, but of *what* and *how*. What can you expect, and how will it go? How *can* it go? How *should* it go? How can families homeschool so that their children grow up to become successful?

Now, we personally don't measure success in money; sure, that's part of success, but we firmly believe that money cannot buy happiness and that there are many other aspects of a fulfilled life. A successful adult is fulfilled, happy, and responsible—just to name a few characteristics we use to define success besides income.

That said, bigger homeschool budgets are not correlated with better education, much less preparedness for adulthood. After all, the United States spends more money on "education" per student than any other country on the planet except Luxembourg, yet we're not even in the top ten in terms of an educated population.[3] Public and private schools graduate young adults who literally cannot read their diplomas. So, money has nothing to do with academic achievement, home or public or otherwise.

Our little family had a tight budget for several years. At the same time, homeschooling was not popular, which was reflected in the scarcity

---

3 - Melanie Hanson, "U.S. Public Education Spending Statistics," Education Data Initiative, last updated September 8, 2023, https://educationdata.org/public-education-spending-statistics#:~:text=U.S.%20and%20 World%20Education%20Spending&text=Schools%20in%20the%20United%20States,operation%20and%- 20Development%20(OECD).

of resources accessible to home educators. However, we were still able to find the resources we needed—even before digital technologies made relevant, helpful information available on demand. Now there is a plethora of resources for homeschool parents freely available on the internet. Not only do we want to encourage parents that they actually can successfully homeschool their children, but we also want to stress that they, as parents, can and will be able to provide an education for their children that is far better than anything the average government-run public school system has to offer.

Every family is different and unique, so what is right and good for one family may not be suitable for another. One particular curriculum or method is not good or bad, right or wrong; it simply may not be the best match for your family style, worldview, or the child's needs. We want to encourage and inspire each family to seek out and determine what fits best and works for them and their children. It's okay to reproduce the traditional public school format at home if that's what meets the needs of your family situation and your children. But, it's also okay not to do that—to do everything differently, or simply mimic the style while adding your specific elements of expertise for certain subjects. We are not going to tell you about "the one right way" to homeschool, because it doesn't exist. Do not expect that from this book. That, in fact, is what the public school system does, and the failure of that one-size-fits-all model has led you here.

Choosing public or private school comes with a trade-off. The parents are under no obligation to "figure it out," because they've outsourced their children's education and preparation for the real world. To choose homeschool, however, is to *insource* all of that, which means it's all on you now—you, the parents or guardians. That's why we wrote this book. We're going to cover why it is your responsibility to not only educate your children, but to also prepare them to be adults—a far greater accomplishment than any single school can provide. We want to inform people who are serious about the education of their children so they know what they're getting into. As we have always said that while anyone *can* homeschool, not everyone *should* homeschool, we also want to scare away those who are fainthearted, for the sake of their children. Regardless of where you currently stand, we have written this book to provide the insight necessary for you to make an educated and informed decision.

We promise that by the time you finish reading this book, you will have a more complete understanding of what successful homeschooling entails and the commitment required to see that through to the end, and will do our best to eliminate as many surprises as we can from the greater decision. We will tell our story, good and bad; our background; how we came to homeschool our children and accomplish it successfully; and the lessons we learned along the way. We'll share what our homeschool developed into for our family so that others don't go into it with ignorance.[4] We will give you a better understanding of what you are committing to so that you can know it is completely worth every bit of effort it takes to homeschool if you choose to do so.

When we started out, we didn't have a handout on how to do what we did. We were most certainly a worst-case scenario for the time, and we still made homeschooling work successfully. Through the years, by making mistakes, making corrections, and constantly refocusing on the direction we wanted to go in, we and our homeschooling evolved over time. We offered more to our children than traditional schools offered. Homeschool is education, yes, but it is also nurturing the family dynamic along with nurturing your children as the independent adults they will become. Homeschool will become your lifestyle. We'll tell you how to create a plan for your family and what obstacles you can expect to face. Our promise is that the person who reads our book will be able to make a knowledgeable decision on whether or not they are prepared to homeschool their children, and at the heart of this book, we hope to teach you not only how to homeschool effectively—but how to parent more effectively.

It is the parent's responsibility to prepare their children to be adults. It is our opinion that much of our society treats children like pets; a novelty that they feed, clothe, and provide shelter for but otherwise leave to watch TV, play video games, or spend hours on social media or with "virtual friends." This sacrifices time that would be better used mentoring

4 - Grammarist, "Home School vs. Homeschool (vs. Home-School)," 2024, https://grammarist.com/spelling/home-school-homeschool/#:~:text=For%20now%2C%20when%20home%20school,t%20become%20so%20without%20trailblazers.

our children in family relationships—something that they will use for the rest of their lives.

We watch parents proudly turn their children loose in public to speak and act in any way they choose, as though behaving badly is a positive trait. We would ask parents, "What if everyone here were acting like your child is acting?" Ultimately, we are informing adults with children what it means to be more than a babysitter. We discuss what a child should be equipped with physically, mentally, and emotionally by high school graduation to successfully enter the world and the global job market as an adult. Under the tight lens of our own society, our children may appear "fine." However, on the world stage, we have fallen behind.

This book may be starkly different from others written by homeschooling parents. In the ones we have sampled over the years, the focus is usually of a religious nature. There are a few secular homeschool books that focus mainly on academics. As it's often said that "kids don't come with a manual," we are writing the manual we wish we'd had as new parents and certainly as aspiring homeschoolers. We haven't seen or heard homeschooling and parenting presented in the way we do in this book. Our supporting information and the "why" is the memoir part, which we think is a good story in itself, because despite starting with nothing as kids ourselves, we successfully put our children on a path very different from our own and from that of our families.

In American society today, most parents seem to have a nonproductive understanding of what their role in their children's lives entail. That may not go over very well with some, but look around, look at the data. Kids are robbing, raping, murdering. The adolescent suicide rate has reached shocking levels. Children and young adults are hurting themselves and each other in record numbers. If parents had a productive idea of what their job is and how to do it, these problems would not be worsening as they are. Again, if you feed, clothe, and shelter a child, you're considered a good parent—despite parts of society crumbling around us. Parents must believe that if they alter their perception and see the value in the challenge of actively raising children, they can successfully pursue what we outline in this book. Your children can avoid being continually subjected to the chaos of the statistically negative masses of the public education system as they learn a more mature and constructive way to live life.

This is the first "do." Understand that first and foremost, you must perceive and treat children like real people, like the future adults they will become. True homeschooling begins at birth. Parents must not give in to the "goo-goo-ga-ga" baby-talk mentality toward their infant child. Speak clearly to your children. They are cute and sweet and impossibly needy, especially for love, but your child is programmed to absorb information rapidly. Don't speak gibberish to them, only to chastise them later for speaking incorrectly. After all, you're the one who taught them how to speak incorrectly with "baby talk" in the first place.

Conversely, your children aren't adults yet; they are still children, and they are always watching their surroundings, constantly soaking up all information in their environment. Exercise patience, communicate and connect with them, meet their needs as they require, appropriately shield them when needed, and along the way, set the standard of how you ultimately want them to act by the example of your own actions. In this and much more, many parents must "become better people," so that they may teach their children by example that which they did not learn from their parents or educators.

We found this part very challenging. We lacked a lot of information and knowledge, so we had to learn in order to teach our kids. This process is exhausting. Parents must believe that their children are worth the effort in order to maintain the fortitude to push through. Parents must believe that they can do it (another reason for the memoir portion of this book). Parents must believe these things with such commitment that they will not be deterred—not if, but *when* they meet challenges and opposition—because inevitably, they will.

So what must all homeschool parents do that is the same? They must learn to see their children as untrained future adults, not as "just kids." It's semantics, but it's a necessary perspective. Parents must recognize that their children rely totally on them to nurture, teach, mentor, and guide them to adulthood. The parent must recognize that they may not be equipped at the moment to provide all these things to their children, and they need to become equipped to do so. For many things, this means learning as you go, because after all, no one knows everything and you cannot learn everything all at once. Parents must recognize when their child is capable of performing new tasks and skills, and the children must be taught and their new skills reinforced while still being allowed to be a child.

But isn't becoming an adult ultimately the act of stripping away childish habits? So, isn't mentoring your child to adulthood really stripping away childish behavior? So, you tell us, what is the job of a parent? The curious nature of children and their desire to explore is the wonder of being a child—let them be a child when appropriate. This does not mean allowing them to act negatively childish. Do teach and expect children to act maturely when appropriate and necessary (events, public travel, etc.). Screaming during a ceremony is not the time to discover how a voice echoes. Plan a field trip to experiment with voices.

Adults can and should be kids at heart when it's appropriate. As parents display having fun in situations that are supposed to be fun, children learn when to be serious and when to have fun. How many of our world leaders can you imagine saying, "Hold my beer," before doing something immature? It is rare. Leaders in society learned the importance of self-control because it instills confidence in those around them. Most children are equally capable of a career at either a fast-food restaurant or a white-collar business—the biggest factor in where they end up comes down to how their parents parented. At the core of truly successful people, we see that they exercise self-control. How many successful people have we seen lose self-control just before they lost everything? You must begin teaching your child self-control by example, from day one. This cycle of **learning/teaching/mentoring** teaches your child to mature, and this cycle is repeated until they begin to continue this process themselves throughout life.

By high school, the child should be able to function mostly independently, with small corrections or sage advice offered as their life becomes more complex. When a child is eighteen, they should be ready to take full responsibility for their life. We know—we can already hear parents groaning disagreement—but what you cannot argue with is the fact that by the time a person is eighteen years old (at least in the United

States), they are considered legally responsible for their actions. One only needs to read the news to see what happens to children who are not prepared for adulthood. What your children need to believe is that if they choose it, they can accomplish it. You are sacrificing part of your life to train your child to become a successful adult who can competently enter the world, you provide the tools for them to do this. Parents must believe they can provide these tools and that the goals they reach throughout the process will totally, 100 percent be worth it.

Parents must also learn to give up some of their own wants and desires to be flexible. We had to figure that out. We had to determine what to teach our children and at what age—and we had to learn how to teach most of it. We were not trained "teachers." We had to learn how to schedule, make a plan, and set goals. By example, you are teaching your children the importance of these concepts as well. You and your children will make mistakes—which is natural and to be expected—which will help you all learn to work through challenges together, so they will in turn be able to handle their own mistakes as adults. Successful or not, the challenge will be met and accomplished on time because you have learned, taught, and mentored your children how to set goals and the importance of a schedule.

Parents must learn how to provide structure within their household for themselves and for their children. Children need structure because it helps them feel safe and secure. They won't need to wonder from day to day what is going to happen next; they will know what to expect. When parents provide a routine and set rules, children can feel more confident in these daily reference points and are able to respond to them the same way every time. Structure provides the building blocks for teaching responsibility, and teaches children how to be a part of the family and what their place is within that family. It also helps parents to know what to expect next—because sometimes you just want your day-to-day life to be easier.

Structure also includes the way that you, as a parent, communicate. Say what you mean and mean what you say; don't dangle carrots in front of your children to cajole them into giving you what you want. Parents should perform at a level that exceeds their children, but the goal is to equip them with the tools to eventually exceed you. We should act with integrity and honesty in order to build trust with our children. We want our children to take this seriously, but we don't want them to take themselves so seriously that they cannot connect and have fun as a family while learning, or are unable to connect with others in their lives. Kids need to be able to take you at your word. Don't be ambiguous. Parents should be a rock that the child can always cling to.

Parents must also learn how to administer education effectively, including life skills (how to teach, what, and when), communication/socialization (active communication with family members and others outside the family), character-building skills (self-control—how to teach and live it, including etiquette/manners, how to dress appropriately, and how to properly present themselves), integrity (such as keeping your word), gratitude, kindness, consideration for others, team building and camaraderie, physical fitness, health, memorization, as well as research and study skills. We address the specific areas of learning as supports, because children must be educated in more than academics. In addition to academics, we will cover life skills, socialization/communication, character building, and activities such as sports and hobby interests.

We won't try to convince you that everything went perfectly for us. We have regrets—things we would do differently. We didn't always provide actionable motivation in the best way. Parents must seek out how to externally motivate their children and how to cultivate internal motivation positively. Adults and children also need physical activity. Knowing your child and their personality, what would they find most interesting? What should they know how to do no matter what? What fits your children and your family? Where do you live, and what resources are available there?

Parents must learn to see value and excitement in their children's interests. They need your support and approval. Activities can be great bonding time—observe and offer guidance when you see them interacting with other people or performing new tasks. Learn about your children's interests and share yours, and take part in their activities if you can. We eventually joined our children in fencing and stage combat, even motocross racing, but we did not try gymnastics with them. Don't compete with them. Don't try to live through your children. Your children want to be with you, and if they want to help, let them. Help them learn to understand how to do something they want to do. Teach and show the consequences of actions. These experiences are sometimes favorable and sometimes unfavorable, but there should be balance, just as we experience as adults.

Join us on this journey, and along the way, you'll get to know us, the husband-and-wife team, not just as parents, but also as a couple who were doomed to failure (according to our closest family and friends). We find this is yet another untold story of the home educator's experience: Set aside parental roles for a moment; there is a married couple here! You know, the couple who met and could hardly wait until their next date or the next phone call? Nurture that relationship just as you nurture your children. Your happiness and fulfillment as a couple are integral to your family's success.

We will share brief scenes and lessons learned from our life as kids, as a young married couple, and our eventual homeschool journey. This way, you may capitalize on our tremendous efforts and challenges and also break out of the technology-centric, zombie-like world we live in, where priorities sit in endless streams of media. You're not going to read this book only to find out that we're antimedia or antitechnology or hold extreme beliefs. On the contrary, we enjoy emerging technology as much as the next person. But we will ask you to reflect on choices, such as choosing to watch a series on television or applying that time to something more lasting.

A certain popular office television series has 201 episodes. If the running time of each episode is forty-five minutes, that's over 150 hours of your life. The average daily time spent watching TV and digital videos in the United States in 2023 was 2.55 hours for TV and up to eight hours for digital videos.[5] Tracking of television viewing habits began back in 1950, when Americans watched TV for an average of one hour and fifteen minutes daily. Americans are now watching between seven and ten hours of

---

5 - Julia Stall, "U.S. TV Consumption: Daily Viewing Time 2009–2023, by Age Group," Statista, July 4, 2024, https://www.statista.com/statistics/411775/average-daily-time-watching-tv-us-by-age/#:~:text=According%20to%20the%20most%20recent,than%20two%20hours%20each%20day.

TV and digital videos combined, daily.[6] Outside of sleeping, Americans spend most of their time watching television.[7] Instead, sit down and spend that time reading with your children.

Our homeschool mindset does lead us to think in terms of quantity of time—because at the end of it all, the clock stops. How many thousands of hours did we spend on things that didn't matter the next day, or any day after? So far, most of our regrets consist of time wasted on pursuits of no value, not putting time into endeavors that truly mattered and were of lasting consequence. Learn to manage time, do new things, enjoy your life companion and your children.

Statistics show that people are currently more lonely than ever. How can that be when a simple click can put you face to face with another lonely person? Can we entertain that what we've been told and taught and accepted as good in life has led to a society disconnected from one another? Mainstream media treats relationships and people like trading cards. It's a sport nowadays to armchair relationships, breakups, hookups, and life failures like it's not a real person experiencing real pain. Is this who you want to be? Is this who you want your children to be?

"Homeschool? Your kids won't learn to socialize!"

The United States has record numbers of children who can't read, write, or do math—surely they've at least learned to socialize in their public schools. We should be the most sociable country on the planet if these people are correct about public school versus homeschool.

No, we have safe places in school because people are speaking, using their voices, and generally communicating—so perhaps the original problem was communication? Now we have historically increased levels of depression, suicide, and violence. The educational policy maker's response is to create more programs that do not actually address the original problems. Now, don't think we're bashing good programs, we're simply asking whether the public schools got better or worse with the

---

6 - Alexis C. Madrigal, "When Did TV Watching Peak?" *The Atlantic*, May 30, 2018, https://www.theatlantic.com/technology/archive/2018/05/when-did-tv-watching-peak/561464/.

7 - Kaia Hubbard, "Outside of Sleeping, Americans Spend Most of Their Time Watching Television," *US News and World Report*, July 22, 2021, https://www.usnews.com/news/best-states/articles/2021-07-22/americans-spent-more-time-watching-television-during-covid-19-than-working.

introduction of these programs? Have our children gotten better or worse with these programs?

We are comparative thinkers. If your home's foundation cracks and causes the roof to start leaking, our public school system's solution would be to pile layers upon layers atop the leaking roof. So much, in fact, that it causes the foundation to shift even farther and the rest of the house to begin shifting as well, resulting in issues like cracking walls. Program after program, and each time, it seems to get worse—do the programs make it worse, or is it that the original problem is not being addressed? We say the latter. The original issue is being avoided. They'll trip over that cracked foundation all day long and never address it.

Furthermore, the corrections they've made reveal an ever-emerging truth: they're going to continue until the system collapses because, for some reason we can only guess at, these people are blind to the results of their actions. There is not a place for everyone in their system, and we would argue that there isn't truly a place for anyone, except them, in their system.

The system shifts the arguments from the original point to something different, such as school violence leading to safe spaces, or hateful words leading to safe spaces, but the hateful words have only increased since then; the system's response to fixing the problem has only allowed it or made it worse. We've said that this isn't a book to point out the obvious and extreme failings of our public school system (including the ever-sacred socialization skills they spend billions of tax dollars providing, which they've obviously failed at as well), but consider this: everything we point out in this book, if you're choosing to homeschool, is all on you now. You have an advantage; you're not responsible for a room full of kids with ignorant, absent parents. Your children will be a reflection of you, well-rounded individuals who will absorb knowledge and wisdom for eighteen years, so that they can enjoy the rest of their years as adults.

We enjoy our relationships with our children. All the years of homeschooling have been rewarded in that our children were ready to be adults, and we haven't needed to continue to raise them or bail them out of tight spots. Our spare room is a man cave that can be a guest room. But what about us? What makes us special enough to write a book on homeschooling, and why should you read it?

We've been together and married for a long time. In Hollywood years we've been together for, like, two hundred years. As a couple, we're not lonely; we're not sad—we're fulfilled and happy, and that's after almost forty years of marriage. Now that we've raised our children, we get to act like kids sometimes, and it's fun!

The years of "sacrifice," as with anything worthwhile, have resulted in us being able to fully enjoy being empty-nest parents. We don't have an adult child living in the basement. It's our second season of dating. We have learned the importance of pursuing and maintaining a good marriage in itself, and with regard to how our children view relationships.

We would also like to be a resource and help people learn to enjoy their partner—to have a great life with each other during child-raising, homeschooling years, and beyond. We didn't accomplish something unique, but we have accomplished something very rare. What may be even more rare is that we are willing to put ourselves out there with the aim of giving parents and families more hope for the future than they have right now.

So with that, here's what to expect when you homeschool.

CHAPTER 2

THE WHY AND THE WHEN

Every homeschool parent has a reason for home education. Most of us have many reasons, but all of us have a first reason. The initial justification. Our "why."

We are no different.

First, let's start with David's why.

WHY DAVID DECIDED TO HOMESCHOOL

My parents were in their twenties and starting a young family. They had a son and a daughter before tragedy struck—they lost their third child soon after birth. It was understandably devastating to the family. My mom later told me the story and included that she nearly "died on the table." That had to rank as one of the worst events in their young lives.

My dad never spoke of it to me or anyone else, as far as I know. Dad stayed singularly focused on providing for his family—that meant work. Inside and outside the family, my dad's exemplary work ethic was his reputation, and he is probably the hardest-working man I've ever known. I remember him being up before dawn five days a week to check on and service all the supermarkets that the wholesale company he worked for had accounts with. He maintained positive relationships with not only the stores but the customers, too. Many of the older ladies knew him by name and he would personally help them as if he worked for the store itself. Occasionally, I got to go with him and help. He was at the stores all day, managing orders to get the merchandise inventoried, priced, and put out on the shelves, in addition to administrative duties. He would get home around sunset, eat dinner, and prepare all the orders to be submitted the next day. He was very good at what he did, and the company he worked for held him in the highest regard. He won salesman of the year consecutively for three years, and when people started complaining, they simply decided to cancel the award altogether.

My parents married young, but I don't know much about their earlier lives. They rarely referred to anything from their childhoods, and even that had its limits of sharing. My dad had a rough childhood, and my mom's mother was in a horrible car wreck that nearly took her life. Most stories came from my mom, whether the anecdotes were about her or my dad.

Dad just didn't reminisce. I knew he played basketball in high school and was a bit of a local star, but that came from other family members and his old friends. From what I'm able to piece together, my dad's family life was tumultuous. My dad's mom had a rebellious streak, and his dad liked to drink alcohol more than occasionally at the local bar where my dad, as a teenager, would often find him and take him home. Although my dad avoided abusing alcohol, I wonder if he didn't substitute work for alcohol with a similar obsession as his dad. He made sure we kids were always provided for and taken care of to the best of his ability. Dad wouldn't be caught spending time at a bar when there was work to be done. In hindsight, the problem was that there was always more work to be done and little time for anything else.

To help support his dad, his mom, and his sister, my dad took a job at a supermarket when he was fourteen years old. He would remain in the grocery business for the rest of his life, almost sixty years by the time of his death at the age of seventy-two. The personal perception never left him that if he wasn't working, he wasn't providing for his family. My dad attended almost two years of college after high school, and he dug graves by hand at night. He married my mom, quit his higher learning, and returned to the grocery business. He knew hard times and faced them by working hard or, if necessary, working harder.

I never knew my dad's dad during the years he struggled with alcohol. I only knew a kind and generous grandfather who delighted in his family. He loved fishing and was a talented woodworker. He would tell me stories for hours. His wife, my grandmother, made fried chicken that we judge all other fried chicken by. She worked for the same business for over forty years. My grandparents obviously changed dramatically from my dad's childhood, but by the age of fourteen, the die was cast for my dad, and nothing was going to change that. Remember this.

My mom was a stay-at-home mom. Mom didn't tell stories of her childhood, either, other than one about her mom, my sweet grandmother, getting into a car wreck and being ejected through the top of her convertible car. It seemed like there was a deep, dark, black hole in my mom's past. Yet no one would ever speak of it.

I've often turned to other members of the family to find crumbs of truth about my parents' past. For example, my grandmother would hold my gaze for a moment after I'd ask, "Did something bad happen to Mom when she was a kid?" After a pause, she'd always look away and say, "Your mom was just always different." To this day, I don't know if there was an event that made my mom different. Whatever it was, it's in a sealed vault.

We had a huge extended family, including wonderful aunts and uncles. I knew two sets of my great-grandparents. My great-grandfather Merle, the sweetest man you could hope to meet, was born in the late 1800s. He would take me to the pharmacy and soda shop to get ice cream. Everyone we saw would greet him warmly, and he was obviously respected in the community.

Grandpa Merle shared many stories with me, and I was fascinated by my family history. I learned a lot about most of my family—just not my mom. I still think that's odd.

My dad worked hard in wholesale, and at one point, he owned his own convenience store in addition to his day job. My mom never had to work, outside of taking care of the kids, until years later by doing seasonal work to earn extra money for Christmas or vacation . I think for my mom to have a job was embarrassing to my dad, like he wasn't good enough. Mom seemed perfectly happy with the arrangement. She was most comfortable at home. When I listened to my parents' after-work conversations, my mom often commented about conflicts she had with fellow employees.

It was four years into my parents' young family when they lost their third child. My mom and dad had a vision, the perfect American dream. Married, three kids, a house, and two cars in the driveway.

That's how I came to be. I was adopted. Mom wanted three kids, and Dad wanted Mom to be happy. It was that simple. Thirty miles from their semi-suburban town was a small farming community. It was the kind of place where everyone knew everyone, and everyone knew everyone else's business. Or tried to.

There, a young mother was struggling. She was raising three kids from two different men in a shack smaller than a studio apartment in the rough part of town. It turns out she was pregnant again — but not from her jealous live-in boyfriend.

Her oldest, a daughter, was a teen at the time and remembered the fights and threats clearly. "Bring that baby into this house, and I'll kill it," he said, and she truly believes the guy would have killed me. My biological mother would later have a fifth child with my biological father. The fourth (me) was the only one she ever gave up. The best I could determine, three of us out of five children had the same father and mother.

When she was nine months pregnant, the boyfriend dropped this young woman off at the hospital. He came back when she called—she exited the hospital without a baby.

"Oh my goodness, he's so cute!" the attending nurse said.

But the birth mother turned her entire body away—a monumental feat after childbirth—and said, "I'm not keeping it."

That was that.

Later that night, two grieving parents got a call—an unnamed newborn was up for adoption. A boy.

Me.

Mom and Dad picked me up from the small hospital, and I became their third child.

What I wouldn't understand until years into my adult life, was that I was expected to fill the shoes of the child they lost. The conclusion I came to later in life was that I was a constant reminder of that loss. My place in the family would never assuage my mom's pain, and in some way, my dad would never forgive me for it. Nothing would change that; I was the odd one out in a large extended family of all otherwise natural-born biological children. Siblings, cousins, aunts, uncles, grandparents . . . literally everyone in my large extended family was a part of the "bloodline," except for me.

My brother was a family favorite. He was handsome, athletic, loud, outgoing, and just the right amount of obnoxious to be endearing. He was the kid who walked into the room, and everyone excitedly said hello. I was the kid who might or might not be noticed, and I was shy anyway. It would take me years to make sense of my childhood. Thankfully, whether I acted out of intuition or knowledge, our children would be raised differently than we—or anyone we knew—were.

TRANSLATING CHILDHOOD EXPERIENCES INTO ACTION: BAD CAN BE GOOD

I did move forward and make positive changes in how my kids were raised, a good thing for anyone. But aspiring homeschoolers, be warned: your optimistic view of choosing to do things differently is often perceived as a slight to those around you. You're effectively saying to people in your life that they're not good enough. Perhaps it's your parents, who followed the well-worn path of everyone else, and your choices are saying they didn't do a good enough job. Perfect strangers who ask where your children go to school don't hear you when you say, "We homeschool our kids." Instead, they hear, "*Your* kids go to public school, and that makes you a bad parent and your kids 'less than.'"

Terri and I would encounter this hostility for many years. People would often draw us into a conversation simply to provide an opportunity to attack and berate us for choosing to homeschool our children or to provide an outlet for their anger about the topic.

You choose your path because of your convictions. Years later, when your critics have gotten divorced, their kids are in jail or rehab, and seemingly everyone is estranged from one another, you'll be vindicated, right? No. The one thing the broken family will still agree on is how much they dislike you. This will happen to many (not all) people who choose to homeschool their children. We had long-time relationships that fell apart and never recovered because people couldn't handle the fact that our private life was private, that our school choice was ours to make, and that we didn't care for a public discussion. On a positive note, these have become excellent lessons about respect and boundaries, both the good and the bad, for our appropriately aged children, as they will be for yours.

I interject these experiences into my homeschooler origin story for a reason. Without realizing it, my thoughts began turning toward homeschool as early as grade school, even though I didn't realize it. I had a fantastic imagination. At the time, this was the source of much of my trouble. "David daydreams too much." While I was trapped in the prison of school all day, five days a week, with angry, life-draining teachers, I dreamed of building things like airplanes and boats. I dreamed of adventures like the freedom of riding my dirt bike through unknown territory or being victorious in a race.

As a young kid, I would also daydream about school being interesting. Fun, even. Completing lessons in my core subjects was necessary, and by myself, I could usually complete them quickly. Our class, however, was based on what I came to call the "lowest common denominator." I would never be free of the assignment any faster than the slowest kid in class. If I was the one who needed extra help, I didn't ask, because who wants to be made fun of or publicly humiliated by a frustrated teacher? Why shouldn't school be interesting and fun? These memories would surface years later when we considered homeschooling.

I was sensitive to the anger of my teachers. It didn't matter if I was the student being yelled at and berated or if it was focused on one of my classmates. School forced me to be someone else, not trying to improve myself, but attempting to fit into a box for the teacher's convenience and approval. In the realm of public education, it seems that educators generally believe we all exist for them. It's about their time, their pay, their convenience, their tenure, their safety, their politics, and their personal agenda. They are willing to sacrifice a child's future to satisfy these personal wants and needs. That sounds harsh, but one only needs to look at the news, read statistics, and look at our mentally ill and deteriorating society to see that our children lack an education that is focused on them. Instead, we have a system whose primary purpose is to create jobs and job security for aspiring or entrenched educators. The public education system isn't going to change quickly enough to be of benefit to our children.

My personal moment of realization for what lay ahead in my life as a father and husband, happened late one night in our tiny one-bedroom apartment. I sat alone, my young wife and infant son asleep in the bedroom. I didn't like feeling helpless, and at that moment, I felt so desperate.

I didn't want my son to be in my shoes at my age, eighteen years old, with nothing. I didn't have possessions of value, and I didn't possess life skills of value to myself or my little family. There was a quickening for me, that my job as a parent was to prepare my son to be an adult.

I had no idea how to do that.

Anecdotally, you protect your kids by teaching them things like, "Look both ways before you cross the street;" "Don't talk to strangers;" and "If you need help, find an adult."Like most things we teach our kids, these adages sound good, and they generally are. This is what I was taught. This is good advice, but what comes after this? What does it look like to do more than ensure your child's safety, give them shelter, and keep them fed and clothed?

This is basically the point that our own parents brought us to and why we were unprepared to do anything except follow the instructions of our parents or teachers. We realized we had to define life for ourselves because what we needed at that point was so much more. We didn't know what we didn't know, but we were determined to find out. We were going to equip our children with all we could. Terri agreed. She was made for this, too.

There may be bits and pieces of my story that match yours. Or perhaps it's almost a word-for-word retelling of your life. That wouldn't be the first time another homeschool parent has told me as much. Either way, I have a why and a when, and you probably do, too.

And so does Terri.

WHY TERRI DECIDED TO HOMESCHOOL

Both of my parents had master's degrees and were employed in the government system. There was no question that education was a high priority in our household, and the state system that provided it was the only suitable form. I accepted school as it was presented, along with the expectations that came with it, and I did well academically—I fit into the box, and I liked school.

I was also a people pleaser. The work came easily to me, and I loved getting the approval and praise of the teacher. But I saw very quickly that it wasn't the same for everyone. The kids who did the best academically (like me) got all the teacher's attention, which in turn helped them to excel even further. The students who (for whatever reason) did not "fit into the box" did not receive help or positivity from the teacher. Oftentimes, these children were completely ignored or received anger, hostility, and disdain because they didn't perform like the good and favored students.

I attended first grade with a girl who always came to school dirty. Her hair was messy, her clothes were ragged, and she smelled bad. We all stayed away from her. She was very shy and didn't speak much at all. The teacher would often yell at her and sometimes even pulled the girl up out of her seat and spanked her.

One day this little girl stopped coming to school. I found out later that she had been living with her mother, who was very sick and couldn't take care of her. They had no friends or family to help. The girl was unclean and unkempt because, at six years old, she was responsible for caring for herself and her mother the best she knew how. Her mother died later that year. I never saw the girl again. However, the teacher remained teaching and was held in high regard as a good educator.

What happened to this little girl? What about her education, her well-being, her socialization—the things educators profess as the irreplaceable aspects of the government-sanctioned public school system? Not to mention the teacher's own individual importance within that system. Who cared about that little girl? Nobody at the school I attended, that's for sure. Almost fifty years later, I remember this very vividly.

That was not an isolated incident. I watched as countless boys and girls throughout my public school education were pushed through the system, treated poorly by teachers, administrators, and students alike without having acquired even an average education and very little, if any, socialization skills. What they were taught is that they didn't matter because they were not the favored students, and they were released unprepared and downtrodden into a world that simply did not care about them. They would have to fend for themselves in whatever way they could. I realized that the system works for those students who are willing and able to conform to whatever standards are in place, and those who don't or are unable to conform must keep their heads down and accept what is given to them.

The children, like that one little girl, are chewed up and spit out, and they don't count or matter. The risk that one of my children could end up like those kids was more than I was willing to take. What if one or all of our children didn't fit into the public school system box and were cast aside? Conversely, did we really want our children to fit into that mold? I knew I didn't want my children to just accept what the world decided to give them or be subjected to the rejection that little girl experienced. I wanted to provide my children with everything I could to nurture each of their unique qualities and abilities. I wanted to enable them to go into the world equipped and prepared to make a positive contribution and difference in society, and yet—that is exactly what many non-homeschool parents believed we were failing to do.

Why?

"Socialization."

It's the buzzword used to argue against homeschooling. Almost every single time homeschooling comes up in a conversation, the first thing people ask is, "What about your children's socialization?" Considering my parents and my household, I should have been (and was) perfectly suited to attend public school. However, my first negative memory regarding school centered around socialization. I have no idea what determined what children were at the top of the group socially, but cliques were already in place when I started first grade.

In order to have friends and be accepted by the group, you had to play the games. This particular game was that one person was singled out each week, and everyone ostracized that person during that time. No one talked to or played with that person all week long. It was understood. Everyone knew it, and everyone complied. Then the next week, they were back in the group and got to join in the "hating" of someone else. We actually said that. "We hate [insert kid's name here]."

This nasty game lasted throughout grade school. Anyone who didn't do it was completely ostracized, meaning that their punishment for non-compliance was not just one week of hatred but every day, indefinitely. I wanted to be accepted by the group, so I went along. Of course I didn't like being treated this way, and I also knew deep down that this was not the way we should treat other people, either.

Everyone, especially children, just wants to be accepted by the people they spend the most time with, whether at home or at school. They just want to know they're good enough, and they'll do whatever they must do to get that affirmation, even if it includes gaslighting, hazing, and manipulation. If this is what people mean by "socialization," then the government-run public school system is the perfect place for their children to be exposed to that.

I would have thought that I was adequately prepared to be a parent. As a young teen, I babysat for several families, and I also cleaned houses for extra money. I had chores growing up, which I did because I was supposed to. As a people pleaser, I wanted my parents' approval, but I also received an allowance and got to hang out with my friends if I did everything on my list.

What I didn't realize at the time was that I was taught to do what I was told, not to think for myself. I was rewarded because I made my parents' lives easier. I wasn't taught how to become an adult myself. I wasn't taught why chores were done or what needed to be completed to successfully run a household.

Largely, this book is about being able to see (and point out) the lessons in life that our parents and teachers let pass by. I was good at doing chores, but to put what I'd learned at home and school together to actually run a home required a totally different perspective.

I was eighteen when our first son was born. I would play with him, read and sing to him, laugh with him, and smile at him. I fed him and kept him clean, dry, and comfortable. I slept when he slept. Although those things are great, I had no concept of what being a homemaker looked like. I didn't know how to manage my time to keep our home clean, wash clothes, and have dinner ready when my husband got home from school and work. I had gone from being a teenager living at home with my mom and sister to being a teenage wife and mom in my own place. This certainly wasn't what I envisioned my life being and was definitely not what I wanted for our children.

Before I got pregnant, David and I had talked about our future; we were planning on getting married and spending our lives together. But our romantic dream life didn't start out like this. Still, we were determined to figure it out. As hard as our beginnings were individually and as a couple, I wouldn't change a thing. Those beginnings helped shape us and our family. As we started down the same path most families take, which leads to public school, our beginnings provided us with a beneficially unique perspective of marriage and parenting that ultimately brought us to the decision to homeschool our children.

HOW WE DECIDED TO HOMESCHOOL, TOGETHER

Our (David and Terri) perfectly imperfect stories made us a fit—as spouses, as best friends, and as home co-educators. When we became parents at the age of eighteen, it became very clear to us both that we were not adequately equipped to be competent (let alone successful) adults and parents. We wanted our children to be better equipped to enter into adulthood than we were. We asked ourselves, What does being a parent mean? We were struggling individually and together with what roles we played as spouses and as parents. In spite of all our years of public school, we didn't know how to effectively communicate our thoughts and feelings with each other or those around us in a constructive way. We each knew in our hearts that we were blind to the task that lay ahead. And we wanted to change that.

SCHOOL BEGINS

Like all good parents, we were excited (and a bit nervous) for our first-born to start school. We had been working with him, and he had all the necessary skills a child needs to start kindergarten. He could dress and groom himself, go to the bathroom by himself, tie his shoes and put on outer garments by himself, sit and listen quietly to a story, be polite and follow the teacher's instructions. He knew shapes, sizes, colors, numbers, and the alphabet by sight and sound. He could already read; he knew his full name, birth date, and address; and he was learning to write. That's normal, right?

We had already begun to homeschool but didn't realize it. Our five-year-old son knew medical terms like *patella, femur, popliteal fossa, radius, ulna,* and *sternum,* for example . . . all the major bones and corresponding parts of the body. We were confident that we had done everything we could do to set him up for success, and now it was time to pass the baton to the school and let them do their "magic."

Although we'd already determined that we didn't want him in the public school system, we couldn't afford to send him to a private school. My mother, for her own reasons, offered to pay for the first year of our firstborn son's tuition at a private Catholic school. Catholic school wasn't exactly what we had in mind, but we felt it would still be superior to public school.

Kindergarten went very well for our son. The teacher liked him because he could read better than any other student and was able to complete his assignments easily without much assistance. He would be required to sit and wait for the other students who needed more of the teacher's attention, so she tried to find books for him to read and work-sheets that challenged him to keep him busy. The busy work continued into first and second grade, which led not only to our son's boredom in the classroom but also to him being neglected academically as the teachers pushed him aside to take care of the other more needy students. This eventually caused problems. The teacher and school reasoned that it was fine for our son to sit and degrade until the rest of the class caught up. It was fine to rob him of his early progress in the interest of the group.

David and I had no idea that anything was wrong. We liked the teachers and thought we had a good relationship and communication with each of them. Each teacher consistently told us that our son was an excellent student. We continued to read with him, and everything seemed normal to us. Looking back, there were changes in his behavior that, had we understood, indicated he was struggling. But we were relying on the school to communicate any problems to us. We thought (incorrectly) that the school would want to partner with us in our child's education. We thought that at the very least, our son's teacher cared about him and his education. They didn't say a word to us. They apparently didn't want us to know.

By third grade, however, the school now wished to discuss with us behavior issues that had developed. Additionally, the school officials decided they should now inform us that he was struggling with math. They told us he was having trouble with multiplication and division. As we looked deeper into the situation, we found he was weak with addition and subtraction as well. We finally came to the full realization that the school had not been doing its job of teaching our child as we'd thought, and his teachers had chosen to conceal from us that he was struggling academically until it became a problem for them. We were also hearing negative and concerning stories from our extended family members about their experiences in the state-run schools which further reinforced our decision to avoid the public school system. We needed more options than public or private education.

Just like you, we knew from the beginning that we wanted to give our kids the best education and chance at a rewarding life. We now understood that if we truly wanted a better education for our children than the traditionally offered public school model, it was up to us to provide it. We made the decision (not lightly) to homeschool. We truly believed we could do it.

But no one else did.

CHAPTER 3

"YOU DON'T REALLY THINK YOU'RE QUALIFIED FOR THAT, DO YOU?" AND OTHER INSULTS AND OBJECTIONS YOU'LL FACE

OPPOSITION FROM FAMILY AND FRIENDS

Opposition to our intent to homeschool began right from the start. According to many people at that time, we were young and foolish and had no business being married in the first place. The consensus was that if we wanted to destroy our lives, that was fine, but we didn't have the right to destroy our children's lives, too.

When we say opposition, we mean hateful, cruel, personal attacks from family, friends, and even the occasional stranger. This is the true measure of how firmly you believe in your ability to take charge of your children's livelihood. In our case, it cost us nearly all of our family relationships. There were periods of years when we had no family ties. We had grandparents who enjoyed their great-grandson, but we had been threatened by other family members to stay away from them. Our little family existed on an island.

As for friends, we didn't have any—not anymore. One of the most popular arguments for public school is the "strong bonds" built with peers, yet the people we spent thirteen years with in the public school system simply vanished. We were ostracized by all of our old friends and their parents, whom we'd known our whole lives.

Would that make you change your mind about homeschooling and bow to the desires of outside influences? You may need to choose which is more important to you, your friends or your child's future. We stayed the course, unsure if we could endure what was to come.

Even before we decided to homeschool, we were constantly reminded by others that we were doomed to failure. This began when a Catholic priest refused to marry us because our union at such a young age would be a mockery of the institution of marriage and the sanctity of the church. Our Catholic family members agreed! As a couple, we decided that we would do a better job of preparing our children than our parents (and the public school) had, and no matter what, no one would come before us or our kids. Not friends, not family, not the church, not strangers, not the media. Nothing was more important to us than our little family and our mission to raise our children to be prepared for the world.

OPPOSITION FROM STRANGERS: DAVID'S EXPERIENCE

Opposition from strangers is an interesting thing to me. A stranger certainly has no vested interest in our lives or the decisions we make. Why are they so passionate about the homeschooling issue? In my view of the world, there needs to be diversity, including homeschoolers. If everyone attended the mainstream school system, everyone would have the same general viewpoint.

Speaking for myself, the responses I get from publicly educated individuals, including those who attended public universities, include similar talking points about numerous topics, including homeschooling. If I try to deepen a conversation about homeschooling, I'm usually met with hostility or at least condescending dismissal. I may find myself in conversation with a stranger, and as soon as the word "homeschool" is spoken, I get a comical facial expression and something like, "Good luck with that. I feel bad for your kids." Or, "Why? My kids go to public school. What's wrong with public school?" To which I may reply, "You had a bad experience with homeschooling?" And no, they haven't.

Somewhere along the line, people have been indoctrinated that homeschooling is bad, and they often repeat what they have heard—things like, "Homeschoolers are religious zealots." This illustrates a detail many people don't notice in life: too often, we're taught something in school, we're told something on the news, or we read something on social media, and then we recite it as fact in an effort to sound informed. If someone attempts to probe beyond these statements, however, most people aren't capable of discussing a topic to the smallest degree to support their position.

We all want to be accepted. Without knowing any different than what we've heard, we argue over things that have no bearing on our lives. We end relationships over these things. To me, abortion is a great example. I've heard a great many people with passionate opinions on the topic, but to my knowledge, few go beyond "my body, my choice" or "abortion is murder." This book is written for someone of either view because the point here isn't what side of an issue you stand on. As a homeschool parent, you're likely to encounter people who can't form an opinion beyond "homeschooling is bad." Part of homeschooling is to teach your children not to be ignorant in the topics they feel passionate about—or to recognize their lack of knowledge and go inform themselves to support their viewpoint.

It seems that most people are willing to argue, but it's a rare person who can do so intelligently. People are most comfortable being told what to think and how to think. These aren't the people to discuss homeschooling with; they don't have an opinion or argument beyond repeating what they've been told. We homeschooled our children to keep their mouths shut unless they can communicate something beyond an opinion. Ever since our children became teenagers, I've known I better have my facts together if I'm going to discuss a controversial topic with them. More than once, they've taken me to task on a topic! It's embarrassing, but I'm proud of them for knowing opposing sides of an issue and being able to intelligently support their perspective with facts.

Very rarely over the years, we've seen negative news that includes kids who were homeschooled. Conversely, we can't read the news on any given day without seeing school killings, predatory teachers, abusive teachers, abusive students, and violence on top of violence across the nation in public schools, along with being nearly guaranteed that a child won't graduate with the ability to compete in the global job market.

Third-world countries are performing better than the United States in public education results, yet there are strangers who will attack you for homeschooling, ignorant of the statistics of our public education system. Do people feel they have the right to insult you simply because you homeschool? Do they believe you're fair game because you're not part of the system? Or do they think they should be advising you? It's a mystery to me.

Just remember, these people are not obliged to take responsibility for the results of their "advice." They certainly will not be responsible for your children in the future. These people disappear after they give their advice—they won't be there when you need help, only when they wish to judge you.

These are the same people who will sue the school system because their child cannot read their own diploma. The public education system teaches us to believe what we are told by that system and to do what we're told to do. Critical thinking is not an attribute they want students to possess, so it simply isn't taught.

If you think you're going to inform family, friends, or even educators that your child takes all of the same tests required of public school students and scores in the top percentiles (in one case with one of our kids, it was the top 0.5 percent) and you think they'll be impressed, think again. Family/friends/strangers may reply, "Well, it's because he/she is so smart," or "He/she got lucky." Of course it has nothing to do with the fact that you homeschool. Yes, we've heard that more than once, and occasionally, we still do.

Honestly, these exchanges are exhausting and a mental distraction of no value. Because "it's none of your business" can come off as more hostile and defensive than we want to be, we took a different approach. Avoiding a fruitless conversation became my main goal of these exchanges. We began to inform people that "our children attend a small private school" or, as they got older, "our teenagers are in college . . . yes, smart kids." No mention of homeschool required, resulting in no further exhaustion and distraction from the good work you and your children are doing. Ultimately, although you owe no explanation to people, be prepared for these types of exchanges.

This hostile attitude towards you and your homeschool will be present on some level throughout the entire time you're homeschooling; it will never *not* be an issue.

OPPOSITION FROM WITHIN YOURSELF

Even if you are the most dedicated home educator, there will be times when you question yourself, your ability, or your decision to homeschool. This is why we strive not to entertain conversations with negative people, no matter who they are. These exchanges will eventually cause you to doubt yourself, and like anything in life, a threat from within is potentially the most destructive. You can do more to destroy your own efforts than anyone because you're the only one who can lose focus and give up.

If you have doubts, what are they? Identify them and address them. Very often, early on, when we didn't know how to do something (usually stacked on top of other things we were struggling with), we would ask ourselves, "Why are we doing this?" We would attack ourselves from within almost daily! Don't fall for it. The public school system has been consistently failing for decades, and school officials keep pushing on like everything is perfectly fine. Children fail tests, no big deal. Children are assaulted or raped, no big deal; it doesn't happen *that* often. Public education is good, in fact. Most of the bad things aren't really "that bad." Kids are resilient! A little bullying is good for them.

What you should recognize and do differently is this: after identifying your doubt or problem, correct it. What do you lack? Find a way to get whatever it is, and then you won't lack it. Homeschoolers must be problem solvers. We don't get decade after decade of endless students to experiment on. We should strive to get it right the first time.

This makes our already difficult work harder. Especially when those in a position to boost your confidence only want to drag you down.

"BUT I NEED ENCOURAGEMENT!"

Years after we first began our homeschool adventures, my (Terri's) mother would brag about my sister's children and all that they were doing in school. Of course I questioned our decision. Are we denying our children all these wonderful school experiences? What are they missing by being homeschooled? And the biggest question of all, "Are we ruining our children?" This particular question plagued me because it was an accusation that came directly from my mother. I learned to use this accusation to challenge myself, and it became a driving force to help me keep going and to the best of my ability, seek to find the path of success that fits each of our children.

A certain amount of self-questioning is natural and healthy. Perhaps a better question is, "What are our children gaining by being homeschooled?" "What do we want them to come away with when we're finished?" By focusing on the positive instead of the negative, we can use these questions to help us improve for our kids. We both knew that what we were doing was right for us and for our family. We knew that we could provide a better and more complete education for our children than they could receive elsewhere.

We kept pushing forward, and we continued to reassess our decisions each year. That helped us to continue without reservation. What was working? What was not? Did we miss anything? What changes needed to be made? Did we need outside help in certain areas? What resources could we utilize for new or more advanced subjects as our children got older?

We never made a blanket statement that we were going to homeschool all our children all the way through school, no matter what. We would simply say that we were homeschooling for another year and would reassess at the end to determine if we would continue the next year. That helped us be accountable for and feel good about our decision to continue, and it also put some people's questions to rest.

IT GETS BETTER IF YOU MAKE IT BETTER

By the time we had decided to homeschool, I (David) had built a significant wall between myself and the world. I was confused by the harsh response our families offered us for not knowing essential life skills that they had failed to teach us. It was their job as parents to equip us for life, but they didn't, and therefore, we struggled blindly. Our experience was a stark contrast to the "family sticks together" mantra. While I was able to acquire an education and job experience, my life skills outside the home were still developing. I think there was an awkwardness about me as I was essentially trying to relearn and overwrite what I'd been taught as a child. I kept everyone at a distance to mask my self-perceived social deficiencies. Every day, for more than ten years, seemed like a battle and it took its toll on me.

I was twenty-seven years old when we decided to homeschool our oldest son. In my viewpoint, it was somewhat about survival, both mine and our son's. I was equipped with what public school had taught me, whatever information I picked up from a hardworking (absent) dad and unstable mother, and lessons learned from my own numerous mistakes in my twenty-seven years. That was it.

CRITICS AND CYNICS

We didn't so much "announce" that we planned to homeschool as much as people found out in conversation at a family gathering. It was obviously the topic of much gossip that evening. As gossip goes, idle talk and opinions bolster the confidence of certain personalities, and finally, we received a statement from a family member akin to an announcement.

"Sooo," they boomed with a smirk. "I hear you two are planning to homeschool your kids." I swallowed, knowing everyone was watching. "You barely made it through school yourself." they continued. "How are you supposed to teach your kids?"

What I recognized, even at my relatively young age, was that our families weren't saying or doing anything out of real concern for us or our kids. One family member, vehement in her outward disdain for me (and also for us as a couple), regularly ridiculed us at large family gatherings for thinking we were "smart enough" to educate our children. She conspired with another family member to compel child services to visit us in an effort to have our children removed from our home, because in their opinion it was illegal and borderline abusive for us to keep our children out of public school.

Think about that for a moment. This same person would provide "party beer" to underage family kids and friends. She was also aware that her own daughter was molested by a close family member and did nothing to protect her daughter from them. Her ex-husband was an unemployed alcoholic. Their young school-aged children reminded me somewhat of Augustus Gloop in *Charlie and the Chocolate Factory*. The same mother who could approach us in the most judgmental, aggressive, and cruel ways would, if her children whined, open a bag of candy for moments such as this. To her, her very young children were obese because of genetics. It was outrageous to suggest that her children's poor health had anything to do with the literal bags of candy she fed them every day as bribes to get what she wanted. This unhinged woman destroyed everything she involved herself in. We took notice.

A ROOM FULL OF ROCKING CHAIRS AND YOU'RE THE CAT

This is a chapter about opposition. My (David) last example is one of the worst, most extreme cases in our decades of homeschooling.

It also takes me back to sheltering my children from those I believed I could trust most. Maybe the first time you decide to relax and leave the kids with a trusted family member, the kids you get back won't be the same. They'll have been exposed to events that will change who they are.

I've spent long hours deliberating whether or not to tell certain stories. How shocking is enough to convey the importance of our point? The point to walk away with is this: those who judge you harshly are showing you how little they care about you and your children. At every turn, when your children succeed, these people will maintain their negativity toward you. Looking back, did the young versions of David and Terri make a sound decision? Did we stand for what was right and good for our children and their future lives? We think we did. Were the many detractors proven wrong? We think they were. If we could change anything, it would be to slow down and live more in the moment being present with our children. To wake up every day more focused on enjoying each day rather than continually living in the future, worrying about what was next.

The extensive adversities you will likely encounter as a homeschool parent can feel endless. It's especially easy to focus on the acts of a poisonous family member, and it's natural to be pulled under by judgments from those around you. But no matter what you do or how you respond, you will be seen by your children. Your confidence in acting as your child's teacher, mentor, and parent may wane, and your child will notice. No part of this journey is about being perfect; it's about being mindful of your goals—your child's future—and noticing anything that is counter to that end.

Look your child in the eyes and see them looking back at you. You are the center of their universe. Those eyes are looking to you for answers. You are the person they were designed to look at and look to for survival. Now look in the mirror. That person looking back at you has full responsibility for that child. What are you going to do to protect them and teach them how to have a rewarding life?

That is *all* that matters.

WELCOME TO LEADERSHIP

I (David) had been taught to care what everyone thought. I'd been taught to do what I was told. I'd been taught not to offend people. I'd been taught to be polite at all costs.

I believe that in general communication, cursing is resorting to the language of the base and ignorant walks of life. Admitting that, I refer back to all of the things I had been taught with a resounding, *Fuck that!* What I think matters. I'll do as I choose. If I've offended you with the truth, that's your problem. Sometimes the truth hurts, but the truth matters. As a parent and a homeschooler, you will also wear the shield of a sentry. Guarding the gates can get nasty. You and your family must come first, always as a parent, but especially in this world of homeschooling.

It's easy to focus on outside negativity, but it's really not about you. You want your child to become their true self, reaching their best personal potential. You help them by providing academics and a learning environment that caters to their individual needs and life goals, developing strengths and overcoming weaknesses. As a parent, you help them by determining what you allow your children to be exposed to and when. You won't allow more than they are prepared to handle, but you will continue to allow more difficult situations as they mature and help them navigate those difficulties as they arise. You will show your children by example, including them in your own problem-solving techniques and allowing them to witness and even be a part of finding solutions for your own challenges.

In the vein of the expression, "We can't appreciate the light without the darkness," we can't effectively prepare our children for their future in a social vacuum without negativity. We, as well as our children, need to be placed in uncomfortable positions. We must be challenged as individuals to become more complete versions of ourselves. The relentless negativity we (David and Terri) experienced made us comfortable with adversity and illustrated to us the importance of teaching these ideas to our children.

On the one hand, we endeavored to raise our children differently, to be different than our parents were, and to be positive and supportive of our children. On the other hand, we wanted our children to be prepared to encounter the kind of adversity that our families offered us.

Clearly, homeschooling involves much more than academics.

CHAPTER 4

INTEGRATING ACADEMICS INTO PARENTING (THEY'RE NOT THAT DIFFERENT)

STARTING WITH STRUGGLE

We can't write this book as though we were the ideal couple executing ideal lives in perfect conditions. People sometimes look at us and assume that we've always led entitled lives. At the very least (to the casual observer), surely we've not lived a life of struggle. But as a couple, we struggled for years to find some semblance of normalcy in our lives and family.

Our first apartment was in the projects, as far as the term could apply in our town. Race wasn't on our radar back then. If anyone lived in this part of town, it wasn't by choice, but survival. That said, our apartment was crawling with roaches and other insects, our rent was $275 a month, and we made about $500 a month.

The first year we were married, we cleared somewhere around $6,000. Our living room furniture was two beanbag chairs. We had a 13" black-and-white TV with rabbit-ear antennas that sat on a plastic Tylenol display that David acquired from a supermarket dumpster. The extent of our decorating was a reproduction *Gone with the Wind* movie poster on a bare living room wall. Dawn dish soap was forty-nine cents a bottle. Dawn was our bath soap, shampoo, clothes soap, and dish soap. We used Dawn for everything because whatever money remained was for food. Our baby used baby soap, but an off-brand.

We both came from decently successful families, middle-middle class. You might think that surely they helped us find our way. Not so much. Anything anyone did to help us always came at a price beyond paying them back. Relatives tried to smoke us out "for our own good." They figured if they turned their backs on us, we would certainly fail, and that was a good thing.

In the days before electronic banking and debit cards, there was one year during the holidays when our paychecks became out of sync with our bills, and our electricity was cut off. Our power company didn't mess around. If one single payment didn't post by the due date, you had three days before the power was cut. We tried calling and telling them we would personally go to the service center and pay the bill instead of mailing it. They never budged. We realized that cutting power was more lucrative than selling it. If they could legally shut it off, they could then charge fifty dollars to reconnect it. Our electric bill wasn't usually more than fifty dollars, yet we paid a lot of fifty-dollar fees in those early years.

ASSAULTED FOR ASKING

I (David) once asked my parents for fifty dollars to get our electricity turned back on during the winter. I was able to pay the original bill, but we wouldn't have enough money left over for the reconnection fee unless we went without groceries. By my observation, fifty dollars wasn't a big deal to them. I was confident the short loan wouldn't be a point of contention.

A week prior, there was a distant family member (let's call him Joe) who'd left a bar and crashed his car while under the influence. It wasn't the first time Joe's drinking and driving had caused problems. Nevertheless, my parents bailed him out of jail, worked with his insurance company, and loaned him a car for him to drive in the interim. Joe also lost his job when he was in jail and didn't show up for work. My dad then gave Joe a job in his company, right after telling me he couldn't afford to hire anyone, and paid Joe a wage that was at least twice what I was making in my current job. My parents provided Joe a place to live as well.

Back to the electric bill. While visiting my parent's home, I discreetly told my dad my predicament and asked to borrow fifty dollars. I promised him I'd pay them back in a week or less. He called my mom over and said, "You want to know what your son is asking for?" My dad often said "your son" to my mom. I always assumed it was a colloquial phrase, not a literal statement. Now I understand that he thought of me as the stray my mom took in.

I then tried to extricate myself with, "I can get by without it. It's just cold at our place right now with no power." Being without power was humiliating enough—having our current struggle advertised loudly to everyone in earshot multiplied that humiliation. But of course, my dad knew that.

My dad grabbed me by my shirt and shoved me against the wall. "You better pay it back, this week!"

I felt a surge of resentment and courage begin to rise in me. "I've never *not* paid you back," I said. "Just like I'm sure Joe is going to pay you back for everything you've done for him since he got drunk, totaled his car, and lost his job. Again." It would be thirty years later before I had my first wreck.

My dad lifted me off the floor as best he could and pushed me harder against the wall. My mom grabbed my face with her fingernails, her eyes filled with contempt.

After I'd asked to borrow the fifty dollars, my parents refused to allow me to back out of my request and demanded I take the money since I had asked for it. I immediately wrote my parents a postdated check for fifty dollars, payable before the end of the week. If the money wasn't in the account, we would also have a thirty-five-dollar overdraft fee. This interaction characterized our early life together, not great, but we were finding our way, very slowly.

WE MATURE, OUR TODDLERS MATURE, WE ALL LEARN

As a couple and as parents, all these experiences are useful. How did I feel when my parents treated me this way? How would I respond if I were in their shoes? I know all too well what my parents did or didn't do, but can I imagine a scenario where they responded differently and what my response might have been?

To a large degree, my experiences were used to define dos and don'ts with our children. I find it necessary to look back on my life in detail. My parents didn't interact with me in caring ways. Sure, they fed me, clothed me, and provided me a place to live, but beyond telling me they weren't pleased or telling me what I needed to do, they had more important things to do.

Integrating academics into parenting doesn't require anything more than constructive interaction with your children. You simply allow your children to be a part of your family's solutions.

I've watched babies bat their sippy cups off the table and squeal with delight. Mom dutifully picks up the cup and gives it back to the baby, who swipes the cup off the table again. Mom keeps returning the cup and cleaning up the mess. If a child can hold a cup and drink from it and bat it off the table, could that same child not hold a cloth or paper towel and wipe up the mess? Our children are saying, "Teach me." All this mom is teaching is that she's this kid's servant. Babies have grabby hands; they'll grasp a towel. Support them with one hand and help them wipe with the other. We can all learn to clean up after ourselves.

If I had a particularly rebellious toddler who persisted, the sippy cup would be placed elsewhere, and a baby bottle would be filled with their drink. Even very young children understand nuances. If they launch the baby bottle across the house, screaming, I respond with, "I'm sorry, Scooter. I'll get rid of the bottle" (not "baa baa."). Perhaps Scooter would rather not have a drink than be relegated to a baby bottle. When Scooter asks for a drink, he gets the baby bottle until he understands not to throw the cup.

"Why so harsh? He's just a little kid, asshole!" Scooter needs to remember these exchanges when he's a much older child. Honestly, in part, you're building in a bluff to use when Scooter is a teenager and you can't control him like a toddler. He has to know when he's a teen that your resolve is not to be trifled with. When Scooter is an adult, he'll realize it was a bluff. Scooter will not get the sippy cup back until he drinks from the bottle and places it back on the table.

Once, one of our children began screaming at us in a restaurant. I swooped him out of his highchair. "I'm sorry, he's a baby," I said as we passed patrons looking at us. "Sorry, he's a little baby," I said as I walked with him out of the restaurant. The other patrons hid their smiles. My son was mortified. He quickly stopped screaming. The more quiet he became, the more earnest my respectful announcement to other patrons. He screamed because he didn't get what he wanted when he wanted it. By the time I was done, he was ashamed. He never tried this demand again.

BE A PRESENT PARENT

Typically, mothers are the daytime caregiver, but I've also been a stay-at-home dad at times. How many parents do you hear talking about how busy they are at home, chasing one or more kids, doing laundry, making meals, changing diapers, and so forth? How many moms say, "My husband goes to work, comes home to relax, and I'm still doing all of these things until after baths and pajamas?"

Ouch.

I've been that ignorant dad. The man she had so much fun with nine months ago, gone with the daily grind of work. I get it. We feel like we're out conquering the world and bringing home the bucks, but our spouses need to feel like something of their old self remains. Their identity has been turned upside down with marriage and family.

Raising three kids and working at home, Terri had reached her limit. I would offer my nuggets of "man wisdom" to her, which understandably didn't bode well with her. We worked it out; I adjusted my employment situation, and she satisfied her desire to go to the office. It was good for her, and I enjoyed not being at a conventional job. It was awesome hanging out with the kids and not a bunch of dudes all day. Terri will tell you later in this book that she regrets the time she spent with the kids not being "in the moment." She wanted to feel "done." She needed to feel like something was accomplished and checked off the list so that she could move on to the next thing. Without thinking about it, she was a "if you want it done, do it yourself" kind of person. She put space between her and the kids to get things done. It wore her out waiting on the kids hand and foot. I don't think she thought about it this way, but instinctively, a job outside the home provided the "done" that she needed.

Terri happily went off to work, and I happily stayed at home. After a week of the arrangement, it was going well. When Terri came home, the house was clean, the laundry was done, and dinner was ready. "This is like a freakin' vacation!" I joked. Marriage 101, don't ever say that. Unintentionally, I made Terri feel "less than," and it hurt her. For that, I am still very sorry.

Read this next part as "child-focused," not "spouse-focused." I told Terri that we had a schedule that included the kids doing their part. Our youngest two were toddlers. If they removed a toy, they were capable of putting it away. If they made a mess, they were capable of cleaning it up. They were capable of dressing themselves because they could certainly undress. I didn't mess around. When it was time for laundry, the kids were responsible for bringing me their dirty clothes, all the way to the washer (I wanted them to see the process), and I'd inspect their room to ensure we had all of their dirty clothes. I required them to accomplish these things. There was no discussion, and honestly, there wasn't much pushback. I didn't yell and count to ten and throw a fit. I knew they were learning, and they had a sense of pride in being a part of the job that Daddy was doing.

The motivation for them to accomplish these things was also because we had a schedule. Breakfast, laundry, cleaning, including dishes—every housekeeping task was complete by 10:30 in the morning. The kids would watch a show between that time and lunch. After we ate together and cleaned up lunch together, we had "us time." I'd get out crayons, paints, glue, paper . . . whatever. We would sit at the table and be artists or builders together. When we completed the chores, we all shared the fruits of our labor, we all had the same fun together, and I wasn't stuck doing "parent stuff" while they did "kid stuff."

Terri was taken aback when, after dinner, the kids carried their dishes to the sink and slid them up onto the counter. If they can't reach the counter, you can lift them up while they hold their plates so that they can still put their dishes in the sink. If kids can hold their plates, why can't they load the dishwasher? I would rinse the dishes in the sink and gently hand them to the two little ones, instructing them where to place them. Yes, it took longer, but really, what else did I have to do right then? They thought it was fun.

You may wonder if everything was strict with our kids on my military-style regimen. Jeez, no. They enjoyed working together. If something wasn't done, everything would stop for everyone until it was completed. Our kids experienced a little peer pressure because, after all, adult life has peer pressure.

Besides television programs and crafts, what did we do? You could ask any of us about "food fight," and we'd all smile. One evening after Terri had gotten home, I'd made spaghetti and French bread for dinner. We were all stuffed and just sitting at the table. I remember the kids all looked happy and content, hanging out with Mom and Dad. Then my daughter "squinty-eyed" me, a look of mischievous defiance. Under her watchful eyes, I put my hand into my leftover spaghetti. "Food fight!" I called out, then threw spaghetti at her.

Everyone froze. Then her round little baby hand burrowed into her plate, and she threw spaghetti back at me with squealing delight. It was on! We were launching spaghetti across the table at each other and laughing to tears. We all had spaghetti stuck to our faces and in our hair. Yes, it was a huge mess, but who cares? It was pure joy as a family. What else did we have to do? Watch television? When it was time to clean up, we all took part in cleaning up the mess. How cool is that? "It's okay to make a mess," we would tell the kids, "just be prepared to clean it up."

This is my perspective on home education: I'm my kid's mentor, not their servant. We did serious work every day (considering our kids' ages), and we played every day. People would often comment about how well behaved our children were. They would also warn us about the terrible twos. Our children were taught responsibility and acted accordingly. Our children didn't go through the terrible twos. Coincidence? I say no.

I built a long balance beam for the kids in the backyard, a "tower" platform they could climb and play on, and of course, a swing set. They were proud to help by handing me nails or screws. Our oldest son could do more complicated things, like use a screw gun and clamp parts for me to weld. We built it all together. As young children, our kids' lives were very structured, but we all had a lot of fun.

These things also translated into a better relationship between Terri and me. She didn't need to come home to chaos or messes or me complaining. She could come home and just deflate, or she could jump in and help. I'd recognized how I, in the past, was able to come home and rest. It was her turn. Seeing that we were all having fun together made Terri want to be a part of it. We were finding our way as a couple and as parents. Our children were learning self-control and responsibility, as well as the rewards for exercising these characteristics.

One thing that Terri never wavered on was reading to the kids. In all of our years as parents with children at home, Terri read to our children every night. Take that statement literally. *Terri read to our children every night.* Before grade school was over for our youngest son, he had read *The Hobbit* and *The Lord of the Rings* by himself. As the kids learned to read, they took part in reading aloud nightly, but Terri still did most of the reading to let the kids enjoy her stories. I read to them occasionally (the kids needed to see that Dad could read aloud, too), but I worked the night shift for years. Regardless, the standard was set that both Mom and Dad read very well.

Terri was getting what she needed at work. She was around others with similar situations and no longer felt alone. She was good at her job, which provided daily affirmation to her as a person. Now she could look at herself in the mirror and say, "I remember you." This change in our lives was a good experience for everyone in our family and represented the "hump" for us to get over as a couple. I understood her perspective better as a stay-at-home mom (men, if we only knew what we think we do!). Terri also understood my professional struggles better. The daily commute in traffic, the grind of the job that wears on you over time. We all need to know that our jobs mean something—that *we* mean something. Whoever's at home needs to know their life is more than dirty diapers and crusty food everywhere.

TAUGHT BY ASSAULT—MY EARLY YEARS

My dad backhanded me in the face for the first time when I was maybe five or six. He slung a large metal belt buckle across my face shortly after that. This was in response to overlooking a pair of jeans for the laundry. The belt buckle blew my lip open and began swelling my eye shut.

The physical abuse was consistent from then on, well into adulthood. Did I do something when I was five years old to deserve being hit by a grown man? Did I do something when I was eighteen years old to deserve the same? I'd never been arrested, no drugs, no alcohol, no partying, no school suspensions. The question might be, What situation merits physical abuse? To many members of my family, it had nothing to do with a particular situation—they believed *I* deserved the physical abuse.

In grade school, my dad grabbed me by my shirt, ripped me out of my chair, and busted my lip open because I wasn't understanding fractions. Looking at it from our parental point of view, what exactly were my parents trying to teach me? Not justice or equality. My parents treated my brother and sister much differently than me. I think back to my dad being so well liked, as that was part of his identity. My brother was well liked also. So, was I to learn that it wasn't what one did or didn't do but how well they were liked? Or was it simply the family blood factor? That was the difference between me and those who got a pass. My mind was searching for normalcy. For acceptance. No matter what action I took, it never seemed to satisfy my parents. It always came back to me being screamed at, shook by my hair, and hit.

Believe it or not, tests still cause me stress today. All I can think of is, "What if I fail?" How nice would it be to be able to sit and just take a test? My parents taught me the opposite. If I failed, I would get punished—physically.

My mom didn't finish high school, but she expected me to do everything she thought was correct simply because she thought it. She watched a lot of television shows that gave her ideas. My parents created this fear of test taking for me.

In contrast, Terri and I showered our kids with tests so that they would learn to be good test takers. It affected how our children viewed the material they learned if they had a test on it. Until kids get through college, tests will determine their status as a student and person. Again, don't focus on how the world should be; focus on how it is and teach your children how to navigate it successfully.

What I realized as an adult was that none of the abuse was for my benefit. It was a manifestation of my dad's frustration that I wasn't what he wanted me to be. My dad solved problems *physically*. He'd been doing that since the age of fourteen. While intelligent, my dad wasn't a teacher. My dad couldn't understand why telling me to do my math homework didn't result in me doing it flawlessly, like he could speak it into existence. He would yell at me and scare me, which didn't result in me understanding the material. When that didn't work, then certainly grabbing me, shaking me, or hitting me would do the trick. The fact that it *never* worked didn't cause him to consider a different approach.

With my shirt in his fist, slamming me against the refrigerator, he once said he'd beat me to death if he found out I was gay. To this day, I've never understood where that came from. Looking back through my eyes as an adult, I believe my dad had *thought* about killing me. I'm glad that realization eluded me for so many years. Your actions will shape the way your children think for the rest of their lives. Think about that.

TEACH WITH SUPPORT, NOT AGGRESSION

When I was in school, I remember thinking, "If I don't understand this, I'm going to get hit." I was distinctly *not* thinking about learning a topic. The thought of my mom grabbing me by the hair and shaking my head, *telling* me to learn something, physically affects me to this day. Neither of my parents ever tried to teach me the material. That was my teacher's job. Whatever teacher I had was beyond reproach by default, so the blame for not learning was solely on me.

When I was able to go back to school as an adult, I worked very hard and achieved mostly A's. My dad, however, didn't share in my success. "Hey, Dad, I aced my ___ test," I'd tell him. To which he'd say, "Oh, so you're better than everyone? You have it all figured out now?" Awkward.

To be a competent parent, remember that simply having your child around you is teaching them. Are you putting energy into building them up? Are you showing them your approval and making a deliberate effort to be pleased with them? All too often we focus only on the negative. Parents need balance, not overly negative but not overly permissive either. Parenting is academics, and academics is parenting. Aggressive behavior puts a person in fight-or-flight mode, where they are incapable of learning. If your child doesn't understand a concept, find a way to enhance their understanding. Help them figure out where the struggle is, and then address that struggle.

My parents missed a lot of opportunities in what they perceived as faults or defects with me.

"David daydreams too much," for example.

As an elementary student, I wore out our encyclopedias, looking up things like boats, engines, and airplanes. When I discovered tools, I quickly understood fractions—32nds, 16ths, 8ths. In modern terms, my mind perceived fractions in *resolution*; 1/4th, 15/16ths, and 28/32nds were just random numbers until I visualized them as something tangible.

Anytime you can identify your child's interests, then relate a subject to something they're interested in, you and your children will find success. As I was growing up, parenting and academics were distinctly separate. For Terri and me, academics were part of parenting. All of our children understood fractions at a young age because we included our children in things like cooking. They never knew we were teaching fractions while using measuring cups, but it happened, and they got to lick the beaters and enjoy some tasty cake afterward. Did we teach it, or did they learn it by example? Who cares? Whatever we did, it wasn't violent, it was usually fun, and learning just happened as a result.

INSANITY: IF IT DOESN'T WORK, KEEP DOING IT!

My parents were content to let Terri and me starve if that's what it took for us to see things their way and implode the life we were trying to build.

I remember not eating so that my son and wife would have enough to eat. No groceries or money for groceries magically arrived for us. We made our choice, though, and the responsibility of providing for our family didn't lie with anyone but us. My parents had every right not to do a damn thing for us. Especially since "family is blood" after all, and I wasn't. We unhitched our wagon and embraced that we were on our own.

While hard, this realization was liberating and gave us something to focus on: our future and how it would serve our children's future. Those who were so critical of us faded away, and our quality of life improved.

We're all held accountable in some way for our actions, good or bad. In hindsight, would I trade the life we've had with any of our detractors from nearly forty years ago? Hell no. I would live my life better. I would strive to be a better person for our children and for my wife. That's what this book is about, making a choice and seeing it all the way through—to the best of your ability. We've had great joy as we've witnessed our children moving on to their adult lives and seeing them flourish. We cherish the relationships that we have with them, which is in sharp contrast to the relationships that we never had with either of our parents.

How will you view the inevitable realization that you will parent your children to adulthood? Will you look at it as a chore, or as an honorable challenge? In how you treat your children and live by example, as well as how you treat others, what will you choose to teach your children? What will you teach them when you're not even thinking about it? If I imagine myself as a young dad and husband hearing the words I'm now saying, it would seem overwhelming. No one can possibly be *that* present every day, all the time. But you have to remember, it's not about being perfect. It's about being mindful and striving to be the best you, every day. All we can do is inform ourselves and commit to the task.

I hope my stories are a catalyst for your growth and development as a parent and educator. We all have our strengths and weaknesses, and I'm in no way excluded. Let your strengths and weaknesses bring to light what you do and don't want to do, as parents and educators who want their children to grow up knowing they are loved, accepted, and important in your family. You'll do this by how you treat them and how they see you treat each other—and others outside your own family.

My goal as an author is to provide connections for a rare perspective that would otherwise take years for new parents to develop (as it did for us). I want to help you understand what factors develop the kind of person your child will become.

My parents' actions and words told me that something was wrong with me, that I wasn't good enough, that I wasn't to be trusted, and that my thinking was wrong. If my parents couldn't see value in me, why would anyone else? My parents' words and actions taught me that the most important thing was for me to live life for the benefit and acceptance of others, not seeking to better myself and my place in life.

CHALLENGING THE STATUS QUO

Later in life when we had our first custom home built, my mom angrily declared that Terri and I had no business building such a nice, big house. When I asked why, she said that my older siblings didn't have houses yet. (Which wasn't true—they just hadn't built *new* houses.) It went against her opinion of my siblings compared to her opinion of me. She needed to be right, and our big custom home proved her wrong on some level. I don't think we siblings kept score.

When I enrolled in school at the age of twenty-one, I was told by my family that I'd fail or not finish. When I graduated at the top of my class, nothing was said by any family, except Terri's mom. Terri handed me an envelope and said, "This is from my mom." It was a card that said "Congratulations," and inside was a check for $500. My mother-in-law may have despised me, but she recognized the value of education and the effort it required. In spite of our vast differences, our children still have a good relationship with her.

Some years later, I heard that distant family member Joe was getting his life in order. Someone contacted me at work on his behalf. I made some calls and was able to secure a slot for Joe in a large company that provided training as well if he wanted it. He took the position, and he did well. After he graduated, my mom called me, excited, to tell me what Joe had done and how he was following in the footsteps of other family members (not me, of course). There was a part of me that still wanted my parents' approval. I told her that I was aware of what Joe had done and that I had helped him get this job and training. My mom's response?

"You'll get there one day."

I'm not kidding. At that time I was being groomed for the president's chair at my then-current company, and I'd been in Joe's place just ten years before. A few years later, I would go on to become a division manager in an aerospace company who subsequently offered me an operations manager position for $350,000 a year. I don't know about you, but to us, that was a lot of money in the early 2000s. My parents never acknowledged that I was even in the same industry as Joe. My mom truly never remembered what I did for a living. She knew I "did something" with airplanes. In her mind, I was something that needed to be fixed, and that would never change.

Is your child's education simply reading, writing, and arithmetic? The topics of your child's education are very important, but these pale in comparison to preparing your children to be the best version of themselves. Those core topics sit on the foundation you've built with them since birth.

Later in the book, Terri shares our academic standards with you. Academics are an important part of your child's life—similar to what gasoline does for a car. But what good is gasoline if you don't have a steering wheel?

Life lessons mean everything to your child's upbringing and who they will become. There's no shortage of people ready to tell you what you do or don't need, but most everything outside of your little family is just noise—especially in the age of smartphones, social media, and polarized and politicized news. The people talking aren't talking from knowledge, experience, or love. They're telling you what to do in order for them to feel important or make a buck. So, listen at your convenience—not theirs.

I was given a good example of this while writing this chapter. A young man earnestly told me all the important things about marriage and raising kids. When he told me everything his wife did for him, I smiled and said, "That's awesome. What kinds of things do you do for her?" He looked at me blankly. "She wants to do it," he responded. "Oh, okay," I said. He was confident he had it all figured out. Who was I to tell him any different? He'd been married six months and had never cared for kids in his life. I didn't have anything else to do at the time, so I listened. All I could hear was how hard his life was going to be when reality came calling. Hopefully, he and his wife committed to the task.

For us, we looked at the lives of the people around us—their homes, their marriages, their children, and the state of their personal lives. Is that what we wanted? No? Then why would we listen to anything they say? My stories speak to an array of points but converge on this: homeschooling is parenting; parenting is homeschooling. The quality of your child's education and life will identically match the quality of your parenting.

My parents provided a torrent of physical and emotional abuse throughout my entire life. No one noticed. Everyone was too focused on their own desires to care about me and my young family. Relatives remained oblivious to drugs and abuse in their own families. This sounds horrible, but it taught me to look at my place in life and at my family through a different lens. How could Terri and I do life differently to remove the crisis that we saw around us? How could we use these experiences in our lives to model a more rewarding way to live for our own children? Our kids didn't know it was all new to us, they just knew that our expectations of them differed from those of their family and peers.

All of the "family is blood" talk was wiped away, and I accepted that tomorrow was up to me, no matter where I came from. Tomorrow is up to you. What will you do today to make tomorrow's homeschool better for your family? How will you see things through a different lens to live a more rewarding life, teaching your children to do the same?

If you're wondering whether my dad ever offered a kind word of approval to me, he did. In our early forties, we flew our children and my parents to Paris for a vacation. He watched me with our youngest son, and then he said to me, "Son, I'm really proud of you."

In forty years, that was the first time he had ever said he was proud of me. Sadly, I didn't care. I *needed* his approval and support when my life was hard and challenging. He was about thirty years too late. But I knew that he was experiencing peace and contentment in that moment that he'd likely experienced very few times in his life. No work, no screaming kids, no crisis, no responsibilities, just being together contentedly for no reason other than sharing life. He and my mom were experiencing our family for the first time in over twenty years. I truly hoped it provided him some form of peace in his heart. To this day, that week in Paris remains one of our most treasured family vacations.

Imagine yourself in my dad's shoes. Your memories of the relationship you had with your kids are not kind to you. You realize that you cannot change the past. You cannot go back and build trust. You do not get another chance to be kind, patient, loving, and build a lifelong connection with your children. That time is gone.

Now imagine your own children in my shoes. No longer caring for a deep, connected relationship with you because you chose to be demanding and harsh in your homeschooling. Your children find their own way in life and now just look at you with pity.

You don't get to choose to have a good relationship with your adult children later; you must make that decision *now*, when they're young and at home. Choose to treat them the way you would want to be treated once they're out from under your homeschool umbrella and your authority. How confident are you in your day-to-day interactions with your children? Are you actively building and continuously fostering trust with them? Remember, it all ties together. You are demonstrating for your children not only how to treat other people by how you treat them, but also how to treat you later in life. You encourage or discourage your children every single day to become the individuals they will someday be.

In the early years, I tried to imagine life from my parents' perspective, putting myself in their shoes. What could their perspective be, and how would I do it differently for the benefit of our children? Consider how concerned you are with the things in life that have nothing to do with tomorrow—like social media, TV series, possessions, convenient friends, gossip news, or even internet porn. Is there anything that has nothing to do with tomorrow that you prioritize over your marriage or your children? Do you favor one child over another or disfavor your children among friends or extended family members?

What do you imagine your children will recall, ten years from now, of your current daily interactions? This way of thinking can help you navigate a good path today. Did you interact with your children for their benefit? Is it for the pure joy of your relationship with them? I imagine this can all sound elementary and full of common sense, but how many articles exist about parents who abandoned their children to the foster system because they couldn't accept the impact the child had on their social lives? I've read too many. What I'm addressing by reliving the stories about my family and my life is that you, parent and homeschool teacher, will have a singular priority in life: providing for your child on every developmental level.

Many parents seem to be most concerned about what their children think of them and how others perceive them as parents. My job is to make sure that my child is equipped to go into adult life. If you achieve this, then your kids will likely love you for the rest of their years. As parents, we didn't negotiate. Does that sound a bit harsh? I bet it does, especially nowadays. I could be overwhelmingly intimidating to our children. I had moments when the anger I learned from my parents came out. I watched once as my young daughter grabbed a handful of her brother's hair and angrily pulled it. Before she realized I'd seen it, I lifted her to her feet by her hair. The complete fear of getting caught and my wordless response terrified her. Though I know my hair-pulling action paled in comparison to hers, she quickly experienced the pain she'd inflicted on her brother. I asked my son if he was alright, and he said that he was. It wasn't brought up again.

When our children got into the world and encountered situations with a boss, a bully, or the police, they were prepared because we'd taught respect at home. What if your children disrespect a police officer? They might get shot and killed. If you want your children to outlive you and have happy, prosperous lives, teach them about respect and authority at home.

They also respect law enforcement. Angry people in authority, including police, did not intimidate our children. Since our children were young, I've not had a need to intimidate them. Lessons were learned, and we moved on. It's not a part of our lives anymore.

Conversely, the public school allows children to be disrespectful and teaches children to take the beating, not to defend themselves and go tell someone after they've been violated. If you get shot, go tell on the shooter? Go to the part-time crisis counselor? Go to a safe place? Generally, it seems they're not teaching kids much of anything useful in real life.

I was taught to fear my dad (and family) through threats of violence. My existence was for their convenience, not my development, and the lessons learned in public school backed this up. As a homeschool parent, you can't teach your children to be victims. You must teach your children to be respectful and command respect. You have to teach them that there are bad people in the world and bad things happen. You will teach your children (we can all hope!) how to confidently handle a predator in public spaces. You'll prepare them for it gradually over time in appropriate doses at an appropriate maturity level. How can you do all of these things? Incorporate them into everyday life. Live these positive characteristics before your children—model them, teach them, and practice them with your children every day as a lifestyle. Attend etiquette classes together. Maybe not the same class, as there are etiquette classes for kids and adults, but you can still experience the growth at the same time. Attend a self-defense class together. Yes, hopefully you will both learn some good self-defense tactics or possibly how to be more socially aware of your surroundings, but you're also teaching your children that we don't know it all, and it's easy and beneficial to learn from someone. These are good lessons. Bring your children into everything you do when appropriate, and make it fun when possible. It's fun for a child to be doing something with you, all while smiling and joking, just as you do with your close friends.

If you're always serious or abrupt with your children or your spouse, but when you interact with a friend or stranger, your face lights up and you speak kindly, what kind of message are you conveying to your family? To me, regarding my relationship with my parents, it said that everyone else was more important to my parents than I was.

You can work together, and that's how you breathe life, love, and happiness into your children. We always want to remember that children are not adults, and they need to have fun and relax. They need to play. When you join your children in play, when you include them in everything you do, you will be teaching them so much more than if you just sit down to teach them their school lessons.

At the age of eighteen, I had no idea what to do in basic life. Let's all raise the bar for our kids. We wanted to celebrate that our children made it to a place they aspired to be. Where do you see your child eighteen years or more into the future? Anything you don't teach them, they'll need to learn later in life through trial and error. Or will they never learn it and blame their shortcomings on you? Every minute you don't teach your children when you could have, they'll spend time making up for your parenting shortcomings. Some parents fall so far short, it can't be made up. When the best a young adult can manage is an entry-level job, I feel bad for the kid. It's 99 percent the parents' fault that their adult child is in a job they resent and are now asking if I want fries with my order.

IMAGINE THE FUTURE

Imagine your young adult child has a real job interview. They walk into an elegant office building and are escorted into a conference room. In this room is a long table. On one side, there are five individuals with binders, and across from them is a chair with a binder in front of it. Your child is getting ready to have their first panel interview.

Instead of a fast-food job, you dream that your child will enter the adult world in a white-collar profession. Better pay, better benefits, and a solid future. It's thoughts like this that you will use to determine what needs to be integrated into your children's education. Was your child capable of preparing for this interview? There are multiple people sitting across from them for a reason. Either your child knows their stuff, or they'll be thanked for their time. Did your child know how to properly prepare for the verbal portion of the interview? Did they know how to dress properly for the interview? People of a higher social status notice details. You don't get to bullshit your way in. Your kid doesn't need to wear a Rolex, but does their timepiece of choice reflect their social status?

When they get a big raise, will they suddenly walk in looking like a goofy character in a movie, or will they understand that properly representing the company matters? Your child must know how to dress, walk, and communicate appropriately for the position and situation. If your child can do this, they'll likely get the job and begin climbing the ladder.

It bears saying over and over: you must prepare your child for success in the world that exists, not the world we think *should* exist. These characteristics are common in successful people, but this scenario will seem unrealistic to some. I'm telling you, it's not. In my career, I've seen many young adults interviewed and hired for their first job who faced a panel of three to five people for their final interview, and the job started well into six figures. A high percentage of the successful ones were homeschooled.

I grew up in the country, wearing blue jeans and logo T-shirts. I didn't know anything about "rich people." Your child must have knowledge about how to appropriately conduct themselves around their peers and superiors. Will you teach your child the importance of professional thank-you cards and the proper etiquette for using them? Will your child be able to sit for a formal dinner that's not really about the food? There are so many intricacies to achieving success as an adult that have nothing to do with test scores or colleges attended. If your children don't learn these things under your care, chances are, they won't. Most kids don't.

WHAT IF . . .

Want an easy way to determine what things your child still needs to learn? Ask yourself, "What if ___?" and insert the common things you've experienced as an adult. What if my child has a flat tire? What if my child needs to cook a meal for an entire family? What if my child has the interview of a lifetime? What if my child is invited to a formal event? The possibilities are endless. To us, your child's personality and interests is what will determine many ideas and suggestions. What unique knowledge will be most useful to their particular interests?

At the foundation, we think that every child should learn how to cook a menu of basic meals. If you take your children to the store with you, let them help with the shopping by telling them why you are buying something. "We use this seasoning to make chili," for example, or "I need buttermilk to make dessert." By the time your child is ready for middle school, they could be making dinner for the family once a week, even if it's with Mom and or Dad's help. By the time they're in high school, they could be excitedly hosting a family cookout on the 4th of July. Now there's a kid with confidence earning high praise from everyone in attendance. I consider it a true honor to provide food for people, and a child can take pride in their role of provider by the grill. Just from cooking burgers! I also see a teenager respecting and interacting with small children and grandmas and providing sustenance to all of these people. How many positive life skills are being reinforced? And you know the best part? You taught your child how, but they own it, and you're proud of them. That encompasses the active homeschool parenting we're talking about.

All of these life skills can be taught by you *or* provided by you. Our oldest son taught himself to cook, and at about the same time, I began learning how to cook outside of chili packets and spaghetti. We have fun conversations about cooking. Generally, he doesn't like my cooking or Terri's, but it's understandable. We lived on the same cheap meals every week for years! Mom and Dad's food isn't good. The die was cast long ago. But he's a wonderful cook and is an equally spirited host who makes every guest feel special. If we had a do-over in this regard, we would have taken a cooking class with our kids. How special is that? Learning a new skill together.

You're reading this book because you want more than fast-food and retail-store job options for your child. You want to look at parenting and education differently than you were taught because you want your children to *be* different. I've read articles on how much cooking can affect a person's ability to attract a quality partner.[8] According to one study, 63 percent of respondents ranked the quality of being able to cook well over

8 - Chris Melore, "Chef Wanted—for Love: Americans Say Being Able to Cook Is the Best Dating Quality," Study Finds, last updated February 28, 2023, https://Studyfinds.Org/Cooking-Best-Dating-Quality/.

all other desired traits in a potential partner.[9] If your child is lucky enough to find someone worth continuing a relationship with, knowing how to cook could be a determining factor. With this research information, how big of an impact on your child's life is knowing how to plan, prepare, and serve a good meal? Life-changing. Do your children understand nutrition and making healthy choices that are beneficial to their bodies? It sounds random, but these are large factors in how your child will be perceived by others, including potential life partners. These will be the factors your children will judge others by as well. Your child will be less likely to judge potential relationships by how physically attractive someone is and more likely to determine true value based on character, maturity, knowledge, and lasting compatibility.

Aside from cooking, what other life skills do you want your child to learn? Can your child maintain their car in good working order? Perhaps maintenance on a vehicle, such as changing a tire, changing the oil, and adding fluids to keep it running properly, should be an educational topic. There are few things that say "irresponsible" or "unreliable" like the person who constantly has to use the excuse that their car is broken down. Neither employers nor potential partners will buy this line more than once.

A study conducted by Harvard University determined that technical knowledge is only 15 percent of being hired for a job. The other 85 percent is based on professional etiquette. This may sound simple, but it's a wide-ranging topic. Teaching your children the concepts of professional etiquette should begin young if you expect to prepare them.

All of these concepts and so many more must be provided by you (but not necessarily taught by you). Are you feeling overwhelmed yet? How do you know if you're capable of being a homeschool parent? When your child is six months old and you feel the same stress as you would over an important work deadline, you're on the right track.

I was in high school when we were married. We went on a honeymoon, and the following week, I started my senior year of high school

---

9 - Marie Haaland, "From Good Looks to Good Cooks, These Traits Are Most Important When Looking for a Partner," SWNS Digital, September 6, 2021, https://swnsdigital.com/us/2021/02/from-good-looks-to-good-cooks-these-traits-are-most-important-when-looking-for-a-partner/.

as though my life were still normal. My life was different, but I was still me, just a lot busier. We couldn't afford a place in the town we grew up in, so our lackluster apartment was about fifteen miles away. I held two jobs that year in addition to school. Anytime I wasn't in school, I was at work, seven days a week. It was the hardest year of my life. The school had approved me for what they called *homebound studies*, but at the last minute, they pulled it and said that since I was physically able to attend class, I had to. Even though I provided examples of students who were in the homebound program, they wouldn't budge. I believe they wanted me to quit because a married father in a small school system wasn't their desired student demographic. I was certain that my family had influenced their decision, but I'll never know.

My public school education was worthless for any job that could begin to support my family. I had no useful experience. If I had no experience to help myself; I certainly had no experience to pass on to our son. I truly didn't know how to take care of my home, from cleaning to cooking. What I did have, and it was invaluable, was knowing how to work on things. I kept our car running, and almost anything that broke in our home, I could repair to some usable degree. These things were self-taught.

Although money was tight, we did the absolute best we could for our baby boy's first Christmas. Terri and I bought a box of snack bars to share because we couldn't afford the luxury of buying each other nice gifts. I had six dollars to spend on our son, and I didn't get paid until late Christmas Eve. I hurried to get to the store before closing, passing the other late shoppers hauling masses of gifts out for their families.

There was nothing left in the store I could afford, but then . . .

I found myself alone in the aisle where rows of Hot Wheels cars hung on pegs. They were ninety-nine cents each. I was embarrassed, angry, and trying not to cry. I bought our ten-month-old son four Hot Wheels cars for Christmas. What is a ten-month-old supposed to do with Hot Wheels? I didn't know, but this sparked a tradition for many years to come that everyone in our family (our children, my wife, and I) would give each other Hot Wheels cars for Christmas. It was like an amusing reminder to never forget our roots as a family.

And I never want to forget those Hot Wheels. Although our two younger children didn't live through these times, I wanted them to know where we came from. More than anything, I never wanted my children to be standing where I was that first Christmas Eve.

That's why we chose to homeschool. We "home-prep-schooled" our children for quality of life. *We* took responsibility for our children's futures because we couldn't trust anyone else with something so important. Our children have never stood in a department store buying Hot Wheels for any reason other than it means something to Dad. When my oldest son was about the same age as I was that first Christmas, I watched him negotiate and buy an oil painting in Europe. He's traveled the world! Our kids will likely never comprehend the emotions their actions cause us to have because of our humble beginnings. The possibility of you experiencing the same joy we have had with our children is what brought us to write this book.

You know that you and your family are the best chance your children have to stand above hundreds of millions of peers who will be pushed through the public education system and left to flounder through life the best they can. You're willing to fight through every tough situation for your kids and for your family. The way you treat your children is the way they will treat their schooling, other people, and ultimately, you. You want them to work hard and keep pushing no matter what, and to not give up at the first sign of difficulty.

Some parents are so concerned with this or that curriculum, or what other people think, they don't bother to ask, "Can I be someone this child believes in and wants to learn from?" You must ensure that you are someone worthy of their admiration and respect. You will provide an environment that creates and develops mutual admiration and respect. You will ask yourself, "Have I made something of myself? Have I proven myself to be their role model?"

What can you do to become the person your children look up to, admire, and want to learn from?

CHAPTER 5

BIRTH TO TODDLER TO KINDERGARTEN

You'll notice that this is one of the longest chapters in the book. That's because birth to kindergarten is incredibly important. Your child will be constantly changing, and you'll be constantly adapting. In my (David's) opinion, this time will most profoundly determine the kind of person your child will be.

I am one of those people who remembers life from before I could speak or walk. These memories are like short videos, snippets of a time and place.

I have a memory of sitting in a high chair at the kitchen table. My dad threw his dinner plate across the kitchen, where it shattered, food flying in all directions. Our little dog and cat happily licked up the mess. Other than that, most of my memories are of my mom. I don't remember Dad being there much, and I assume he was always working. Whether he was gone out of necessity for work or a desire to avoid home, I don't know.

Monday through Friday, we had a routine. Mom smoked cigarettes, talked on the phone, and watched soap operas while I found activities to occupy my time. None of my memories include my mom doing things like taking me to the park or playing outside with me.

I remember our dog, Pamela, strangled herself on a rope and died in the backyard one day. My mom didn't notice all day. My brother found her when he got home from school. He said she was hard and stiff.

Another time, when I was about three years old, I snuck a pack of cigarettes. Because my mom and dad smoked so much, I thought it must be great. I shared my exciting discovery of cigarettes with a boy named Mike two houses down who'd come over to play. Later, Mike's mom smelled the smoke on him and called my mom. My mom asked me about it, and I showed her the pack of cigarettes. Understandably, I don't have a memory of Mike ever coming to play again.

I also have memories that carried emotion for years. One day, as a toddler, I was in the front yard exploring. My mom was watching TV and said I could go out as long as I stayed in the yard. There was a Spanish-style brick house across the street that, for some reason, captured my imagination. I looked both ways and crossed the street to explore the ornate brickwork that extended from the house.

I didn't see any cars or people. After exploring behind a curved brick wall, I turned to leave. A known bully in the neighborhood named Allan appeared, grabbed my overall straps, and pulled me between the two houses. He told me not to scream. Roughly, he pulled my pants down, then slapped my junk around. He threatened me not to tell anyone or he'd hurt my family, and then he ran off. In my memory, through tears and shaking hands, nothing existed in the world except reattaching my overall straps. I knocked on the door of my house, but no one came to the door.

When my mom finally broke her attention away from the TV, she knew something was wrong. I told her what happened and who did it. I also remember my brother laughing at me. "Did Allan slap your dinky around?" I was confused. Why did I feel scared if the incident was funny? My brother was six years older than me. It seemed to me that very soon after the incident, not only did everyone in my family know, but my siblings' friends also knew. I felt embarrassed and ashamed. What I learned was that my mom was not really there for me. My dad never spoke of the incident, but I recall my mom facing him in the living room, talking and pointing. But I was left to process it by myself.

More than once in my life, people have observed, "You have trust issues, don't you?" Personally, I wouldn't call them issues, I simply learned from a very young age to be discerning of people. It would have been healthier for my mom and dad to teach me this, but instead, Allan taught me at a very young age, whether I was ready or not.

As parents, we are everything to our own children. But are they *that* important to *us*? Are they more important than whatever is on your phone, tablet, or television? When they stick a hairpin in the outlet, will you recall that you were engrossed in reading about a royal scandal?

I (Terri) recently saw a mother out walking in our neighborhood while her two younger boys were riding their bicycles. What's wrong with that? Just like David's mom was so engrossed in her TV shows, this mother spent the entire time looking at her phone. She had no idea what was going on with the boys; she just followed them like a zombie, staring at her phone. She was not present. She was not engaged with her children or interacting with them. She was passively babysitting. Maybe she *was* the babysitter, not the mother, but that's unlikely.

Put the devices away. Make time to interact and be present with your children. That's part of building a relationship with trust. Do your children know they can count on you? Are you their biggest fan and cheerleader? Hug them and hold them, play and laugh with them, but these are just a few things that create love and trust, allowing us to bond with our children. When they're riding their bikes, encourage them. If not, they'll notice you're not paying attention to your surroundings, so why should they? If they get hit by a car, will you blame the driver?

What are you doing with your children that's building a relationship with them? If you were in David's parents' shoes, what would you do differently to let him know that he was important, special, and wanted? Do you do that with your kids? How are you showing them that they are loved and accepted and that they're an important and valued member of the family? Can you remember your parents doing anything like this with you? Did you feel like you were wanted, needed, and included? Or as an adult, do you look back and wish your parents had made more effort toward building trust with you?

Actively including your children in your daily activities of life goes a long way in developing a relationship of trust with each of them. The more effort we, as parents, put into building a foundation of trust with our children early on, the easier and more manageable it will be to get through the harder stuff later. We work through things together, and by example, we model that we will not give up until we get it worked out.

Children absorb everything we model. Just like young David.

I (David) absorbed information about what I saw my mom doing, the pets we had, where our house was, and the color of the telephone my mom talked on that was attached to the kitchen wall. I have memories of being in my crib in my parents' bedroom, and I *still* remember a dream that I had at that age. Every memory forms your child's perception of who they are, the world, and their place in it. When does homeschooling begin? When does the task of parenting start? Even before the cord is cut.

YOUR NEWBORN

When your baby is born, they're completely dependent on you for everything. Everything you do from now on is parenting, teaching, modeling, mentoring, and it's all imprinting onto the psyche of your child. This is when you begin the process of bonding with your infant. You begin building a relationship, creating a bond of safety, love, and trust with them—or you don't. You set the stage that all future teaching will be built upon. How you begin is of paramount importance for the success of your children's future homeschool education and life. This may sound quite dramatic, but the very amazing thing about having a baby is that building a strong foundation is a very natural and enjoyable process if you put some intention into your interactions.

The first interaction you have with this tiny human is when your newborn baby is placed into your arms for the very first time. It's the most emotional and wonderful event I (Terri) have ever experienced. I've had the privilege and absolute pleasure of holding my own newborn baby immediately after their birth on three separate occasions. It is a memory with each of my children that I cherish and have never forgotten. Of course I remember the ups and downs of each pregnancy. Of course I remember all the months of morning sickness, gestational diabetes, and painful swelling of my legs and feet. Of course I still can remember the hours of intense contractions and pain before each child's birth. But the complete and overwhelming joy of holding each infant absolutely over-shadowed all the trials that came before the moment our babies were placed in my arms.

I cradled each of our babies right after their birth as David cradled me, and we both looked adoringly into the faces of the tiniest, most beautiful human beings we had ever seen. After each baby was born, we kissed their little cheeks and touched their soft heads. We gently rocked them and spoke words of love and tenderness to them. Nobody had to tell us to do this; it came naturally, as it does for most parents. For those parents whose instincts don't come immediately after birth, they usually experience it very soon after, within days.

Nonetheless, we were nervous about leaving the hospital and taking care of our first baby all by ourselves. The realization quickly set in that very soon, we would be completely responsible for keeping this baby alive. Although nurturing our newborn infant son did come naturally to us, moving and handling our son so as not to hurt him, feeding him, bathing him, and changing his diapers did not. We needed help!

ASK FOR HELP

David and I were eighteen years old when Blake, our first baby was born. Like most brand-new parents, we had no idea how to properly take care of and meet the daily physical needs of our precious son, so we asked the nurses at the hospital to teach us. It's part of their job, so don't be afraid to ask. They were very kind and patiently worked with us before we left the hospital. They also gave us some literature to take home to read.

Six years later, when our sweet little girl, Jessica was born, we'd forgotten most of what we once knew and were unsure of ourselves again. Changing a little girl's diaper is also very different than changing a little boy's! Once more, David and I asked the nurses who were attending us to give us some hands-on training, which they gladly provided. Both times we asked for help not only because we were nervous, but also because we wanted to ensure we weren't missing anything. We wanted to provide the best care for each of our children.

You don't need to know everything, but you are responsible for recognizing when you don't know something. Ask for help and figure things out as you go.

You'll realize many times throughout your homeschool journey that you don't know what to do. That's okay, just ask around. Find someone who knows the information you need and is willing to teach you. Ask other parents who have already homeschooled their children to mentor you. Find a community of like-minded homeschoolers you can partner with to assist with subjects you're not well versed in, and share your own expertise and experience with the group.

There's a saying that goes, "You don't know what you don't know." As with parenting, in homeschooling, you'll encounter new situations that you didn't foresee. For many things, you can look ahead and start preparing for a known obstacle. But other times, you'll find yourself in a challenging situation before you realize you need help. Ask for help as soon as you realize the need. Don't put it off. It's when we wait that we get in over our heads. Time passes and other matters arise, pushing back the first issue, leading to a snowball effect. Tempers flare, and a lot of things get blown out of proportion when two tired parents and their stress are involved. When we found ourselves in this type of situation, we were unable to stay calm and make good decisions. Notice I didn't say *if*; I said *when*. It will happen. The sooner we recognize a need and seek help, the easier it will be to get back on top of things. Make a point to keep searching until you find the help you need.

YOUR SPOUSE

Ask your mate for help. Sometimes we neglect to let the person closest to us know we are struggling, but communication is key. Calmly and kindly verbalize what you are thinking and feeling. Listen attentively to one another. Include each other in your challenges, share the load, and help each other. That is what marriage is for—to have a partner to walk the road of life with. Someone you know you are safe with, who will share your burden as you share theirs. Someone who will always be there for you and you for them, to encourage and uplift each other. That one special person to enjoy the journey of parenthood together.

Ask each other what you can do to help, and don't expect your spouse to read your mind. How can they know what you are thinking or feeling unless you tell them? They can't, and they don't, no matter how obvious it seems to you. Don't just tell them the baby needs changing and assume they'll go do it. Ask nicely. Verbalize how they can help. For example, "Hey, honey, I'm struggling and need your help. Could you check the baby and change her diaper, please?" Or "We're out of milk. Could you go to the store for us, please?" You may think that sounds simple. In theory, it is. But it's not enough to just think it's a good idea—you must actually do it. You must recognize when you are not communicating and change that.

Sometimes we think things but don't speak them out loud. Sometimes we just say, "We're out of milk." But we don't let the other person know we need their help in getting more. We just expect that if we make the statement, they'll go do it. Then we get upset if they don't. It's unfair and unreasonable to expect your spouse to know what you are thinking. Conversely, you don't know what they're thinking, either. You might guess correctly sometimes, but no one truly knows what another human being has on their mind. So ask.

Now, look at this as a homeschool parent. Each interaction with your spouse, whether positive or negative, is what you're teaching your children by example. Unfortunately, our oldest son remembers clearly the destructive interactions between David and me. Because, "Duh, why would I say the baby's diaper needs to be changed if I didn't want you to do it?" No one is immune. Make a conscious, deliberate decision every day to create the kind of interactions with your spouse that will teach your children the importance of treating others with kindness and respect. The example you provide today is how they will treat you tomorrow and into adulthood.

FAMILY AND FRIENDS

Ask trusted family and friends for help. Of course, we learned that the first thing to always be aware of when asking for help outside of you and your spouse, is your own safety and the well-being of your family. If you or your spouse don't feel good about someone or a particular situation, listen to your gut (or your spouse's gut). You may not be able to say why, but if something doesn't feel right, just exit the situation. Don't be afraid to walk away anytime someone or something doesn't feel right. Always be mindful and vigilant at all times for the safety of yourself, your marriage, and your children.

If a person seems too interested in your spouse or your child in a way that makes you uncomfortable, distance yourself and your family from that person. It's your job to vigilantly guard your marriage and family. If you have family members who can and will help and you trust them, ask. If you have a friend or neighbor you trust, ask. If you don't know anyone, look for someone to help you. *Everyone* needs help from time to time. It's important to have people in our lives whom we know we can trust and rely on when we need help. This is true with a newborn as well as with homeschooling and with your marriage. Surround yourself with good, trustworthy people with whom you can share your life and who will encourage you and help when challenges arise. You'll soon find that through your growth, *you'll* become the trusted friend who can offer sound solutions to those less experienced parents.

DON'T GO IT ALONE

David and I did *not* ask for help once we were home with our newborn. We were young. We didn't have a great relationship with our families, and we felt alone. So, we tried to do everything on our own. It caused a lot of problems and made our life much harder than it had to be. Please spare yourself the misery and ask for help sooner rather than later.

If you're able, find a group with other new parents so that you can share your ups and downs. It helps to know you're not alone. It also helps to hear how others are handling challenges with their children. Don't feel obligated to take all or any advice from others, but remember that learning about different options helps us to make better and more informed decisions for our own families.

If you can get help with chores around the house to take the load off, do it. Occasionally, hiring a cleaning service to clean your home while you relax with your children can be money well spent. Anytime you are able to take a little time out for yourself, do it. Always make time for your spouse, regularly. Take time to share, laugh, cry, and be alone together to continue reconnecting, nurturing, and growing that first and most important relationship—the one that started the adventure of having a family! Remember, your spouse came first before the kids, and your spouse will be there after the kids have grown up and gone into the world. You want that relationship to be mature and strong. You'll be a happier and healthier person when you have a good marriage, because when you and your spouse are happy and healthy, you'll be able to meet the needs of your children better than when you're not.

Get any help you need to make this happen, even if that means seeking out a professional marriage counselor. Don't wait until things are bad. Think of a counselor in the same way you get a check-up at the doctor. You don't wait until you have a major medical condition. You get check-ups to catch things early. Do this with a marriage and family counselor you both feel comfortable with, and you'll fast-track your relationship's maturity.

We knew we needed help with our marriage, so we went to see a counselor. I think we ended up going to seven different counselors over the years before we found the one who truly helped us. We realized that basing our relationship on the example our parents provided was going to destroy us. My (Terri) parents' marriage ended when I was young, and David's parents' marriage wasn't loving, even if they were a good public couple. We had to be shown a more healthy way to relate to each other and build that mutual bond that provides fulfillment.

To be successful with your homeschooling, you must be healthy—physically, mentally, emotionally, and spiritually. You, your spouse, and your marriage need to be healthy because you, as parents, are responsible for the health and well-being of your children. David often refers to his mom lecturing him about healthy food and life choices while she ate cheese puffs and smoked cigarettes—you can't help your children stay healthy when you or your marriage are sick.

Whatever it takes for your situation, keep searching until you find the right help for you and your family. David understands that we all have our weaknesses, but perhaps if he witnessed his mom eating well, exercising, and quitting smoking, her advice would have meant more.

When we realized we needed help with our homeschool, we started asking around in our community. Through a friend of a friend, we found a school that we partnered with to help us get it right for each of our students, along with other homeschool parents who encouraged us and helped with our challenges. It took almost three years of searching to find the best people to assist us, but when we found the right fit, we knew it.

YOUR BABY STILL NEEDS YOU

The very basic needs every human being has—besides the need for food, water, clothing, and shelter—are to feel safe, loved, heard and wanted. Every day, as parents, we make a choice of whether or not to continue to nurture our children like we did in those first moments. Every time we interact with our babies, we have an opportunity to strengthen the bond with them or weaken it and tear it down.

When we would feed our babies, we would hold them close (breast-feeding or bottle), look down into their eyes, speak their names, and tell them how much we loved them. We would sing or hum to them and rock them as they nursed, kissing their little foreheads. We called it a "sniff-n-smooch," because we couldn't help sniffing their tender skin when we kissed them! They may not have understood the words we spoke to them, but they understood by how we held them, touched them, looked into their eyes, smiled at them, and spoke to them that they were safe, loved, heard and needed. They were cherished, special, and important to us. This is the message that we want to communicate to our children when they are born—and for the rest of their lives.

We parents do not have a moment to lose. Inadvertently, you can lose one opportunity, and then another slips by unnoticed.

And then another.

Before you know it, years pass, and the children are as distant as roommates. Parenting is a "now" endeavor. "I'll get around to it" works with cleaning out the garage or rotating the car's tires, but your children need you to engage right now, no exceptions. Your personal life takes a back seat to their development into an adult. Wake up ready to be a parent or don't, but whatever choice you make, understand that your child rapidly absorbs the world around them and their interactions within it. You might be embarrassed to learn what they recall one day.

In the younger internet days when everything was new, I (David) recall seeing a photo of a mom on her hands and knees in a parking lot, twerking in a skimpy outfit for onlookers. She had successfully encouraged her young (approximately kindergarten-aged) daughter to join her. Mom and daughter in a parking lot mimicking a sexual position. It broke my heart. I don't consider myself a prude; most everything has an appropriate context. I felt, however, that maybe your daughter should be able to fill out a job application before she's taught to sexualize herself.

You are not expected to know all the answers to be a parent. Keep it simple with a single-minded focus on your children and your task as their parent. What is the right way to start the day? "Get your ass up!" or "Good morning!" accompanied by a smile and a hug? Early on, your child won't understand the words, but neither does my cat. They both understand, however, the emotion behind them.

Parenting (and homeschooling) is providing the correct and successful way to be an adult by example. You can "teach" until you fall over dead, but talk is cheap—example reigns supreme. Look at families together; parents and their children walk the same way. Do you think that Dad sat his son down and "mansplained" the proper family walk? "Son, our gait is a proud tradition that dates back to your Pepaw Jones in 1865." No, it went something like this: "Honey! Little Scooter took his first step today!" Every day after, little Scooter wanted to keep up with you. Scooter wanted your approval. Most of how Scooter lives life, he does just like his parents, all the way down to the way he walks.

The first years of a child's life shape who they will be for the rest of their life. Who they *believe* they are is reflected to them in their caregiver's eyes. Are your eyes looking at your children with judgment, criticism, or indifference, or are your eyes smiling down at them with love, kindness, and encouragement? Do your eyes say to your children that you love being with them or that they're a nuisance to be tolerated? Whatever they see reflected in your eyes now is who they'll believe they are. They'll either flourish in life because they were seen and cherished, or they'll struggle because they were worthless in the sight of their most important people.

If you find your eyes are less than positive, you can change that—do it now. Who are the people your eyes actually smile at? Notice your interactions with your spouse, your children, and people outside your family. Give your best to your spouse and children by going out of your way to be kind, loving, endearing, and encouraging. Change this now, because you can't go back and undo it later.

Make a point to smile not only with your face but with your eyes. Let your children know, with every advancement, that they are wonderful and that you're excited about them and their progress. This is easy with babies because they're so cute! When an infant starts lifting their head or they roll over, it's easy to be proud. We laugh, we clap, and we rejoice constantly. We want you to let that same enthusiasm last their entire lives—make a point to be your kids' biggest fans!

We counted everything out loud all the time with our babies. When we would get to the end of our counting, we'd say, "Yayyy!" and clap our hands or gently clap their hands together until they began doing it themselves. When we would change their diapers, we'd raise one of their hands and say, "One hand!" then raise the other and say, "Two hands! Yay!" When our little girl was born, her six-year-old big brother would join in. We would repeat the same activity with their feet and their eyes. They loved it! They kicked their legs, wiggled their arms, and squealed with delight. We would repeat this game with everything we could find. We'd put our finger on their nose and say, "One little nose! Boop!" They loved playing pat-a-cake and peek-a-boo. Their big toothless grins were contagious. They may not have understood all the words, but they enjoyed every minute, and so did we.

Each time we repeated these games, associations were made and connections formed in their brains. We would do this with things of the same color, big things, small things, different textures—with anything and everything descriptive, you can make a game of it. Are you formally teaching them? Not in the traditional sense, but you are teaching them every moment of every day! It's your choice to have lots of playful fun or to just walk around saying, "This is an orange;" "This is a door;" "These are your feet." I know that sounds silly—who would do that with their baby? Exactly! You wouldn't. So, why do this with your older children? Why can't learning be fun? You can make it that way. Do it! Even as a young lady, our daughter would come help out with a task like cutting vegetables. We would say, "Thank you, Jessica!" She would smile really big and say, "Yayyyy!" and we would all laugh.

IMPLEMENTING A ROUTINE, NOT JUST FOR ADULTS

Creating and sticking to routines at home is the best thing you can do for yourself and your children. When the time comes to start teaching academics, it will be much easier if you and your children are already accustomed to routines and a schedule. Maintaining daily routines will set you up for success and reduce stress and anxiety for you and your kids, both in everyday life and in your homeschool. Conversely, if you fail to create and follow daily routines, it can and will cause significant stress in your life and make homeschooling much harder than it needs to be. Stress can also put you and your children at higher risk for heart disease and negatively affect your overall health. On the other hand, an effective routine can help reduce stress, which can lead to better mental health, more time to relax, and less anxiety. If you are not already in the habit of specific daily routines, it will help you and your homeschool to work toward implementing them. Do it from the very beginning of your children's life with you, and keep doing it throughout their lives and your own. You may always have to work at it, but it will be normal and easy for your children if that is how they are raised.

FEEDING SCHEDULES AND MEAL ROUTINES

We learned early on that setting schedules and routines was very helpful. I remember for each of our babies, after we brought them home from the hospital, we would feed them on demand, as you do starting out. But in time, we had to put them on a feeding schedule. I breastfed each of our babies from birth until they were between nine and twelve months old. For the first few weeks, they would wake up and want to eat, suckle for a few minutes, and then go to sleep. They weren't really getting that much milk because they would go right back to sleep. I'd put the baby back in bed, and they would wake up and want to eat thirty minutes later. We'd repeat this process nearly twenty-four hours a day. It didn't take long for me to become exhausted. Finally, after doing some research at the library and asking our baby's doctor and some people we trusted, we decided it would be best to get our baby on a feeding schedule. I implemented the schedule gradually over time. The baby would wake up and eat and go to sleep. Then the next time he woke up, I would wait fifteen minutes before I would get him to feed. The next time, I would push it out to thirty minutes, and then forty-five, and so on until we got up to three hours in between feedings. Yes, they cried, and yes, it was very difficult for us to just let them cry, and it disturbed the whole household. But it really didn't take that long for them to adjust, and when they would feed, they would eat a good amount, and their little tummies would be full so that they weren't hungry for about three hours. This was better for the baby and for me. They were more content and would sleep longer, and I could get more rest.

We were learning each child's temperament and personality, and at the same time, we were also teaching them to conform to our will. It did not hurt them to wait a little longer to eat, and it was better for them and me because they were learning not to eat constantly, whenever they wanted, but to wait for a set time to eat. This becomes more important as our children get older and even more so into adulthood. They need to learn self-control, and it's never too early to start. We also didn't want our children to always have a snack in their hands, which could lead to obesity and impulsivity. Having scheduled times to eat, along with helping your children make healthy food choices, teaches self-discipline early on and benefits them into adulthood.

Maintaining a good routine and set times for each meal helps give structure throughout your day, especially while homeschooling. Additionally, planning your meals ahead of time will help take the stress out of mealtime and will help you maintain a more healthy diet. As a baby grows and moves from bottles to sippy cups, from formula to baby food, it is beneficial to have set times for meals when they sit together with you at the table to eat. The more meals you are able to have together as a family, the more time you have to connect and interact. This is an excellent time to make a habit of putting away all electronic devices so that you give your undivided attention to each other. Make a point to ask each member of your family questions about their activities or something learned or interesting about their day. Ask about what went well and what didn't. You can have a conversation with your baby even though they may not have the vocabulary to respond in words; they will communicate and interact in whatever way they are able. If you develop this habit early on, it will be easy to maintain throughout the child's life; if not, it is harder to implement as they get older and more time passes. However, it is never too late to start good habits that will build up your family, and it is always worth the effort to do so.

With our first baby, we had no concept of regular mealtimes or eating together at all. David was still in high school, so he left early in the morning, was gone all day, and then worked at night to support us. We only had one vehicle, so our baby and I were stuck in our apartment all day every day. I slept when he slept, and we ate when he was hungry. We had no structure to our day, and consequently, I did not accomplish much. I became depressed and lonely. After attending school all day and working all evening, when David got home, he was exhausted. He had already eaten at work. Consequently, we really didn't connect much during that time, and we grew apart.

The more babies you have, the more you realize the importance of a schedule and routines. By the time our youngest was born, we would have two meals together most days. Blake was seven years old by this point, and he helped us with our eighteen-month-old, Jessica, and our newborn,

Joshua. We were learning how to get on a schedule and put routines in place to enable our home to run more smoothly. The better we got at it, the less stress and more enjoyment we could have with each other. Getting to this point doesn't necessarily come all at once—it certainly didn't for us—but we kept working on it, making improvements with time. When we began homeschooling, maintaining a schedule and establishing routines became even more imperative.

Routines such as your sleep schedule and bedtime habits affect your mental sharpness, emotional well-being, and energy. Maintaining consistent times for waking and going to bed can help you get better rest. The same is true for your children.

BEDTIME ROUTINE AND SLEEP SCHEDULE

I (Terri) did well with our bedtime routine. This was something my mom did with me and my sister. Every evening from as early as I can remember, at the same time each night, we would have our bath and get on our jammies for bed. We would brush our teeth and get in bed, my mom would read us a story, and then we would say a short bedtime prayer. She would kiss us goodnight and turn off the light. Sometimes she would rub our backs for a few minutes. I am thankful that my mom made us keep a regular bedtime schedule, and I looked forward to this time with our children every night. It was such a sweet time of bonding together. It was a time just for them, without distractions or interruptions. We didn't have cell phones or iPads back then, but this is a good time to put those away. It is important for their safety that they have your undivided attention, but it's also so that they feel your love and joy at having this special time set aside every evening just for them. It is comforting for them to know they can count on this time together every day. Our kids were always excited to take their bath each night because we made it fun with bubbles and toys. We spiked and swirled their hair with the shampoo suds. When they are babies, naturally, you will bathe them yourself, but as they get bigger and are able to do more, you will train them little by little to do it all themselves. They love to "help" Daddy and Mommy. Our big helpers. We would call out their body parts as we washed them, make funny sounds, and sing songs like "head, shoulders, knees and toes," and point to each corresponding part. I'm afraid I am making it sound quite mechanical, but it wasn't at all. We had fun, they had fun, and they were learning without it being like a lesson where they had to memorize a bunch of stuff. We would play a game and say, "Where's Blake's eyes?" or "Where's Daddy's eyes?" And they may or may not be able to show you, so you take their hands and cover their eyes or yours and say, "There's Blake's eyes," or "There's Daddy's eyes!" Laugh and clap their hands together; make it a game of peek-a-boo. It doesn't take long for them to want to play and start doing it themselves because you are smiling and laughing and cheering. Babies, toddlers, kids, and adults—we all enjoy and are drawn to smiling, laughing, and cheering. It is just how we are all wired.

This is the perfect time to teach your children good hygiene habits. If you do the same things every time in the same order, they will quickly and easily learn to reproduce your actions without you telling them to do it—it's all in how you present it. If you make it fun and enjoyable and the time spent together is pleasant, they will happily do it to please you and show you how big and grown up they are. If you see hygiene as a chore and treat it as another thing that has to be dealt with or as if it is mundane, they will learn not to care, they won't look forward to it, and not only will it not be a bonding experience, but it most likely will become a point of contention. You'll end up fighting them to get their baths completed whenever you decide it is necessary, and getting them to go to bed will also be a fight.

READING TO YOUR BABY

My mother instilled a love of reading into my sister and me with our bedtime routine. Consequently, we (David and I) started reading to our kids when they were babies. We made a point to hold them and read to them every night before bed as part of their bedtime routine. Holding your children while reading and snuggling with them is a very important part of showing them your love and affection. When you cuddle with them while reading, they feel safe and connected, loved and warm in your arms. We would hold them on our laps, with the book we were reading that evening right in front of them so that they could see. When they were babies, it was usually hard books that they could reach out and grab and touch. Or puffy plastic books that they could hold on to with us. We would point to the words as we read them and read in an animated style. Again, it is all in how you present it. If you read to them like it is a chore, they won't develop any fondness for it, but if you animate your voice and enjoy reading with them, they will learn to love reading themselves. It does not matter at all to them whether you can read out loud really well or not. The more you do it, the better you will get. We would read different children's books, including lots of Dr. Suess; the older Golden Books; books about animals and nature, shapes, colors, sizes, families, and lots of other different things; tactile books; Mother Goose nursery rhymes; Aesop's Fables; the Serendipity series; animated Bible stories; even tongue twisters. All kinds of different subjects that we had fun with. Each time I would read Dr. Suess, I would try reading faster and faster without making a mistake. It was funny when I'd mess up, and we would all laugh.

Reading to your baby every day is exceedingly beneficial to them. During the first year, a baby's brain is growing more than at any other time in their life. Not only will reading to your child help create a sweet bond of love and affection between you and your baby, but there are many academic benefits for your child. Not only will this help set them up for success in homeschool and in life, but reading is also very beneficial to their social and mental health as well.

Benefits of reading out loud to your babies include the following:

- Helps their brain to develop
- Helps them learn their native language and develop speech patterns
- Helps them learn the sounds of language and meanings associated with words
- Introduces them to uncommon vocabulary and sentence structure
- Acquaints them with rhyming and repetition
- Builds their listening, memory, and vocabulary skills
- Introduces them to things like numbers, colors, letters, shapes, and sizes

- Helps them develop a larger and more complex vocabulary by age two
- Teaches the importance of communication and presents a wonderful social element of communication
- Provides information about the world around them
- Enables them to be more likely to read on time or, in the case of our children, early

Consequences of not reading to your child include the following:

- The brain develops less, which can lead to a smaller brain.[10]
- They develop speech and language skills at a slower pace.
- They have lower language comprehension, smaller vocabularies, and lower cognitive skills than peers.
- They are less likely to be able to read on time, leading to decreased literacy.
- Poor literacy skills are shown to lead to behavioral problems, drug use, and are associated with a higher rate of poverty.[11]

Children who are read to as babies are more likely to be able to read at or above grade level later in life, but those children who are *not* read to as infants are likelier to *not* be able to read beyond a third-grade level, a sad state that is linked to academic failure later in adolescence. Furthermore, a student who cannot read on grade level by third grade is four times less likely to graduate by age nineteen than a child who does read proficiently by that time.[12]

---

10 - M. D. De Bellis, M. S. Keshaven, D. B. Clark, B. J. Caseey, J. B. Giedd, A. M. Boring, K. Frustaci, and N. D. Ryan, "Developmental Traumatology. Part 2: Brain Development," *Biological Psychiatry* 45 (1999): 1271–1284.

11 - Sherri Gordon, "Why Reading to Your Baby Is Important," Very Well Family, last

updated November 21, 2022, https://www.verywellfamily.com/why-reading-to-babies-is-important-5189827; National Center for Education Statistics, US Department of Education, Office of Educational Research and Improvement, *Literacy in the Labor Force: Results from the National Adult Literacy Survey*, 1999, http://nces.ed.gov/pubsearch/pubsinfo.asp?pubid=1999470.

12 - Sarah D. Sparks, Study: Third Grade Reading Predicts Later High School Graduation," Education Week, April 8, 2011, https://www.edweek.org/teaching-learning/study-third-grade-reading-predicts-later-high-school-graduation/2011/04.

We attribute our children learning to read before starting kindergarten to diligently reading to them every day. We encouraged their learning as we pointed to the words. We spoke with animation and asked them questions about the story. They learned to listen carefully to be able to answer the questions. Our children caught on and quickly wanted to read themselves. They developed a love for reading that they still have to this day. Their vocabulary was larger and more complex than that of most other children as a result of how much we read to them. I remember having a conversation with Jessica when she was about eighteen months old. She was speaking in full, complex sentences using big words that she had heard in stories we had read. People were amazed at how "grown up" our children sounded because they could speak so well and form sentences coherently. They were not necessarily any smarter than other children; they just had been exposed to a much larger set of vocabulary words and experiences through the stories we had read to them. We continued to read out loud together as a family from birth all the way through high school. As they got older, the books we read became longer, and we introduced increasingly complex literature. Our routine evening reading time was a time of connection and adventure that we all looked forward to.

Implementing reading into your bedtime routine helps to calm both you and your children down as you cuddle up together and become still to listen to a story. The precious time you spend holding your little ones while reading and discussing a story enables them to feel safe and connected to you. It helps both you and your child wind down from the day and provides a transition from being up, awake, and active, to slowing down and getting into bed to go to sleep. Reading daily to our children models and nurtures a love of reading—they learn to love it, and they want to imitate us by learning to read by themselves.

CHILDREN ARE YOUR MIRROR

I (Terri) remember noticing our six-year-old son had stopped smiling and seemed sullen. How could this be? He was always such a happy little one. As I thought about it, I realized I had stopped smiling at him. I was pregnant and was sick most of the time. I was also working outside of the home. At the end of the workday, I was exhausted and didn't have anything left to give my family. I had allowed the circumstances of daily life to take my smile away, and it was reflected on my little boy's face. Remember, children are a reflection of what they see and have learned from the people they are around the most, and hopefully, that is you, their parents. Whatever you wish to see in your child, you must model to them; you must live it before them. That is how they learn. If you see your child behaving in a way you don't like, look in the mirror and evaluate what you need to change in your own behavior, because your child is just reflecting and imitating what they have learned from you.

Soon after I realized how sullen Blake was, his baby sister, Jessica, was born. When Jessica was born, we smiled and played with her constantly, just waiting for that big, toothless grin to shine back at us. We delighted in her smile, and we did anything we possibly could to get her to laugh, which in turn made us laugh. We all enjoyed playing with our sweet little baby girl and eliciting as many smiles and giggles from her as we could. At the end of every school day, we would go pick her big brother up from school. As soon as she saw him, she would start kicking her little arms and legs in her car seat and smile so big! He would go straight to her and kiss her and hug her! She adored her big brother. She helped bring us closer as a family and reminded us how much we had enjoyed our son when he was a baby. She gave us back our smiles.

Do you remember when your little ones were babies and you smiled at them all the time? Remember when you looked forward to playing with them and hearing them laugh with glee? No matter the age, our children love to see us smile and hear us laugh just as much as we love to see them smile and hear their laughter. As our little ones get bigger and they start moving around and getting into things, we can begin to lose our joy and get frustrated with the natural changes that come with growth. We can—and often do—allow life's burdens to encroach upon our own mood. Sometimes we lose our smile and stop laughing. We get too serious and self-focused. We stop having fun and enjoying life. Your family members are the most important and amazing people in your life; they are yours! Don't allow your smile to go away, cherish them and let them know how special they are to you. Make a point to have fun with and smile often at your children, and smile not only with your mouth, but with your eyes genuinely from your heart.

MULTIPLE CHILDREN AND ADDRESSING SPECIAL NEEDS

Jessica was our little sunshine, and her daddy, Blake, and I all doted on our precious new baby. We tickled her and laughed with her. We loved our new little baby girl. She was a firecracker! She was stubborn and sometimes a challenge. But we all loved her and enjoyed every moment with her. We would all take turns reading to her. Blake would sit and hold her and play with her. We would sing ABCs and 1-2-3s with her. All three of us were busy showing her every little thing we could think of to teach her. She loved it! She loved every bit of attention we gave her and readily drank in all the information we were sharing with her.

Jessica learned to speak very quickly and seemed older than her actual age. She was born with a lot of hair, and by the time she was a year old, her hair had grown long, below her shoulders. It was twice as long as that of her twin cousins of the same age. To me, they still looked more like babies, but Jessica looked more like a three-year-old than a one-year-old. We had taught her to do many things on her own, which she was proud and happy to do all by herself. She was a capable little one, and she quickly became very independent. I began to relate to her as if she actually were older.

Jessica was only nine months old when we became pregnant with Joshua, our youngest. Gradually, throughout the pregnancy, my attention toward Jessica started to lessen. As with my other pregnancies, I was sick. In the last few months, the bigger I got, I carried and held her less. I was tired. I was more focused on managing my pregnancy than giving Jessica the attention she had been receiving from me before. Once more, I allowed life and circumstances to distract me from being the mom she needed me to be. To me, it was barely noticeable, a gradual decline, but to her, she felt rejected by her mother, and she didn't know why. This is something all children do: they blame themselves when they sense something is wrong or different with one or both of their parents; they wonder what they did that caused the change. But of course, she did not have the knowledge or vocabulary to tell me how she was feeling.

Jessica was just eighteen months old when Joshua (Joshy b-squashy, we called him) was born. It was not on purpose, but she took a backseat when he was born. I put all my energy into taking care of him. I didn't think at the time that I had cast my daughter aside, but I now realize that she felt that way. I believe that she felt this newborn baby had moved in and seized her place in our hearts. I am sure we included her because I remember doing so, but most of the attention had definitely moved from her to the new baby, simply because a newborn requires more attention. At the time, I didn't understand that what I was doing was hurting Jessica. Sure, I recognized she was jealous, but I ignored what I saw happening to her. I dismissed it and discounted her feelings because I hadn't realized the damage it was doing to her then and how it would affect her for the rest of her life.

I refocused the teaching techniques we had used with Blake and Jessica onto Joshua. Jessica had already learned all the basic stuff, so she listened and played with her toys while I was reading, singing, and teaching Joshua the ABCs and 1-2-3s, but I didn't continue to focus as much attention on advancing her learning. Because of her jealousy, she refused to join in the "fun" of teaching her baby brother like her older brother had done with her. I failed to include her as the "important and much-needed" big sister. I neglected to spend quality alone time with her to let her know that she was still special to me, that she had not been replaced in my heart. This fueled her jealousy and resentment toward her little brother. Her big brother was her buddy, and he saw what was happening and shared her sentiment of resentment toward the baby.

After Josh's birth, I was able to find a job that would enable me to work from home as a medical transcriptionist. The office was about an hour's drive away from where we lived. Most of my energy went to my training and being at work all day. The faster I learned my job and became good enough to type the required ninety to one hundred words per minute, the sooner I would be able to do my work at home. In the evenings when

I got home, we would eat dinner, do our nighttime routine, and then start the process over again the next day. It took about three to four months to become proficient enough at transcription before my boss would allow me to work from home. During that time, the jealousy that Jessica was experiencing was not on my radar unless she was acting out. While I just dealt with the symptoms as they occurred, sadly, I failed to address the root cause of the problems. This is called *reactive parenting*, and it often makes the situation worse.[13]

I wish I would have made a point to set aside quality time daily with our children individually, when they each would have my undivided attention to show them they were special and important to me, that they were loved and accepted by me. Doing so would've positively affected all of them. It lets your child know they are seen and gives them identity. Now I know the importance of both parents setting aside one-on-one time with each child. Studies have shown that spending as little as fifteen minutes of quality time per day with each child is linked to fewer behavior problems in school.[14] In our family, this practice could have avoided problems in the future by helping us develop a healthier relationship with our children. Creating space to spend quality time with each child outside of teaching was a foreign concept to me back then. My parents did not do this with me that I can recall, and I thought all the time I was spending teaching them was way more than what I'd experienced growing up. I was proud that I was spending—what seemed to me—a lot of time with them. But it wasn't focused on them as an individual person; it was focused on teaching. If you recognize this special time is lacking with your children, it is never too late to make a change and start spending sweet, quality time with each of them. This focused attention shows them very clearly that they are seen and important enough to you to slow down and join them in their world for some one-on-one time.

---

13 - Claire Lerner, "Responsive vs Reactive Parenting: It Makes All the Difference," Lerner Child Development, August 9, 2018, https://www.lernerchilddevelopment.com/mainblog/2018/8/9/responsive-vs-reactive-parenting-it-makes-all-the-difference.

14 - C. Opondo, M. Redshaw, E. Savage-McGlynn, and M. A. Quigley, "Father Involvement in Early Child-Rearing and Behavioural Outcomes in their Pre-Adolescent Children: Evidence from the ALSPAC UK Birth Cohort, *BMJ Open* 6, no. 11 (2016), doi:10.1136/bmjopen-2016-012034.

I do believe that had I taken the time to sit with and hold little Jessica right then when I recognized her jealousy, to visit with her and play a bit with only the two of us, it would have made a big difference to her. But as I have reflected on my actions throughout the years, I have come to realize that this first rejection she experienced led to many years of Jessica feeling insecure, not accepted, not good enough, not seen—"invisible," as she would tell me when she was older. It is heartbreaking to me to finally understand this now after it is too late. But it is my hope that by sharing my mistakes with you here in this book, you will pay attention, learn, and subsequently avoid this same heartbreak with your own children—a heartbreak that I will have to endure for the rest of my life, simply because I was too busy and self-focused to slow down and be present for my children when they were young. The insecurity and rejection Jessica was experiencing would cause problems for her later in her childhood.

WHAT EXACTLY DOES "SPECIAL NEEDS" MEAN?

Merriam-Webster's online dictionary defines *special needs* as follows: "any of various difficulties (such as a physical, emotional, behavioral, or learning disability or impairment) that causes an individual to require additional or specialized services or accommodations (such as in education or recreation)."[15] Every human being has special needs in one form or another and at different times in their lives. It is somewhat unfair to only consider physical or mental disabilities as special needs, although we do acknowledge that the most commonly understood meaning of *special needs* is represented in the definition just given. The whole point of homeschooling is for parents to be able to address whatever special needs each of their individual children may have regardless of the severity, whereas in the common form of Western public and private schools, it is not feasible for all the needs of all children to be met. Invariably, some children get left behind or lost along the way. Although there are some

---

15 - *Merriam-Webster*, s.v. "Special Needs," last updated July 8, 2024, https://www.merriam-webster.com/dictionary/special%20needs.

teachers who genuinely care about their students, the fact is that even the ones who do care are not able to meet all the needs of every one of their students, and the ones who don't care not only don't meet the needs of their students, but they may even do harm.

In our family, "special needs" manifested in several forms. When Blake, our oldest, started school, he was very capable, well-behaved, and mature for his age. He could read well, write, and do basic math. He needed to be stimulated and provided with materials that would challenge, inspire, and propel him forward in his learning. We handed the torch of Blake's education to the school, believing they would take it and run. Instead, the teacher sat him in a corner to read by himself while she worked with the other children. His learning stagnated as his individual needs were not being met. Neither David nor I recognized what was going on at school. He was pushed through those early grades with only what we had taught him before starting school to pretty much go it on his own. They thought him capable and not in need of any help. This led to problems with math for him.

Because Jessica felt rejected, she became withdrawn, shy, and insecure as she lost the boldness and spark she'd had as a baby. My cure for that was to send her to a well-known local preschool. I thought being around other children, in what would surely be a wonderful learning environment, would help draw her out of her shell. She would have fun and learn at the same time. What could go wrong?

I didn't know that being in that environment actually made it worse for her. I later learned that she shrank back from the other kids; they latched on to her insecurity and bullied her. She bravely endured every day because I wanted her to go, but it was ultimately to her detriment, emotionally and academically. Most young children do not have the words to tell us what is going on with them. We must take notice when we see a change in their attitude or behavior—when they lose their spark, the light in their eyes. Again, I did not pay attention. I chose to ignore what was right in front of me, and neither David nor I recognized what she was going through.

Joshua was like any normal little boy with lots of energy. There was a fad going on in the 1990s that basically labeled every kid with energy, usually boys, with attention-deficit, hyperactivity disorder (ADHD). A close family member advised us that we needed to put Josh on Ritalin to control his energy because they were doing that with their boy. Other friends and couples in our family on both sides also did the same thing with their boys. While we acknowledge there are some children who may genuinely need medication to help with a disorder such as ADHD, we did not believe Josh had a disorder that needed to be chemically controlled. We believed he was an ordinary little boy who needed to run, jump, and play, but also needed to learn how to sit still and concentrate when appropriate to do so. We refused to go the Ritalin route with him. To our knowledge, three of those kids ended up in jail as teenagers. Is there a connection? Seems possible. They're totally unrelated families. Back then, as politely as possible, we said, "Fuck off—stay out of our business." Our kids, our choices. We weren't looking for a conforming child. We were looking to realize his abilities and desires, and bingo, we found it. His mind wanted to be challenged, and as homeschoolers, we did just that! He found his "why," and his mind calmed down. In a very short time, his personality calmed; he was focused and seemed to be a few years older in maturity. He's still one of the kindest and smartest people you could ever meet.

We recognize that what I (Terri) have shared with you isn't considered special needs per se. I'd like you to consider that "special needs" encompasses whatever unique "special need" each child has. As homeschool parents, we are problem solvers by nature. We set out to work with each child to identify challenges as they arise and to overcome them regardless of severity. That's what good parents do. There's nothing inherently "wrong" with the child; they may just learn differently. The sooner we figure that out, the better we homeschool parents can support them in the way they learn best so that they can capitalize on their unique strengths. We want each individual child to reach success in life, whatever that may mean for them, so we do whatever it takes to help them achieve that.

Every state has programs available to help parents test children in several key areas of growth and development, and then help parents create and adjust homeschool plans specific to each child's needs. It is up to you, the parent, to find whatever assessment is necessary that will identify your child's needs and meet those needs so that they can overcome their individual obstacles.

However, we will admit that we don't have experience with exceptionally severe special needs. From our limited viewpoint, we would treat this child with the same consideration as any other child. They may not progress as other children do, but your lessons to teach them are the same, appropriately taking into account their individual needs for their unique situation. We would look at their abilities and contrast this against the life they will likely be able to live as an adult, and we would focus on their skills specific to that task. From our perspective and how we evaluate with a homeschool mindset, we would recommend that you look to the results of testing assessments on this child. What does research say they likely will be capable of? This really isn't any different than how we look at any other child; the information is just more limited to specific special needs.

There are so many stories of children who have overcome their disabilities and lived amazingly full adult lives, despite what the "professionals" pronounced they could or could not do. So, it's up to you, as parents, to endeavor to understand what your children are capable of and then help them to reach as high as possible based on their own abilities. Testing should be used as a tool to help us gauge where our children are, physically, mentally, emotionally, and academically. We figure out what appropriate goals are for each child, and then we move forward from there with a plan to achieve those goals. Use the assessments as a guideline but not necessarily as the only rule. We know that most parents do this naturally; we just want to break the process down.

One aspect of having a special needs child that I (David) find extremely important is communication. Even with our oldest son (who could easily communicate with us), we still didn't know what was going on at school. With a special needs child whose difficulty lies in their inability to communicate, I would find it very hard to confidently send them off to strangers. Admitting my ignorance, my singular focus would be, if possible, communication. Thinking about it, though, that's what we do with any child: we talk and interact until we form an understanding between one another, then build on it.

All I know is that all of our children are special and deserve all the love and attention we can provide for them to live their best possible life, and it's beautiful to get to be a part of that.

INCLUDE YOUR CHILDREN IN EVERYTHING

You can and should include your children in almost everything you do. It doesn't matter what the task or subject is. Converse with them about whatever you do as you do it. Speak enthusiastically to them about washing the dishes and folding clothes. Explain how you are repairing or maintaining your vehicle and why. Tell them all about the stocks you picked and what is significant about them.

Tell them stories.

What about that huge fish that got away? Show them pictures of family and share your favorite stories and memories. Point out animals as you drive down the road, walk along in the park, or hike down a trail. Mimic the animal's sounds and laugh when your child tries to mimic you. Hug them and tell them that they are great! Pretend you are on a cooking show and explain everything to them as if they were your audience; our oldest granddaughter and I (Terri) had a great time with our "cooking show."

I (Terri) was taking an anatomy and physiology class in college, and at the age of two, our son would go with me to class a few evenings a week to study. We'd get a life-size skeleton (it was a plastic replica), and he and I would learn the bones of the body and skull together. I would point to some part of the body and tell him what it was. I would explain what I was learning to him. That helped me to learn what I was studying. Anytime I could, I would point out a body part and ask him what it was. He, in turn, would point at something and ask me what it was. He was modeling what he saw me doing. It didn't take long for both of us to learn and remember every single bone. He loved it. We were doing it together, and people were amazed at how much this little guy knew.

Even if your children don't understand a word you are saying, they love the interaction with you, and eventually, they will understand. Their minds are continually absorbing everything around them, especially what you say and do, as well as your emotions and attitudes. When we talked to our babies, we would include as many descriptive words and sounds as we could—blue sky, green grass, soft blanket. We would lift them up into the air and say "Up!" with a lilting voice, and then we would lower them down and say "Down . . . " with a droopy voice, repeating this multiple times to elicit their glee and laughter. Their incredible brains are taking everything in, and they make associations and connections very quickly. Delight in your children. Enjoy them. Make what you are doing into a game that causes them to laugh. Make it exciting and fun. It doesn't need to be elaborate or complicated. It can be done simply with your cheerful voice and a smile. You can apply what I'm saying to any topic you can think of in many different ways. If it is enjoyable and interesting to you, it will be to them as well.

LEARNING TO WALK

I (Terri) don't remember learning to walk do you? David actually does, because he remembers how he didn't like how baby shoes felt on his feet! But even still, no one starts out in life already knowing how to walk.

The way we are with our children when they are learning to walk is such a great example of teaching. We model walking every day—our babies see what we are doing and want to be just like us. We do little bouncy exercises with our babies to build strength in their bodies and legs. We hold them up and encourage them to stand; we cheer them on. We clap when they pull up to something and as they start to creep and crawl. With each skill they conquer, we celebrate. By doing so, we are bringing attention to and reinforcing the behaviors we want them to continue. When they fall down, we don't tell them how naughty or stupid they are or how disappointed we are in them for falling—of course not! We say something like, "Uh-oh!" with a great big smile and help them get up to try again. We keep encouraging them until they learn how to walk on their own.

I do not ever remember saying to my toddler that they could not walk or would never be able to do it for any reason, because we expected that they *would* learn to walk. We helped them as they mastered the necessary skills of walking, and then they moved on to learning to run. It is a very natural—and gradual—process. An individual skill is learned, and then another and another, gradually building up toward mastering the whole. Can we, as parents, use this example as a template to help us with our teaching of every skill and subject? Is it possible to emulate this example with everything else?

Make it your own. Find your own example that you can relate back to, like this one, to help with everything you teach.

When our baby boy had gotten big enough to pull up and stand using the dishwasher door, he would watch me put the dishes in the dishwasher. I would hand him a spoon and show him where to put it in the basket. As he did this, I would tell him all about that spoon. It was a big spoon, a little spoon, a silver spoon, a slotted spoon, a soup spoon, a wooden spoon. There was a whole family of spoons, and each had a job and was an important part of the family. And I would praise him for a job well done! He was my big helper, and he loved being a part of what I was doing. With time and repetition, he learned each task to the point that he could do the dishes by himself at a young age.

Now let's apply the example of learning to walk to learning math skills. I think it goes without saying that you are not going to try to teach your kindergartener how to do calculus. Most likely, they will not possess the vocabulary or the prerequisite understanding to be able to proficiently master this subject. Instead, you must start with very simple terms and gradually progress as they gain understanding. The way we taught our children math was to start counting everything out loud with them when they were babies. We would cheer and make the "Mwaa, ha, ha, ha," sound that the Count from *Sesame Street* would make when he finished counting. "One cookie, two cookies, three cookies. Mwaa, ha, ha, ha! Three cookies! Yayyyyy!" As soon as they started speaking, they would try to imitate what we were saying to them over and over again. We would keep progressing with them until they were able to count things themselves. Gradually, they could count to ten, fifteen, twenty.

We then would start using items to teach addition and subtraction. For example, we'd put one pretzel stick in front of them and then another and say, "One plus one is two! Two pretzels!" And then count them, "One, two!" They don't need to understand what that means; they will learn and come to an understanding the more you repeat the process with them. We'd do the same thing with subtraction. "Two pretzels. Mama has two pretzels. One, two. If Blake eats one pretzel (give it to your child to eat), there is one pretzel left. Two take away one is one. Two minus one equals one." You are introducing them to a language, the language of mathematics. Make it fun! Be delightful! Count their stuffed animals as you and they put them away. Count their blocks as you stack and build together. Count nesting cups and let them figure out how to nest them. Count trees, buildings, or traffic lights as you drive places in the car. You get the idea.

Just as you wouldn't try to teach your kindergarten student advanced mathematics, you also would not and should not expose them to sexually explicit adult content or violent subject matter at an early age.[16] It is our job as parents to protect our children from all content that will harm them mentally, emotionally, and spiritually, just as we protect them from anything that might harm them physically. It is up to us to decide at what age they are mature enough to handle sensitive information and how much information they are able to handle at any given time or age. We must limit their exposure to questionable materials and only allow age-appropriate content. What does that mean exactly?

It probably means something different for each child. Just as you would wait to move on to a new concept in math until they are proficient at the previous concept, you must only gradually expose them to the darker things of this world at a pace that they are mature enough to handle. We don't want our children to be so sheltered that they cannot function as adults once confronted with the world's atrocities. We must, however, correctly discern when a child is mature enough to handle certain knowledge in an effort to protect their innocence as long as possible. It is up to you, as parents, to make wise decisions on how to deliver this sensitive information in a way that protects their hearts; enables them to discern between right and wrong and good and evil; and teaches them to

---

16 - Jill Christensen, "Children and Screen Time: How Much Is Too Much?" Mayo Clinic Health System, May 28, 2021, https://www.mayoclinichealthsystem.org/hometown-health/speaking-of-health/children-and-screen-time.

make rational, logical, well-thought-out decisions to help them navigate the world they will be living in as an adult. It is your responsibility to make decisions that protect each child and prepare them for the world they soon will encounter as adults. They don't get to decide. That means you must control their access to the internet and social media, and must also monitor everything they watch on television and online. This may sound overbearing, but you can never go back once they have seen too much too soon. You can *never* reclaim a child's innocence once it is gone. Make the choice now to limit TV time, tablet time, phone time, computer time, and video-game time.

LIMIT MEDIA USE

The American Academy of Pediatrics (AAP) discourages media use for children under two and otherwise says that children should be limited to no more than one hour per day of screen time. Furthermore, the AAP also recommends that adults limit their own screen time to less than two hours per day.[17] This is one way you can model self-control to your children.

The Mayo Clinic maintains that too much screen time leads to the following:

- Obesity
- Irregular sleep
- Behavioral problems
- Emotional, social, and attention problems
- Impaired academic performance
- Violence
- Less time for play

The whole point of homeschooling our children is for us to provide them with the best education possible and prepare them with life skills to sufficiently and effectively navigate the world they will be living in as adults. Some television and electronic media can be educational and

---

17 - Jill Christensen, "Children and Screen Time: How Much Is Too Much?" Mayo Clinic Health System, May 28, 2021, https://www.mayoclinichealthsystem.org/hometown-health/speaking-of-health/children-and-screen-time.

entertaining, but it should be the exception, not the norm. Most media consumed can and should be family fun time, not electronic babysitter time.

When you do allow your children to use some form of screen time, always keep them under your careful supervision, participating with them so that you can be there to answer any questions they may have or turn it off if the need arises.Not only did we limit screen time, we also carefully monitored what media our children consumed. Some people wrongly assumed that we were the religious zealot brand of homeschoolers—not just a religious family but viewed through the lens of what anti-homeschoolers viewed as religious zealots—and therefore forced our children to watch only religious programming.

We didn't.

The only remotely religious programming that comes to mind is the *VeggieTales* cartoons. The kids couldn't wait for each new video to be released. We enjoyed the programs with them and still drop random quotes or sing Silly Songs like the Stuff Mart Rap, The Hairbrush Song or I Love My Lips to each other. We didn't have video-streaming services besides cable when our kids were young; we had DVDs and VHS tapes. If it was in their video collection, they could freely watch it. We screened literally everything our children had access to before they watched it. And no, the kids weren't made aware that we did this. Otherwise, it was a mix of PBS-style programming and Disney-type movies. The point was that we screened everything first to catch any topics or references that might cause the child to ask questions for which a full answer was not appropriate for their age. It took a lot of work.

I recall their grandparents' anger when we informed them our children were not allowed to watch certain "kids" programming that they had in their house. If the grandparents turned it on anyway after we were gone, our kids would leave the room and piss off the grandparents all over again. Remember the importance of sheltering your family? Kids shouldn't have to deal with this. We had family members who didn't care what we said; they did not respect us, and consequently, our children were not allowed to visit alone anymore.

We had one family member who actually encouraged our children to lie to us, saying that it was okay, because that family member knew better than we did. Our children told us what happened, including the lie, and we calmly thanked them for being honest. Some discussions don't need to include the kids. We dealt with it. Although we could have done better over the years, we succeeded in being more open while encouraging our children to be open and honest with us, more so than either of our parents had done with us. You'll never be perfect, but striving every day to gain ground in regards to trust will leave you better prepared and strengthen your relationship down the road.

The more you visit and engage with your children, share their experiences, and create a safe atmosphere where they feel free to be honest with you, the better it will be for everyone in your family when tough situations arise as your children mature.

YOUR BIG HELPER

Once again, *appropriately* involve your children in everything you do. Be curious and foster curiosity in your children. Tell them about it, model how to do it, touch it, taste it—let them experience and explore whatever you are including them in as much as you can for their age and benefit. Help them to participate in activities so that they can be a part of what you are doing and be your helper—your big helper. Continue repeating this pattern until they're able to do each thing, bit by bit, on their own. Hug them, cheer with them, and show them how proud you are of their accomplishments. This pattern, at its best, should be a lifelong process—just like the process of homeschooling. Everything you include your babies in helps prepare them—and you—for homeschooling when they officially start school and are introduced to academics.

After our little ones could walk, David and I built on that by including them in helping us with simple tasks around the house. It was fun and easy for us and exciting for them. They naturally wanted to do what we did. They liked picking up their toys and putting them in the toy box after playing, because they were our big helpers.

We don't want to just train our children to accomplish tasks; we want to teach them how to think and do for themselves and discern the world around them. Each of us has patterns of thinking and making decisions.

How did we learn to do that? What criteria do we use when making decisions? These are the thoughts we should be considering to help us foresee what to teach our children.

As soon as our children were big enough (but still unable to walk), I (Terri) would pick up a toy and put it in the toy box as they watched (modeling), and then I would hold our baby over the box to allow them to drop the toy they were holding into the box (practicing). I would pick up another toy and repeat the process—it was a game. Each time I put a toy in, I would cheer, and each time they put one in, I would cheer. Soon, they would cheer for me, and we would cheer together every time a toy was put in the box. Once everything was put away, we would cheer and say what a good job we did.

Once each child was big enough to walk over to the toy box themselves, then I would ask them questions as we were picking up toys, such as, "What's next?" or "Do you see anything else to pick up?" Asking questions helps them learn to think about what they are doing, look around themselves, and make a decision on what to pick up next. If they missed something, I would help them look around until they found the item, teaching them to develop the habit of looking around to see if their task had been completed.

Additionally, as you mentor your children, they are learning to socialize with you and others through the conversations you are continually having with them. They will learn to smile and enjoy doing tasks together as you smile and have fun doing things with them. They also gain approval, acceptance, knowledge, and life skills from you.

Conversely, if you only talk to them (or at them) when you are telling them what to do or are angry with them, they will learn they are no good and become sullen, withdrawn, resentful, and even combative. They will learn what they see from you and parrot that, or even act out to those around them. Whatever you live in front of your children every day is what they will become as adults.

This is because your children want to please you. Make up your mind to be easily pleased with and by them, *let* them please you. Look for ways to deliberately be kind and laugh with your spouse and each child daily. Hug them and express your love for them every day. Sing and dance with them. Run, jump, and play with them. Read to them and recite nursery rhymes with them. Yes, when I say "them," that includes not only your children but also your spouse! Keep this up throughout all their years before they leave the nest. You will be able to accomplish much more in your homeschool if you already have the foundation of respect, love, enjoyment, and acceptance in place early on.

I (Terri) wish I'd realized what I'm sharing with you now, back when our children were growing up—because as they got older, I failed to continue that natural learning process. I did not persist in talking, smiling, having fun, and mentoring our children as they got older. I got lazy and did things myself because I didn't want to take the extra time to instruct and model processes to them. I did not include them, nor did I persevere in working with them; I just told them what to do while I did other tasks. I easily slipped into complacency without even realizing it, because I was getting more done by "delegating responsibilities." I did get more done, but I was no longer nurturing our relationships. As a result, the bond we had formed early on was weakened by me not staying connected with them the older and more capable they became. They began to have resentment toward me, which has continued in the background and under the surface of my relationships with our adult children. This is one of my greatest regrets.

Look forward in time, learn from your mistakes and our mistakes, and recognize the importance of constantly seeking to cultivate a healthy relationship with each of your children by nurturing that special bond of love and trust from immediately after birth and onward. Sometimes (maybe even oftentimes), this will seem very difficult and challenging, but always, *always* remember that every bit of effort you put into creating and growing a good, healthy, special, and long-lasting relationship with each child will be well worth it during your years of homeschooling, and long after they leave home and are no longer under your care and supervision.

What kind of people do you desire to see your children become? What kind of people do you want them to be to you when they are adults? Become that person for them and to them. One step at a time, make changes that will reinforce love, kindness, respect, relevance, acceptance, and important values and skills to your children that will set them up for success in relationships and in life. Work toward mastering the character traits you wish your children to possess. The best way to master a skill is to teach it. You are determining what you want to teach your children; you are endeavoring to learn specific traits and impart what you learn to them so that they can do just that—master the skill to turn around and teach others. Little ones imitate and practice what they hear you saying and see you doing on their stuffed animals, action figures, or dolls; they repeat what they have heard to their siblings; they share their knowledge, good or bad, with other students in the co-op, church, or playgroup. One day, they may even set up a tutoring business, which is what our youngest son did in college to make extra money. It's up to you. You set the stage. The time from birth to toddler, and from toddler to kindergartener, is the prime time for implementing healthy habits and patterns that will enable you to effectively teach your children throughout the rest of their time at home.

MOVING TO THE COUNTRY

My (David) parents had spent a few years paying off ten acres of land they bought in the country. Once it was paid off, they worked with a builder and had a custom ranch-style brick house built on their land. It was a four-bedroom, three-bath house with a two-car garage, and they had two cars to park in it—my parents' dream was coming to fruition. The day we moved, the bully and molester Allan was standing at the end of our street, I assume watching the movers pack our things into the large moving truck. I just remember seeing him standing there watching us as we drove away. It scared me.

As far as the larger extended family went, we now had the big place. Lots of parking, a lot of room for large family get-togethers, and a fireplace that topped off the holiday charm. My brother and sister had received brand-new Honda Z-50 motorcycles the previous Christmas, and they now had private land to ride them on. My brother and sister would also each have a horse within the first two years of being at our new place, but each of us had our own bedroom.

My parents sprung for new furniture for their bedroom and our living room, while my brother received the unused furniture my grandmother had bought for her own guest room before my grandfather passed away a few years before. I think she was proud to pass it on to my brother. My sister received furniture from another grandmother's bedroom, and if memory serves correctly, my dad stripped and painted her furniture. It had to have been from the 1930s or earlier—very curved and ornate woodwork. To me, it was just my grandmother's bedroom set painted an antique white, but it was nice. Just perfect for my sister and her things, as it was girly—I was excited to see what I was getting!

At the end of the first week at the new house, I was put in the smallest bedroom with a mixture of leftover furniture from our old house. That would never change. When I was a teenager and was allowed to temporarily move into my brother's room (long after he'd married and left home), I used the furniture my grandmother gave my brother. My mom made it very clear, however, that it was still my brother's room, even though I only wanted the room because it was farthest from my parents' bedroom.

I remember that seemingly every kid in the neighborhood had a motorcycle or dirt bike like my siblings, and most of the kids were around my siblings' ages. I say "neighborhood," but it was a mile-long loop. Every resident had at least five acres, and every home had to be at least 1,800 square feet. It was a private community—our closest neighbor was an eighth of a mile away—so seeing people riding horses and dirt bikes down the gravel road was a normal thing. My brother and sister would depart and ride with the neighborhood kids all day. Essentially, we had access to two hundred acres if we counted Farmer Brown's land. Farmer Brown was a crusty old cattle rancher who was used to seeing the occasional stranger riding across his land, and he didn't mind as long as we respected his property and didn't harass his livestock. As far as safety and freedom went, my parents chose the perfect place.

Of everything that was going on in our lives at this time, I have memories of seeing people and families doing things but not many memories of us or our family doing things together. My dad started stretching miles of barbed wire for a horse fence and laid out the plot for the large pole barn he wanted to build, but these were things I saw from a distance.

What I had to do was stay away so that I didn't "get hurt." It was never revealed to me how or why I'd be hurt. I wasn't told or taught what to watch out for or how or why some work was being accomplished. "So you don't get hurt," was the sugar to make the truth more palatable: my dad simply didn't want me there. I just saw him and my brother working together and doing what looked like cowboy work, and I wanted to see what it was all about.

I didn't have a dirt bike or a horse or friends. I was considered a twerp, a nuisance, a frump, and an annoying son or little brother. (My mom actually called me most of these names, among others.) I was unwelcome. Depending on the day, my mom would be watching soap operas or the *Phil Donahue Show*. She was always going to watch enough television or watch enough talk shows so that her life would be right and make sense. She never did. It was a household sin to interrupt the lessons or insight my mom was going to learn or gain from her talk shows, and so I would depart the house for the "woods" to explore.

The "woods" seemed like a massive mystical forest to me back then. In reality, I was fighting through weeds and oak trees on close to twenty acres. I'd hear my mom call my name, and I'd run back to the house. She'd be standing in the driveway with my dad and ask, "Where have you been?" At a very young age, I began to question if the obvious answer was the best answer, so I would reply, "In the woods."

"Who were you with?" my mom or dad would demand.

I'd shake my head and try to make sense of the barrage of questions. It was as though I'd done something wrong. I didn't have any friends, so it seemed obvious I was by myself. My dad and brother didn't want me with them. My mom didn't want me interrupting her show, and if I sat in my room, they'd say, "Don't sit around in your room all day." So I would reply, "Nobody was there. I was by myself down by the creek." Mom and Dad would angrily search my face for signs of dishonesty. They never would reveal the motive or reason for why they approached me this way. Predominantly, my memories from that time in my life are of tearing my way through weeds and vines, climbing trees, and usually, at least one of our dogs tagging along for the journey. I knew something wasn't right in our family dynamic, even at that age. I knew that my existence was a part of it, but it would take decades to conclude why and gain some understanding.

In my earlier grade school years, my sister did the dishes while my mom watched her shows, and my brother fed the animals. Mom usually cooked dinner, though, as Dad worked. When he was at home, my mom would say, "Your dad has worked all day for you guys! He shouldn't have to do anything but relax." Parenting by guilt was the household norm. Mom and Dad would sit in their chairs, drink iced tea, smoke cigarettes, and watch TV.

My most useful contribution in those years was to remain out of sight.

I learned at a young age to avoid my parents to the largest extent possible. Dad was all about the threatened "backhand." He'd quickly raise his hand like he was going to hit me and then scratch the back of his head, because he thought it was funny to see me jerk my head back in fear. Since my dad did actually backhand me, however, he was only reinforcing that he could hit me in the face at any time for any reason, or even none at all. My mom would lecture me literally for hours about a healthy diet (as she gained more and more weight) that she learned about on Donahue, while eating from a bag of cheese puffs and drinking iced tea. Her fingers, lips, and cigarette butts would be stained orange while she passionately lectured me about eating "right" and being healthy. I'd do anything I could to avoid Mom or Dad's brand of family time in daily life.

In contrast, by the time our oldest son started kindergarten, he could take his dirty dishes to the sink and load the dishwasher with little instruction. He dressed himself appropriately, could separate his laundry, and get his clothes out of the dryer. He could read at a mid-grade school level and even name every major bone of the human body by its correct name. We had a lot of fun with our son as we did things together.

He wasn't forced to be a housemaid, and much of what he did at a very young age could be frustrating because he was slow-going and we were young parents. It would have been easier to do it ourselves in many cases, but getting things done wasn't the only goal—teaching him how to do these things for himself was the goal. We also played with Ninja Turtles, Hot Wheels, Barbie and Ken dolls, Atari 2600, and Legos. We did messy crafts at the kitchen table covered in newspaper. We made a zipline and swing sets and balance beams . . . and on and on. There was seemingly no end to the shenanigans we could drum up to occupy our time together.

Terri and I were young and ignorant as parents, but we interacted with our first son every day. That was the secret to our success as parents and him as a person; we developed relationships with each other. We treated him like a mature person most of the time—maybe even too often. We had eras or seasons when he was obviously stressed out, and we realized that it was in large part due to the stress of the expectations we'd placed on him. This was in sharp contrast to what I experienced when growing up as a result of our attempts to parent differently, due to how my parents made me feel as a child. My parents demanded perfection but never defined the goal. Really, there was no goal. They simply demanded that I do exactly what they said, when they said it—*because*, they said so, for their benefit, and they also wanted me out of their way.

My mom once decided to give the horses (which she rarely visited) some fresh fruit and noticed there was dried urine crusted onto the male horse's phallus. My mom came in and demanded that I clean and scrub the urine from the horse's . . . business. I flatly refused. When she grabbed my hair in her fist, shook my head, and dug her fingernails into my face to force me to look at her, but I still refused, she told me to sit in my room until my dad got home. My dad whipped me with a belt—and then told my mom that her idea was ridiculous.

My refusing to obey her command was disrespectful, and therefore I deserved to be whipped, but Mom's demand was absurd. None of these exchanges made sense to me. My dad never instructed me what the correct response should have been, just that my response deserved violence.

My mom later brought it up again to my brother with my dad there. I was quietly at a distance. My brother laughed and said, "Hell no! I'm not jacking off a horse to get dried piss off his dick!" He and my dad laughed at my mom's suggestion—to her face—only for my mom to start laughing, too. What exactly were they teaching my brother? What were they teaching me? Did my parents comprehend what raising children meant, or were they just keeping us as pets, like so many horses, pigs, dogs, and cats?

BIRTHDAYS ARE SUPPOSED TO BE SPECIAL

My brother's birthday is a week after mine. My mom has always wished me a happy birthday on my brother's birthday. Our parties were always held together, always on his birthday. As an adult, I told my mom years ago that if she couldn't remember my birthday on my birthday, then she shouldn't bother. I'd delete her text or decline her call if she called on my brother's birthday. While in recent years my mom's condition has declined from Alzheimer's, she hasn't wished me a happy birthday on my birthday, or on my brother's birthday, for at least twenty years. I've also had years that passed with no birthday wishes from any extended family, so it seems I have an incredibly forgettable birthday. But that's okay, because after writing this book and Terri reading my story, my last birthday was the first birthday a cake was made just for me. Not store-bought, but baked and decorated just for me. Terri put up streamers and had party favors, and the cake was covered in toys! I was moved by her sentiment, especially because my parents never did that for me.

This is why we celebrated birthdays for each of our kids, because we both remember how we felt about our birthdays as children. Terri's mom always made her and her sister special cakes, and it meant a lot to Terri. Mine never did, and it affected me as well. The details of life can have a long-lasting impact on your children, good or bad. To this day, any birthday wishes from extended family, if they arrive at all, arrive on my brother's birthday—even from my brother, which I think is funny. They also arrive, every single time, with an apology for "being busy" and that my birthday slipped by . . . but the wishes always arrive on a day, amazingly, that never slips by, and when no one is ever busy—my brother's birthday.

The point is this: what you start now, at this young age of your children, you're likely to continue without thinking.

My parents and family obviously thought that either I wouldn't remember that they did this every single year, or they simply accepted that good enough is good enough. I learned that they were okay with making me secondary to my brother. Because isn't that the truth?

It's what my parents taught my brother and sister and extended family: the firstborn comes first—and by the way, the stray kid's birthday was last week. Make sure to wish him a happy birthday, too, so that the truth isn't so obvious.

My brother is a good man, who works hard and takes care of his family. I'm not offering platitudes, and my observations aren't his fault. He knows what his parents taught him; what could possibly be wrong with that? What kinds of things will your actions as a parent teach your children? About two thousand days will pass between your child's birth and kindergarten, and I've given you a glimpse of what I learned in my two thousand days—was I ready for kindergarten?

WHAT ABOUT KINDERGARTEN?

What exactly is significant about kindergarten? Yes, a child is still young and impressionable, but it's not that big of a deal . . . right? Kindergarten signifies the age at which a child is beginning their independence. If they're sent off to school, they're on their own for at least half of the day. If you want your homeschooled child to at least be on track with their peers, you must prepare your child to be appropriately independent for their age by the time they reach kindergarten.

In kindergarten, I was impossibly, awkwardly shy as a result of what I was taught; no one in my family seemed to want me around.

Why would I expect anything different from anyone else? What was this new teacher going to demand of me?

The only thing I remember being told was that I was starting school, and that I needed to do what the teacher said and get along with everyone. My young mind didn't process the thoughts in those exact words, but that's what I was thinking. Besides being forced to stay off the radar, my parents taught me violence, but I'd still rather my mom sling a belt at me, than face the unknown.

With the perfect clarity of hindsight, my path going forward as a kindergartener makes sense to me as an adult. I was never a bully; instead, I was the quiet kid who would—one day soon—meet a bully with a violence that earned me a reputation as a tough kid. That violence was the consequence of what I was taught at home from the age of molested toddler, to the time I became an insecure kindergartener.

Like me, our oldest son, Blake, went to kindergarten. I recall us telling him that he was growing up and was going to be starting school, and that was exciting! He was going to do the things that he already did, like read and color and listen to stories, but he was also going to meet new kids and make friends. He did, and I think he liked kindergarten. Terri and I went to school with the same kids for thirteen years and have no lasting bonds. Those all ended when we married. Our children have formed relationships based on individual thoughts and interests, not pack mentality and popularity learned at school. For that reason, our children have friendships that span their entire adult lives.

Parents must encourage their children to be the best version of themselves. This is something that is accomplished by complimenting their strengths in character and offering encouragement in areas where they are weak. If your child seems a bit greedy or selfish, create instances of giving to others for their benefit in order to nurture a better balance of giving and acceptance within your child. We shouldn't always be expected to share, but we do need to recognize moments where sharing is appropriate.

Beyond these necessary concepts needed for constructive socialization, your child should be able to dress themselves, go to the bathroom sanitarily, wash their hands, and communicate effectively regarding their basic needs. If your child cannot do these things, then you are telling them that their care is being transferred to a stranger because they're incapable of caring for themselves. Meanwhile, their peers who *can* do these things will look down on them as weird, or "less than."

Our children were potty-trained no later than age two, but in the past couple of years, I've read articles about teachers at kindergarten through second-grade levels having to change the diapers of their students. These are not special needs teachers, but average schoolteachers. I hope you're as shocked as we were that there are parents and teachers out there allowing school-age children to defecate on themselves like animals—this is Basic Parenting 101! We want to encourage you to raise the bar so much higher for your toddlers and kindergarten-age children. If you look at this child as a future leader of their generation and the need to prepare them accordingly, you can ask yourself, "What if all kids conducted themselves like my child[ren]?" Or, you can ask, "What if everyone in sight were acting like my child?"

Would that be good, or would it be chaos?

In my experience as a dad, regardless of how different each of our children were, their traits of self-governance were nearly solidified by kindergarten. Even though our children can't understand that we still see those kindergarteners in them today, that particular aspect of their personality is unique to them alone, and will be with them for their entire lives.

Homeschooled children most likely won't have to experience the separation anxiety and independence of going to kindergarten at a school, but we should still teach them to be independent for their age as if they were going to a public school. Of course, you will oversee and direct them, but everything you do with them should be pointing them toward their future independence and capability to function in the world as an adult. Teach and expect them to have a daily routine to address their own personal needs. It truly is a joy to have your little one working happily alongside you, rather than running around and getting into everything while you are trying to get something accomplished. As homeschool parents we are given the unique opportunity and much more time with our children to continually cultivate that happy little independent coworker/helper in our children because we choose to homeschool.

BE UNITED AND BE CONSISTENT

In our writing, we consistently reinforce the need to self-evaluate as a parent, and as a couple. I think this is one of those concepts that appears easy, but in the moment we often either reason out poor actions or responses, or one parent may "break the rules" on a whim, negating the other parent's effort.

But why shouldn't we be able to act on a whim? We are the parents, after all.

For Terri and me, early on, we had this cycle. She would be strict, and I would be the parent who would "sneak" candy. Terri would see this and blow up. She was trying hard to work on something specific with our son. I would relent and step in line, but later, she would decide to take our son to the ice cream shop for a treat to curry her own favor or reward him for a perceived success. I'd "stepped in line," but she'd jumped off the track. "Seriously?" I'd blast at her. She was confident, "You give him candy all the time. You're making me look like the bad guy, so I wanted to get him ice cream!" Yes, this was a vicious cycle. If our children see us do things behind our spouses' backs, what exactly are we teaching them? That one piece of candy can teach that lying is okay, and that not doing what we're supposed to do is also acceptable. This teaches them that the parent whose wishes we're disrespecting is undeserving of respect and honesty. All these instances add up over time and make lasting impressions that shape who your child becomes as an adult.

So, you and your spouse need to be in agreement and on the same page, and then you must honor and respect that agreement. If you would like to do something different, that also needs to be agreed on. We're not talking about one spouse answering to the other, we're talking about consistency. We all know about the "if one parent says no, I can go ask the other," trick, so as parents, you must present a united front. You're teaching them from the very beginning what a healthy relationship should look like, and rather than teaching your child wiggle room or manipulation, you're teaching them that you and your spouse are one and the same. It doesn't even matter if your significant other is a bit of an idiot in your viewpoint; you're teaching your children to enter this with you next time—the vicious cycle.

So, at this point in our children's lives, we're (hopefully) a unified couple. Terri and I weren't consistent with our first child, but we'll press on because we know you will be. What can we do instead of sneaking candy and buying random treats? The years before kindergarten are the years for you to get a head start on school, without officially starting school. This age is when you're laying a real foundation for your children to build good habits and academics. Organize your child's room and train them to keep it that way. Begin to organize your home. Begin buying and organizing supplies for school. Begin using the space and the resources with your child to strengthen your bond with them. Passively teach them the skills they would otherwise not learn until kindergarten and first grade.

How do you think your class area will function? Where will your books and supplies be stored? You should already have scissors, pencils, crayons, paper, a dry-erase board with markers, and various crafting supplies. Your child can have coloring books in the place where their textbooks will be stored, for example, to get in the habit of going to that place to get what they need. Are we secretly teaching numbers? Maybe you'll use a label maker to number coloring books so that you can tell them, "Let's color in book number three today." When it's time to put the book away, you can say, "Let's put it between books two and four."

What if, at a young age, you introduced your child to pictures of classical art? The paintings are beautiful (not the scary ones). Picasso is known for Cubism, but he was also an incredibly talented painter of realistic subjects. Picasso also had a "Blue Period." What if you shared pictures like this with your child and said, "Let's color page ten like Picasso, using only blue colors!" What if you had identical coloring books and said, "Let's color like van Gogh in oranges and yellows!"? Wait a minute, you're using different colors, too! Ask, "What colors are we using?" The children are now learning to read and recognize the colors of the crayons. As they progress, you can ask, "How many colors did you use?" The child can then respond with the number of colors and name them. If you place a print of *Femme assise* on the table, your child is also learning to compare colors and identify specific areas of change. They're learning to recognize details.

To accomplish this, you must create and use a schedule. More than likely, your spouse is at work and adheres to a schedule. Whoever is at home should also be on a schedule. If you're simply at home making sure the child doesn't poison themselves or burn the house down, you're just the babysitter. The fair balance of work is that everyone works on a schedule. When the employed spouse gets home, you both take part in the activities of the evening because you've both been "on the clock" all day. The spouse who works outside the home needs to do activities with the children as well (they get to leave work, so whoever is at home all day also deserves a break). This is serious work. You can see how this endeavor is more than just typical parenting. That's why we say that homeschooling is a lifestyle. But it's worth it for us, our marriage, and our children's futures.

Recap? You're teaching numbers, colors, artists, organizational skills, and a schedule—and this is just as a toddler.

The best part?

You are spending quality time with your child, not staring at your phone while they mindlessly watch television or play video games. Set a timer that is realistic for your child and modify the timing as their focus improves. You'll need to work up to your child being able to focus for a full school day, but eventually, their school day could be as long as six hours. Let's try to get our kids to half that by kindergarten. You can do art, read stories to them, and play with tactile toys like building blocks. And of course, we also need recess, so let's get outside and play, move our bodies! This homeschool thing looks like it's as much fun for the parents as it is for the children!

The key to all of this for you, as parents, is to stay on schedule together. Start planning and get your marriage into teamwork mode!

CHAPTER 6

STICKING TO A SCHEDULE

The phone rings. I (Terri) stop what I'm doing because a friend or family member wants to visit. Often, it's my mother-in-law; she wants to advise me on the newest parenting technique she learned about on a television talk show, but I try to tell her that I am working. She just continues to talk, as she cannot appreciate the fact that despite working from home, I cannot have a four-hour-long conversation about her one-hour TV show.

Growing up, I was taught to be polite and respectful, listen to adults, and do what I was told. I was not really taught to think for myself nor set boundaries when necessary, so I really had no idea how to handle this situation. All I knew was that the longer I continued this conversation with my mother-in-law, the longer it would take for me to complete my work, and ultimately take time away from my family. I tried to politely explain to her that I needed to get off the phone, but again, she did not seem to understand the importance of or respect what I was saying to her. This was not new. Even before I worked from home she would call me at my job, but in that case it was much easier for me to tell her I could not visit.

I began working from home as a medical transcriptionist in 1995. This was an important step for our family because it enabled me to stay at home with our children and earn an income at the same time. We saved so much money when we no longer had to rely on strangers to take care of and raise our children while we worked.

In 1995, we were nine years into our marriage. We had three children; a third grader, a three-year-old, and a one-year-old. At the office, I had gotten very proficient at transcription to the point of being able to get the required daily amount completed in five hours or less. The great thing about my new job was that I could choose my hours at any time of the day or night, so long as I completed a certain amount in a twenty-four-hour time period. Working from home was going to be a breeze!

So I thought.

When I first started working from home, I spent a minimum of eight hours daily, usually more, getting my work done. There were so many interruptions and distractions all the time that it took forever to finish. It seemed I never stopped working because I would sit down and start typing, and just then, there would be another phone call, the doorbell would ring, or one of my children would need my attention. Other distractions included pets, meals, dishes, and laundry, which called out to me constantly.

Not being on a schedule, not setting boundaries, and not maintaining a good command of my time put a strain on our family and our marriage. David would get home after working all day, and I would say, "I have to work," and disappear while he took care of our kids and cleaned up. As I typed into the evening, he would get the kids' baths and get them ready for bed. I would stop long enough to read to them, but then go right back to working. Eventually, David would go to bed without me. He finally pointed out to me that when he stayed home with the kids while I went into the office, everything was done early in the day, every day—as you can imagine I did not receive this well. Of course *my* situation was different from his. He didn't have to work every day when he was home with the kids. To keep my job, I had to type Monday through Saturday and complete the required amount of work every day. Between what I had successfully accomplished at the office and what I thought was the intent of David's comment, I realized that I needed to be on a schedule.

I also needed to address interruptions. It's just one phone call—why make such a big fuss? Family and friends call or come by; that's a good thing, right? You may even want to talk to them at the time of the interruption. At best these interruptions were counterproductive to our goals, our family, and our kids; and at worst, they were destructive.

We were not just at home hanging out; we were taking care of business, managing work and school for myself and for our kids. Every day, the interruptions and distractions would happen, and I would get more stressed out. Day after day, the stress added up. I knew it was taking way too much time to complete the amount of work required for me to stay at home, and as a result, I realized these interruptions were stealing time away from my family. I wasn't able to truly be there for my kids, I wasn't there for my husband, and knowing that just made it worse. The more stressed I became, the more out of proportion my responses to my family became. You can see how something like one seemingly harmless phone call can become a destructive force when multiplied daily by other distractions. If left unaddressed over time, that destructive force can cause damage to your marriage and family, and we were no different.

So finally, it all blew up. "Why were you not able to get your work done during the day so that we could spend time as a family together at night?" my husband would ask me. At the time, I got angry, of course, because of the confrontation, but mainly I was angry because I knew he was right. Ouch!

All of this comes down to schedule and priorities. What do you value most? What is your top priority? Your outside relationships or your own family? Do you put your marriage and your children first, or do you allow others to rob you of your time and energy so that you have nothing left to give your family? Yes, we can and should make time for family and friends, and of course, we have work commitments that must be met. However, we must also learn to balance outside influences and set limitations, so that our marriage and our children do not suffer at the hands of people who do not care nor take responsibility for us. I had to set boundaries for myself, for my kids and husband, for my work, for our family and friends, and later, boundaries for school. If we were going to make this work, we had to get these dynamics figured out.

As we've said before—every family is different. What works for one family may not work for another, so you should base your decisions on your priorities for your family and your homeschool. What is most important to you? What are your short-term and long-term goals? Determine what works for your specific situation. Decide what is going to benefit your family most and enable you to reach the goals you have set. Then, keep figuring it out as you go because in time, your situation will change—especially as your kids grow up. You should grow as your kids grow. As you do, you will find better and different ways to do things. Continue refining along the way, and adjust to what works best as you progress.

Personally, I found that it was very important for me to set exact times for work, school, and family time. If I didn't, work or school would never end, and that wasn't good, either. I thought about how our lives were when we both worked outside the home. We had to be at work at a certain time, and lunch was at a certain time. Work ended at the same time every day, and we went home and had family time.

This concept also applies to homeschooling, and is exactly how I patterned our days.

I would wake up several hours before everyone else to get in some uninterrupted work—it was so early that nobody ever called! Then, everyone else got up to start the day. We did schoolwork in the morning and had lunch at the same time every day. I was able to finish my remaining transcriptions while the little ones were napping, and then we got in some playtime. No matter what, school and work had to be done by a certain time every day—no homework, no extra work after that time. It was important to David and me to have dinner together every night, a special time set aside to be together and interact as a family. Sometimes there were exceptions, but for the most part, we kept to this schedule for the next fifteen years. It made a huge difference for all of us to know what to expect each day. It gave us a framework to balance work, school, and family so we could accomplish our goals and meet our collective and individual needs.

At my best, when I found that sweet spot that worked really well for our family, I would get up at 3:00 a.m., exercise for thirty minutes on the elliptical, get dressed, make some coffee, and start working at 4:00 a.m. I could complete all my transcriptions for the day in the next four hours. Our little ones were now in middle school, and they were responsible for getting themselves up, getting dressed, eating, and sitting at their desks, ready to start each day by 8:00 a.m. We did not say it, but their morning autonomy was in preparation for them to successfully function as adults in society, just like the rest of us.

I would finish my work, and then we would start our school day. Usually, we were able to be done with all the teaching I needed to do for them by our lunch break, and if they had anything else to do, they would do it after lunch. I would grade their work during this time each day.

It's important to make time to grade the work that you expect your children to do on the same day. By doing so, you are regarding their work as important and respecting them as people. How can you tell them it's important to complete their assignments if it's thrown into a pile and left to sit? While I would return their work to them to make corrections on their own, I think it is much better to make time to sit down with each child and go over the corrections. This can help you to identify any problems they may be having. They can ask questions if there is something they don't understand. It is good feedback for them and you. Then, make sure you record their grades in your gradebook and *they* file their daily work in the appropriate notebook. This was our routine every day. You will be rewarded with newfound time each week if you are diligent with the recordkeeping and filing process daily. Keeping everything organized and current will help considerably when it is time to record their grades each quarter and at the end of each school year. It is not fun to try to play catch-up; it hurts you and them. I speak from experience!

The rest of the day was open for us to do extracurricular activities. As David said earlier, he remembers that when he was in grade school, he would never be done any faster than the slowest kid in class. In contrast, our children were done when they completed their work neatly and correctly. Compared to their public school counterparts, our children did more work in half the time because they were rewarded for their diligence, and they did not have to wait on twenty other students.

Another part of getting organized and sticking to a schedule also included implementing weekly menus for breakfast, lunch, and dinner. We shopped and prepared food on the weekends so that we were not distracted throughout the week. Meals were already planned, and each of us would take a turn preparing a different night's meal. In the early days we were on a very tight budget, so having a plan helped me to get all we needed each week with limited resources. As time went on and our finances increased, I adjusted as necessary. Sticking to our weekly meal plan was key, and very helpful in keeping to a schedule. David and I still plan our meals for the week because it avoids the whole back-and-forth of, "What do you want to eat?" "I dunno, what do you want?" This way, either of us can go into the kitchen and make a healthy meal, stress-free.

This may seem like a lot of work. Why put so much effort into a schedule? You haven't even mentioned teaching school. How does having a schedule relate to homeschooling?

So glad you asked.

Having a schedule so that you properly manage your time allows you to focus on teaching when you are ready to teach. It enables you to give your undivided attention to your children and their education, which is critical if you are all going to be successful. In order to reach your goals for each child, it is imperative that you have a plan and stick to a schedule for school. My mentors would say, "If you fail to plan, you plan to fail," and they were right.

Think of it like a map. If you want to get to a specific destination across the country, you don't just start driving in any direction because it feels right, and then expect to get where you want to go in any reasonable amount of time. You get a map or use a GPS and set your course so that you end up where you want to be, and can get there as quickly and efficiently as possible. Homeschooling is the same way. If, for instance, you want your children to go to college, they must have a specific knowledge base before they can be accepted into a college. You look at where you want them to be by the time they graduate high school, and you make a plan so that they arrive at that destination in the allotted time, which is usually considered to be from birth to eighteen or nineteen years old. The great thing about homeschooling is that if your child excels in a subject, they are not anchored to every other child in class. You have a schedule and a lesson plan, so your child can perform lessons ahead or extra projects they enjoy and be rewarded for their natural abilities. Conversely, if they need more time in any area, you can give it to them and adjust as needed. Sticking to a schedule allows you to have extra time when—not if—challenges arise.

College is the path we felt was right for our children, but that is not the only path. You will find which path suits your family and each child best. The point is to figure it out, make a plan, and set a course. Don't worry—you can modify things as you find it necessary to do so, but by setting your course early on, you will have the freedom to be able to adjust easily as you go—while still knowing you are going to reach your goals. If you don't make a plan, you will likely run into so many problems that make it difficult to accomplish anything on a day-to-day basis, much less reach your long-term goals.

Specifically, you should have an overall twelve-year plan for each child. When we first started homeschooling, we did not have a plan for our oldest, Blake. We knew the basics and just did what we thought he needed for the grade he was in. It wasn't until we joined the homeschool program at a local private school that we realized and understood the importance of planning ahead. Blake was beginning his seventh-grade year when we first made his plan. For our younger two, we had an overall plan for grade school, middle school, and high school—-and we had a plan for each grade level. We started by looking ahead, then working backward.

What are the requirements for college admission at your state colleges? I (Terri) recall when I did a four-year plan as a high school freshman. The guidance counselor asked me if I knew what I wanted to do after graduating high school. I said I wanted to go to college to become a doctor. So, in ninth grade, with the counselor's help, I decided that I would take four years of math and science, as well as all the other classes I would need to take each year in order to exceed the minimum requirements for college admission. What do your children need to accomplish academically each year? I based our children's planning on my past experience and followed the guidelines set by our mentor school, but there are many resources available on the internet to help you do this. Do an internet search for a twelve-year plan; that's a good place to start.

Let's look at the subject of math. By the time I was in high school in ninth grade, I was enrolled in Algebra II. To be able to succeed in that class, I needed to take the prerequisite classes of Pre-Algebra and Algebra I. Because I took those two classes in seventh and eighth grade, respectively, I was able to start ninth grade in Algebra II, so I decided to take Geometry, Analytic Geometry, and Calculus to round out my four years of math.

Now, look at what a child must learn in the years before they take Algebra I so they may successfully handle the course material. You wouldn't expect a first grader who hasn't learned their addition and subtraction math facts to be able to do complex equations. There is a specific and proven path that incrementally teaches a child what they need to know in math from kindergarten to sixth grade that will prepare them for Pre-Algebra by seventh grade—if that is the path for them. Some children may not have the aptitude or drive needed for higher math, or they may have no interest in the subject. That's okay, I am just using my path as an example. As adults, we need to be able to do basic math for many reasons, and I'd say that for most people, having an understanding of at least algebra and geometry as an adult is important for everyday life. Also, if you make this plan when they are a baby, and then somewhere along the way, you realize something in it is not realistic for your child for whatever reason, you can change it. But now you have a framework that you can use and make changes as needed to better suit each individual child.

Part of your planning should also include those character traits and values that are important to you and your family—figure that out. Like the example David gave about the interview, what type of character should your children develop by the time they leave home? Do you want them to go through other people's stuff and take whatever they like when they visit the home of a relative or friend? Or do you want them to respect other people's property as they would want their own property respected?

You have to teach that from the start to all of your children. There should be things that they are not allowed to get into of yours and of their siblings. They should learn that they cannot have whatever they want whenever they want it. It is good to learn to share when playing with blocks and common toys, but there should be some things that are theirs that they do not have to share, ever, such as their special stuffed animal, or anything they buy with their own money. You would not share your spouse or your car because someone says, "Now give that to your neighbor—it is good and right to share!"

Think about what you are teaching in terms of being an adult. How do you want to be treated? Teach your children to treat each other and you in that way so that they learn how to treat other people. If you allow them to take whatever they want and get into whatever they want until they are eight years old, the mold is set, and it will be very difficult to change that. Identify those traits that are important to you and incorporate them into your child's everyday life and teaching. If you do this, you will reach your goals—but you must actually do it. Take the necessary time not only at the beginning but throughout their childhood to make a plan and add or revise along the way, and you will reap the benefits. If you don't make the plans and use them, you will have constant problems, so review your plan each year. Keep what was good, get rid of or make changes to what was not so great, and add in what needs to be added. Things do change along the way, and that's to be expected, but having plans already in place (just like having a weekly menu) will help reduce your workload and keep you focused on the path to successfully get your children to their desired destination.

The scheduling, planning, and organization I shared earlier in this chapter did not happen overnight. It took years to develop and refine to find what really worked for us. We didn't know what we didn't know, and we hope this book will save you much of that same struggle.

Please do not feel like you must have the perfect schedule right off. You probably won't. I only share ours to say that it *can* be done. We started changing one thing at a time. Because we could see early on that time management was very important, I started with that. We tried different ideas and if something worked, we kept it, but if it didn't, we moved on to try something else. Maybe we read an article that illustrated some good points, or we heard what worked for another homeschool family. I found that getting up early to complete my typing is not only what I preferred, but was what fit best for our family and our homeschool. I knew other transcriptionists who preferred working at night. What is right and works for us individually and for our families won't be exactly the same, but we are all trying to accomplish the same goal. Over the years, I met many different homeschool families. While each was unique, the one thing that successful homeschool families all had in common was that each worked hard to find a schedule that suited them and enabled them to succeed. We each love our spouse and children, and we want the very best for them, right? Of course we do! That is why we work so hard to find the solutions, to find what is most beneficial for us and them, and we continually keep on making adjustments as we grow and change to best suit our family. It is often trial and error—but isn't that true of everything in life? I think this is especially true when it comes to creating a schedule, setting boundaries, and limiting interruptions.

So, what happened with my mother-in-law and her calls? It was obvious that she did not understand or see value in what we were doing, nor did she see the importance of properly managing time and a schedule—perhaps because she did not have those values for herself. Once I figured out a time schedule for myself, I set boundaries for everyone, including my mother-in-law. I let her and everyone outside our family know that during the weekdays, we would only be available from 11:00 a.m. to 11:30 a.m. during lunch and after 4:00 p.m. That gave us enough time to get work and school done. I also let them know that they could call, but I would only answer the phone if it was during our break time. They could leave a message, and I would get back to them after 4:00 p.m. If they wanted to come by, I would only answer the door on our break periods. If they came at a time when I said we were busy, I would not answer the door. Believe me, at first, no one liked my new rules. It is not pleasant to get stern with anyone, but if someone loves and respects you, and if they have the best interests of you and your family at heart, then they will understand and honor your boundaries.

Remember that you are not setting boundaries to be mean to anyone; you are setting them to benefit your family and for your own sanity and peace of mind. That was not the case with our extended family. They did not respect us or what we were doing. So, they pushed me and made life uncomfortable for us for a while to see if I would consistently follow through with the new rules. Does this sound familiar? It is very much like a child testing you to see if you will be consistent—except they're adults. You (the parents) are the protectors of your marriage, family, and children; you are your children's greatest advocate. You must constantly be aware of anything that would cause harm and stop it immediately. You must always seek what is healthy for your marriage, family, and children above all else. You will become stronger as you set boundaries and enforce them with yourself and with others. When those outsiders saw that we were serious and would not give an inch, they backed off and eventually respected—or at least observed—the boundaries we set.

As our little ones got older and had their own schoolwork to do, it became even more important for us to maintain a good working schedule so that each of our students could have the individual time they needed to learn and be successful. It does seem daunting to teach one child, let alone multiple children of differing ages, but with a good plan and consistent schedule, it's not difficult. A consistent schedule relies heavily on each child learning, maturing, and accepting increasing responsibility for their lives and routines as they grow older. By the time they are young teenagers, your specific attention to each child during school will be in assisting their learning. You've taught them how to manage their day; now it's hopefully time to observe, correct, and allow them to exercise adult responsibility.

CHAPTER 7

MULTIPLE CHILDREN, MULTIPLE AGES

FIRST, SECOND, AND THIRD GRADE— BALANCING TEACHING MULTIPLE AGES OF CHILDREN

In the earlier years of our homeschool, I (Terri) would be working at home, transcribing medical reports in the afternoon. I needed to be able to listen and type uninterrupted in order to get all my work completed, but our kids would come in and just start talking to me. I had to stop what I was doing, ask them to repeat their question or request, and help them with whatever the issue was. When their need was met, I could then return to my typing; I had to rewind the audio and get my mind back into the concentration of my work to continue typing. If this happened too much, I was unable to get my work done quickly. Finally, we came up with a system of building on the need for recognizing and respecting the needs of others.

If our children only needed to yell, scream, or cry "mama!" to get attention, they would never understand what quality time was, only manipulation. To avoid this while teaching respect and patience, our children were taught to approach me (if I was busy) and gently place their hand on my arm or my belt. I would obviously notice their presence, and when I could stop what I was focused on, I would respect their need by thoughtfully giving them my attention. They would get in trouble if it was petty—like not sharing a toy or other child conflicts. On the other hand, if it was an emergency, they could run in and raise their voice to get my attention, and I would respond immediately. We had to teach them what "emergency" meant. This system taught our children the priorities of interaction.

They learned that not everything requires Mom to be involved, like squabbles about sharing. They could learn to resolve these conflicts because if I was interrupted for truly insignificant things, we talked about it after my work was done. They could potentially be punished for trying to manipulate a situation by threatening a sibling with "telling Mom." These instances were viewed as lessons. Punishment then was something like being in time-out for three minutes, or however long their actions delayed my work. Not everything needs to be dramatic; just teach gentle consequences. We would also complement them afterward when we saw that they were patient and respectful in other areas, using the same technique of building mutual respect and trust between us and our children.

WORKING TOGETHER AND ONE ON ONE

When we started homeschooling, our oldest was in fourth grade, and our youngest were four and two years old. We would sit around the kitchen table and the two little ones would have measuring spoons, plastic and wood shapes, or letters to play with, while their older brother did his school lessons. Making space for each child to learn and be a part of the experience is truly not that difficult.

We included our little ones in Blake's lessons, and I (Terri) taught all three of them as if the two younger ones were a part of the class and learning along with their older brother. They didn't know they weren't in his grade. They didn't care because they got to do what their big brother was doing. He had to do the work assignments that accompanied his lessons, and they were busy doing their "work"—coloring, building with blocks, and listening to what we were talking about. We would even occasionally use the sifter to dust white flour on the tabletop for them to draw on with their fingers.

Put simply, you recognize what subjects lend themselves to including the younger siblings, and you let them be a part of it. Are they going to learn the lesson? Probably not, but you never know what they will pick up. Continue the activities you started with your children earlier, like art and coloring. By now, you could even introduce paints, play dough, and as their hands get stronger, modeling clay; this is a great time to introduce or reinforce the concept of primary colors and mixing colors. Remember Picasso's Blue Period or van Gogh's *Sunflowers*? Your child can begin comprehending mixing a color and changing the hue. How fun is that?

Do they have blocks? Can you instruct them to arrange five blocks and then ask them how many blocks there are? Remove one, noting, "That is one-fifth of the set. If you remove two, how much is that? Two-fifths, or five minus two, is three." Then move on. They don't necessarily need to know its fractions or math, the main thing is that they are included. They are learning to play quietly while we are having a lesson. They are not getting into trouble. You do not have to monitor them in the next room or put them in front of a screen to keep them occupied; they are right there "learning" with you. This was one way that we began teaching our children patience at an early age.

We say to do these things young because the younger they are, the more your child focuses on you specifically. They're less distracted. Create and nurture curiosity about the world around your children. Encourage them to explore nature, and explore it with them. Go outside and listen to the songs of nature. Look at insects and different animals together. Look small and look big. Explore high and low. Climb trees with them and trek through the forest, be in awe of the beauty of nature with them, but first and foremost, be safe! It's all fun and games until you're face to face with a poisonous snake, but that's a story for another day. Explore books. Explore different foods, tastes, smells, and textures. Learn how things are made, and then try to make them. Listen to music together. Plant seeds now, and if it's fun, they'll want to keep doing it with you later.

My entire family listened to country music, except my sister; she liked disco, too. I (David) was starting to discover music at a young age; we had a piano, and my brother and sister took piano lessons. My dad had a guitar and took lessons off and on, too. By mid-grade school, I liked AC\DC, Nazareth, Judas Priest, and of course, Black Sabbath.

In some weird turn of events, I discovered classical music through big band music like Henry Mancini. This stuff was old and out of date when I discovered it, but I liked it. Classical music caused me to see patterns in my mind. Am I weird? I don't know, but I think it helped me in some way with memory and understanding more complex ideas as a kid. I'd put an eight-track tape into the stereo and crank up Beethoven when my parents weren't home. My dad and brother thought I was weird for listening to classical music. Honestly, I think my dad thought that if I listened to classical music, I must be gay or at least not normal. Times were very different back then, but I still thought people were weird for listening to songs about whiskey, bluetick hounds, and pickup trucks. Everyone in my family was a country music fan. To each his own. But again, I was the weird one. Big deal, right?

My mom believed one could meditate their way to clarity. She forced me to listen to endless hours of self-improvement tapes as she watched TV, smoked, and ate cheese balls. Am I saying that if you listen to classical music you'll be imparted with the knowledge of the universe? No, not necessarily, though classical music can help you focus. Listening to the melody of the piece requires focus. Each instrument can be singled out and focused on while your mind follows the notes up and down. Your brain will begin to pick out patterns. To me, it's relaxing, but also, there isn't a singer forcing me to relate to bluetick hounds or think about booty, booty, booty. Classical music allows me to have free thoughts—my own thoughts—and I also listen to instrumental blues and jazz music nowadays. What foundation will you lay for your children? Will you ask the current popular entertainers to tell your kids how to think and feel and view the world, or will you take charge and allow your child's mind to develop with thoughtful, intelligent intent? To this day, I listen to hard rock and classical music, but I would hold off on music that can plant adult ideas in little kids' minds—at least until sixth grade. There's enough time to allow a little corruption later; there's no need to hurry at the expense of their development.

Alongside activities for the younger children, you should also encourage the older children to help teach their younger siblings. Blake would practice his reading skills by reading books out loud to his sister and brother. He would also mimic how we taught him to read by interacting with them, showing them pictures, and pointing at the words as he read. He was learning how to teach what was modeled for him. When there is a more complex subject or the older children need uninterrupted time, then do that part during the little ones' naptime.

These are just a few ideas to include your little ones in your teaching and make room for your older students as necessary. After a while, you get into a routine and can see the things that are working and change those that are not. We believed that common respect for each other could be taught here as well. It is a continual dance of learning to give and take, and also teaching your children how to give and take to respectfully make time for one another so they can all learn. Recognizing the needs of another and accommodating them in a way that constructively places priority for someone else takes thought, and it takes effort, but it is not that difficult. Just continue to work at it.

Just as it is important to include working with all your children together, it is also crucial to give them each one-on-one time. It is easy to get lost in the process of always trying to do everything together, but I would discourage parents from allowing this to happen. While I encourage you to work together with your children and as an entire family, I also understand we can get caught in the trap of always doing everything together. Again, although it is important to strive for time together, (I can't stress this enough) it is equally important to make time to spend individually with each child, both with their lessons and outside of teaching and school time. If you don't make time for each one individually during their lessons, monitor how they are doing, watch them work, and ask them to describe and explain what they are learning and doing, you can easily miss the difficulties they may be having. It sounds like a lot, but it's really not.

Just like in a business, you plan a specific time on your calendar to meet with important clients. Your children are your most important clients! Plan time to sit individually with each child during your school day, then plan time to spend with each of them outside of school and lessons to talk about things they like, what is important to them, or what is on their mind. Let your children know that while you are with their brother or sister, they are not to interrupt. When it is their turn, they will get the same undivided attention from you and respect from their siblings. By enforcing this, you are teaching respect for your time and others' time, as well as patience to wait until it is their turn.

AUTO MECHANICS SKILLS

Terri read to the kids every day, and as they each grew into this age range, she would have them share their abilities by reading stories aloud at lunch. My (David) contributions were only sporadic, academically speaking. Instead, my contribution was mainly life skills, but I would also read out loud to them when I wasn't working.

Years ago, the manufacturer of our car had a recall, so we had to buy the part. Even at a discount, it hurt financially, and I was angry. Being angry wasn't going to solve anything, so I endeavored to make it a positive, to make it worth the expense. "I really need some help. Will you help me fix the car?" I asked our youngest son. He was more than willing to be a part of the solution. I have a photo of Joshua at the age of six sitting on the front of our car with the hood up, and he is holding a socket and ratchet. He was removing the intake manifold from our family car. Of course, it took longer to include him, but he could proudly say, "There was a recall on our car's intake manifold, and I replaced it," because he did replace it. I assembled the tools and "took care of other things" while guiding him in the task. I was able to spend time with my young son and teach him about car maintenance. When it was complete, I thanked him for his help, told him he saved us money, and paid him for his work. For any work done outside the purview of daily home life, we compensated our children in order to teach them that their efforts had value—that they had value.

I did this with all our kids. The following story doesn't pertain to the age group of this chapter, but it does apply to allowing your children to help at a young age. It illustrates the results of the effort. Our oldest son had helped me work on our cars from the time he could walk, literally. Then, when he was in the sixth grade, the clutch went out in our truck. I was a supervisor at work and on a strict schedule, so I told my son, "I need your help. Please get your schoolwork done as quickly as possible. I need you to remove the transmission in the truck so that we can replace the clutch when I get home."

When I got home, his schoolwork was complete; the truck was safely up on jacks in the garage; and the driveshaft was on the floor, with the transmission on blocks under the truck. I was so incredibly proud of him—and thankful! I had told him, "If at any point you don't feel safe or you're unsure, just stop," and I knew he would. It was a really big ask of a sixth grader, but he did it, and now we could finish it together. I changed clothes and guided him on how to replace the clutch and reinstall the transmission. Again, it took longer, but because he'd completed the transmission task earlier in the day, he deserved my time to learn the rest of the job.

My overarching goal was for our children to understand their vehicles and be comfortable performing maintenance if it served their interests. I also wanted them to never consider being an auto mechanic as a career. I was an airline mechanic at the time, and being a mechanic was a thankless job with little opportunity for advancement. Years later, our son's Porsche needed a clutch replacement. I chuckled and asked him what it cost. He laughed, too, and said he was quoted $3,500! I said, "Ouch." My son casually admitted, "I did it myself. Less than $500 for the clutch and a couple of hours, it was done." I nodded knowingly. Those moments of including him in the work I did for our family out of necessity paid dividends. It improved his quality of life as an adult, because he was in control of his own life.

In the past year, he thanked me for teaching him these things. He said it instilled in him the confidence to work on anything mechanical, and he's become a very competent mechanic. Because we share a respect for one another and are comfortable communicating, he took the time, out of the blue, to call and thank me. Thankfully, he doesn't and never has worked as a mechanic. He has a nice, clean desk job. Each of our children learned unique skills that I began sharing and teaching them at a young age. Over the years, they have built on those skills, and now they teach me. All of our kids are wonderful. We enjoy deep technical conversations on everything from engines to theoretical physics. These relationships are precious to me.

Speaking from the standpoint of a dad, what in the world do you do with a daughter, though? While our daughter could change the oil in a car, change a tire, change an air filter, and properly detail the vehicle, she wasn't interested in learning more. That was fine, and I didn't force her to. My experience could easily be applied to her interests. So instead, we talked about textiles, jewelry, makeup, and art. I could recover a dope and fabric airplane, safety-wire airplane hardware, and even paint airplanes. We would sew; make wire jewelry; and draw on large pieces of paper with crayons, charcoal, and paint. I didn't care whether it was "boy stuff" or "girl stuff." It's commonly said that boys marry their moms and girls marry their dads. If that's true, even if my daughter would marry a bad boy, she would still expect him to cook and sew—at the bare minimum!

WEAPONS SAFETY TRAINING

I grew up in the country. To me, it seemed everyone at least had a shotgun. So, when each of our children were six years old, starting with Blake, I planned to teach them how to shoot guns. We still lived in the country and we owned guns, but we weren't "gun nuts," per se. Even still, our children's safety was a top priority, because how many children are killed by curiosity with regard to firearms?

Once they reached six years old, I had each child take a stuffed animal (not their favorite) from their collection and proudly accompany me to a place in the country. They weren't going with me to shoot; I was going with them to shoot. They were each excited when it was their first time. Each child willingly set up the stuffed animal, and we backed up to load the gun. When it was all ready, I squatted behind them and helped hold the heavy shotgun against *their* shoulder. I helped them take aim. "When you're ready, put your finger on the trigger and slowly pull it back," I instructed. Each of them did, and then the gun blasted against their shoulder and sent them back against me with a loud boom.

The stuffed animal vaporized into flying stuffing. Each was shocked and on the verge of tears. "This is what guns do," I said. "Never touch a gun without me there." They each nodded earnestly, and they never did. But they all did want to keep on shooting with Dad.

As teens, they each shot and killed an animal and had to clean it and prepare it for dinner. Just once. Otherwise, I wasn't really into hunting as an adult. I continued to build on this experience by taking them to the range to shoot as they grew up. I wanted them to understand firearms because of the country and world we live in. As there are a lot of firearms in our country, it's my opinion that this is a critical knowledge set.

Did this make our kids "gun nuts?" No, but they all know how to safely handle firearms or notice when someone else is being dangerous and irresponsible. Our oldest son is an avid shooter, and I enjoy the conversations we have and the things he teaches me. While our daughter obtained a concealed carry permit when she was twenty-one, she only shot at the range to stay proficient as she saw the importance of practicing to maintain her skills. We enjoyed doing it together. On the other hand, our youngest son built his own AR-15 (which stayed in a locked safe) because he enjoyed the task from a technical point of view, even though he isn't an avid shooter at all. Ultimately, guns don't scare our children, and they can recognize unsafe situations when firearms are involved. If our children encounter a situation with firearms involved, they likely won't panic, and that was my goal.

We will begin to talk more and more about marriage as the book continues, but this is a good place to also say that I introduced Terri to firearms. Together, we trained to a more advanced proficiency, and are now peers in this subject. I'm not the "Well, little lady, I'm the big man who will guide you because of your lady-ness with these big guns," kind of guy. We have real adult conversations that can sometimes be about firearms. I teach her, she teaches me, and we challenge each other. How cool is that? It's okay if you're not into guns because guns aren't the point;

it's about having a common topic where you can exist as peers within your family.

It is so tiring to try to make my family believe that I know absolutely everything and that my judgment is infallible. If I can't remember how to position a bolt to the bolt carrier to insert a cam pin, I can ask my wife. Our ladies (and children) get as much joy out of being helpful on a topic as we men do, which is why it's so beneficial to do things together as a family.

MOTORCYCLES

Another thing that grew out of this shotgun-wielding age range with the kids, was that our children were told that I would teach them to ride a motorcycle when they could ride a bicycle without training wheels. They each learned to ride a bicycle at ages three, five, and four, respectively, so by first grade, they all could competently ride a motorcycle (dirt bike). In everything, safety was the first lesson. We showed them, in a real way, that we trusted them to handle responsibility. They were proud of what they could do and acted accordingly, as the responsibility of using things like guns and dirt bikes matured them. Jessica loved riding together and having fun together. Enjoyable experiences built our relationships and our bonds as a family. Today, only our oldest son is an avid motorcycle rider, but that's another story. Like when they were young, we still bond over the activities we shared so many years ago, and we still share the joy of riding. That's time well spent. And again, all of these things started when our children were in early grade school or younger.

Look at your own children, and resist the urge to look at other people's children to gauge what you should be doing with yours. The bar in our country and society has been kicked to the ground. What are they capable of? When you have knowledge about a subject or topic and can determine if your children possess the necessary traits to be introduced to something, give it a try. Let them fail. Let them experience the consequences of their actions. You can control the situation so that the fall isn't as bad as it could be, so that they learn lessons early and quickly.

When I was in the third grade, I drove a car for the first time . . . without my parents' knowledge. When I was in fifth grade, I learned to drive a manual transmission car . . . without my parents' knowledge. As a twelve-year-old, my mom had picked me up from my private school, and we were driving home. In the past, Mom had experienced episodes having to do with high or low blood sugar. I don't recall the specifics, but I know that it miraculously disappeared at some point. I yelled out that she was running off the road. Mom slammed on the brakes, half-on, half-off the two-lane country road, and she knew she was not fit to drive. We weren't anywhere near a payphone. "Don't worry, Mom—I'll drive," I said. My mom looked at me, confused, and I backed it up, remarking sheepishly, "Dad lets me drive sometimes." She had a Subaru with a manual transmission. I helped Mom buckle up in the passenger seat. I slipped into the driver's seat and smoothly, safely drove us several miles home and parked straighter than she ever did in the driveway. Knowing Mom was just going to lie down and rest, I was happy and scot-free. Mom wouldn't be lecturing me or giving me random tasks like scrubbing the driveway.

Then my dad got home. I heard them visiting, and the first thing I made out was, "He drives great. Drove us all the way home. He said you let him drive." Dad was furious.

"I let him sit next to me and steer!"

Damnit! I thought. My dad burst through my bedroom door, grabbed me by the shirt, and lifted my face toward his. "Where did you learn to drive?" All I could think about was taking a hit to my face. "You taught me." Dad doubled down with two hands on my shirt. "I let you steer! I'm only asking one more time: Where did you learn to drive?" As best I could, I meekly shrugged my shoulders. "We haul hay, Dad. I've driven the truck." The truck was an old Ford with "three on the tree," and I only ever used first and neutral. "I also ride motorcycles with a clutch." My dad shook his head. I continued, "I dunno—I've been driving some with you, and I see how you do it, too."

I'm embarrassed to tell a lot of my stories, though this is the point of this book: challenge your children at their pace, or they'll find ways to occupy their time and feel challenged. My decision was to lie or get my mouth busted open. Of course, I could've just let my mom and me sit on the side of the road for a few hours, too, but ultimately, like I'll say several times, I did what I thought was best, and then told my parents what they wanted to hear.

In regard to my dad, being king of the universe, the best way out for me was to give him credit for doing something supposedly exceptional (facilitating me safely driving myself and my mom home because he equipped me to drive). I know his gut told him it was bullshit, but he said, "Thank God you didn't kill your mom and yourself. Never do that again." Roger that. Mom had totaled two cars by that point in her life and my dad had totaled one, so all I did was nod agreeably.

The following year, my sister and I drove over a hundred miles away to a family wedding (in the car my parents got for her). On the way home, my sister had a serious allergic reaction while on the interstate. It was raining. We hit a guardrail, and the car spun down the two lanes. We came to rest sideways across the road. My sister wasn't doing well, and as I was looking at two semitrucks coming straight for us, it was the only time I've been thankful for the 55 mile-per-hour speed limit.

"Push in the clutch!" I yelled.

She did. I put the car in reverse and yelled, "Floor it!" Amazingly, given her condition, she didn't stall it. I saw the semitruck trailers beginning to slide sideways as we exited backward to the median. Remember, it was raining. As soon as the front tires cleared the lane, I pulled the emergency brake with everything I had, trying to avoid being stuck in the mud. The car stalled, and the semitrucks blasted by us. "Fuck! What happened?" I asked my sister. She seemed better, but still out of it. "Switch out," I said. "I'll get us home."

She didn't argue. Though I was shaking from adrenaline, I was more worried about her. There wasn't a hospital or even a town nearby, and cell phones were still several years away. We traded places, and in first gear, I gingerly pulled out of the grass and onto the small inner shoulder of the road and watched for traffic. I accelerated onto the interstate and drove the remaining eighty miles home.

I already knew there was no way out of this predicament. The car was damaged. My sister was sick. She had the presence of mind to ask if there was anything we could do to "fix it." I laughed and said no. The front fender and door were crunched and scratched to the metal. "Dad's gonna kick my ass for driving," I said. My sister was my ally. We'd get bitched out together.

"He drove from where?" my parents asked. My sister told them. "Thank God you two are okay," my mom said. My sister said what happened to her, as far as she could remember. I told my parents the sequence of events, and they weren't sure if they could believe that I told her what to do so fast that we didn't get hit. "What way did you drive home?" they grilled. I told them that I took a specific exit to avoid busy roads because I didn't want to get pulled over. My sister's and my stories correlated. They found it hard to believe that I was capable of doing what I'd done, but they let it go.

After that, my sister would let me use her car. We would leave home together, happy brother and sister, to "go to an arcade or the local drive-in for a Coke;" in reality, we'd meet up with her boyfriend, they'd go out on a date in his car, and I'd take her car to my girlfriend's house. Win-win. A part of our common bond was the overbearing, controlling nature of our parents, specifically our mom.

"Control" is an illusion for overbearing parents or authority figures. No matter what, your children will find a way to explore who they are. I first rode a motorcycle without my parents' knowledge when I was four years old; I drove a car without my parent's knowledge in the third grade. Your children will also begin to develop their personal relationships with each other, depending on their age gap, in this same time period. What are your kids interested in? What do they *seem* to be interested in? Recognize it and act on it. It doesn't have to be a big deal—as a matter of fact, just see if they respond. If you want to truly be a part of their lives, sometimes you will have to follow their lead.

For our grandkids, I've exposed them to several things (after first asking their parents for permission discreetly, of course). I took them out and let them drive the boat down the intercoastal with lots of other boat traffic. Of course, we had a safety brief first, and I told them that if I grabbed the controls, just sit back, no big deal. Their smiles never faded, and the stereo never got turned down. Of course, we've also ridden motorcycles, and while we didn't shoot stuffed animals, we did learn gun safety and recited the safety rules, then went shooting. I told them that anytime they wanted to shoot, they had to recite the safety rules to me or Grandma, and then we'd take them shooting.

We've also talked about school shootings and what to do if they hear "that" sound. "You need to be a leader. Get other students to help you and throw a desk through the window to get out. You may even need to tell your teacher to get out." We are fun grandparents—intense sometimes but always fun!

The foundation your children will develop through the first half of grade school will result in their growing independence as they wrap up grade school. In a sense, this should be one of the most intense periods of learning in your child's development because between birth and third grade, you are their anchor. Their focus is on you and relies on you in a way it never will again. You must capitalize on it. The fourth and fifth grades are when your children are going to exercise their own independence and create a more complex view of what they know. They'll start connecting the dots. It will end an era.

"That's crazy," you might think. "They're little kids." This is true to someone as old as you, but think back on your childhood and adolescence. In chapter 10, which covers the age range when your kids' hormones kick in, you'll see that if you've not done your job up to this point, it's on you (like it was on us).

CHAPTER 8

FOURTH AND FIFTH GRADE (NINE TO TEN YEARS OLD)

Fourth and fifth grade bring back two distinct memories for me (David) that played a large role in why we ultimately chose to homeschool. These memories also encompass my self-imposed rule as a parent as something to avoid with our children at all costs.

In the late 1970s and early 1980s, motocross had become a real industry, with factories spending millions to support teams, and it was only growing. I didn't have anything more than a Honda minibike, but I rode it like it was a factory race bike—I lived and breathed off-road motorcycles. I wanted a real race bike so badly, beyond my ability to even describe on the page. I'd have agreed to almost anything to get it.

Before YouTube and the internet, I was doing not-normal things on motorcycles, like jumping over cars. When my parents noticed yet another part had broken off the minibike (that I couldn't repair without their knowledge), I'd tell them that I wrecked or hit a tree or didn't see the creek and rode right into it because those things were okay with them. Supporting their belief that I was stupid was my golden ticket, as I knew the fact that I was actually airborne over the heads of my friends (who were excitedly watching my crazy antics and bolstering my school reputation) and landing so hard that I eventually cracked the engine mounts and broke off lights and fenders would not be acceptable to my parents. So I learned to repair what I could. They didn't see my fast, high-flying riding as a talent. Nowadays, these riders are called freestylers, and they enjoy wide and popular coverage by the X Games.

I have one single photograph of me on a motorcycle as a child. My mom refused to take any pictures of me otherwise. I never came home hurt, but I would occasionally wreck and tear my pants, in which case they would ask where a certain pair of pants were. "I dunno. I think they're in the laundry." The pants were, in fact, long gone. Evidence disposed of. (Before you judge me too harshly, jeans were about four to six dollars a pair for Levis, and my parents got a discount on that from the store where they bought them.) My jeans often got demolished by barbed wire, angry hogs, or rambunctious horses, so when my motorcycle riding finished off an old pair of jeans, it was a rare event that simply condemned an already ragged pair of pants. Riding, to me, was pure freedom fueled by adrenaline. It was absolute calm in the middle of a storm that I was in control of, for good or bad. I'd say it was the first thing that I was passionate about and a true escape from everything else that was my life.

LIES, ALL LIES

As a young child, like when I walked in the woods, I'd tell my parents the truth, and they would accuse me of lying. If I'd told my parents the truth, I would have lost the bike and probably been smacked around, or I could've just lied and enjoyed the ride as long as possible. In this case, I chose to lie rather than lose that outlet in my life. I'm just being honest on this side of life looking back, although it's decades later.

With my parents, what they taught me was that truth and lies were irrelevant. They wanted to hear something specific. A teacher could lie to cover her ass, and my parents always believed the teacher. I told the truth and got in trouble. My mom could lie to my dad about what she had been doing all day (watching television); she'd get whatever he needed tomorrow. No big deal. I watched family members at gatherings lie to each other seemingly all night. I had a teacher in eighth grade beat my ass bloody (literally) with a red oak board because he said I hadn't turned in my homework. I'd tutored a group of students in class; everyone in class, including the teacher, knew I'd done the lesson. I told the truth; he lied. My parents thought my bloody underwear and future ass scars seemed excessive but assumed the punishment would make up for "whatever I'd gotten away with." Even when I was beaten bloody, my parents admitted that the truth didn't matter. I once watched my dad tell quite the whopper twice on the same day. He knew I knew. He knew I noticed. I cashed that check right then, and my dad left me in peace for a couple of months. I even got to ride my motorcycle. To this day, his secret has stayed safe with me.

This reflection on my own life as a child was an invaluable guide to how I would do life as an adult and parent. If my parents never offered a goal or positive outcome for me to work toward, then I would work toward the outcome that was the least undesirable. My parents were only happy when they got what they wanted. Seemingly, they were least happy when I was happy, so I did what made me happy and then lied to them, saying what they wanted to hear, which made them happy, and there was peace. I was taught this by my parents and family, but especially by the family members who thought their secrets stayed secret. They'd be mortified to know what I know.

As a parent, I had to *want* my own children's personal happiness and fulfillment. In my motorcycle fantasy era of grade school, my parents had an opportunity like none other. In reflection, it would be the only true opportunity they had to bring us together or create a divide that would never heal. I say "only" opportunity because as parents, not all of our children had one big single interest; only one of our children did. My parents had it dropped in their lap with me, I practically begged for it.

YOU WANT SOME CANDY, LITTLE BOY?

In my district, the school administered IQ tests every year. It was at least a state thing, but the scores were ranked nationally. All I knew was that I had to take the school test at the end of every year, and I always ranked highly. In the fourth and fifth grades, my scores were in the top 2 percent nationally, yet this wasn't reflected in my schoolwork. Grade school didn't have an A–F grading system. My memory is that we had an *E* for excels, *S* for satisfactory, and *U* for unsatisfactory. I would get all Es and Ss. The IQ scores and grades didn't have any meaning to me, beyond that I wouldn't have to do the work again. Good enough was good enough—in my estimation, as long as I got passing grades on my report card, life was good. My parents begged to differ but never explained why—besides demanding that's what they wanted to see. My brother and sister were not straight-A students, but my parents wanted straight As (Es) from me. I didn't care at all what was on my report card, because as far as I was concerned, the teachers gave me work and I did it because it was required; now let's move on. There was no greater motivation to do any differently.

My mom was into higher-power meditation kinds of things. She said that I only used 4 percent of my brain and that I could—and should—unlock more of it. She didn't and couldn't do so herself if she had to, but she truly expected me to do so—to the point of screaming in my face and pulling my hair to accomplish her will. It seemed that for herself, my mom believed the answer was in the bottom of a bag of Cheetos or on talk shows. She lived by the old saying, "Do as I say, not as I do." Her target with me was always moving, largely based on the daily television she watched. What she told me to do from day to day or week to week could change dramatically.

For every S or U that I received, I'd get hit with the belt, but I could live with getting whipped four times a year. It was three lashes for a U and one for an S, and I was always guaranteed a U for student attitude. It was six or eight lashes for each nine-week period, and I simply accepted it. Later, in addition to the belt, though, if I didn't get perfect scores, they'd take away my motorcycle for the next nine-week period. That was a bit different, but I had to accept it because our report cards were partly based on the teacher's opinion, in cases such as "student attitude." Unless you were a favorite, you'd get a U, because that's how that generation of teachers was, generally speaking. There was nothing I could do to change the fact that I'd get beat with the belt and lose my motorcycle every report card for having passing grades.

This practice began before fourth and fifth grades, but in this window of time, a life-changing deal was struck. My parents said that if I got a perfect report card, they'd buy me the brand-new race bike I wanted.

Well, alright then! Now that they pushed a button I could understand, true motivation spoke to me.

I worked my butt off to ensure my grades were always Es. Every day, I came into school ready for the challenge to learn the material and turn in clean, accurate work. I avoided trouble by not running on the playground or climbing on the equipment because inevitably, some kid would hurt themselves, and everyone around them would be blamed by the bitchy old teachers. I went out of my way to be polite to my teacher. I didn't bring her any apples or chocolates, but I didn't antagonize her, either. In my mind, there was no other way to appease the adults around me.

I swear that I can remember my emotions the day report cards were going to be handed out. My mind went back over everything, searching for any bad assignments, any infractions at all. My heart was pounding in my chest because I couldn't think of a single bad thing. I was about to get a brand-new race bike! I could smell the tires; I could feel the rough seat, the grips in my hands. I could jump over a bus and not break anything on my new bike! The teacher handed me the report card. I opened the tiny envelope and looked at the grade column, E, E, E, E . . . "Student Attitude: U."

Really? Not even an S? Just go straight to U?

How bad could my attitude really be? Surely, my parents wouldn't count the arbitrary student attitude score against me. I had perfect grades, but in my heart, I knew it would be used against me. I'd seen my mom come to the school to visit with my teacher recently, which was odd. She also left and didn't give me a ride home, which meant she was hiding the visit from me. I saw her through the classroom window while on recess. She was never at the school when I was doing average, but now that I was working hard, here she was at the school before report cards came out? Although I'm unsure of what my parents' motivations were, I do believe that my mom had something to do with the teacher giving me a U for attitude. While I wasn't a favorite, I simply wasn't one of the kids who acted out in class.

That evening, my parents sat at the kitchen table. They both seemed to know what my report card said already. They were expectant, and if it had been in my lexicon then, I'd have said my parents seemed smug. My dad made a show of opening the little envelope, eyebrows raised, as if he were truly anticipating the results like some gameshow host. He looked at the card and handed it to my mom, and they calmly delivered to me an oddly rehearsed speech that began, "Well, now we know you can do it . . ." I responded with, "Do I get the bike? They're all Es." My parents pounced, and my dad jumped up. "They are not *all* Es!" my dad angrily yelled and made a show of holding up the yellow card and pointing at the *U*, driving his finger into the card over and over as though my face could be next. I was desperate. "I didn't get in trouble. I got good grades. She's mean to everyone except the [pretty, rich] girls." My mom went off on a two-hour "better self, better attitude" speech, and Dad was ready to take my shirt in his fist and hit me if it looked like I wasn't listening.

The problem with my attitude wasn't ever specified by the teacher or my parents, so there was really nothing to correct—I just needed to be less like me and keep doing what they wanted. The bike was off the table since I utterly failed . . . but I was told to keep up the good grades, and "one day we'll see." With my parents, "one day" meant *never*. Yes, I was also grounded from my current motorcycle for getting a U for student attitude on my report card. While I don't fully recall, honestly, I was also probably whipped with the belt for the U as well.

ONE DAY . . .

My mom has proved my perception over and over since I was in grade school—she's been saying she is going to get her guest room cleaned up "one day" . . . for thirty years. My parents didn't tell me "good job" or encourage me for what I had accomplished; rather, I was in trouble for what I didn't accomplish. If I received average grades, I'd be lectured and punished. If I worked my butt off and got perfect grades, I'd be lectured and punished. What do you think my response was?

Apathy. There was nothing to care about. My parents' power of manipulation only worked if I cared. They manipulated anything that I cared about to the point that I just quit caring.

In response to me flatly not caring anymore, my parents shipped me off to a charismatic Christian school to get my attitude in check. My parents didn't attend church or read the Bible, but my mom was certain that Jesus would solve her problems with me and get my heart and mind in the right place. My dad still just wanted my mom to be happy, so he agreed. As a parent myself now, I think a deal is a deal. As a grade-schooler, I'd have been open to my parents saying, "You did well, son, really good. We need to see what Mrs. Smith thinks is wrong with your attitude." Because of that omission on their part and the fact that my mom secretly visited Mrs. Smith during the week of report cards, I knew they'd lied to me, but now I knew what to watch for. I also resented my angry old teacher more than ever.

Reflecting on the memories of a child through the eyes of an adult and applying those observations to myself and the lives of my own children has taught me so many things. Good, life-changing things. After denying me the motorcycle, my parents went on to celebrate both my siblings' sixteenth birthdays over the next couple of years (the siblings who got brand-new motorcycles for Christmas years before). My parents took them out of school and went car shopping. They were treated to a special birthday lunch and each got their first cars. They later received letter jackets and class rings and all of the fun things high schoolers look forward to.

I didn't get any of it.

On my sixteenth birthday, I got high by myself, and when Dad got home from work late that night, he put a bag of supermarket fried chicken on the table for me to eat—if I wanted it, but I'd already eaten and gone to bed. Since my brother was married and moved away, there was no birthday to celebrate. Happy birthday to me.

When I got my first W-4 job at the age of sixteen, I bought a sports car. It was beautiful, a metallic blue 1979 Camaro with a moon roof. (I know that by today's standards, it wasn't a sports car, but it wasn't an Oldsmobile or pickup truck, either.) It was the nicest car at our house. I paid for the car, my gas, and my own insurance (all of which was about $200 a month back then; I made $3.32 an hour).

The first weekend I had the car, my parents did the "kitchen assault" and took my keys. They decided to go visit friends in another state for the weekend. My parents often took my car because, as they said, I owed it to them. I'd have the car detailed for a fun weekend with Terri (yes, when we were sixteen; we were high school sweethearts). My parents would vindictively "thank me" for cleaning my car for them to use (without asking, threateningly demanding), and they would return it full of smoke and cigarette butts and ashes and the occasional fast-food trash.

What were my parents trying to teach me through this? Nothing. There were so many opportunities for good, but since they weren't looking for it, they didn't see it. I had no value to my parents. My parents would reveal over and over what they were watching for. They wanted to validate their desire to lash out at me because their real son died.

Not only was my mom's target for me in constant motion, but her perception of reality was in flux as well. I'll say over and over that no one saw the reality of our home life. Everyone took my parents at their word, and it was just how life was behind closed doors.

Years later, when my mom lectured me about my smoking—she also complained for years about her own "bronchitis," which magically disappeared—I retorted to her that I wished she would have been this passionate about the subject and realized this when I was a little kid, when she would smoke in the car with the windows rolled up; or sit in her chair in the house, chain-smoking cigarettes all day; or when she and Dad would take my car and leave their cigarette ashes and butts behind. "I never did that!" she would proclaim in shock. Nobody is perfect, but it's times like these when you realize someone's mental health is in question.

Years later, after I'd exited the picture, most everyone else got a dose of the mom I knew and grew up with, and I'm not ashamed to say that I've enjoyed it more than I should.

As a child, she would constantly accuse me of stealing and lying and anything else that could be accusatory and hurtful. As an adult, the first time a family member called me up and emotionally told me what had just happened with my mom, I said, "She's always been that way." They said, "Well, no! Not like this!" I asked, "Did she pull your hair out?" There was silence.

"No, why?"

I responded, "Well, you're lucky—she's gotten better." Click. *I don't give two fucks what she did to you as an adult, motherfucker. What about what she did to me as a* **child**? I was offended. Later, from another family member, I got a big information dump—my mom had eventually attacked every other close family member, and all those people who had stood in judgment of me when I was a defenseless kid were shocked and surprised. I laughed until there were tears in my eyes. It wasn't that I thought their hurt was funny or took any pleasure in their pain. I thought, *It's finally everyone else's turn to share in my reality.* If I dealt with it as a kid and didn't turn out too fucked up—surely they could handle it as adults.

MOM'S FINAL ATTEMPT . . .

Much later in life, my mom lost her license to drive because of her deteriorating mental health, and when enough time had passed and it was obvious she would never drive again (after about a year), I asked about her car. It was literally the car that was driven to the store by an old lady once a week and maintained on a schedule. It was also the only car that she hadn't wrecked in some way. We had recently considered buying a second car, and it occurred to me that her car could possibly be the perfect grocery-getter for us.

One day, as I was driving a rental vehicle from Las Vegas to San Diego, my mom called to visit. I was driving a newer model of the exact same car she had sitting in her driveway. My drive usually took about four to five hours, depending on traffic. After talking for about an hour, I had the thought, and I asked her, "Hey, has anyone asked about your car, Mom?" I knew that I was last in line if anyone else had already asked. That's just how it has always been. "Well, I can't drive anymore, so it's just sitting," she replied. I said, "Well, if you're not going to drive again and if no one else has asked about it by now, I'll buy it from you. Just tell me how much and we'll write you a check."

Mom was aghast! "If you want my car, you can have it!" she said. What? She had surely mistaken me for someone else, someone distinctly not me, at least. I told my mom that I didn't want to take her car; she had invested a lot of money in it and should realize a good return on that investment. Never mind that the last four cars she and Dad owned were given to them, which they in turn gave away to "blood family" prior to my dad's passing.

Right then, my mom and I struck a deal. She was happy that she'd have a nice pot of money to play with and that it wouldn't be a burden on us. I coordinated with other family members who lived near her to help her take care of the title. I made arrangements to fly into town several weeks later at the agreed-upon date; we would make the exchange, and I would drive the car home over a thousand miles away. However, during that time, unbeknownst to me, someone else asked about the car.

When I got into town to pick up the car, I called my mom. "Well . . ." my mom hesitantly said. "I didn't know anyone else would be interested in my car." *Oh my God, here it comes,* I thought. Seriously? Still? "I asked you if anyone else was interested in your car, and you said no, and we made a deal. Here I am." She said, "Well, another family member asked about it. His son's girlfriend needs a car." I looked at her and said, "Okay, Mom. So, the deal is off?" I was momentarily hurt, and now I needed to make other travel arrangements to get home. It had been hard for me to even ask my mom about the car in the first place, as I'd learned throughout my life to avoid putting myself in a position where my parents would choose me last. However, even as an adult, I guess I still hoped to find some kind of normalcy with my mom.

She broke this deal with another: "Let's wait and see what happens." Trying not to laugh, I responded, "Are you seriously still saying that, Mom? Someday never comes with you; it's a cop-out. Someone else, anyone but me, will get the car, and you'll be so proud to see them take it, knowing it's going to some undeserving kid you don't even know—just as long as the stray kid you adopted doesn't get it." I asked her how many promises she had broken to me that involved this family member, and then I reminded her of the big ones.

I wasn't angry. I'm still not angry. Unlike her and my dad, I could afford to buy my own cars. I was just sad.

In all the years since I was a kid, nothing had changed, and my adult reflection on when I was a child had been accurate. Blood family reigned supreme. To me, the car wasn't a car; it was a representation of a relationship. My mom told me loud and clear, one last time, that we didn't have one. Her word meant nothing, and a nameless kid, a friend of a friend, outranked me. I learned that the relationship my mom had developed with me as a child has continued in the same manner, and will continue in the same manner for the rest of our lives.

LET'S NOT DO THIS

As a parent, especially as a homeschool parent (since we are with our children so much more), our interactions with them are so incredibly important. Not everything is binary; yes or no, good or bad. We need to teach our children through example, honesty, integrity, and respect; we need to illustrate to them why these are important traits to strive for. For these early years, Terri talks more about schedule and technique with our young children, but what was most profound to me at this age, was just how much my mind absorbed information and emotions from birth through grade school. As I look back, I'm astonished at the rate at which my brain absorbed information and how solidly it was retained. If there's a time to strive to be an attentive parent for your kids, it's during the years from birth through grade school.

If there's a time to be the best you can be for your lasting relationship with them, it's after this. If you lie to or betray your children, they'll never forget it, and it will be the simple, uncomplicated memory of a child—you lied to them. Period.

PARENT LIKE IT MATTERS, BECAUSE IT DOES

My unbreakable rule as a parent is not to dangle carrots for my children or grandchildren. If I make a promise, I will figuratively bleed, if necessary, to follow through. Of course I've made promises that, for one reason or another, I failed to follow through on, and there've been some biggies. My reasons were usually work related, but even a legitimate reason is still an excuse. Not following through with your children teaches them to expect promises to be broken. It is teaching your children that they can make promises and it's fine to break them if they have a good enough excuse. No, if I break a promise for any reason, it's still a broken promise. I'll apologize sincerely and pay it back with interest. What I do know

now, is that I can take our kids at their word. If they say they'll do something, they do it. If we say that we'll do something, they can count on us doing it. Nothing is more important than trust, and I had to lie and be lied to by those closest to me to learn this valuable lesson.

With regard to school, I'd tell our children why having good grades was important in a manner appropriate to their age, and any rewards offered were to accomplish something special, outside of normal responsibilities. Do you get a gold star for going to work every day? They won't, either. Employee appreciation day is payday. I should say again, keep in mind that you are preparing your children to be adults. I don't know about you and how things work in your life, but for me, when I accomplished a nearly "impossible" task at work (even if it literally made the company millions), the reward, at best, was "Good job! Thanks!" To them, I'd done the job I was hired to do. It really is that simple.

We're not preparing our children for what we think life *should* be; we're preparing our children for what life *is*. Because we held a preparatory point of view on homeschooling, our grading expectations were a little different, especially from those of my school and my parents. Our expectations were very high, but it wasn't expected that our children would meet everything perfectly because to us, that mimicked adult life. You work as diligently as possible, to the best of your ability, and we identify the weaknesses as well as the strengths. Sometimes it's wonderful, and other times you fall short.

We would reward our children for their overall performance for the week (kind of like how we get a paycheck; they had something to look forward to as well). Did they get up and show up for school on time? Did they complete their work with intent? Did they accomplish their other responsibilities, like dishes or feeding the dog and cat every day as needed? We all woke up and had a job to do. In the same way that some people go to the club or bar on Friday after work, Terri took the kids for lunch at the burger and ice cream restaurant, or we went to the theater for a movie or bought a new-release movie. This is adulting. We get up and do life, even the parts that suck, because it needs to be done.

We began teaching our children this at a very young age. Reaping the rewards of being an adult is part of the fun of being an adult, so we should teach our children this as well. There are countless nuances to everything we did or recommend, and that's what this book is largely about. Your children learn to be self-motivated each morning because they can get the requirements out of the way, hoping to enjoy their personal interests and their family. Usually it works out, but sometimes it doesn't. They'll learn to adjust their decision making and try again. When they do, the reward is something special for everyone, like dinner and a movie (the reward also results in spending time together as a family, and they're excited for it!).

Continuing the theme of adulting, use their personal successes as an opportunity to allow your children to make decisions. For example, create a list of restaurants to choose from. Allow one family member to make their choice. It isn't required that everyone likes all the choices, but you can tolerate a restaurant your child likes for their self-satisfaction of choosing where to eat for the whole family (no complaining or taunting allowed by anyone). Additionally, they also get to choose the movie. Everyone has a regular turn on the schedule, which teaches respect. (Hint: As the adults, you're going to give them choices of movies they're at least remotely excited about and interested in. Don't pander, but also don't choose a restaurant or movie that only a mature adult will appreciate, or that's inappropriate for the youngest age of child.) While Terri and I enjoy animated films, this is also why it's good to have spouse "date nights," too, to enjoy dinners and movies for adults. You and your spouse also need private time to discuss your efforts and each child. It's important to be adults together, not just teach adulting—you might be embarrassed to know what little ears hear at home.

IF YOU TALK THE TALK, WALK THE WALK

This decision-making scenario was recently tested with our youngest tween granddaughter. To her surprise, Terri and I asked her opinion about where to eat in her city. She proudly picked out the restaurant she wanted to go to with Grandma and Grandpa. She recognized the restaurant's name and knew that people talked about it, but she had never been to it. Unknown to her, it was a white-tablecloth-and-crystal five-star restaurant—not a place one would usually take children. What do you do?

We chose to honor her restaurant decision. It was a blind menu (no prices). I told her that she wouldn't find chicken strips and to just order what looked good. She chose a filet mignon. She felt special sitting in this beautiful restaurant with all of these dressed-up people. The waiter treated her like a young lady, and she acted like a young lady. We enjoyed a wonderful meal. She didn't know what to think of having her soda in a crystal glass. She kept looking at her grandma and me as if she were wondering, *How could this be normal?*

It was fun to watch her body language and facial expressions. Later, when the bill came, she looked over her grandma's arm to see the amount. My tip alone would be more than the average restaurant bill. Her eyes couldn't have been wider; her face was red and her mouth opened, but no words came out. She's never at a loss for words, which made it even more funny. She looked at me for some response. "This is where you wanted to go for dinner," I said. I swear her face got more red. "I didn't know it was going to cost that much!" She was embarrassed. Honestly, we were a little surprised, too. "We asked where you wanted to go, and here we are. Enjoy it!" I said with a smile.

Besides feeling a little out of place, I know she felt special. She felt special being there, special for getting to go there, special that her grandma and grandpa took only her, and special that she got to order whatever she wanted—no kids menu and no imposed budget. She was a young lady and was treated more like an adult than a child. Through that lens, was it worth it? I say yes. To me, it was more than a meal. We exposed her to something new that created new desires and expectations for her life going forward. Will it accomplish world peace? No, but it's one little thing in a string of many little things over years that characterize our relationship with her, and will shape the woman she'll grow up to be. We want our children and grandchildren to never feel "less than." We want them to want nice things and not just accept what someone is willing to give them. We'll do everything we can to equip them to reach those goals. So, strive to succeed.

As young parents, however, five-star restaurants weren't in the budget. These lessons taught don't require much money, though. Allowing your child to take part in decision making when they have the maturity to do so is all it takes to teach this. As they mature and grow and respect your decisions, their freedom to make decisions also grows.

YOUR CHILDREN WILL BECOME THE WORLD'S FUTURE LEADERS

I covered a lot in this chapter with my stories. To me, they all have multiple viewpoints that speak to the same point, the least of which is the perspective that I was a victim—I wasn't. Life isn't fair. I recognized years ago that some people, like family member Joe, will get endless assistance, but at what cost to themselves or their personal development? Do I think there is a more constructive way to learn these lessons? Absolutely, and that's why we parented differently, and why we decided to write this book.

Children need to understand and experience successes, rewards, failures, consequences, and punishment. In life, they will experience unfairness and injustice. Your lessons will teach them how to handle all these things in a positive way. This is the world everyone lives in and the one successful people flourish in. Our world badly needs leaders, people who step out of the chaos and provide stability through their actions and words. Will you teach your child to simply conform, or will you teach them to be their best—to be a leader?

Beginning in high school, our children were drawn toward leadership roles. Our sweet daughter taught a fencing class to young children who loved and respected her. She then went on to be a team leader throughout different activities in high school, including the legal debate class, Mock Trial. Our sons were the same, and they continued to excel and lead throughout college and into their careers. It's not about being "the boss;" it's about success for everyone. I taught our children that every job comes down to one simple task: your job is to make your boss look good. Do that, and you will rise. But what does that mean exactly? I mean that you should know and perform your job without being told or corrected, recognize when your boss will have questions, and be prepared with the answers.

And of course—I have a story. At one company I worked for, the chief executive officer (CEO) was having a bad day. A few large defense contractor reps were showing up for a tour, and the CEO's staff members were either not at work, or came unprepared. The CEO came to my office in the morning and told me about his predicament. I was a division manager, and he asked if I could conduct this tour on top of my own deadlines.

"What is the tour about?" I asked. In the same way that a dinner isn't always a dinner, he told me the goal of the tour.

"We don't have the facilities for that," I replied, fascinated with what his answer might be. He told me of the land the company had purchased and the money they set aside for infrastructure. With a tired but hopeful look, he asked, "Can you work with that?" I nodded, somewhat amused, thinking this might be a fun challenge. "I can work with that." Terri brought a suit to my office and used the outing to take the kids out to lunch.

After a catered lunch in the conference room for our visitors, the CEO called me; he was ready. I arrived, introduced myself, and apologized to the group for missing lunch. I told them we had unforeseen difficulties that were now resolved, and I was free to show them around the facility and answer any questions they had regarding a possible expansion. I was going to do everything possible to make the CEO look good. If there was a shit sandwich, I was going to eat it for him. To get my legs under me, I started the tour in my shops, and it continued across the twenty-five acres of buildings and facilities.

To get this new business meant we'd triple our earnings, seemingly overnight. We would have to scale impossibly fast to meet their minimum contract requirements, and their toughest questions were regarding this obstacle. I confidently told them that our unknowns were construction contractor schedules, but that the officers of the company had everything in place to pull the trigger. I told them, "As an example, for operations, every person in my shops is capable of supervising a crew." I told them that specific detail was intentional by management (to make my CEO look good), when in fact, it is just the way I function as a supervisor. I want all of my people to see the big picture as much as is appropriate. To our visitors, we did this in preparation for this growth. I told them that personnel-wise, we could successfully scale to meet requirements within weeks. Meeting the requirement over a quarter wouldn't cause me (as a manager) to lose any sleep.

The CEO couldn't have been more pleased. He was in a bad situation, and I shouldered part of that load to put him in the best light possible, and I delivered. Why wouldn't I? I had a vested interest in the success of the company, too. Honestly, I was surprised at the comments he reported from the corporate representatives. They enjoyed their tour! It would be maybe a year later that we had a meeting where he brought up grooming me for "the chair" of president. This story is meant to illustrate what making your boss look good can mean.

This can be taught by parents to their kids. Though I learned the hard way, this is just one story from countless examples in my life of advancing by doing my job with integrity, doing it well, and truly focusing on being a good representative of my boss and the company. Before you let yourself think I've gotten lucky, I have been faced with "opportunities" to make a lot of money, stupid amounts of money, if I could just shelf the honesty and integrity for a time. If, in my younger days, accepting money from my family came at a price, what would the price be for accepting money for breaking the law? I can confidently say that I never look back and wish I'd taken the money. There are stories I'd like to tell for entertainment value, but sometimes, it is best to leave the past in the past.

I will make one story exception. I worked in the airline industry and was interacting with either a maintenance rep or a pilot; I can't remember that detail. It was the weekend, and I was called in for a plane that had been diverted to us for a maintenance issue, but we maintained that particular airline's fleet. I evaluated the discrepancy and informed them of my findings. It wasn't a huge deal, but it would take a couple of days to resolve, partially because it was the weekend. Since our facility didn't have to perform the permanent repair, I informed him that there was a temporary fix that I could perform and they could fly out that day. However, airline policy wouldn't allow a temporary fix while continuing to transport passengers.

I was offered several thousand dollars in cash to perform the temporary repair but sign it off as a permanent repair. Have you ever heard a story of a crash and they report that the plane was inspected and the fault was found, but they're not sure why it was never repaired? This is how that happens. "Well, the next person will find it. Take the money." *You're choosing* not to do the right thing and blindly expecting some stranger to choose to do the right thing, and then hoping it works out while putting lives in danger, all for a few bucks? But people do it every day—everyone from airline mechanics to police officers to politicians. We, as individuals and as a society, have to choose to do better in order for things to be better. By homeschooling, you're teaching your children not to be selfish, greedy pieces of shit, devoid of integrity, and how to be the solution, not the problem.

If you perform in your job and don't rise, then thank the employer for the experience and move on. If your integrity is constantly challenged, move on, because a job has to be more than pay. Our own children have found their success and are held in high regard, because the foundation for these personal qualities were laid in grade school and reinforced after that.

But how did I come to learn these things in spite of my upbringing? As life kept slapping me in the face; I kept reflecting and correcting while teaching our son lessons as we kept moving forward. I wouldn't knowingly change anything that affects my life with Terri or our children, but I can't imagine where I might be if it hadn't taken me fifteen extra years to learn how to be an effective adult.

So, remember that race bike where my parents said, "We'll see?" Well, I never got it from them. Not surprisingly, "one day" never came, but my mom said if I saved my own money, I could buy a bike. I saved money I earned from cutting and selling firewood and taking care of neighbors' horses, and when the time came to get the dirt bike, she refused, modifying the deal to include that I had to buy the most expensive riding gear (because it was the safest). It cost half as much as the bike—I gave up.

You can see how backing out on her agreement about her car much later in life wasn't really a surprise. Whether it was saying she would be somewhere at a certain time or following through on something she said she would do, the best thing for me to do was to have no expectations at all. I think that's sad.

After several years of marriage, Terri and I began to get our feet under us financially and organizationally. We were emerging from the worst that our lives together had been since getting married, and Terri surprised me with my first real race bike. She knew what I wanted; it was the beast to rule them all, a Maico 490 Sand Spider. On its release, it was the fastest production race dirt bike ever built.

While dating, I had introduced Terri to the man who offered me a sponsorship ride as a kid years before. His name was Howard, and he owned a dealership. Terri went to Howard's shop and bought me the bike for my birthday. Our children were raised riding dirt bikes, and I still ride with my oldest son every chance we get, dirt and street. Sadly, I was forced to sell the Maico to continue my education after a few years of owning it. But now, I have two off-road race bikes in my collection. Blake and I have ridden across deserts, over mountains, and across the salt flats at Bonneville, all wonderful memories.

My last motorcycle road trip with my daughter was to the Florida Keys. For her, riding was always about the adventure. In 2023, our oldest son entered the annual Barstow-to-Vegas ride with me. Terri and Joshua drove the "chase vehicle" with parts and supplies. So many cherished memories from something so incredibly easy. I'm sad for my parents that they didn't see the opportunity or value in my young interests, or even in taking an interest in me, but I'm grateful to have that connection with my own family. Terri even has her motorcycle license and has her own on- and off-road bikes. Our adventures aren't over yet.

SO WHAT DOES BEING BENEFICIALLY DIFFERENT LOOK LIKE?

You and your children will navigate grade school, laying the foundation for the academics that will prepare them to learn more advanced aspects of their subjects. When we started homeschooling in coordination with a private school (more about that later), Blake was in seventh grade, Jessica was in first grade, and Joshua was in kindergarten. Jessica and Joshua and I (Terri) would count to one hundred every morning by ones, twos, fives and tens. We would look at the calendar and say what today's day and date were, what yesterday's day and date were, and what tomorrow's day and date would be. Sometimes Blake would do this with them instead of me. Each of the kids would read out loud from a portion of the Bible. We would read every day, with the goal of reading through the entire Bible in a year. Even though reading the Bible didn't become an important daily habit for them as adults, as children, they read words and stories that are complex, even for some adult readers. They all got really good at reading the Bible out loud. Jessica told me once that none of the students in her college classes could read out loud very well—they weren't confident at all, and they stumbled and stammered when they tried. The professors would usually end up calling on her because she could read out loud so well, because reading aloud in our family was normal. I had learned how to teach Spalding phonics and Shurley Grammar for Jessica and Joshua, but I included Blake in their training as well because I felt it would be of benefit to him. He has told me, while discussing this book, that he felt it was a good decision to include him, and he still remembers some of the grammar jingles as an adult. I do, too.

As Jessica and Joshua learned their math facts, we started doing timed tests. The goal was to reinforce what they were learning so that they could easily do basic math functions quickly. Over their grade school years, they both worked their way up to math-fact timed tests with one hundred questions every morning. The goal was to complete all of them and be 100 percent correct in two minutes. We worked up to this over time. They would add more facts as they became more proficient with each type of operation. The older they got and the more they took the tests, the better they were able to successfully complete them. Ultimately, we mixed addition, subtraction, multiplication, and division facts in a single one-hundred-problem test—daily.

This tool was meant to strengthen their math capabilities, but I also thought it would help normalize test taking, so that they wouldn't be nervous in testing scenarios. It can be a worthwhile tool to use, and it can accomplish those goals for some children. However, I learned many years later that the way I used it with our kids was not especially valuable because the expected outcome was to get 100 percent correct in two minutes. I was pushing them for the grades, not necessarily making sure they learned the lesson. It actually ended up setting them against each other, competitively speaking. On the outside, this looked great, and for some students, it can be a very good technique. They were doing it; they were performing to my standards. But in hindsight, it was not helping them the way I thought it was, nor in the manner I intended.

Joshua had an aptitude for math. He naturally seemed to catch on and understand quickly, so he excelled, and this daily math-fact quiz was easy for him. Jessica, however, was not as adept at math, and it was a burden for her. I found out years later that the way I did this was not beneficial to her. She was penalized for her level of ability and felt she was less than Josh because he was younger and easily succeeded at the timed tests and at math in general. This was not known to me while we were homeschooling. Josh helped Jessica so that she appeared to me to be succeeding at math as well. It would have served her better to go at a slower pace to help her succeed, build her skill, and become surer of herself. I was not attuned to her individual needs and she did not always feel that she could come to me, as I had not earned her trust across the board. Again, this is in hindsight.

It is our job as parents to figure out what works and what doesn't work for each child. To use what works and stop using what doesn't. Learn from your mistakes, help them learn from their mistakes, and move on. Be kind—to yourself and to your children. Set them up for success—don't give it to them—help them to become successful, and build their confidence through their own successes, building on each success as they go. Just like our example of learning to walk; you couldn't do it for them, but you assisted them in success after success until they could do it on their own. Yayyy!

I really wish to emphasize what happened with Jessica to you and how, from a very young age, through a series of oversights on our part as parents, we caused her to feel unseen, not good enough, alone. We didn't mean to, but we were just barreling through life, overlooking and not paying close attention to what was going on with our children. We were focused on the finish line. "Get it done!" It is important for you, as parents, to understand the strengths and weaknesses of your children. To discover their unique qualities and the things that they are interested in. To understand what drives and encourages them, what hinders them, what lifts them up and what brings them down, what gives life to them and what steals life from them, because everyone is different. Some people thrive and get energized being around other people; some do not—it drains energy and life from them. Some love sports and physical activity, and some love sitting down reading a book. Figure out ways to nurture what they love and search out unique ways to work in the stuff they don't find as interesting but still need to learn. Find the subjects they love that each can easily succeed in and set them up for success.

I am not saying to eliminate subjects your children don't like. We all must do things in life we don't like. I'm not saying Jessica shouldn't have learned math because it didn't come easy for her and she didn't enjoy it. Compared to the average student, Jessica was very good at math. In our household, Jessica wasn't the strongest. What I am saying is that I should have helped her to become successful at a pace that she could manage and found ways to teach math to her that she could relate to better than just doing problems on a page. She loved cooking; perhaps, had I understood what she was experiencing, I could have taught her more math by doing something she loved. Like we said in earlier chapters, you do have to plan and prepare for the finish. You must set short- and long-term goals in order to reach them, but stay focused on the here and now with each child. Make every effort to stay present and connect with them on a daily basis, and don't let the close relationship you fostered with your babies slip away as they get older.

I genuinely believed (and still do) that all of our kids were exceptionally intelligent, and we pushed them accordingly. Before giving them a math assignment, I would work all the problems myself. I felt that I couldn't ask or expect them to do something that I could not do myself, but if I could do it, then they could, too. In my way of thinking, this was the right thing to do. For me, this mindset worked growing up—it still does. But for Jessica in particular, it was a continual reminder that she did not measure up. It came across that she was being compared to me as a constant standard that she had to live up to; that I expected her to be able to do whatever I could do just as easily. Math was a strength of mine, not of hers. Without realizing it, I was trying to fit her into who I was, not seeing her for who she was. It was an unrealistic expectation that she would not be able to attain, not under those circumstances. I really missed the mark with her. I saw hints of this throughout her life, but I did not pay attention or recognize the pain I was causing her, especially with math. Make it your passion and lifelong goal to study and understand your children. If they learn like you, fantastic! If they don't learn like you, it is up to you to understand that and learn how to teach them most effectively—**or to find someone who can.** Sadly, with Jessica and math, I did not do this. This is the point and beauty of homeschooling. We can tailor our teaching to each child's way of learning if we will take the time and make a point to do it.

On the other hand, spelling and English grammar were a strong point for all of us. We had a good daily schedule set for spelling. Believe us when we say we hit the ground running every morning. On Monday, they would receive their spelling words using the Spalding phonics method. We would work the words into their lessons, and they would write sentences using the words. We would take practice tests Tuesday through Thursday. They would practice spelling out loud and writing any words they missed on those days. If they got 100 percent correct on the Thursday test, they didn't have to take it on Friday, and we would go for a walk to our local ice cream store to get an ice cream cone on Friday. They recited their Latin roots, their phonics sounds, and their grammar jingles.

Additionally, our kids also practiced handwriting and cursive skills daily, despite public school students no longer learning cursive at all. A three-year-old child can recite Latin and phonics as well as a thirteen-year-old. They can hold a crayon and "practice" their own letters, and as they "pretend write," they will develop the fine motor skills needed to hold a pencil and actually write. You'd be surprised what the youngest can pick up by the time they "start school" if they have been included in their older sibling's lessons; they just have to be there listening to absorb some or most of what's going on. We possess the unique luxury, ability, and opportunity to provide so much more interaction, learning, and attention to our own children in the homeschool environment than what they could ever get in a socialized public school setting. We are able to be fluid and move with our children as their needs dictate, according to their abilities and situation. That is the beauty and importance of homeschooling—we meet our children's needs as they arise and grow with them to help them reach their best. This includes allowing them to advance beyond their grade level when they are ready so that they don't have to wait for their peers in a large-classroom situation.

Our youngest, Joshua, was taking math-fact tests before kindergarten—because he wanted to. He tested (state testing) at a high school level in reading while in the third grade. By fifth grade, all of our children were reading at a college level. Remember the statistics? If children don't excel at grade school assignments by the fourth grade, they're in trouble, possibly for the rest of their lives. We didn't know this statistic then.

When Joshua went to the university of his choice after graduation, the admissions advisor remarked, "We have a new high school graduate ready for college! And he wants to be an engineer!" They reviewed his transcripts and looked blankly at Terri and our son. "Oh my gosh, we have a special one here." Indeed they did. He began his university studies for mechanical engineering as a junior. This day was made possible by recognizing his desire to learn as a child and capitalizing on it. We allowed our children to advance as they chose but required them to always maintain, at minimum, the expectations of their grade level as per national requirements.

So, what now? You've successfully gotten a child through grade school, they're on track and surprisingly mature and intelligent for their age, and now you're thinking, "This is amazing!" Oh no, Mother Nature has some challenges in store for you. The reason we keep stressing grade school is because your children are approaching the hormonal roller coaster, and when that time comes, their ability to absorb information will change and be slower than what you're used to. Your children are going to become more interested in life outside your little family; they'll desire to see and be seen by peers, express interest in making more mature friendships, and care more about how they dress. Our little babies leave grade school and want to become adults.

CHAPTER 9

SIXTH THROUGH EIGHTH GRADE (ELEVEN TO THIRTEEN YEARS OLD—AWKWARD/ PUBERTY SEASON)

TERRI'S TAKE ON SOCIALIZATION

Although this is an important topic, the question of and the discussion about socialization are way overdramatized. What I (Terri) see, is that when homeschool parents address the subject of academics, they put a lot of effort into making sure they get it right for their kids. However, parents typically do not put the same effort into addressing the question of their children's socialization or fail to address it at all. That is what has made people so upset about homeschooling in general.

The narrative that established public school proponents would purport, is that the only guaranteed way a child will successfully learn to socialize is by spending six to eight hours a day, five days a week, with other humans of the same age who also do not know how to socialize—all under the care and instruction of adult strangers. If you actually think about that statement, it is absolutely absurd. It is a lie they tell us so that we will blindly send our children to their public schools so that they can indoctrinate them into accepting a certain level of socialism. Nobody is born knowing how to act in a way considered to be socially acceptable in the society they live in.

What actually takes place for every human being at some point is that we are forced into situations where we must talk to other people, and we practice talking to and interacting with each other. This includes being able to talk to the opposite sex in a more personal manner, leading to dating and, eventually, marriage. As with all learned skills, they must be taught how to do this.

Every human being makes many mistakes as a little kid, especially when it comes to communication. We may say whatever comes to our mind, or we may not speak much at all, it all depends on a child's personality and how they are treated at home. I have seen and experienced children who talk nonstop at home, but when placed in a school setting, they do not say a single word the entire time they are there. We have all witnessed kids in school who were excessively shy and absolutely could not talk to a person of the opposite sex to save their lives. We all know of children who were ostracized; those kids who were pushed away and left out by the other kids at school, the so-called only way for them to learn to socialize. They did not actually learn to talk to and interact socially with other people until they moved on from school and found people they felt comfortable socializing with, but eventually, most of them did learn. We may have encountered these same people later in life and thought, *Whoa, what happened to them? They sure did grow up and are so different!* While these people just needed time to mature and find their path, they probably did not find their way primarily from their peers and public school.

As we get older, we learn what is socially acceptable from the people we are around—whether that is being mean or kind, making cruel jokes at another kid's expense, or standing up for the kids who are picked on.

Babies who do not have human contact at all (due to their environment) outside of having their basic needs met—such as those historically reared in punitive orphanages or institutions—do not and cannot learn how to do the things civilized humans do. Way back in the thirteenth century, there was a study done to see what language babies would learn to speak if they were never spoken to, but the scientists never found out because the babies died from lack of human contact within four months.[18] That is how we are created—we learn from the people around us through the context of the relationships we have with them.

Sixth grade was an especially hard time for me. At eleven years old, I was, as most sixth graders are, gangly. I was at that awkward in-between stage of growth, where everything in my world was changing. In my mind, I was ugly, and the other kids seemed to think so, too. I was not one of the popular kids. Being good-looking seemed to have something to do with popularity at my school. My parents got a divorce around this time, I had to get braces on my teeth,and I didn't know how to take care of or style my hair—but I wanted to learn.

I just wasn't comfortable in my skin.

I was the firstborn daughter of a single mom who did not prioritize fashion or makeup at all. She dressed basically the same way and wore the same minimal makeup for decades. So, she was not interested and not willing to try to help me. I was determined to figure it out on my own; I wanted to wear makeup, get my ears pierced, and shave my legs. I saw these things advertised in magazines, and they obviously made these models look beautiful, which would clearly help me to become popular—I was sure of it. My mom said I had to wait until I was thirteen years old before I could do any of that. I didn't really have any fashion sense. As a little girl, I either wore dresses, jeans, and T-shirts or matching shorts sets. By this age, I had started to think boys were more than just other kids. I noticed some were kind of cute, and I began to have secret crushes. My body had started to develop, very slowly, but I wanted to start wearing a training bra. I was very aware of being flat-chested and thought that possibly, the padding of the training bra would make me less so.

---

18 - Digma, "Frederick's Experiment," accessed July 14, 2024, https://www.digma.com/digma-images/video-scripts/fredericks_experiment.pdf.

Our school had a program that required all sixth graders to sample classes in art, band, choir, and drama. To my memory, we tried each course for two weeks to see what we liked best. It was required that every student select at least one fine arts class, so I chose band. I wanted to be in Jazz Band, but in order to be in Jazz Band, I *also* had to be in Concert Band. My schedule and the fine arts requirement grew more than anticipated. My mom had played the clarinet in school, so I chose clarinet for Concert Band. For Jazz Band, I chose the alto saxophone because it had a rich, full sound and just looked cool. Our band director was tasked with the unfortunate job of teaching a bunch of first-time music students how to play their different instruments. We had to learn to read music, understand the timing of the notes, and follow his direction as a director. The goal was for all of us to read and play the notes on a piece of music at the same time as one cohesive unit by the end of the year. I cannot imagine having that seemingly insurmountable challenge, nor do I want to. This particular band director was a creep and a jerk. He made fun of students for any number of random reasons that came to his mind, especially girls. He would humiliate us in front of our peers. I clearly recall the first such instance of him singling me out in the group for that day's humiliation.

My mom had taken me to our local department store called TG&Y. This was before Walmart and Target were the main national chains they are today. I had earned some babysitting money, and I had enough money to buy a new shirt. Looking through the clothes in the juniors department at TG&Y, I came across this scoop-neck T-shirt I just had to have. I still wear scoop-neck shirts to this day! It was made of a soft fabric and had a picture of a Persian cat's face that covered the entire area on the front. It was the most beautiful and fashionable piece of clothing this eleven-year-old had ever seen.

The only problem was that even the smallest shirt available was a little bit too big for me. In order to wear the T-shirt, a girl needed to have at least some boobs, something I did not have. Even with my little padded training bra on, I was still flat-chested. I bought it anyway and decided I would just keep adjusting it so that it wouldn't slip too low, and it would be just fine—so I thought. It would make me look beautiful, like the women in the magazines.

The next school day, I wore my new shirt. I was super excited to wear it, even though it required constant adjustment. I would be beyond embarrassed if anyone saw even the tiniest portion of the bra I was wearing; that would be the worst thing I could imagine at that point in my life. So, I just kept on adjusting all day long. The last class of the day was Jazz Band, which consisted of sixth, seventh, and eighth graders combined. I sat in the front row with the other saxophone players. As we settled down to start class, I glanced at my shirt to make sure it was in its proper placement. The band director looked down at me from his podium and said, "Hey, Terri, what are you looking at?" I innocently responded, "Nothing." To which he replied, "Yes, I see that." He then started laughing, along with all the other kids in the class. It took me a minute to realize what he meant, that he was referring to my chest and that he and my peers were all laughing and staring at me. It was a cruel joke at my expense. I wanted to cry, but that would have been an even worse embarrassment, so I just sat there, humiliated.

Every kid goes through this awkward stage. Every human being has something they are insecure about, and some people are insecure about a lot of things. Talking to other people is a common insecurity. The minute you open your mouth, you are subject to another person's judgment that says whether you are accepted, rejected, or dismissed—of no consequence. It is scary! No one wants to go through rejection or being dismissed. We all crave and need acceptance. We all need to know that we matter, that we have value, especially to the people around us.

Dr. Glenn Hill says in his book *The Connection Codes*, "The #1, fundamental, foundational, most pressing human need, is Identity. We cannot go without identity for very many seconds without experiencing harm, sometimes extreme and lasting levels of harm."[19]

But if identity is so important, then why don't we teach it? When we have identity, we know we matter to those around us; we gain confidence. We are more willing to speak to people even if they might reject us because we know and are secure with our place in the world. Our strong

---

19 - Glenn Hill and Phyllis Hill, *The Connection Codes: The Blueprint & Tools for Creating the Relationships You Crave* (self-pub., Dr. Glenn Hill, 2021).

identity allows for adverse interactions from which we easily recover because of our secure and safe position of identity that is already established. We know who we are to them. They are the most important people in our lives. They are the people that matter. They are our family.

As homeschool parents, we need to learn about it, live it, give it to our spouse and children, and teach it to them, because communicating with other people is a skill. We are not born with advanced skills; we have to learn them and practice to improve. Sit down and practice conversations with your children. Like many things when they're young, you can make a game of it. When something is fun, we learn and retain information more easily. If we look at a child's tea party, this is what is happening—practicing etiquette and socialization skills.

We taught our children how to communicate properly with people in order to get what they wanted. Blake was three years old when we started teaching him how to order his meal at a restaurant. We would ask him what he wanted to eat and then tell him what to say and when to say it to the server. After repeating this process many times, he was able to order by himself and answer their questions with little effort, still as a very young child. If he didn't know the answer, he would look at us, and we would tell him what to say. We were there to guide him and teach him. It did not take long for him to figure it out and answer for himself.

We did this with all of our kids. We taught them that they should be respectful to the person serving them and trained them to look directly into people's eyes when speaking to them. We instructed them to enunciate their words and speak loud enough to be heard and understood. The point of speaking is to clearly convey your desire to the listener in a manner that they can easily understand.

We continued this process with other business activities as our children got older. I (Terri) took them to the bank to open their own checking accounts. They had earned their own money, and we wanted them to learn how to manage it and use a checking account to keep track of their spending. I told them what to say when we got to the bank. Just like we did with ordering food, we went in together; they went to the teller and told them they would like to open a checking account. Then we sat down with a banker and when the banker would address me, I would politely refer them to our teen to continue the conversation. I was right there to help when needed and sign the paperwork, but they were conducting the business—and what a great opportunity for our kids to practice interacting with adults in a professional manner. We would make regular trips to the bank for our children to make withdrawals or deposits to further practice their skills, and after every trip, we would sit down with each of our children and show them how to make the entries in their ledger. They were required to keep their account balanced, so we explained what would happen if they wrote a check or used their debit card when they didn't have enough money in their account. They learned about interest as well.

Again, it does not take much repetition for children to become proficient and comfortable with the process. The point was for this to become routine and easy for them so that when faced with finances as adults, they were already used to it. Neither David nor I had any kind of financial training from our parents so consequently, when we were first married, we had bounced checks along with overdraft charges and had to learn the hard (and expensive) way about credit and collection agencies. We wanted our children to learn money management from us rather than learn the hard way from angry strangers.

When we went shopping, our children could use the money they had saved to buy what they wanted. They would interact with the cashier and conduct business on their own with one of us there if needed. They understood sales tax and how to quickly approximate the percentage off on discount items. They could figure in their heads how much change to expect to receive and were aware of the correct amounts ahead of the cashier. It's not that we really expect people to shortchange us when we go to the supermarket, at least not in the United States, but knowing what to watch for and being aware of the situation helps your child to catch mistakes or true cases of fraud immediately, rather than realizing it too late to do anything about it. Knowing how to calculate financial transactions mentally is especially useful and important to prepare them to travel abroad so that they don't get swindled. We also taught our children how to return items to customer service by themselves when they needed to. These lessons included how to respond when someone is being combative, disrespectful, or just a total jerk.

Another way we taught them socialization skills was for our children to make telephone calls to request information and make their own medical appointments. As with the other skills, we would talk about what they might expect ahead of their conversation. For example, have them pretend to call you, and then ask them questions they might be asked to help them practice before the actual conversation. Make it fun. Use different and funny voices. It's easy to have your child call you on your phone with you acting as a receptionist or secretary and role-play their first calls. Creating a fun atmosphere helps take the fear out of the unknown and gives them confidence to step up and take on new challenges. It also helps make connections with them. You'll be there, so reassure them that if they feel overwhelmed, you're there and can take over if they need you to. Your kids can witness the things you do as a parent and they'll have more respect for you—beyond the fact that you're the adult and get to make all the rules.

As you learn what your children enjoy, encourage them each to start taking more and more responsibility for and ownership of their own interests, whether that be activities or projects. Help them learn what arrangements might need to be made and what goes on behind the scenes. Encourage them to make the arrangements themselves instead of you doing everything for them. They can learn so much by doing things they love and interacting with people on a regular basis, which builds their confidence. Get creative—as Ms. Frizzle would say on the TV show *The Magic School Bus*, "Take chances, make mistakes and get messy!" Interestingly enough, the web says that this is also good dating advice!

SOCIALIZATION—DATING AND SEX

This leads me to one specific area of socialization that we have not mentioned, speaking to someone in a more personal manner with a romantic interest in mind, or dating and sex. Our goal as parents was for our children to be better prepared for adulthood than we were. We did pretty well with a lot of stuff, but not all. Our children were confident and able to carry on a conversation with anyone they met, regardless of age or sex. However, the subjects of dating and sex were areas that we were less successful with. I (Terri) don't remember getting any instruction at all from my parents about dating and sex. At my school, I was socially awkward, not pretty, and not popular, which caused me to be somewhat withdrawn. I learned about sex and dating mostly from TV shows, movies, magazines, and other kids. The Catholic church that we attended taught me that it was wrong to have premarital sex, drink alcohol, smoke, or do drugs; and in addition to that, it was essential to obey the Ten Commandments. Obviously, I did not listen and obey.

My parents were friends with a couple they knew from work, who had a daughter a grade older than I was. They lived about three hours from us, and occasionally we would go visit them at their home on a beautiful lake. She and I had a lot of fun together. We would write letters back and forth (this was long before email) and became good friends. Beginning around sixth grade, my mom would let me spend spring break with her, as her parents had a boat, we would ski all day. I always enjoyed being with her and her parents.

My friend was a cheerleader and was very popular at her school. She made a point to "help" me transform from a gangly, awkward teen into a confident young lady. Over time, she instructed me on how to pick out nicer, more fashionable clothing. She taught me how to do my hair and makeup. She coached me on how to talk to boys. We would call her guy friends from school; she would listen in on the telephone landline (before cell phones) and tell me what to say. I would "practice" every time I visited her, and I started getting more confidence to talk to boys on my own. That is how I learned to talk to guys.

We did very well in helping our kids develop interaction and communication skills with people on a general basis. All three of our children could go into any situation and hold a meaningful conversation with adults and younger children. We continue to get compliments on how enjoyable it is to be around our children because they can effectively communicate, but we neglected to provide them with sufficient interaction with their peers throughout their childhood.

I think one of the biggest complaints I have heard from our children and from other homeschooled kids as adults, is that they were kept away from other kids and not allowed any real time or opportunity to actually develop close friendships or develop skills of interaction and socialization with their peers—skills such as how to be a good friend, how to discern whether someone is or is not good friend material, problem-solving skills in close relationships outside of family, and skills for dating and choosing a good life partner.

Due to this, unfortunately, none of our children really developed good or lasting friendships until after high school. We didn't communicate any (or very little) instruction on what a good candidate for marriage might look like or what being a good spouse would entail. Because we did not get that from our parents, all we really offered our children was our example as a couple, which was not always that great. If I'm honest, we were still trying to figure it out for ourselves. I would say we failed to act—to provide instruction. What little we did do, we did primarily out of fear. We left our kids to try to figure it out on their own. Just like we had to do.

You might think, "Well, what's wrong with that? We had to figure it out; why should they be any different?"

Do you want your kids to experience the heartbreak of broken marriages and relationships because you failed to give them the knowledge and understanding that would enable them to choose a partner who would stand by their side, walk through life with them, and be committed to them for the rest of their life? Do you want your child to have to learn the hard way that they are a jerk, and that their spouse and children cannot stand to be around them? Do you think it is acceptable to just skip over this training in their childhood so that when they leave home, they go wild and try everything or implode and try nothing? No, of course not!

If you do nothing to prepare your children in the area of intimacy, they can and often do become resentful. You set them up for anger, rebelliousness, and all kinds of trouble and heartache if you do not work diligently to give them the tools they need to navigate intimate relationships.

Every parent wishes for a better life for their children than what they experienced—but wishing is meaningless if no action is taken. At the very least, we can and should tell them stories of our journey in the areas of close friendships, dating, intimacy, and marriage—what we did right, what we did wrong, what we learned. I would say (and would ask you to consider), that these areas are the most important areas of each person's life, more so than academics and career path. Choosing the right mate in life can be the difference between succeeding or failing in all life's endeavors.

David and I chose wisely in terms of a life partner—but not because we knew what we were doing. We were stupid, hormone-driven kids doing stupid kid stuff, left to figure it all out on our own. Even though we both thought we wanted to get married to each other (after graduating from college of course), in the end, we chose to get married because I was pregnant. That's not an optimal way to start a marriage. It is only by God's grace that we got together in the first place but also that we stayed together. There were numerous occasions throughout the first ten to fifteen years of our marriage where we both considered divorce. That is *not* what we wanted for our kids. However, we foolishly did not make the effort or take the time to teach them any better way; we just left it up to them to figure it out on their own once they left home, just like we had to do.

Leaving dating and intimate relationships up to your kids to figure out on their own is like throwing them to the wolves. Actually, I would say it is more like throwing them into the ocean and expecting them to swim without teaching them to swim first—they are going to drown. This is definitely one area in which we failed our kids. As a result, they have had to learn hard life lessons. Do not think, "Oh, that's a good thing." No, we don't think so. Not for them or for us. Our hearts break anytime we see our kids suffering, and yours will, too. The weight of knowing we neglected to give our kids adequate opportunities to develop dating skills, engage in social interaction, or provide life instruction in intimacy is sometimes very overwhelming, and a heavy weight to bear. We had diminished ability to sit down and simply teach them for a variety of factors, but at this point, would they even receive it if we were able to give advice or instruction?

We, as parents, are responsible for teaching and mentoring our children in everything. It is the most important job you will ever have, and it is not always easy. Is it possible to teach them everything? No, of course not. That is why it is so important to plan out the things that are most important to you to teach your children over the course of their lives while they are in your care. You cannot possibly prepare them for every difficulty that will arise in their lives, but you can give them the tools to navigate and work through life's challenges for themselves.

That is why we are bringing attention to as many topics as we can in this book—to help you make better, more informed decisions for your own family. This is another difference between what we're illustrating in this book, versus indoctrination, whether in the public school or homeschool. Indoctrination only tells your children *what* to think. We're describing laying a foundation for your children to teach them to determine answers and solutions for themselves. You may not always agree with them, but they are learning to speak their informed mind and not blindly repeat what they've been told to say.

Teaching your children to socialize with the opposite sex for a more personal interaction is something that grows over time throughout their lives. It goes hand in hand with teaching them to take responsibility for their own actions. They need to understand that how they treat others and interact with others is important, and that they are personally responsible for those interactions. How do your children see you, their parents, treating each other, conversing and communicating with each other daily? How do they perceive you interacting with them and their siblings? What about with people outside the home? Your daily interactions set a pattern for them to follow. How did you learn to communicate with your spouse when you first met? Did you flirt? Do you still flirt with each other? In all honesty, most parents do not teach their children how to communicate with the opposite sex; they leave that to the school and the kid to figure out on their own. It's up to the child or young adult whether they do it or not—the parents just hope everything will work out.

As parents, we must not overlook the most important relationship your child will ever have in life: the person they will choose to marry, share the rest of their life with, and raise children with. It takes deliberate planning ahead of time. Don't wait until the day it comes up and then think you are going to be able to give them one quick "talk," and all will be well. It takes careful consideration of your interactions with each other and how you and your spouse live your love for each other daily, in front of your children. This means deliberately being kind to one another and speaking with love, honor, and respect for the other, even when there is tension, and teaching your children to always respect and honor the other parent, even when they are not around. This all begins when they are born and should be a part of everyday life. Be flirtatious and playful with your spouse, have fun together and do it around your children. Show genuine affection for each other in front of your children. Hug and kiss each other in front of them. (Don't be gross, though.) Express love freely to each other. Tell your children stories about how you two met and the fun things you did before you got married; tell them your embarrassing moments, too. Talk about the things you talked about that drew you to each other and how you enjoyed spending time together. Bring attention to each other's good qualities, qualities you want your children to notice and emulate. Answer their questions appropriately for their age and maturity. Tell them about your feelings, and let your children know what they might expect as they get older, what things they will experience, and how they might feel. You will have to determine the appropriate content to tell them at what age for each child's maturity level in order to construct an overall picture for them, so that they will have a road map they can refer to. But ultimately, the responsibility is theirs.

Just like all of us, your children will have to put themselves out there and take chances for themselves. They will make mistakes and mess up and be embarrassed. Teach your kids—over and over, throughout life—that it is okay to make mistakes, that everyone makes mistakes. That everyone goes through feeling awkward when speaking to and getting to know people they're attracted to. It is just part of life. We try, we make mistakes, we learn from the mistakes, and we try again. As with learning to walk, you cannot do it for your child; they must get up and keep trying until they learn for themselves, but you can (and should) be there to support, mentor, and cheer them on as they struggle through the learning process.

Did we do these things with our children? Nope. We did not plan or prepare ahead of time what we would say. We did not think about the character we would like them to have or what kind of character they should look for in a spouse. We did not consider how we lived out our marriage before them, either. Neither of us had a good example from our parents to start from, and the word *mentor* was unknown to us and not part of our vocabulary. We didn't have anyone we could go to for help or guidance. All the people we had previously looked up to, turned away from us; the people we thought were our friends were no longer around. We were trying to figure out our own growing and maturing issues as we went along the path of life together. As the adults in our lives said, we should have failed. We think they wanted to see us fail; at least that is how they acted toward us.

I think the very fact that it seemed the whole world was against us made us even more stubborn and determined to succeed. We have worked through very difficult personal and life experiences over the course of the last thirty-eight years and have emerged as better people because of those experiences. We had to learn how to treat each other with kindness and respect. We literally had to learn to become friends. We had to decide to get back the love and fun we had when we were dating. It took years of counseling and practicing for us to "grow up." We had a lot of baggage that had to be unpacked, but we continued to work toward a better relationship every day. And we still do. It is an ongoing, lifelong process to become the best people we can, for each other and for our adult kids.

Even though we struggled with life and with marriage, we did do better than our parents. Was it the best? No, but it was better. People used to say to us, "You cannot be around each other twenty-four seven; it is not possible." We wondered, "Why not?" Because to us, that's very telling of that person's relationships. Of course we understood the importance of having friends and outside activities, but we also felt it was important to learn to get along with each other. Socially, the isolation that accompanied the COVID pandemic was not a big deal to us. We were already around each other twenty-four seven. The months we spent at home together were enjoyable.

Over the years, we had to learn to get along with coworkers and other people. Our children would have to learn to get along with people they'd encounter and be around for the rest of their lives. Why not learn to get along with the people you are supposed to be closest to, your family? Although the lessons came late, we hoped they would provide valuable experience and knowledge for our children's future relationships.

As our children got older, my (Terri) parenting was not deliberate and turned more into reactive parenting by fear than through love, especially when it came to the topic of sex. My greatest fear was that they might follow in our footsteps of getting pregnant at seventeen years old, without an education and without the means to live and support a family—and also without the maturity and skills to have a good marriage. I was completely focused on the negative, on what I did not want to happen. I was so effective with my message of fear that what our children actually came away with, sadly, was to avoid having children at all. I learned this from them much later.

Do not parent by fear or negativity. Focus on what you do want to happen. Focus on the positive, the things you want your children to learn. Don't let cultural norms dictate how you treat and parent your children. Do not assume they are going to be rebellious and disrespectful as teens, because it doesn't have to be that way, you must only choose to create the type of relationship with them that does not promote that kind of response. Continuously and diligently build trust and respect with your children by communicating and connecting with them. Deliberately and thoughtfully work to model and impart the lessons, qualities, and characteristics you find most important for your children to learn for their future adult lives and relationships. When they are old enough, the goal is that they will be ready to take responsibility for themselves and their actions. They will have the courage to go out, take healthy chances, and risk embarrassment to find the right person to spend their lives with.

DAVID'S PERSPECTIVE ON SEX

I (David) have feared this chapter from the time we decided we would write a book. Teenagers, hormones, and sex—at least in regard to the years of raging hormones and the idea of what will develop into the sexual side of your child. Hopefully, your middle-school-aged children aren't sexually active, but as with academics, your child needs to have a healthy foundation to build on later. We didn't want our child's knowledge to be based on the talk of other kids, pop stars, the media, or internet porn. Shockingly, I read an article in the past year where a grade school girl was performing oral sex on boys in their public school classroom—times have changed in a short period of time. How did a grade school girl not only learn this, but also view it as of no consequence to do it publicly?

In my grade school, a girl named Amanda told me to look under her desk; two boys near her smiled and nodded and whispered, "Look under her desk!" I did. The girl's bits were exposed under her dress, and she used her fingers to imitate the women she'd seen elsewhere. To my recollection, I thought it was weird. Why was she doing this? Girls and boys were different—I knew that much—but my "sex switch" hadn't turned on yet, so Amanda's action didn't mean anything to me. When we were at recess, a troupe of teachers walked earnestly across the playground and escorted Amanda back to the building. Ultimately, it was revealed that Amanda's dad had multiple magazine subscriptions where the "pretty women" her dad liked to look at exposed their bodies in this same way. Amanda wanted to spend time with her dad, but Dad wanted to spend time looking at porn. Amanda wanted to be accepted; she wanted to have value as a person. Young children watch those closest to them and adapt. If she exposed herself explicitly, she could possibly get 100 percent of a male's attention. How strong is the instinct for a child to seek a connection with their parents? I've seen children do some crazy things because nothing was more important than a connection with Mom or Dad.

THE CHRISTIAN SCHOOL AND SEX ED

At my grade school age, contrary to the girl I recently read about in the news, I didn't have a clue about porn or that oral sex was a thing. In this regard, my life changed considerably, relatively innocently, for me in the sixth grade. My parents informed me that I'd be leaving my school and attending a private Christian school. Surely a Christian school could get me where I needed to be as a person and push me academically. The school used a curriculum that is, surprisingly, still available on the market today. I cannot believe it's still being published! In my opinion, it was useless then and still is today (and no, I won't say which one it is). For me, it was a school-year vacation. I memorized Bible passages every week, and I learned about worldviews provided by the Christian Bible, the Quran, Catholicism, and the Orthodox Church. Of course, according to the teachers at the school, their Christian views were right, and everyone else was influenced by the devil. Students were encouraged to "speak in tongues" and flail around during parts of our daily church sermon. If you're not familiar with this tongues phenomenon, watch a video of it. Who am I to say if it's a direct line to God—like having two cups and a string—but in this school, if you didn't jabber like an idiot, you obviously embraced the devil.

Like my parents, these good Christian people were teaching children to lie to be accepted. We teach what we know. It's no wonder the Christian Church in the United States has experienced a rapid decline amid abuse and scandals. It was a cesspool of abusive corruption for decades because that was what they knew. It was a pastor I'll call Fred who taught me this. In a group, he was on stage to perform for the crowd, but at the flip of a switch, when no one was looking, Fred—and shockingly, his wife—were pure fucking evil. But hey, Fred and Mrs. Fred got a free ride for earnestly telling people they'd pray for them. When no one was looking, though, they preyed on them. Remember, whom can you trust? The nasty Fred couple had almost everyone eating out of their hands. I say "almost" because there were times new people would show up and not stick around. They saw this sick couple and their little band of followers for what they were.

Back at the Christian school, a married couple who were on staff asked if anyone listened to rock music like AC/DC or Led Zeppelin. A few of us raised our hands (you know, answering honestly). We were pushed into a circle by the altar, and everyone else surrounded us to pray the devil out of our souls and plead for Jesus not to throw us into the pit of hell. The school couple then told us to cleanse our homes by removing records and tapes that "were of Satan or the devil." The school was going to host a bonfire to burn it all while praying and singing. Yes, let's breathe burning toxic gas to get closer to God. I considered taking all of my parents' albums and burning them because after all, the school they sent me to told me to do it. Wouldn't that be funny? I knew better and chose not to. How do you think we responded the next time we were asked? I lied my ass off.

It was a small Christian school, and by my estimation, I oddly felt like a predator in a petting zoo. The boys, up to seniors, were the worst bullies I'd ever encountered, but they were just spoiled, sheltered rich kids. I'd been raised on a different diet than Bible scripture and rich, accommodating parents. I'd been raised on a healthy dose of anger and violence that taught me to always watch for the next threat and meet it head-on. After all, what was going to happen—you're going to beat me? I was *told* by my parents that I better not fight . . . or else (I'd be beaten—belt, fists, fingernails, whatever). But I was *taught by example* to use violence by my parents, and perhaps occasionally by a sibling. As each of my siblings knows very well, I had my moments, too.

On a bus ride to a game, a high school boy named Todd, who was sitting behind me, grabbed my ears and pulled them, not letting go while laughing with his loser buddies. The pain was searing. It wasn't the first time Todd had physically hurt me at school. Accepting the pain, I ripped out of his grip, jumped over the seat, and mercilessly beat him up. When I was pulled off him, he was bleeding and crying. I thought Todd was a little bitch, especially when I got in trouble for the altercation, not him. I secretly made fun of him after that. There were several fights for me that year. His equally spoiled buddies tried to right the wrong, but these kids weren't taught to think for themselves; they just secretly bullied and "told on" people. I never backed down. They might have been able to beat me up, but it would come at a cost.

One boy, Kenny, was older than me and a "bad boy" as far as the school went. Kenny attended the school on a "scholarship." His family was poor, but attended the church. In the sanctuary one day, Kenny pushed me out of the way for a seat. I told him, "Back off, Teddy." Well, Teddy was a large obese boy who was often made fun of. There were also whispers that he was gay. In the early 1980s and in church, Teddy was anything but popular. I was new and simply got my names mixed up. Kenny took it as an intentional jab on my part and shoved me back over the church pew. Damn! Kenny was strong! I jumped up on the pew and headed right back at him, all the while under the watchful eyes of Jesus on the cross over the altar. If I wasn't going to hell for the impossibly long list of "you're going to hell" actions, I was certainly going to hell for this one. Kenny and I swung our fists into one another. I couldn't beat this kid, and I knew it. We were both bleeding. I put him in a headlock and pulled him to the ground. If I learned anything from my older brother, it was that I had a chance to hurt him in a ground war. We were finally yelled at and physically pulled apart by school staff. I told my side of the story to the principal, who pulled out a board, told me to bend over, and gave me three swats. Kenny and I ended up being friends that year. He liked motorcycles, too. Consequently, I was also friends with Teddy. He was a large quiet guy who was pleasant to visit with if you took the time to get to know him. He knew I didn't care if he was fat or gay (if that was the case). I just liked people who were kind and didn't hurt me, and I enjoyed being kind to kind people as well.

THE GIRLS AT THE CHRISTIAN SCHOOL

On the other side of the Christian-school coin were the girls. They were forced to dress a certain way, act a certain way, say certain things, and essentially deny any individuality. The school staff, such as the married couple, would randomly measure skirt lengths and shame a girl (implying she was a whore) if her skirt came up "short" (even half an inch too short). I think the guy just liked the control he had over young girls. Especially being able to force them to get on their knees. He was creepy. For an age-appropriate young man like myself, I recognized the true nature of the girls. We boys went through it, too, though. Act a certain way, say certain things, always carry a Bible, and say "Praise God" when someone shares a success—and *bingo*! You're a good kid.

A few older girls perceived my flexible values, it seemed. These girls sought me out and started flirtatious conversations. When they would help out in my class, they would lean over my chair and press their breasts against me to "point out" things in my lessons. Sometimes after a day's sermon, a young lady would "praise God" and hug me. Occasionally, I'd get a discreet kiss on the neck or cheek. It wasn't brotherly love inno-cence. It was raging girl hormones. It was adolescent exploration, and we both knew it. The school had a very strict no-touching policy, but in the name of God, it was accepted. Apparently, there was a God, and he did positively answer prayers sometimes. Among the teachers, I was an average student but rebellious and a bit arrogant. To the boys, I was either a cool friend or kind of scary and violent. To some of the girls, I was a "player" (which was bad), or I was a trusted confidant, kind of cute, and also "safe." Bonus points for being safe. Sixth grade at the Christian school definitely contributed to my development as a young man. I'd kicked a senior's ass, which built my confidence, and when not under the watchful eyes of Jesus in the sanctuary, I learned to speak in tongues under the guidance of the older girls. Praise Jesus!

BACK TO PUBLIC SCHOOL

At the end of that year, my parents never told me what happened or why, but the following year, I returned to my regular public school. I think my parents realized that the school was a bit charismatic and overbearing for their expectations, and I'm sure the school mutually agreed that they'd like to see me go. Between sixth and seventh grade, however, my brother got married and left the state. My sister was right behind him in age, so she went to school but also had a good part-time job (she did her best to be at home as little as possible). For the most part, it was my mom and me at home.

I played sports in school so oftentimes, I was able to at least go home later because of my after-school sports. Seventh grade wasn't anything special except for sports. I had a reputation for being a tough kid or a bit crazy, depending on whom you asked. The older kids would try to bully me, and I'd double down. Again, were they going to beat me any worse than I'd already seen in life? I still didn't think so. That was enough to earn a reputation as a bad boy. I never actually fought in seventh grade, that I recall, but only because I didn't have to.

Just like in sixth grade, the girls, some in my class and some older, saw something in me. It had to be—I don't think I was that handsome. Though unlike Terri's perceived experience, for good or bad, I was popular in school. I certainly had friends, but I wasn't attached to a group. I wasn't a childish boy who would "kiss and tell," either. A girl could practice her suggestive flirting with me and know that I didn't feel the need to tell everyone about it. The same went for me. I could flirt back and be an awkward guy, and they wouldn't call me out on it. I was an early bloomer, but I wasn't alone. At thirteen years old, having known as long as it mattered that I liked girls, I was developing the ability to interact on a suggestive, more adult level. And I can't feign innocence—it was exciting. One popular, older girl in particular lifted my T-shirt at school and pointed out the line of hair that had grown down my abdomen to my belt and asked, "Is this the trail to adventure?" I responded, "You know it." I smiled like I totally knew what she meant. I didn't, but I liked the idea of the interaction and her pretty smile as she said it.

THE DIFFERENCE BETWEEN CHRISTIAN AND PUBLIC SCHOOL

This is my takeaway as the adult me who raised and homeschooled three children: the Christian overlords at the charismatic school believed that forcing children to perform and act the way they demanded was the answer, but the middle school and high school girls at the Christian school had the same curiosities and desires as the girls in the public school I attended. What I noticed, though, was that when the Christian kids believed they had a real opportunity to explore, they usually went overboard (because who knew if you'd get another chance). The public school kids had regular opportunities to fraternize but no guidance, so it was relationship after relationship on a seemingly weekly basis of who was together and who wasn't. They learned to gossip and exclude, whereas the Christian-school kids learned to conceal and hide, but neither was a good option. That's my "in a nutshell" of the contrast between the two schools of kids . . . Individually, the kids were the same. The two good kids were the same; they're all just kids. Be a good guide for your children in this angst-filled, confusing time of life.

I knew one public school "good girl" who was raised like the Christian schoolgirls. Her mom made it clear that I wasn't a good person and gossiped exhaustively about me as good Christians did in "my neck of the woods." A couple of years later, this mom got her daughter paired up with a "good Christian boy." The pair were soon on the girl's pink sheets of her brass bed, rounding third base for home, when the gossip mom busted through the door and stopped the game. According to the rumor mill, he was tossed onto the gravel driveway with no shirt and his junk hanging out of his jeans. From what I know about the mom, her daughter is probably still grounded. I felt bad for the two kids. They were good kids. The mother who took joy in passing judgment on others under the guise of being a good Christian woman was now the subject of gossip; I hadn't laughed so hard in a very long time. Behind her smile, she was not a kind person. It wasn't long before she was back to her old self, harming others to feel better about herself.

Speaking to the overarching points made in this book, as a middle school kid, I thought it was odd that the mom was "so nice" and always smiling, but the humble dad (also very kind) was very quiet and rarely ever in the house. Being on this side of life and looking back, that mom controlled everything. Ultimately, I think the dad was the biggest positive influence on who the kids became. They're good people in spite of their mom.

To follow up on my own tumultuous teen years, some years later, when I was part of an aerospace maintenance crew, we were celebrating winning a contract, and the older crew members thought a trip to the strip club would be a fun way to celebrate. I gathered this was their celebratory default setting. Terri blessed my participation, and I attended my first strip club.

The crew amassed on one side of the main stage and, seeing my discomfort, put me in a chair closest to the stage. They couldn't believe I'd never been to a strip club, and I can only imagine how uncomfortable I appeared since the guys were having as much fun making fun of my discomfort as they were watching the show.

The song ended, and the DJ hailed the next dancer: "Center stage, we have Brandy! (enunciated Brrraaandeeee) Let's hear it for this sexy dancer!" Brandy walked around the stage as Metallica's "Enter Sandman" blasted through the sound system. She made it to my side and looked down at me as I looked up at her . . . We went to school together—at the Christian school. Awkward. This particular snippet of memory includes seeing a barely dressed, attractive young woman on stage; my coworkers whistling and catcalling behind me; and the smell of stale cigarette smoke and beer in the air. I discreetly excused myself before Brandy really got going on stage. I'd rather remember her as an innocent, judgmental church girl.

As an example, these are some of the stories I shared with our kids. Not to bash strip clubs, for instance, but to illustrate how easy it can be to do something you thought you'd never do and to share my realization that it could only be "fun" if I was anonymous. Doesn't that kind of feel wrong? What did it mean that this girl was embarrassed to see me? What did it mean that I was embarrassed to see her see me?

Rather than telling our children that they'll burn in hell if they do this or do that, I told our kids that they could *do anything*, but they were responsible for the consequences of their actions. It falls in line with knowing that I can't control what my kids do, but I can inform them, and every time Dad or Mom's words ring true, they're more likely to remember our words and choose not to learn the hard way. Perhaps your kids will think, "Not only do Mom and Dad have a lot more life experience than I thought, but I don't want to know what they know . . . or how they know it."

Really, wouldn't this be the definition of a good kid? One who can walk in wisdom from the experiences of another, avoiding damaging their own character or reputation in the process? The families I saw in church thought it was most important to look good, to hide the past as much as possible. But I had no reason to hide anything from our children—they would just find out about it anyway. Instead of saying, "Because I said so," I began with, "I'll tell you what I did and what happened," or "This is what I've seen." Aside from the fact that they can't imagine I'm not embellishing, if they do proceed, they tend to proceed with caution. "Hey, you should enjoy the freedom to fuck up as much as I did. Knock yourself out." There is no more information I can provide. As a parent, I had to accept this.

It could be considered that demanding conformity of a child doesn't necessarily stick with what I've seen in life. I ended up being neighbors with another girl from the Christian school. She was divorced and had many different guys at her house on a regular basis. When she suggestively flirted with me once, she said she had to make up for lost time, and she "knew how I was" in school (based on reputation and gossip). So, the overlords dictating how this young lady should act didn't stick. She was a girl who considered me a player at school, but when she had the chance, she made me look like an angel. The point isn't to judge her sexual partners. My memory was that she was a happy, friendly girl in school, and later in life, she looked tired and unhappy, but somehow, thought that fucking as many people as possible would make her happy.

It turns out that the "trail to adventure" girl in public school was sexually molested at home and wanted to hook up with normal boys at school to feel normal and accepted.

Another girl from public school was whipped with a coat hanger when her mom found out we were boyfriend and girlfriend, even with no sex involved. She never spoke to me again, and I later heard that when the girl arrived at college, she was nearly expelled for her extracurricular activities with alcohol, drugs, and crazy sex adventures. Last I heard, she was on marriage number three. All small-town gossip.

Many "good girls" I knew are now repeatedly divorced single moms who date like they're still in high school. The "good boys"—not the "dangerous" and "predatory" boys like me—are also repeatedly divorced and cussing about how much child support costs. I'm not judging these people, but rather observing actions over time between demanding authority figures and the kids involved. Was the good girl really the good girl to her benefit? Was the good boy being the perfect boy in his parents' and teachers' eyes to his benefit? What does "good" actually look like when it's benefiting your children? I'd already walked my road for good and bad, and those memories I'm sharing now helped Terri and me, as parents, to try to understand how to best raise our teen children.

WHAT DID WE DO WITH OUR KIDS?

We are a product of who we're taught to be, and our true, unique nature. My parents never discussing the topic of sex and dating with me probably wasn't a productive choice, and my parents never talking about teen pregnancy *definitely* did not benefit me. So then, where is that defining line between rules and personal freedom that is most beneficial to our children?

Parents who ruled by fear and threats seemed to be an equally unproductive choice. Terri and I, in hindsight, took the path of too much honesty, too much reality with a desire to inform our children. That translated into them being unsure whether they wanted to have children at all. Our kids all went to college and didn't overindulge with alcohol or snort lines of coke at college (sex) parties, as far as we know, but they also largely avoided developing serious relationships.

Our youngest son, Joshua, was a senior in college as an engineering major. I saw his Facebook page once, and many of his friends were attractive young women who were also engineering majors. He was an adult, and I respected his privacy, but I had to ask, "You know all these girls?" He said yes and started telling me who wanted to study with him, who he tutored, who'd asked him out, and on and on. "Beauty and brains, son, put yourself out there," I said. He's a really handsome young man. He shook his head, "Nah, I'll get out there later. It's time for school right now." I really started to reflect on how we raised our kids because I knew young women like these wouldn't be unattached for long.

In an earlier story about Joe (the family member who was drinking and driving), I referenced a wreck of my own, noting "that it would be thirty years later before my first wreck," and I feel the need to insert the side story here. I was driving Joshua's Volvo, I was T-boned, and the car was totaled. I gladly gave him my pristine five-speed manual 2008 Mustang Bullitt to drive. We had restored it to its showroom glory, and it had less than forty thousand miles. It was loud and ridiculously fast. "Josh, take it—chicks dig it." I laughed. Seriously, Terri loved driving or riding in that car. She enjoyed the compliments she'd get, and same with me. It was just a Mustang, but it drew attention.

Joshua took the car and used it for the commute to college. We told him that we would sign the title over to him and that he could have the car if he wanted it. He didn't. I had wrecked his Volvo; it was eventually replaced with a Volkswagen, as Josh is a practical man. The fact that attractive, successful college women chatted him up a lot more around the Mustang or asked for rides had no influence on the way Josh lived life.

We were deficient as parents in teaching our children to explore outside the friend zone. When our youngest was a young college senior, he dated occasionally but didn't let anyone get too close. Our kids were always comfortable around both sexes and were never creepy or awkward. In their upbringing, we never addressed actually exiting the friend zone. To them, everyone was "friend zone," and that's where people stayed.

We're a product of the influences in our lives. We are also going to be who we truly are, eventually (not who we try to convince people we are). When I hear about a preacher or priest assaulting or molesting people, it doesn't surprise me. They are just regular people posing as something more virtuous. If I've seemed a bit harsh on the church, it's because I've known more than one woman, girl, or young man who was molested by a "person of God," ranging from pastors to youth pastors, with deacons in between, and that's just the Christians *I've* been around. Should we hold back about the two boys who were caught in the boys' bathroom with their fingers up each other's asses, masturbating with each other? Shockingly enough, that incident happened at a religious private school. In some way, your children need to know all of this exists in the world, but at the right time and place. They need to know how to guard themselves against anyone who would take advantage of them, but not in a way that they walk around afraid all the time.

Do you really think this information should be entrusted to people who can't teach basic math to a grade-schooler? That's the point that we are making over and over. You are picking up the mantle to successfully instruct your children in what others are failing at. Character, discernment, and life skills—you'll teach your children these things instead of blind indoctrination. Who are your children "safe" around? That's for you as a parent to determine. Good luck!

Every living creature is designed to have the instinct to reproduce. Our children are not excluded, and live in a highly sexualized world. Your children must be able to develop their sexuality, and the foundation to build upon begins with influences from a very young age. At the appropriate age, they need to be comfortable and safe visiting with their peers, regardless of gender.

With our kids, I focused on a perspective of not sexualizing people in general—but moreso women—unless it was appropriate. That went for our sons and daughter.

I'll explain.

To our sons, "sexualization" was only appropriate at casual events, like parties or clubs, and by this, I mean noticing and approaching a person through physical attraction. This distinction is important, as we want our children to understand that you don't do this at a professional function. If you find a coworker attractive and want to see if the attraction is mutual; if you want the chance to try connecting on a deeper level—the things that really matter in a relationship—then that is for somewhere besides work.

To our daughter, our message was to not sexualize herself in the workplace or in any professional environment—ever. Don't dress in a way that accentuates and invites people to check you out sexually. Yah, yah, I hear you. Men should be respectful no matter what a woman wears. Let me walk into an office full of women with my shirt open halfway down my chest, showing my (imaginary) heaving pecs, and take note of all of the women *not* looking at me. I've had women say and do things to me in the office that any man would likely be arrested for. It goes both ways, just saying.

If you're going to homeschool, be sure to teach your children about the hypocrisy in society. Professionally, be responsible and respectful of everyone, and any other time it's up to you—bearing in mind the reputation you want to maintain. This is the biggest innocence and is the hardest to choose to let go of with your children. How many times do you hear that someone seemed so nice until they assaulted someone? Should this young woman or young man have clued in on certain words or quirks in personality? "They just seemed down and wanted to talk in a quiet place."

Your children must be equipped to recognize risk and identify sexual cues; they need to be able to identify scary, creepy, or dangerous people.

So, what do I know about assault or predators? Female friends of my older siblings propositioned me for the first time when I was about twelve. I had two female teachers, two mothers of girlfriends, and one female barber proposition me throughout middle and high school. I once had a male "family friend" who requested my help and then tried to drug me with a spiked beer. The first red flag being that the work he needed help with suddenly didn't exist, and then I saw him put a pill in the beer. Alcohol wasn't my thing, thankfully. I left, and we never saw him again.

Except for two, the women were divorced. I only point this out because their approach was different from that of the married or unmarried women. I never accepted, but the instances taught me social and sexual cues, for better or worse.

All of these things were filed into my bigger picture of life. Over the years, looking back, I've come to believe that

1. sex is easy to find, but
2. sexual diversity (random quantity) comes at a price.

Sex in a true relationship is a gauge, a meter that subtly can indicate the state of a relationship. It's not a measurement of quantity, but of mutual desire. I've crossed paths with a lot of people in my life, and one consistent factor I've seen is that the more casually people treat sex, the more likely they are to not have fulfilling long-term relationships.

Why would a young adult endure a significant other or spouse who occasionally doesn't feel sexual when they do? After all, there's plenty of people willing to have sex with them. When sex represents something more than lust for both you and your committed other, you share a deep connection that is unique to your relationship. Of course, mutual lust in the relationship can be a lot of fun, too. All of these lessons were passed on to our children. We never said, "Don't do it;" we said, "This is the likely outcome if you do." For good or bad, the rest was their choice.

I was very blunt with our teenage daughter when she was at that young age. I told her that she could get in over her head really fast. I was not always going to be there, and not everyone was nice or even reasonable. I told her that every man she met in the world would first look at her sexually and while it's not wholly true, it happens more so than not. I felt, however, that if she held that view, she would be less likely to find herself in an unwanted situation. It was up to her to be the kind of person she wanted to be, and she was responsible for her actions.

Even though my daughter was a young teenager, it broke my heart to have that conversation because I cherished her sweet innocence, and I was getting ready to partially destroy that innocence with knowledge that would change how she viewed the world and also inform her of how the world would view her. She was shocked at the things I told her, but in time, she decided that I had been overly gentle and told me as much, but she also said that she felt our talk(s) had saved her from some bad situations where other girls were hurt. All you can do is do your best, but base it on knowledge, honesty, and experience.

Like I said before, this is a hard conversation, and it has been one of the hardest conversations I ever had with our children. You must choose to expose your children to the darker adult world.

Your children will view you through their lens of innocence. That's partially why teens treat their parents with disrespect or even disdain. *You can't possibly know as much as I do!* they think. Let's have a chat, then. If I told you everything I've seen, you would need counseling for post-traumatic stress disorder (PTSD). You ought to carefully reveal to your children a glimpse of your adult side and uncover your knowledge of this world to them. Give it to them bluntly—but only enough to get the point across. There are some things I've seen that I'll never tell my kids. Every kid thinks they're the first to be there, so enlighten them enough to let them know they're in an impossibly long line of people who also thought just that.

I mentioned that we believe "baby talk" is destructive to your child's development. This applies to the sex talk, too. You know, "Well, when a mommy and daddy really love each other," or "Mommy swallowed a watermelon seed," or any number of other ridiculous things I've heard people say to describe where babies come from—it is the same as baby talk. It's minimizing one of the most important topics you need to seriously discuss with your children.

Every young child is going to ask Mommy or Daddy where babies come from. Obviously, we're not going to describe copulation to a two-year-old, because their next question will be along the lines of, "Where does candy come from?" Our answer would be that it's an amazing thing and that we'll discuss it in biology class in school.

I like to compare my way of talking to our kids about sex to the way I talked to them about driving. Driving is wonderful! You'll have the ability to hit the open road and take yourself anywhere you want while listening to the music you like! Most parents stop there. For driving, I showed our children pictures and videos of car wrecks with bloodied and broken bodies, whose lives ended when a person's head parted their torso. I did this because it's what my driver's ed teacher did, and I remember it vividly to this day. Over one hundred people die every day in car wrecks in the United States.[20] To a kid, it's just a number; your child can't comprehend it. They see people "die" all the time in movies, but it looks different when your child sees someone's body cut in half with their intestines hanging out of a windshield. There are "only" thirty-six thousand traffic fatalities each year in the United States.[21]

Getting back to sex, by comparison, there are 460,000 sexual assaults every year in the United States, one every sixty-eight seconds.[22] Boys are not excluded, however the most affected group in the United States is young women aged eighteen to thirty-four.[23]

How important is understanding healthy relationships, social nuance, self-defense, safe sexual standards, and so forth? All I can say is that I wanted our children to want and be fulfilled with a healthy sexual life when it was appropriate, but they also needed to appropriately understand

20 - https://www.google.com/url?q=https://www.nhtsa.gov/press-releases/early-estimate-2021-traffic-fatalities&sa=D&source=docs&ust=1728956791864909&usg=AOvVaw2hta2JLStWYhQ_Q5nkwKvd

21 - https://www.nhtsa.gov/press-releases/early-estimate-2021-traffic-fatalities

22 -https://www.nsvrc.org/statistics

23 - https://www.nsvrc.org/statistics/statistics-depth; https://www.google.com/url?q=https://rainn.org/statistics/victims-sexual-violence&sa=D&source=docs&ust=1728956791866743&usg=AOvVaw295lhxT-6NHH9p_Ke-9nJXH

that the world is a dangerous place. You be you, child, but do it safely. Terri and I hit the paper but missed the bullseye on sex and relationships. This, to me, is the most challenging topic for a parent and homeschooler.

WHAT ABOUT SOCIALIZATION?

To be socialized, children must socialize. Not the public school brand of socializing; as there are almost fifteen thousand reported sexual assaults in public schools yearly—almost half of which are completed rapes. Your children must be provided an outlet to safely socialize appropriately with peers their age. To us, the younger children begin to socialize, the better. Boys and girls around each other as toddlers is a good place to start. We've known children who were molested at a young age or whose parents exposed them to graphic music or videos who, while around other children, had predatory tendencies, even as toddlers (kids learn by observation). Otherwise, kids are just innocent kids.

As a guideline, however, I would recommend that you be present with your children while they are playing with other children. Don't let them be alone in their bedroom, the bathroom, the basement, and so forth. Involve them in something you are doing that is fun, like baking cookies or making crafts, all the while having conversations with them—or even let them help you do something you need to get done. Be outside in the backyard with them or go to the park and play with them; don't just sit on a bench and watch from a distance.

If we were homeschooling today, we would try to have multiple groups that our children visited with on a rotating basis. Once a week, we'd have an outing, and each week in the month would be a different group. Again, young children are like sponges; they can be influenced quickly, positively or negatively. Let them encounter different dynamics and not be taught an exclusive social circle, and if your child's actions toward others or their treatment from others within a group is unacceptable, remove them right away and talk about it. They still have other groups to play in, so watch your child as they play and interact with and guide them according to your most important values. There is a balance.

You don't want your child to dread field-trip day because they're going to be mom-splained or dad-splained for hours after. It's a chat in the car and then let it go. Spouses, don't feel like you'll add any value by reinterrogating your children if your spouse has already done so. Don't say grace before dinner with, "Dear Lord, please protect little Scooter from the evils of Danny Smith and his inbred mama and give me self-control so that I don't break a foot off in her fat ass. Amen." Like everything, it's multifaceted. With this approach, you've likely just embarrassed your child by gossiping openly at the table. Additionally, you've taught them gossip, name-calling, threats, and worst of all, that they can't trust you. They won't want to tell you things because you can't be trusted with it. Or if their view is different from yours, they'll learn that this is how they can expect you to talk about them. When they don't confide in you, you might think, "Oh my God, I just don't know why Scooter didn't come to us." Maybe because fifteen years ago, you started teaching Scooter, the toddler, that you were not trustworthy. Consider this approach instead: "You know what, Scooter? I think what Danny did to you wasn't very nice. It wasn't good manners of him nor his mother to not apologize. How about next week we'll just go to the museum (something constructively fun) and see if some of the other kids want to go?" Your child nods happily. "You know what else? We don't have to be around people who treat us poorly, whether it's someone as young as you or as old as me! We have a choice." Then, your sweet, well-behaved child will smile up at you and nod their head—conversation done.

This takes us into the awkward teenage years of your child; where you still need to provide appropriate venues for them to socialize. You'll still need to discuss their socialization, such as things you noticed or heard; hopefully, you've built a healthy foundation of socialization in them at a young age. You are not doing this to judge or keep them under your thumb; you're doing this to guide them toward the social skills of a civilized, successful adult.

In concert with this, take your teenagers with you to appropriate adult venues to socialize and practice their skills with adults. We like formal events such as benefits, the ballet or orchestra, a political dinner, or a special event at the museum—anywhere your young teen will be exposed to a culture that encompasses formal attire, socialization, and etiquette. Your child will absorb a lot of information from the people around them. This doesn't sound terribly fun, but should your teenagers practice social skills at a rave, or at a stuffy adult event? I suppose that depends on where you see your successful child spending their decades as an adult. Don't get me wrong, but as much as we love the orchestra, we still aren't beyond going to a good rock concert or inhaling exhaust fumes at a race.

HOW ABOUT ACADEMICALLY SPEAKING?

When Blake was in sixth grade, we continued teaching him from the textbooks we had purchased for sixth-grade English, math, science, and history. We knew we needed help to continue our homeschooling because as he got older, the material was getting more challenging for him and for me (Terri). He also started pushing back a little more with age and I began to feel like I was drowning. If you struggle, if you don't have confidence in what you are doing with your children, they will pick up on that and push you to see if you fall down. It is important that you approach your teaching duties with confidence.

Knowing how to do something is one thing, but teaching someone else how to do it is quite another. Up until this point, teaching grade-school-level subjects seemed pretty easy for us, but it was clear to me that as Blake advanced, I would need to get help teaching the upper-grade levels. Finding the support that you need will give you confidence to continue. If you don't get the help you need, each day will get worse until you either get help—or quit altogether.

We knew we didn't want help from just any school or organization. We wanted and needed the kind of help and accountability that would set us on the right path and see us through all our years of homeschooling to come. I have a tendency to be inherently lazy. When people are watching, however, I perform and want to please them; therefore, I knew it would benefit our homeschool to have someone to hold me accountable. I needed that. There were not a lot of options for homeschoolers during the 1990s. The internet that is available now did not exist in its current form at that time. We were most concerned that our children would not be accepted into college because we homeschooled them, but we were determined to find a way. We searched for about two years before we found a fully accredited, local private school that had a program created to assist homeschoolers.

Accreditation was significant and very important to us. We knew that true accreditation for any school is a long and difficult process. We also knew that after receiving accreditation, the school must continue to demonstrate that they are maintaining high standards. It is beneficial to consider accreditation when you are looking into online schools or whatever resources you are considering. You want to know that whatever you use to help you teach your children will actually provide the kind of education that will enable them to effectively enter the job market and world scene. If you want your children to have the option to go to college, accreditation is of particular benefit to your homeschool for the following reasons:

- It shows that the school has demonstrated a history of trustworthiness.
- It shows consistent quality in programs and ensures that the institutions uphold the highest academic standards possible.
- It opens up avenues into more colleges and widens eligibility for more college scholarship programs.
- They do the grade reporting, recordkeeping, credit tracking, and provide the transcript for each student.
- They provide protection of your homeschool rights and help you abide by state laws.
- Full accreditation ensures that all courses within a homeschool institution are of high academic standard and will count toward your child's diploma, particularly Advanced Placement (AP) and dual-enrollment (high school and college credit) courses.

We felt confident that this school could help us to provide the kind of quality at-home education that we deeply desired to give our children. Because this school was officially recognized through accreditation, colleges would accept the transcript our kids would receive from them. This was huge to us, especially me! Just knowing I would receive assistance with their transcripts took a lot of pressure off my mind.

Before we started with this school, they performed aptitude testing for each of our children to assess their grade level academically. We started working with an advisor who met with us and our children. She helped us set overall academic goals for every grade for each child. She scheduled time with us to get to know us and each child. She became our trusted mentor and, in time, our dear friend. Our children trusted her as well and still think very highly of her now as adults. She made a huge difference in our family and our homeschool. It is very important to have at least one person, a mentor, outside of your family whom you can trust to help you navigate homeschooling—without bias. Someone who will hold you accountable and help you work toward the best interests for each of your children. Sometimes we are simply too close to a situation to be objective, and it helps to have an advisor or two that you know you can trust to give words of wisdom and equitable guidance.

The school required that each homeschool family enrolled in the homeschool program participate in a week-long conference called "Prep to Teach Week." It included multiple workshops throughout the week with time built in to work on your own. This conference was presented by the teachers and administrators of the school to provide quality training to us moms (and the one father present) that we needed for the upcoming year. The enthusiasm of these teachers was contagious. They modeled for us the way they taught in their own classrooms. It was a very enlightening and encouraging experience to be around teachers who truly cared for their students and were willing to share their knowledge and experience with us.

Prep to Teach Week is where I learned how to teach Spalding phonics to my children. All the parents who would be teaching this course had to take the class. Our instructor was a sweet and gracious woman who modeled not only how to teach this phonics program, but also the love she had for children. We had to learn everything in this program, and as we learned, she modeled how to teach it properly. It influenced me greatly to see how this teacher actively, truly cared for us, her students. These dedicated educators helped me learn to be a better teacher to my own kids. Prep to Teach Week was the foundation that I would build upon as a teacher myself. A few of us would participate as speakers each year to do exactly what we are hoping to do with this book: encourage parents not only that you can homeschool, but it can be accomplished with so much success, you'll wonder why everyone doesn't do this. More than anything, Prep to Teach Week offered reassurances that we weren't alone, we had help if needed and that we could be successful.

I would estimate there were at least fifty families represented at the first Prep to Teach Week that I attended. In addition to training, this conference brought us in contact with a homeschool community that was previously unknown to us; we had been isolated up to that point. I was able to interact with other homeschool moms and learn from them. It was beneficial to hear the different stories from other moms with kids of all ages—what worked for them and what didn't work. We could ask others how they managed their homeschool and get ideas from them. Sometimes I would think an idea sounded so good I wanted to try it with our family, only to realize it didn't really suit our family like it did theirs. That is not to say the idea itself wasn't good, simply that not every idea works for every family—and that's okay.

The conference week also allowed uninterrupted time to work on lesson plans. We prepared plans for each child for every subject, for the entire school year. Our advisor was there to help us and would check our work to ensure we were ready to start the new school year. This is a very important step that should not be overlooked. Having the whole year's plans prepared ahead of time will enable you to stay consistent throughout the year and complete each subject in the time frame you desire. As always, you may wish to or need to make adjustments to your schedule as the school year progresses which is much easier to do if you already have the whole year already planned out. During the summer, before this prep week, each family had made the decision of which curricula we would be using and obtained all of the teaching materials we would need for the upcoming school year. Each subject that I was planning would have a page that would go into my planner binder. I am sure you can do this digitally, but I liked to write mine out in pencil so that I could easily make changes throughout the year when necessary. Each sheet was divided into thirty-six weeks total, four nine-week sections, which is similar to the schedules at traditional schools, but you can choose the schedule that suits your family best. Textbooks are usually arranged for a student to accomplish the entire book in one school year, so we would just divide each subject up to fit evenly throughout the time periods. I would also include holidays and breaks that were similar to those of the local schools. That way, if we needed a little extra time, it would already be built in. It is better to have extra time built in and not need it than to not include it and need it, so be your own friend and advocate—build your schedule in a way that will benefit your family.

The year we traveled to London and Paris for two weeks we could only go during the school year. So, we were able to adjust our schedule to complete all our lessons before the trip so that we could take that time off. We also tailored our lessons to study about the historical places we would be visiting. Our trip was very memorable because we looked forward to seeing each site we went to. It has become a family favorite.

KEEPING RECORDS

If you have not started keeping daily records of all your children's work and grades, which (for Blake) I had not, now's the time to start. Before we started keeping records, I always felt behind and unsure of what we were doing from day to day. School and daily life felt hectic, aimless, and disorderly. I would anxiously wonder what needed to be done next and if I was doing all that we needed to do.

Our advisor, Marilyn, taught us how to get organized so that we could consistently keep good daily records. She showed us how to set up our notebooks for every subject and how to teach our children to set up their notebooks. Learning and implementing organization for yourself and then teaching it to your kids is imperative for their success and yours. This will enable you to keep accurate records of everything they do and give them something to show for their hard work.

Whatever work you require of your child, you must grade it. Every single piece. If they are required to do the work, you must always grade it—*always*—without exception. "Inspect what you expect," is the saying we were taught. Make a point to grade each day's work before the day is over, and then record the grades in your grade book. It is good practice to grade their work as soon as possible, go over it with them, and have them make corrections. The intention here is to help them understand why they made the mistakes and for them to learn from their mistakes. I would give our children half credit for each one of their corrections. This practice can be a useful tool to catch and correct misunderstandings early if used properly, and it also enables your child to move on to the next lesson with confidence. Take your time with them and give them the encouragement they need to grow. It is worth your time and effort for their personal growth and success, and if done with kindness and consistency, you will build trust and goodwill between you and them.

Your children should also keep a record of their assignments and grades at the beginning of each subject's notebook; we had a specific page for this that we placed in every binder. You and each of your students should maintain a daily practice of teaching a lesson, completing any assignment given, grading and correcting the assignment, recording the final grade together, and finally, placing the completed assignment in the appropriate place in their notebook. By doing so, you form a good habit in yourself and them, and you never have to worry that your or their work is not current and up to date. It is much like a scrapbook, and I would even encourage you to teach your children to make and keep their own scrapbooks. They can show their dad (or mom) and grandparents what they are doing, and if the time ever comes that you must show proof of their grades or work, you will easily be able to do so. At the end of the school year, our homeschool group would have a night where all the children would proudly showcase their work for everyone to see. It is a fun time and helpful to have a special event to work toward and look forward to at the end of each school year.

Middle school not only brings with it academic advancement for your children, but you—as a teacher—will also experience a higher workload to challenge your teaching. You will begin to be much busier than what you are accustomed to with grade school children. Your children are going to be faced with more challenges, from increasing difficulty in their subjects to hormones changing, and the resulting interactions will add to your and their daily stressors. Please take time to visit with and explain to your children the expected changes that will occur in their bodies and thoughts, and why. Explain hormones. Tell them of your own experiences and how you felt about it growing up. Let them know what acceptable behavior is; let them know what unacceptable behavior is. Explain the consequences of their behavior. Encourage them to come and ask you about anything that they notice is different. Do this before the changes begin, so that they will be aware and not be taken completely by surprise.

I (Terri) did this kind of halfway with Jessica. I did tell her what to expect. I also told her that her mood would change, especially during a specific time of the month, and that it was usually not pleasant. However, I expected her to still treat us and other people with respect. We all have bad days, and that's okay, but it is not acceptable to take it out on everyone around you. She learned to do this very well, but I wasn't as thorough as I could have been. I didn't build up our relationship so that she felt safe coming to me with her feelings, fears, and worries. As far as the boys were concerned, I did not really talk to them about any of life's changes, not that I can recall—I left that up to David. Back then, I felt that the dad should talk to the boys and the mom should talk to the girls. Although there are parts of the conversation that are better suited for the same-sex parent, I think there is room for both parents to be involved in the conversation. If not together, then separately. It is important for kids to hear from both their parents on these matters (if both parents are available), and it's good to share our experiences at that age and talk with our children about those experiences. We want to share with them and encourage them to share with us by always working toward building trust and connection between you and them.

MAKING CHANGES

One of the most difficult parts of being a parent is changing as they change, growing with them. It is not an "if they change" proposition; it is a "when they change" inevitability. Our children were no different. I (Terri) had taught our children all together as much as possible. David and I found that our youngest son had quickly advanced in math, so we thought that if he was willing to do extra work one summer that he could catch up to his older sister, who was a year ahead of him in math. Having them on the same math schedule would lighten my workload. After asking Joshua if he wanted to do this and was willing to do extra math during the summer, we asked our advisor if she thought that was a good idea or not. Our advisor helped us work on a plan that would get Joshua on the same math level as his older sister.

We had to reassure our daughter and our son that they were on track and let them know it helped me out to have them on the same workload. Her younger brother was catching up to her—was she stupid? Was he catching up to her because he's so "smart?" These dynamics must be realized and addressed. Your children need to be reassured. Our daughter was the middle child; she felt left out and sometimes "less than." She was also an alpha personality. We needed to consider these personality traits and craft the most constructive way to inform the kids of what we were doing and why. Jessica didn't need to perform at a higher level, but that would be her natural response—self-imposed stress to do more, to be "better." Her brother was just more naturally adept at science and mathematics. Jessica was so damn intelligent. I'm not trying to be nice here. She simply needed to understand that and accept it without comparison. On the other side of the coin, we didn't want to inflate Joshua's ego to his detriment. They each needed to accept themselves today and, while being healthy, strive to be their best selves.

Joshua could have graduated school and entered college at fourteen as an average college student. He took his first ACT test in eighth grade, and he scored in the high twenties. Academically, he *could* have gone to college, but *should* he? We felt this wasn't the right choice because although he was mature for his age, the college influence wouldn't have been constructive for him and it would have definitely affected his sister negatively. I also think that it wouldn't have been a healthy dynamic between the two brothers. As I (David) write, I can see how it may seem that I've gone off track on the topic of teaching, but like we've said over and over: homeschooling is so much more than academics. Recognizing priorities and maintaining balance are paramount. If your child is a prodigy in one area, that gives you the ability to focus on other areas, but not without considering everyone else as well. If we, as parents, do this well, we will assist each of our children according to their individual needs to help them become their best selves. This takes a lot of consideration on our part; it requires actively parenting and loving each child uniquely for their own self, staying connected no matter what, and truly delighting in them and their journey of growth and discovery on the way to adulthood.

The school we partnered with was an excellent fit for us, but that doesn't mean that is what would be a good fit for you or is even available in a similar form. I think by now, we have said it enough and you get the idea that *you must find what works best for you and your family.* We would highly recommend that anyone wishing to have a successful homeschool carefully consider the following, which will assist you in every way to be the best homeschool for your children possible:

- Become active in a homeschool community of like-minded families who will help and encourage you and your children, families who will reassure you that you aren't alone and you can be successful in your homeschool endeavors.
- Find at least one trusted mentor who will hold you accountable and help guide you on the right path for your family.
- Find good, kind, caring teachers who will model to you how to teach—hopefully, they will be a part of the homeschool community you are active with.
- Look for genuine accreditation; there are programs that say they are accredited that actually aren't. It is up to you to do the research to prove the validity of claims that are made by schools or curricula.
- Do your research on curricula and teaching materials. There are so many resources available, and they all look good. Take the necessary time to find a good fit for your teaching style, taking each child's learning style into consideration.
- Purchase your materials far enough in advance for you to review and plan for the upcoming year—or return them and get something different if they don't fit you or your child.

- Set aside uninterrupted quiet time so that you can plan and prepare for the upcoming year.
- Choose a schedule that best suits your family; this can and may change as situations arise, such as an unexpected illness or a move to another state.
- Get yearly grade-level aptitude testing for each child and an interpretation of the results. The best time to do this is toward the end of the current school year to give you time to make any adjustments for the upcoming school year.
- Make a point of getting organized with notebooks and keeping daily records for you and your children.
  - Daily/weekly/yearly planner
  - Gradebook
  - Notebooks/binders for every subject for each child. Show them how to set up their own notebooks, and help them if necessary—*do not do it for them*!
- Plan an event near the end of the school year with family, friends, or other homeschool families in your community where your children proudly showcase their work, special projects, and hobbies. Plan and prepare for it from the beginning of the year so that your kids are thinking about what they want to present. Get and keep them excited about it all year long!

Because of your diligence in making adequate preparations before your children enter the ninth grade, you and they will have a much smoother transition into high school than waiting until after they are already there. You and they have put in the necessary time, research, and effort, planning and preparing for the last four years of their homeschool adventure—now it's here! It's time for your children to start high school!

CHAPTER 10

NINTH AND TENTH GRADE AND BEYOND

As a result of extenuating circumstances in my (David's) family, my parents decided to move me to a city a hundred miles away. It was the summer before my sophomore year of high school; my dad transferred within his company, and I enrolled in the large local high school. I had no friends, and I didn't live near any kids my age. My mom stayed at the household I grew up in. I think it was a marital separation for them, but as usual, my parents kept their private life private; they didn't say it out loud if it was. Either way, Dad was always at work.

This was a bad year for all of us, but it was my most self-destructive year. I'd had a concussion my freshman year in football, so my mom managed to remove me from sports. She badgered and dictated to the doctors about what "she knew" was wrong with me, to the extent that it would negatively affect my life for years to come while ultimately, proving to be false. Other events also pushed her to want me out of sports, so I had no dirt bike, no friends, no car, and now, no sports. I was almost sixteen with nothing to occupy my time or look forward to.

Upon arriving at the new school for pre-enrollment, I was pulled aside by the vice principal and told that I was in the top ten on their "blacklist" of bad students. He was threatening me, but I wasn't sure what the threat would produce. Another teacher pulled me aside and said they were good friends with a teacher from my previous school and that they "knew all about me." It sounded like a threat from this sports-car-driving teacher. I quickly realized that for the first time in my life, I was one of the "loser" students.

Overnight, I went from athletic, popular, and active to less than nobody. My parents avoided me, my family avoided me, the kids at school avoided me, and a few of the teachers preemptively threatened me based on my reputation and gossip. So, how important is a person's reputation, really? I taught our children that reputation is everything. During this same period, there were other relatives in my extended family who were busted for drugs and DUIs, totaled their cars, and had questionable consensual sexual encounters of a predatory nature—all very hush-hush. Conversely, my personal life was public knowledge to the whole extended family, and they didn't try to veil their contempt for me.

I was alone. Nothing anyone could say or do to me could ever be bad enough in their viewpoint. However, there was one elderly family member who understood me and held a quiet disdain for the actions of these other family members. I knew that he could see more than my young mind could comprehend. The wisdom in his eyes always seemed to look straight through me. In his way of letting me know that I wasn't a bad person or alone, sworn to secrecy, he filled me in on the sordid details of those other extended family members. Those same family members who endlessly criticized and judged me and, ultimately, my own family. The dad that my dad never wanted to be like, my grandpa, ended up being the father figure I desperately needed to help me through many of my darkest years. Also, it was funny and quite interesting to see the juxtaposition of the outward actions of these people toward me against the backdrop of their own family secrets.

Back at the new school, I befriended the outcast kids. We were all very different but had that one thing in common: we were not welcome or wanted. No one saw value in us as human beings. We didn't fit in their world, so we, as outcasts, created our own little world. I had nothing to look forward to and nothing to lose, so I did whatever I wanted. To be honest, I didn't see a point in trying to maximize my years in this world. The last half of that school year, I smoked weed more days than not, I didn't eat breakfast or lunch, and I often skipped dinner. This year was a bit of a dichotomy; I was at peace because my parents weren't around for most of this time, but I was also alone and coped with that fact by keeping my mind hazy with drugs and alcohol.

I went from looking athletic to a skinny druggie. I remember smoking a joint before school photos. I'm obviously stoned out of my mind in the photo. The school didn't care; I was never called out or in trouble for being stoned in class. Looking back, I wonder what the people around me who were *supposed* to care were thinking. Why didn't someone say to me that they cared and wanted to help me (how, I don't know)? Or was I actually left alone in hopes that I might solve everyone's problem with me by ceasing to exist?

Healthy communication wasn't something my parents equipped me with, but every day was a new day for possibilities. I had two "friends" in this group who tried to commit suicide. One succeeded after days of being brain-dead. The other wasn't successful but was committed to a psychiatric hospital. Another boy raped his little sister and was sent away to a juvenile detention center. The island of misfits was shrinking. In the end, I had one main friend, Luke.

Luke was a clean-cut "good kid." His parents were very wealthy. His stay-at-home mom practiced the kind of oppressive religion I could recognize immediately. Luke brought home good grades and took out the trash. He kept his room immaculate and knew exactly what his parents needed from him to leave him alone. Luke discovered what I'd discovered: his parents were happiest when he wasn't around. What they didn't know—hidden behind his demure innocence and expensive, preppy clothes—was that Luke had the biggest pot farm I'd ever seen (not that I'd seen many), growing deep in the woods behind their house.

Despite his parents' wealthy status, this kid was melting down from the battle of wanting his individuality but needing to act a certain way to make others happy. Luke confided in me that he thought of ways he could kill his mom. He hated her constant controlling, bitter attitude that was supposedly based on the love of Jesus. Luke also talked about killing kids at school.

You would never guess that this clean-cut "rich kid" was fighting a battle in his mind that could affect so many people. I'd steer him away.

"Dude, you know you'll get caught. Just get through high school and tell them to fuck off."

Luke wanted his mom to feel the perceived pain she put him through. He wanted, for once in his life, to be the person in control. Thankfully, Luke didn't follow through. He did eventually move out, though, telling his mom and dad he hated them and wanted to cut all ties. I heard a few years later that Luke died in a car crash. Maybe all of their money and Jesus were enough to compensate for failing their son, but as a parent myself, I doubt it.

Sophomore year, I binged on drugs and alcohol; no one noticed or cared enough to say anything. I am thankful I didn't die. That year was full of things that would have an effect on my future perception of family, life, and kids. One teacher, a tall, thin woman more than twice my age, insisted she give me a ride home in her shiny sports car one day. I agreed to avoid the usual walk. In the driver's seat, she hiked her skirt up nearly to her panties, stroked her thigh with her fingertips, and smiled at me. "You can touch me if you want to." What do you do with that? I shook my head and thanked her for giving me a lift home.

Reputations aren't always accurate, but mine would lead to some interesting propositions. Two girls in my art class at the same school asked me to be their first, together. I wasn't innocent, but a threesome wasn't something I'd ever thought of. Call me naive. The interesting thing about this year and the school I went to was that while I was one of the "bad kids," it was the "good people" who propositioned me. I always declined, despite my reputation.

How does this tie back in with whom to trust, who is good, and who is bad? Should you protect and shelter your children from people who will expose them to questionable things before the right time? The only way your children can understand the implications of the darker sides of life is if you talk to them about it. Gradually and continually, little by little, expose particularly sensitive subjects to them in tiny chunks according to how much they can handle over their lifetime. Don't talk *at* your children like my mom or Luke's mom, but actually take an interest in your children as individuals and have conversations with them. My approach as a parent, rather than emphasizing right or wrong, was simply focusing on the implications of a certain decision. Our children were smart enough, like most kids, to determine whether something was good or bad.

For example, if you do drugs, your professional choices will be limited; or if you are promiscuous, you'll have a reputation that could determine how people view and treat you. You can't complain about it after you've earned it by your actions. Considering the sad case of Luke, can your children understand that school is just a speck of time in their lives? It seems like the whole world is in view at this age, but I think it's by design. They should have a clear understanding that the rest of their life is being built upon a foundation formed by the decisions they make while growing up. Children without guidance aren't standing on a solid foundation. Children should feel secure and confident, but instead, most children today are trying to find something to grab ahold of as they enter adulthood.

CONTROL

I've debated with myself whether to touch on this topic or not. It's a hot social button that's full of emotion. The topic is public or school shootings. As a frame of reference, I'm a person of extremes, who understands that people want and need to feel wanted and in control. So, school shootings don't surprise me—not when you have a child who is raised with no self-control. A child who is dictated to. A child who is an outcast. A child who was not mentored by loving parents and family, but treated as a pet to take care of and left to "figure out" life for themselves without guidance. I'm honestly surprised that extreme school violence doesn't happen more often in today's day and age.

If you look at the shocking suicide rates of kids nowadays, what percentage of them decide that if they're going to die, they'll die in control and "show" everyone that they matter?

Inherently, people seek justice and equality, especially teenage children. Inequality like this has started revolutions—why wouldn't it occasionally result in a school shooting? Judging by the numbers, the public school condones violence against kids—because this violence is only getting worse. The statement, "Violence is against our policy," spewed by the school's public relations officer is seen for what it is (bullshit), because the next time a similar incident happens, the response is no different—"Violence is against our policy." Nothing has changed. Children go to the same schools I went to, with the same types of kids and teachers I had in school. The school is still full of the same hypocrisy I dealt with, and if you have a child who is absorbing their surroundings and seeing that certain people get away with certain things while they or others get in trouble for less, they're eventually going to act out. The public school teaches kids to be predators or prey, and the prey unjustly suffer the consequences at the hands of those who are predatory, and the school administration either turns a blind eye or is also aggressive to our kids. They've obviously given up on solutions and accept that whatever sounds good in the moment is good enough, and the violence against our children will continue, and some children will continue to act out violently with no recourse… and the schools will continue to say "we don't condone these actions".

You, as a homeschool parent, must guide and mentor your children to succeed and thrive in a world shared with—and often controlled by—these people. This part of high school is the time when you ensure your child's individuality carries into adulthood. You should discuss all of the darkness while teaching your children that they are always in control of and responsible for their own lives and actions—and what being in control of their life looks like. It is our job to teach them how to make good decisions. They need to understand that every decision they make is a choice—their choice—and learn to accept responsibility for those choices and actions. If their decisions resulted in either good or bad consequences, then they accept responsibility, positive and negative, for their own actions—because nobody can make them do anything. They chose this for themselves.

Departing from the more negative commentary, you must also remind your children of the good in their lives, their accomplishments, and their uniqueness as an individual. How they can contribute and make a positive difference in the world around them. You will reinforce what you admire about them and how excited you are to see the adult they will become. It goes both ways in that regard. Your instruction is always truthful, however painful or uncomfortable, but your praise and confidence in them will counter the bad in the world, improve their contribution to those in their lives and ultimately, contribute to their contented happiness in life. Everything you have taught them since birth is going to settle into who they will become as adults during these years.

ACADEMIC PLAN AND CAREER OPTIONS

CAREER APTITUDE TESTING

I (Terri) strongly recommend that as early as sixth grade, but definitely no later than the summer before each child's freshman year, that parents make time to find several good career aptitude tests that assess your student's personality, what professions would be most suitable for your child, and which jobs or career paths would not be a good fit. The resulting analyses may not necessarily tell your child exactly what the perfect profession is for them, but it can help to eliminate many occupations that are likely not a good fit for your child. Sometimes we have to work backwards, and by that, I mean work through elimination, narrowing down career options to provide a direction of interest that helps your child find their best fit. You may be able to remove several industries, job fields, and careers so that they can focus their attention on the areas that are most interesting and fit their character and personality. By knowing your child's interests, the direction they most likely want to go after high school, and what jobs they have an aptitude for, you will be better able to establish a four-year plan that will prepare them for college or the vocation most conducive to their personal interests and success, as well as adhere to your state's requirements for graduation. Conversely, you can direct them away from fields that are not suitable for them. For example, if you recognize that being around people drains the life out of your child, then you would not advise them to train for a position in the career fields of customer service, retail, or hospitality-related industries. Anything working directly with the public or interacting with large numbers of people will likely be eliminated, because your child is not drawn to that.

You and your child should research all viable career options, which will lay the foundation for planning their next four years. Do this together *with* your student. I recommend utilizing a trained individual or service that can interpret your child's test results and assist with developing a four-year plan. You and your student should discuss different job fields of possible interest, research the descriptions of these jobs or career areas, and even consider the demand of that career field through employment outlook reports. In all of this, your student should be involved in and take responsibility for helping to prepare their own four-year plan; you will guide and mentor them as your knowledge and experience allow.

WHAT IS A FOUR-YEAR PLAN?

A four-year plan is a schedule that outlines every course necessary for each semester, quarter, or trimester, etc., of 9th through 12th grades in order to be prepared to continue their chosen adult path after high school. The point of developing a plan at the completion of 8th grade is so that your student does not get to the end of their senior year with incomplete requirements for post-secondary education or college admission. A good four-year plan will ensure a smooth graduation and successful academic transition from high school to adulthood.

Looking at this more closely, to graduate from high school and be eligible for college admission, each student must complete a set number of credits during their four years of high school. Credits are a numerical value assigned to each course in high school and college. You must research and know the credit requirements to graduate from high school for where you live. If your child is going to attend college, you should also examine college requirements for admission to help you plan accordingly. Because high school credit requirements for graduation vary by state in the United States, it's possible that your child may choose a university whose admission requirements exceed their high school graduation requirements.

There are programs online that can help you and your child create a four-year plan. However, because there is such an overwhelming amount of information available online, I would not recommend arbitrarily using these online resources. It can be difficult to find the information that is directly applicable to your students and narrow down what is appropriate and applicable for your homeschool, state requirements, and the admission requirements of the university of their choice. It can get confusing. If you want to ensure that your children are prepared and meet all applicable requirements for college, you should seek out assistance from other successful homeschoolers or a homeschool association with a proven track record. They will help you and your child find the best courses and construct a good four-year plan.

Other options to consider asking your advisor about are Advanced Placement (AP) classes and dual or concurrent enrollment. If your children intend to go to college, AP classes and dual enrollment (being enrolled in high school and college simultaneously) can help with college admission and with scholarships. Your advisor will be able to help you and your child decide whether either of these is a good choice for them or not. We will discuss these options more in the next chapter. Each of our children began taking college classes as early as was allowed at the time.

Our homeschool mentor was a big help to us at this stage. The school we worked with had graduation requirements already in place that were in accordance with our state mandates, so they helped us create a plan that fit each of our children individually and prepared them for college. I am so thankful we had this resource and did not have to figure everything out on our own, and you will be too. Having a good advisor makes all the difference; the difference between just getting through homeschool, and really making a positive lifelong impact for your children and their future.

In addition to the specific courses and credits required to graduate, each student must maintain a minimum grade point average (GPA). If you have not already started keeping a record of your child's GPA, you must start in their ninth-grade year. If you choose not to keep records in grade school, you should start no later than sixth grade. I strongly recommend starting as early as first grade. I don't think it is good to teach only with grades and testing as your main focus. Grades are a tool that provides both you and your student a measurement of their knowledge, understanding and successes and where they need improvement. Another reason to start early is to give yourself and your students time to practice and develop good habits of keeping timely and orderly records. If you wait until sixth grade or later, it may be a shock to you and much more difficult to be consistent. You may also find gaps in their knowledge that went undetected because you were not measuring their progress by keeping appropriate and adequate records.

Keep in mind our theme of what our job as parents is: we prepare our children to be adults. The four-year plan is no different. You are guiding and preparing your child to make these decisions for themselves. Activities like creating the four-year plan for their life after high school is where the rubber meets the road. Help them make sound, reasonable decisions by explaining the reasoning behind your recommendations to help teach discernment. Nurture their ability to make decisions by setting the requirements before them, choosing electives that are available, and then assisting your child to construct their own four-year plan. Guide, mentor, encourage, and assist, but make no mistake: this is for their life, not yours. The plan is theirs, for their future—for their life.

Each year, you and your student will review their four-year plan to determine if anything needs to change and to verify that your child is still on track to achieve their set goals for graduation. If your child's interests change, the plan will need to be modified to accommodate the new direction. While we are actively encouraging them to take responsibility for planning their own life, this could be frustrating and even require an entirely new plan. The silver lining is that your child will be better equipped to perform more work on the four-year plan themselves (and then gets to live with the repercussions of their decisions). How great is that?

Throughout this book, we primarily speak from the perspective of preparing for college because that is our experience. But what if your child doesn't really want to go to college? That's okay! College is not a good fit for everybody. There are other options available if your child has different aspirations besides college.

VOCATIONAL OCCUPATIONS

We were having a conversation with our grandkids, and one expressed a desire to avoid as much school as possible after graduating from high school. College, at this point, is not in their plan at all. My advice was to suck it up and go to college anyway, but if not, at least specialize in something through technical training. While there are many jobs available that do not require a college education, they do, however, require a license or certification. Depending on the field of interest, a license or certification can typically be accomplished in a shorter time frame than a college degree. While it may even be possible to get hired as an intern or apprentice to be trained in an occupation under a skilled technician, vocational training after graduation can also be obtained through the military.

If your child chooses to go the military route, they still need a solid, well-rounded education in order to achieve a high score on the Armed Services Vocational Aptitude Battery (ASVAB) test—the test all applicants must take before enlisting in the military. These are generally for enlisted jobs—no fighter pilots here. The lowest scores offer a few opportunities, such as motor transport specialist (bus driver), plumber, infantry (ground-pounder), or food service specialist (fast-food worker). The higher your score, the more opportunities there are for leadership and some truly interesting career fields and opportunities to further your education. Like public education, it's a good fit for some and not others, and the commitment is between two to four years of your life depending on which branch you enlist in. However, be forewarned, failure to honor your commitment to the military could result in a dishonorable discharge, which is akin to a felony. Your civilian opportunities will then be limited to transportation specialist or food service specialist for the rest of your life. With your child, research statistics for the military, research their requirements, mission, and political leanings to determine if it is a good fit for your student.

That said, the military is not for everyone. Another option your student might consider is to obtain instruction at a vocational technical school. They offer training that can enable your child to immediately enter a vocational career upon graduation from high school.

VOCATIONAL TECHNICAL SCHOOLS (VO-TECH)

If you know your child is more interested in a trade rather than going to college, an alternative is the local vocational technical school, also called "vo-tech." During high school, most vo-tech schools offer classes in a variety of trades to students, free of charge. This is not a substitute for academics; it is an option to supplement your child's homeschool studies. The benefit of getting specialized training from a vo-tech during high school is that the student will be prepared for real-world working experience right after graduation. However, if you do not plan ahead and obtain the classes offered while your child is still a high school student, then they will have to pay for an adult vocational school. So, if you know your child is interested, why not get them into the training of their choice early on? At the very least, they will know by the end of the classes whether they really want to go into that field or not. David took a computer programming class at our local vo-tech school, which has served him well, even though he chose not to go into that field. Some classes offered at vo-techs include construction, mechanics, childcare and education, carpentry, agriculture, cosmetology, drafting, welding, food preparation, health care, and criminal justice.

David obtained many aviation-related certifications, among others, that allowed him to uniquely stand above the majority of other job seekers in the aeronautics field, and he has been very successful in his line of work. He will share, however, that because he did not have a college degree, he was unable to advance into upper management later in his career when the opportunity presented itself. I (Terri), on the other hand, had obtained an associate's degree with an emphasis in the medical field. This training facilitated the at-home medical transcription job I held for thirteen years, which helped make it possible for me to homeschool our children. We know a lot of people who, after choosing not to go to college for whatever reason, years later decided to get a degree. Even now, we may choose to go back and continue our higher education as well. On this side of life, however, getting a degree only gets harder the longer you wait. It will never be more convenient than immediately after high school.

It doesn't matter what direction your children decide to go after they graduate from homeschool; what matters is that you, as parents or caregivers, actively and continuously choose to nurture and educate them the entire time they are with you so that by the time they leave your care, they are equipped to go out and meet life's challenges head-on to make a positive impact on the world and the people around them. Part of that process is preparing the documentation they will be required to present to attest to their education, which includes a transcript, résumé, and any verifiable supporting documentation.

I (David) wanted to take a graduate-level mathematical statistics class for a job I had as a project manager. I was in my early twenties. When the college asked for my transcripts, I told them I couldn't get transcripts in time. The fact was, I had an average high school transcript and a few college classes for flying. I'd taught myself higher math. We didn't have a television set or other entertainment. When I couldn't sleep, I read Terri's college math books and learned the concepts that my public school failed to teach me.

Nothing in my past indicated a readiness for calculus-based statistics; the highest math class I took in high school was Algebra I, so I requested a placement test. Upon reviewing the results, I was told that I could take any math class at the college, and ended up earning a B in mathematical statistics. That said, while you might be capable of doing the coursework, you still have to meet credit requirements. Being allowed to take a class and getting a degree are two entirely different things.

The last university I applied to admitted: "We're in the business to make money; you have to take a minimum number of credit hours for us to give you a degree." Many of those credits they wanted me to take were ones I had already accomplished or were simply electives. The totally new information I'd receive for the degree was less than eighteen credit hours. Much like my grade school days, I just want to get the work done and move on. But no—even forty years later, I have to wait on someone else or do it over and over, waiting for someone to tell me they're happy just so that I can get on with my life. Each time I've thought, *I can work this out*, then contacted the university to enroll in classes, they've changed the requirements yet again, and I'm forced to choose work over school. I cannot guarantee that I'll have an internet connection every day or every week, but these people think everyone works in a cubicle and goes home to high-speed internet every night. No, even in 2024, education is not easily accessible to everyone.

TRANSCRIPT

A high school transcript lists all the courses a student has completed, what credits they have obtained, and what grades they have received. Students are required to submit a transcript when applying for college, which admissions offices use to determine their eligibility for acceptance to college. These high school transcripts are also used to determine students' eligibility for various scholarships, so ensuring that a high school transcript is complete and looks professional is critical to promoting your student's future success. Even if a homeschooled student intends to go straight into the workforce, having a complete and well-written transcript is still extremely important because they may choose to attend college later in life, or employers may even ask to see their high school transcript.[24]

Both David and I have had to produce our educational transcripts for jobs we applied to, many years after graduating from high school and taking college courses. Do not neglect to keep each child's transcript complete and up to date throughout high school. It is crucial to obtain advice and guidance for creating and diligently keeping up your documentation before your children start high school.

Learning how to prepare a transcript from other successful homeschool parents can be tremendously beneficial. I was able to find a good program (via app) that was recommended by other homeschool parents in our group, and it was extremely helpful for us. First, I typed in our school information and the school year. Then we entered each student's information, which included immunizations. (Some colleges do ask for

---

24 - Coalition for Responsible Home Education, "How to Obtain a Homeschool Transcript," 2024, https://responsiblehomeschooling.org/guides/resources-for-homeschool-parents/homeschooling-high-school/how-to-obtain-a-homeschool-transcript/.

immunization records. If you chose not to immunize, just state something like "Immunizations not given for xx reason" on the transcript.)

I would enter all the assignments along with the due date, and then I just added the final grade for each given assignment. I chose the parameters of our school year, and the program generated well-organized, nice-looking transcripts for our children. Additionally, with this program, I could print out a page with each student's assignments for the week. I could print out reports of extracurricular activities they participated in. I could run reports of their work for each subject, as well, to easily present it for the school's examination or even the state, if asked.

The school that we worked with also created a transcript for us. Because they were an accredited school, when they presented our children with their transcript, they were attesting, "We have examined all this student's work, and we verify that they have earned the grades shown in accordance with the requirements set forth by this state." Sometimes it is more beneficial to have a transcript from an accredited school, because it's not unreasonable to imagine a public university insinuating that as a parent, you've lied to try to make your child look better. While his stellar ACT score couldn't be falsified, our oldest son was denied honors housing at a state university because he was homeschooled. Regardless of which option you decide to utilize, just make sure that whatever you choose has all the information needed to adequately represent all of the student's hard work to the review board they present it to.

RÉSUMÉ BUILDING

One of the best things you can do for your children and yourself is to start keeping a running ledger of their accomplishments. The ledger is a concisely written record of your child's achievements in chronological order so that you will be able to use it to build a résumé when the time comes to do so. Higher education institutions may require a resume as well as any job they apply for. In conjunction with the ledger, encourage and help each of your children get into the habit of keeping a scrapbook. When you add to their ledger, have them there with you to take part and "help." While you are recording the event in the ledger, they can put in the scrapbook any mementos from the activity, draw a picture, and put in newspaper articles or photos they have—anything that is special about that event that they would like to note or keep. A scrapbook can be a good place for your child to journal as well. It is a great place to record life milestones, and it's fun to look back together and see the progress your child has made over time. The point is to do it together and make it fun so that they look forward to doing it every time they have an event!

Both David and I kept scrapbooks growing up, and we enjoy looking back to see what we included and what was special to us in our younger lives. Unfortunately, neither of us encouraged our children to keep a scrapbook. I'm not sure why not, but we didn't, and I now wish we would have. As I look at other people's examples of scrapbooking, I think this is something I might want to start doing again as an adult—perhaps David and I can put together special memory books for ourselves and our kids. I still think that would be a beneficial project.

Create a binder specifically for the running ledger. Include a divider for each school year beginning as early as grade school. You will want to include everything they do and organize it in such a way that you or they will be able to recreate any of their activities on a résumé for submission at any time. Just like, as professionals, we keep a record of our accomplishments, special training, awards, jobs and job titles, community service, sports, special interests, and activities, you will do so for your children. You will teach your children how to do it, and eventually, they will take over. The ledger is not going to contain pictures or memorabilia. Those items will be kept in their scrapbooks. Remember that the entries are to be concise—just the facts, ma'am! Number and date each entry, and include a short explanation of what activity they did; an address or location of where the event took place; a contact person's name and phone number(if available); competitions and awards received; how many people they helped; jobs they held and the dates (no matter how small); mission work; community service; and other projects completed.

We did not make a point to keep an up-to-date record with our kids, so when it came time to "remember" and prepare applications to universities, we had to work a lot harder to produce and assemble all their information. Learn from our mistake: it would have been so much easier had we consistently kept a record over the years. Include everything they do in the ledger. Most likely, everything that you have written down on the ledger will not make it onto an application or résumé, but that is a decision that will be made later, long after the event has already passed. If it is all there, your child can easily choose what is most relevant for whatever application they are submitting.

David is a good example of why to do this. His resume is so vast with knowledge and experience that he cannot possibly list everything, and not everything is applicable to a specific job. David reviews his records to support his application for a position. He has proof for what is on his CV. Instead of having to pad his resume or outright lie as he has seen people do, up to 75% of his experience is left out because it isn't nec- essary to support his application for the position. In large part, this is because he has kept detailed records of his employment and education experience. Another detailed aspect of record keeping David mentioned was when he applied for his first security clearance many years back, at the time known as the SF-86 form. This form demands detailed informa- tion for the past 5-10 years minimum. If you didn't keep detailed records, good luck. Additionally, if your child was arrested, did drugs, drove while intoxicated or was fired from their jobs or otherwise sucked at life, don't bother. Poor decisions have repercussions for many years to come. Some- times for the rest of their life.

If you submit an application for admission to colleges, they will require the data you have recorded. It is much easier to look back at your well-kept records and take the appropriate details from it than it is to try to remember or attempt to search for the specific information, sometimes years after the fact. This will become most important after their junior year. Even if your child does not intend to go to college, they will still need this information to apply for jobs and other areas of training as the need arises. It is a valuable tool that will be an asset to them, regardless of the path they choose.

Sometimes we can get so busy with all the details of homeschooling, it can be easy to become isolated, focusing on your own world as you work through the challenges, but be careful. You and your child need to guard against becoming complacent as you near the end of your child's home education and avoid thinking that you are done because you and they are on track, they can do it by themselves, or because you feel like you are nearing the end of the journey.

This is not the time to begin relaxing, thinking that because you only have younger children to worry about, or feel like you've set this one older child up for success, that they are now on their own. No, not at all! Academically speaking, they may be on track, but all the areas mentioned earlier must continue to be cultivated, and it is still your job, as a parent, to work on your child's behalf and guide them to get the most out of the time before they graduate high school and go out into the world. The last four years—especially the junior and senior years—are the most important academically and require that you maintain your focus and dedication to their preparation.

CHAPTER 11

JUNIOR YEAR AND ADVANCED ACADEMICS

I (David) have watched the institution of education over the past few years and honestly cannot believe what I'm witnessing. The ignored physical assaults on our children are a travesty, and while students' test scores continue to plummet, teachers' unions and school boards continue to ignore the primary function of their jobs. I've collected hundreds of these types of headlines over the past two years from an array of news outlets. I've seen a lot in my life, some too shocking to tell in this book or possibly anywhere, but what I see happening in our public schools is shocking—because it's being normalized in our society.

I've read over and over that teachers' unions are increasingly "flexing" their muscles politically. These ever-powerful educators are hiding behind children to accomplish a political goal? So, if your child is fortunate enough not to be bullied, raped, assaulted, pimped out, or forced to endure a polarizing teacher who rants and demeans them, then at the very least, the children in the public education system will be used as political pawns. I put this uncomfortable truth here because it's likely your home-schooled child will be starting college courses by this time in their life. It's one thing to evenly educate your children to think for themselves, but now that you may be sending your child to a state-run college, their peers and educators will be older and more influential.

For the kids who slipped through the propaganda cracks, now is the last chance for the education system to fold them into the fray. Our own children experienced an array of politically motivated one-sidedness in college. Our youngest didn't experience much that we know of, but the university commencement speech was decidedly politically motivated. All of these college graduates, up to physicians, had to endure a rambling speech that wasn't inspiring for anyone except the speaker. Here's the reward for years of hard work and tens or hundreds of thousands of dollars: "Listen to my personal politics!" As a junior taking a few college courses or when your senior becomes a college freshman, it's up to them to endure the environment of college, and hopefully, you've prepared them for it. Stay vigilant, parents!

RECOGNIZING AND OBTAINING HELP WHEN NEEDED

The older your children get, the more advanced their skills become and the more that is required of us, as teachers, to meet their needs academically, socially, and physically. Now more than ever, it is crucial that you have solid advisors and mentors guiding you and your children. We didn't suddenly decide that we wanted or needed to get help with specific subjects; we gradually became aware that our students were advancing academically, surpassing my (Terri's) abilities to teach specific subjects. We sought out alternative teachers who could offer more enriching and comprehensive courses than my limited knowledge could provide, which presented me with a great opportunity. I found that when the teacher allowed it, I could participate and advance my knowledge right alongside our children.

A crucial ability that your children must master before graduating from high school is writing. Being able to competently communicate their thoughts to others is of utmost importance, regardless of what path they choose to take when they embark on their own life's journey. You have worked hard throughout your kids' early years, enabling them to read well and comprehend what they read—but are they able to write? Are they able to investigate a topic, write a research paper, and give a speech presenting their findings to an audience? A senior thesis is required for all high school students to graduate. It can be anywhere from 30 to 125 pages, depending on the department and subject matter. This is one area where you do not want to skimp, so if you are not an expert in teaching writing, please do your children and yourself a favor and find someone who is and can help you. Their future may very well depend on how well they can write. We mean this literally. We know there are apps and of course A.I. that can make the most ignorant of people sound socially acceptable. These are backups at best. Neither of these can mask stupidity at a board meeting. Your student needs to know how to effectively communicate in real time.

When our kids were younger, I obtained training to teach them the parts of speech and how to construct and write simple paragraphs. In time, our children grasped how to write three-paragraph essays. I knew that developing the ability to write well and appropriately was vital to their lives, as writing well enables your children to communicate their thoughts effectively to others to accomplish their goals. Because we wanted our children to write well, we turned to our advisor to give them more advanced and comprehensive training, and she transitioned them from simple essays to more involved writing and research papers. She incorporated reading very complex literature, including epic poems such as Homer's *The Iliad* and *The Odyssey* and John Milton's *Paradise Lost*, into their writing repertoire. They learned to write in different styles and creative methods to impart their thoughts onto paper. As a result of their extensive training, each of our children was able to test out of Composition I and II in college through taking the College Level Examination Program (CLEP) test. They easily wrote papers for their professors throughout their courses of study.

A lot of people struggle with simply knowing how to write. Because they do not know how to write well, it keeps them from successfully reaching their goals. Knowing how to write well took a huge weight off our kids' shoulders and enabled them to focus on learning, rather than figuring out how to write the many papers college professors required of them. Writing well has served and continues to serve our children well in their adult lives.

Even if your child does not go to college, chances are they will need to write something to someone at some point in their lives. For example, I had a friend who needed to write to a judge because a relative decided to sue her for ownership of 125 acres of land that she had inherited from her parents. She had to learn how to write to the court and communicate appropriately to retain her property. Knowing how to write well to effectively get your ideas across to a person or people is an invaluable skill your children will utilize for the rest of their lives. It could help them get the job or the proposal, retain their rightful property, or possibly even win the attention of someone they admire. You never know!

Acquiring at least one or two years of a foreign language class was required when our kids were in high school. With Blake, we used a popular German curriculum. It was a good program and we were able to work through it; he learned what it taught and easily completed the requirements for graduation. Even though the instruction Blake received from the German curriculum was good enough, we still felt we could have done better for him. Like us, if you have multiple children, you will make improvements as you learn better methods of teaching.

When it was time for Jessica and Joshua to take a foreign language, we decided to get a native-speaking French tutor. We were fortunate to find a wonderful French tutor from France with a degree in English. She made learning French fun, which always helps when learning new concepts. She would play word games with us in French, and we would sing songs and recite rhymes and tongue twisters in French. She incorporated all the things that help babies develop language into our sessions. She used several strategies to help with pronunciation and gave us opportunities to apply our language skills to retain the material. Learning a foreign language on your own from a book, recordings, and computer programs works just fine, but having a native-speaking tutor was a great experience for us. I feel we benefited much more from personal interactions with our tutor than simply using a curriculum. Afterward, we were able to take a trip to France, and we got to practice what we learned. We didn't speak

French fluently, but we could communicate while we were there, which definitely enriched our experience.

In addition to learning French, we also took an art history course in preparation for our trip to France. Our school mentor, Marilyn, taught this course, in which we studied the architecture and history of famous sites like the Eiffel Tower and Notre Dame, as well as learning about the artwork and history of the Louvre and Versailles. While going to France was a wonderful experience for us, it was further enriched because we were now seeing, in person, all that we had studied. We got a totally different experience experiencing the grandeur and majesty of these iconic landmarks. You really don't have a feel for the size of a landmark, painting, or statue until you are standing before it in person—I was completely astonished by the size of Leonardo da Vinci's *Mona Lisa*.

Joshua quickly moved through math, beyond my ability to teach him. We found our state's school of science and math, which was designed to educate academically gifted high school juniors and seniors in advanced mathematics and science. He took Calculus I and II and Physics I and II. These college-level classes offered him the challenge that I could not. As your children take college-level courses, not only does it prepare them to go to college, but it also increases their ability to get in. When a college recognizes that a student has successfully completed higher-level courses, they are more likely to accept their application for admission because they know the student has the ability to handle the classes they will encounter in a higher learning environment. If the admissions review board doubts that a homeschool student is not equipped to succeed at their university they will deny your student's application in favor of students they believe will be successful. Their statistics depend on the success of the people they admit. So it is to your child's benefit to be prepared for the scrutiny of the universities they apply to.

The same is true for dual-enrollment courses. Dual enrollment, also known as *concurrent enrollment*, enables high school students to take college courses taught by college professors at their high school campus or at the college. What makes this program desirable, especially for homeschooled students, is the opportunity to experience going to college while still in high school under your watchful eye. We chose for our children to go to and be on the college campus to take the courses offered concurrently. Programs like this are usually sponsored and paid for by the state, so the student does not have to pay for their tuition. Some states even pay for their books. Once the student passes the class, they earn both high school and college credit.

As the person responsible for laying the groundwork for your children's lives after high school, it is beneficial to understand early on what colleges are looking for so that you can guide your child appropriately.

According to the Armed Services Vocational Aptitude Battery (ASVAB) Career Exploration Program, the things colleges are looking for on an application are as follows:[25]

- Good Grades: A 2.0 grade point average (GPA) is required for most college admissions and scholarships, but in order to be competitive, your student should strive to maintain a 3.0 or higher.
- Challenging High School Curriculum: Students should take harder classes that either prepare them for college-level work or are on par with college-level work, such as Advanced Placement (AP) classes or dual-enrollment courses.
- Strong Standardized Test Score: Although some colleges have made the ACT or SAT tests optional, it is a good idea for students to take one of them to show the admissions board that they are willing to go above and beyond the requirements. This will help the student stand out from others, especially if the score is strong.
- A Well-Written Essay: The essay showcases the student's personality and gives the admissions officers a glimpse of the unique qualities they will bring to their campus.[26]
- Extracurricular Participation and Leadership Skills: This includes involvement in activities of interest, community service, missions, or sports. Extracurricular activities also show time-management skills, creativity, commitment, team-building

25 - ASVAB Career Exploration Program, "What Are Colleges Looking for in High School Students?" updated July 1, 2024, https://www.asvabprogram.com/media-center-article/54.

26 - ASVAB Career Exploration Program, "10 Tips for Writing a Strong Essay," updated July 1, 2024, https://www.asvabprogram.com/media-center-article/52.

and leadership skills. It is better to be consistent and show growth in one or two activities than to have many activities, but no real growth or leadership.

- Diversity: "Colleges emphasize a diverse class because different perspectives allow students to learn from one another," says Monica Inzer, vice president for enrollment management at Hamilton College in New York.[27]
- Enthusiasm for the School: The school wants to know that the student is excited to be there and will be an enthusiastic and productive member of the campus community.
- Letters of Recommendation: These letters will need to be obtained from a mentor, coach, or someone outside of your school (not a parent) who knows the student well and can speak to their academic performance, creativity, problem-solving ability, commitment, and leadership skills. Be sure to ask several people well in advance of the time you need the letters.

We were not aware of all these factors before our first child got to his junior year of high school. We feel very fortunate that we had the great mentor and school support that we did, or he would not have been prepared in these areas.

JUNIOR YEAR

If your child is planning to go to college, they must prepare their application packet for college admission the summer before their senior year. Each packet they prepare will be submitted in the fall of their senior year and will include their transcript. Junior year of high school is the last complete year that will be on their transcript, and it will have the biggest impact on the admission officers' decision as to whether or not to allow your child to attend their university. This is the year that should contain

---

27 - Josh Moody, "Diversity in College and Why It Matters," *U.S. News & World Report*, March 31, 2020, https://www.usnews.com/education/best-colleges/articles/diversity-in-college-and-why-it-matters#:~:text=-Diversity%20often%20means%20race%2C%20ethnicity,term%20can%20extend%20even%20further.

the most challenging coursework and is also the time that should shine as their strongest academic year in terms of a high GPA.

COLLEGE APPLICATION DEADLINES AND SCHOLARSHIP DEADLINES

At the beginning of and during your child's junior year, they should be researching different universities to decide where they want to apply. Every college has an application deadline; it is an absolute must for them to get their application packet completed and submitted before the deadline. If they miss the deadline, they will most likely not get admitted for the following year. The same is true for scholarships, but they all have different criteria and different deadlines, so you must do your research early on.

TESTING: ACT, SAT, AP, ASVAB, CLEP

It was the fall of 1985. I (Terri) was scheduled to take the ACT test. I called David, who was my boyfriend at the time and said, "Hey, I'm going to take the ACT test. Do you want to go with me and take it, too?" He said, "Sure." And off we went. It amazes me that he was able to go in with me and take the test with very little advance notice because when our kids took it, we had to register, pay, and reserve a spot by a certain deadline before the test date—you couldn't just show up and take it—but somehow David managed it in less than a week back then. He didn't even know what it was when I asked him.

That is because nobody cared enough or thought it was important enough to give him that information. Nobody told him.—not his parents or anybody in his family and certainly not the school guidance counselors. That was one thing that my parents encouraged me toward, a college degree. David's parents did not encourage him in that direction at all. As a matter of fact, they did not see it as important and even looked down on people who had a college degree. As far as I was concerned, it was a given; we both should and would go to college—no questions asked.

Neither of us really knew the importance of taking this test or what impact our score would have, we just did our best. I knew we needed to take the test to apply for college, so we did it. I think we both took the ACT twice that year and scored a twenty-one, which was and still is the national average. Not bad, not exceptional—just what was needed to be accepted to our state universities.

Blake, our oldest, had been working with our state representative, and that's where he found out about an ACT prep seminar being held locally. He signed up, and that started our homeschool ACT journey. At this point, it was already his junior year, so we had him take the test as many times as they offered it. Blake gained insight to help raise his scores, and was able to achieve much higher scores than ours before he graduated.

Consequently, because of this new knowledge, Jessica and Joshua started taking the ACT test when they were in the eighth grade. We knew they would not do well overall because they had not been taught all the information that they would encounter on the test. So, we told them not to worry about their score and just do the best they could. We wanted them to get used to taking the test, because part of the difficulty of test taking in general is overcoming anxiety. We hoped that by taking the test multiple times, they would get used to it, and gradually, as they gained new knowledge, they would be able to do very well. And they did. As middle school kids, their first scores were high enough to enter a state college.

I spent a lot of time working with Jessica and Joshua on specific skills that we learned from the ACT prep book Blake had received, such as ways to read the math word problems and quickly discern the equation and an understanding of what answer they were looking for; learning the process of deduction and elimination; and recognizing which answers are not correct right off, which can save a lot of time. Noticing the wording of questions and being able to quickly find the answers in the reading comprehension paragraphs was another biggie. In the science section, tips included eliminating the pieces of information that are not pertinent to the question to enable them to focus on only what it is asking for. That sounds easy, but there can be a lot of information in a problem that is extraneous to solving it, and some of the answers to choose from correspond with that other information. It can be tricky. We did not have them take the essay portion every time. They averaged taking the test two to three times per year, and we had them take the essay section only one time per year. We focused so heavily on reading, English, and writing from such a young age that, in our opinion, it wasn't necessary for our children to practice the essay portion as often. This proved to be accurate.

It is much easier to practice taking the ACT or the SAT test now. In this section, I have included some links to free testing that your students can take as often as they want. They will be able to obtain their grades and even access study materials to help improve their scores.

The Free ACT Official Online Practice Test option, offered by ACT testing company, has the following features and benefits:[28]

- Students can take official ACT practice tests in all four subject areas.
- Students will know exactly what they missed and what they didn't with a score report.
- Students can access related resources to improve their skills based on what they missed.
- Students can retake the test as many times as they want.

Free SAT Diagnostic Tests

Varsity Learning Tools offers options for SAT test preparation. The website notes, "Explore the Varsity Learning Tools free diagnostic tests for SAT to determine which academic concepts you understand, and which ones require your ongoing attention. Each SAT problem is tagged down to the core, underlying concept that is being tested. The SAT diagnostic test results highlight how you performed on each area of the test. You can then utilize the results to create a personalized study plan that is based on your particular area of need."[29]

Varsity Learning Tools also offers free practice tests. The website notes, "Our completely free SAT practice tests are the perfect way to brush up your skills. Take one of our many SAT practice tests for a run-through of commonly asked questions. You will receive incredibly

28 - ACT, "Free ACT Practice Test and Resources," 2024, https://www.act.org/content/act/en/prod-ucts-and-services/the-act/test-preparation/free-act-test-prep.html.

29 - Varsity Tutors, "Free SAT Practice Tests," 2024, https://www.varsitytutors.com/sat-practice-tests.

detailed scoring results at the end of your SAT practice test to help you identify your strengths and weaknesses."[30]

The Princeton Review is another program that offers a free practice SAT test. Its website notes, "This test emulates all the features of the Digital SAT, such as highlighting, computer-adaptive scoring, and a built-in calculator, so you'll get a great introduction to the testing experience. After the test, spend some time reviewing the Princeton Review's score report, which breaks down your results into areas of strengths and areas in need of improvement. Each question has a thorough explanation, which allows you to use questions you got incorrect or struggled with as learning opportunities. This will also help you determine what to focus on studying next."[31]

AP CLASSES AND DUAL ENROLLMENT

AP, Advanced Placement, is a program of classes developed by the College Board to give high school students an introduction to college-level classes and also gain college credit before graduating high school. Although most students plan to take AP classes because they know it will improve their admissions chances, there are other benefits of taking AP classes in high school as well. Students can save some tuition money by taking AP classes in high school since they can earn college credits without paying college tuition, while getting a head start on their college requirements. Many colleges also look at AP experience when deciding on whom to award scholarship money to, so AP classes may improve your student's chances of receiving scholarships. This can help show the admissions staff that the student has a more strategic and thoughtful approach to their college application. Our youngest son, Joshua, took AP Physics I and II and AP Calculus I and II at our state school of science and math. When he enrolled in college, they counted these classes toward his college requirements for an associate's degree. Not every class counts for

---

30 - Ibid.

31 - Princeton Review, "How to Prepare for the Digital SAT," 2024, https://www.princetonreview.com/college-advice/how-to-prepare-for-digital-sat.

college credit, so you and your student must do the necessary research to determine if it is worth it in the bigger picture for them to take AP classes.

Another program that enables students to earn college credit in high school, as mentioned earlier, is dual or concurrent enrollment. In most states, both two- and four-year institutions offer classes that are accepted for both high school and college credit. This saves time and money for students. All three of our children benefited from concurrent enrollment. At the time Blake was in high school, it was more difficult for homeschoolers to take classes concurrently. We had to work harder and longer to get him into the program. Consequently, Blake was not able to take as many classes before graduation as his younger siblings. However, the experience alone was still valuable to him. It demystified the unknown of higher education and provided a smoother transition from high school to college. Blake recognized that the work he was already successfully doing in high school would effectively serve him well in a university setting.

Six years after Blake, it wasn't as difficult for his younger sister and brother to get accepted into the concurrent-enrollment program and take classes. Jessica took more classes concurrently than her older brother and Joshua was able to earn enough college credits while in high school that when he graduated, he needed only one semester to earn his associate's degree. Because Josh had been taking classes with our local community college, he simply continued taking classes there to wrap up his associate's degree and then transferred directly to a partner university to complete his bachelor's degree in mechanical engineering. Taking classes concurrently made it much easier for him to move into college life because he had already experienced it in smaller doses. That move wasn't as overwhelming as it can be for a student who is experiencing college life for the first time all at once.

Today, because homeschooling is more accepted, it is much easier for students to take advantage of the concurrent-enrollment programs that are available. Do research on what your state offers before your children enter high school so they know what is available to them. Students must meet set criteria in order to take advantage of this program. Your student must have it in mind when they start high school so they can adequately prepare ahead of time.

ASVAB/ROTC

There are also job opportunities in the US military. If your child is interested in a military career, look into the ASVAB test or the Reserve Officers' Training Corp (ROTC). Where their interests lie will help determine which branch they choose. The ASVAB test evaluates a person's aptitude for careers available to those who enlist in any branch of the military and the ROTC is the path to enter the military to become an officer while attending college. If your student wishes to enter into the military elite, start researching military academies that offer high-achieving individuals a more specialized and rigorous training, but have the most difficult entrance requirements. The five military academies are West Point, the Naval Academy, the Air Force Academy, the Coast Guard Academy, and the Merchant Marine Academy.[32]

High school isn't just about taking as many high-level classes as you can and spending all of your time studying. AP and dual-enrollment classes may look good on college applications, but so do extracurricular activities and community involvement. Regardless of the path your child chooses after graduating from high school, being involved in other activities shows the college board and potential job interviewers that a student is well-rounded and diverse, which will add value to the campus community. So, students should be sure to leave themselves time to socialize and relax outside of their schoolwork.

Investigating your children's interests and abilities before high school enabled you and your student to create the four-year plan that has brought them to their senior year. Because you helped them prepare ahead of time, this year will consist of tying up all the loose ends to bring their homeschool journey to a close. The better prepared you are beforehand, the more smoothly this year will go for you and your student. It goes by very quickly

32 - Gain Service Academy Admission, "The 5 U.S. Military Academies," 2024, https://www.gainserviceacademyadmission.com/service-academies/.

CHAPTER 12

TWELFTH GRADE—SENIOR YEAR (COLLEGE PREP AND GRADUATION)

This chapter makes me (David) think of a line from *A Tale of Two Cities*, "It was the best of times, it was the worst of times . . ." When I was eighteen years old, I sat in the small living room of our one-bedroom apartment and desperately wanted our firstborn baby not to be in the place I was at my age. I have a photograph of me wearing my cap and gown, holding our son, at my high school graduation. I was very proud that I'd accomplished what my family and others said I'd fail at, graduating high school with a wife and child.

Looking back on that day, I just shake my head; I was just a kid holding his baby. My parents' advice to me at that time was to get a job at a supermarket and "stick with it." I suppose that worked for my dad—that's all they knew. Terri and I didn't know what the future held, but we were determined to push through it all and change the future for generations to come. We made life-altering decisions, broke bonds with family and friends, and stayed the course no matter what to ensure that our children were not only better prepared than us but better prepared than their counterparts and peers.

Not being boastful, only honest, by the time our children graduated from high school, they accomplished so much more than we did that we can't possibly list it all. Our goals for them to be better prepared than us had come to fruition.

Our first son, Blake, walked the stage to receive his diploma with real-life experience, both good and bad, under his belt. He worked as a page at our state capitol and worked directly for one of our state representatives as well. He volunteered for our town's police department. He went on two mission trips to Mexico and helped build houses. He was an accomplished fencer in foil, raced motocross and BMX, built a car engine, and spoke a decent amount of German. In addition to this, he had a successful business building and repairing computers to generate his own income. He was able to attend some college courses as a high-schooler. This was the best we could do . . . and it was much better than where I had been at his age. He scored a thirty-one on his ACT and was readily accepted to a good state college, where he went on to earn a bachelor's degree with a major in business, as well as a double minor.

Our daughter, Jessica, followed in her big brother's footsteps with many accomplishments. She scored a twenty-nine on her ACT. She spent time working with our state governor and worked on volunteer teams to clean and rejuvenate our city's parks. She was a professional model and voice actor appearing in radio commercials and television ads. She enjoyed gymnastics and stage combat as well as performing in Renaissance Faires. She qualified for the fencing nationals in sabre and played the piano beautifully. Like her brother, she completed some college classes during high school. One of her favorite activities was coaching the young students' fencing class. The children loved Coach Jess just as much as she loved them. She also had a business producing and selling her own custom earring designs. In high school, Jessica participated in Mock Trial classes, which led to a state championship. Later, while in college, she worked with a state assistant district attorney (ADA) and other influential attorneys toward her life's goal and passion of becoming a lawyer who represented and protected children in the entertainment industry.

Our youngest son, Joshua, continued on a similar path as his older siblings. Like we said earlier, he was accepted to an elite state school of science and math where he completed Calculus I and II and Physics I and II during his junior year, and he was able to complete an associate's degree in math and science within six months of graduating high school. He scored a thirty-one on his ACT, and like his sister, Josh was also a professional actor, obtaining a role in a full-length feature movie. He joined with her on volunteer projects cleaning and rejuvenating the city's parks. He was an accomplished fencer in epee and enjoyed gymnastics and stage combat as well as performing at Renaissance Faires like his sister. They choreographed their own fights and even performed together. Josh apprenticed under the chief armorer, building, maintaining, and repairing all the weapons and equipment of our fencing club. He also tutored adults reentering college to earn extra money.

Like we mentioned in an earlier chapter, we were able to provide a private tutor for Jessica and Joshua in French for two years, so they spoke a good amount of French by graduation. They also had a private tutor for English literature and poetry. All three of our children tested out of English Composition I and II before beginning college. As we've mentioned already, each of them scored at a college level in reading and comprehension before completing grade school. Early accomplishments like these make big contributions later.

Our two youngest took their driving test when they were fourteen and a half to obtain their street motorcycle licenses, which required taking the full written driver's test. Our youngest son also earned his open-water SCUBA certification, and together, he and I (David) have explored shipwrecks and caves in lakes and the ocean.

Regarding those who homeschool, the popular narrative is, "You're religious zealots whose kids won't be able to socialize." Hopefully, we're painting a much different picture of homeschooling than the "mainstream" wants you to see. The fact is that by the time our children entered middle school, they far surpassed most graduating high school students academically, and we had responsibly exposed them to enough of the adult world for them to understand many of the paths and pitfalls. They could effortlessly socialize, seemingly with anyone. When our children blew out their eighteenth-birthday candles, we were confident that they were equipped to tackle and achieve the life they wanted. It's incredibly hard to say goodbye, but they had outgrown being confined to what we could offer as parents.

We would always be Mama and Daddy, but we were also peers in the adult world. We respected our children, and they respected us. Our parenting spanned nearly twenty-five years. Looking back, so many aspects of their senior year seemed difficult, especially letting go, but there isn't a day that goes by that we don't look at the last year of their high school careers with both fondness and sadness. We could have done better; we could have done more. Not by pushing our children harder, but by pushing ourselves harder. By being more present and emotionally available in everyday moments. Also, by making a point to enjoy them and the time we had with them more. You don't realize how quickly and absentmindedly you move through life until you reach a big milestone. You suddenly realize eighteen years went by way too fast.

We think back over the years to giving them their baby baths and their little feet kicking, wrapping them up in a warm towel and holding them in all their helpless innocence, then seeing them succeed in walking or riding a bicycle for the first time, writing their first paper, having their first friend crisis, sending them off to their first ACT test (in middle school), or watching them communicate in a foreign country. Perhaps you'll feel as we did: they're amazing! Our children are amazing in spite of us, and I wish I would have done life better for their benefit. Was I as shitty and worthless as I was told growing up? No, thankfully not-- but as a dad, I could have sucked less more often.

So here we are, writing a book because we don't get a do-over. Slow down and be in the moment with your children and family. It is so hard some days—all of the noise of life is vying for your attention, and most of it just doesn't matter. Terri has talked about having a schedule and this is why that schedule is important. You'll know how much time you're devoting to your children and family, and during that time, nothing else matters. We are, I think, a close family. It all comes down to this twelfth-grade year. Did you do the thing, or did you not do the thing? There are no do-overs. We cherish every moment we get to spend with our children. We also respect their personal private lives, and this began the day they graduated. If I had to describe our sons, I'd say they're like me, just a better version. Would they homeschool their children? Yes, I believe they would.

Twelfth grade is the paperwork year. Wrap up loose ends and prepare for what comes next for your children. There shouldn't be much, if any, parenting—only guidance. Terri and I differed on whether our children should have jobs as teens. I was strongly against it because I feel it indoctrinates kids into thinking they must work for someone else. I agree that kids need to be able to earn money as part of the adult experience, but I put my foot down on the "kid job." Each had their own business or were hired for jobs like commercials or radio spots—no varying schedules dictated by an immature boss in a dead-end job with ungrateful customers. Regarding first jobs, our oldest son worked for the National Aeronautics and Space Administration (NASA) at the university he attended; our youngest son continued tutoring adult university students and consulting on fabrication projects as an engineer; and our daughter worked at a law firm, performing receptionist duties and paralegal work.

For me (David), if you've not done it by senior year, it's too late to do much. This is the year you should have in mind when your child is an infant, because this year is as much for you as it is for your children. Think about where your child needs to be by twelfth grade. This is the year you prepare to say goodbye to your child. When you're angry, frustrated, distracted, or hopeless, think about where you want to be during this year and get over it.

DIPLOMA

A high school diploma is a document issued by an educational institution verifying that a student has completed the educational course of study required for high school graduation. The school that mentored us did award our children an official school diploma. As a homeschool, it is up to you whether or not you create and issue your students a diploma. It is not a document that is required, but is more for personal accomplishment. You are free to choose one way or the other.

TRANSITION FROM HOME TO WORLD

You've been parenting, teaching, and mentoring your child for the last eighteen years. You and they have already had conversations about what this transition is going to look like for them. Hopefully, the conversations have consisted of plans—plans you both have excitedly shared about moving into the next phase of their life called adulthood. These plans should have been in development for many years and evolved— it should be nothing new at this point. Together, you and your child have already mapped out what this year and the upcoming transition will consist of. Whether they will be moving out to live at college on their own or sticking around for a while longer to get their career going, you all have worked hard to plan and prepare for this exciting time in their lives.

We cannot tell you what this time should look like because there is no single correct way—every family, every parent, and every child is different. It is going to look like what you make it look like, what is right for you and your family and your situation. Because there were six years between our firstborn, Blake, and his younger siblings, there were many differences, including a better financial situation for us. We had learned much from his journey and were changing things along the way according to their needs and what we had learned with him.

We all tend to work exclusively from our own life experiences, which heavily influence how we teach our children. Because of the struggles David and I had encountered earlier in our married life, our experience taught us that in order for our children to get the jobs they wanted and make a viable living on their own, they had to get a college degree of some sort. As far as we were concerned, obtaining a degree was the best and expected path for all our children. We believed this path would be their best chance at being successful later in life. Consequently, everything we discussed and planned with them was in preparation for them going to college; I don't even remember there being an alternative discussion at all.

It is very difficult to break out of the mindset of our past experiences because it is all we know. That's not necessarily something we have to do, but I do think it is good to allow your children the opportunity to think outside of the box of your experiences. It is good to entertain and explore different path options and help them figure out the course that will fit them best.

Much has changed in the world since our children graduated from high school. Do I still believe a college degree is important? Yes, but higher education has changed, and the job market has changed. Obviously, if your child wishes to become a doctor or a lawyer, they will be required to complete a specialized degree in those fields, but there are many possible paths to success today aside from a college education. The career decisions your child makes will determine which direction they go.

For most parents, the firstborn child is the "experiment" child. That just means we have no idea what we are doing and we learn a lot from them as they grow up, and we also grow and change with each successive child.

Suffice it to say, our firstborn was no different. We had not done a lot of research on what the transition to college would look like, nor did we plan accordingly. Neither of us had that experience. Remember, we went straight into marriage, family, and the workforce from high school and attended college later. Our ignorance and bad decision making forced us to acquire student loans to pay for our education. We were still making payments on them when Blake graduated. Unfortunately, we did not seek out advice or instruction on how exactly to pay for a college degree—all we knew from our experience was that our children could take out student loans, just like us. In our excitement for his future and our perceived accomplishment of completing our task of educating him, we sent Blake out to navigate on his own. It was like saying to him, "Okay, we did our job; now it's your turn, kid—go!" We completely dropped the ball right there. I wish we had walked with him instead of thinking that he would get what he needed from the college advisors. Sadly, because we did not provide the financial guidance or seek the help Blake needed, he is still paying on those student loans. We both regret this.

Don't be like us: seek sound advice and assistance with financial aid for college long before your child gets to their senior year. Find someone who knows the ins and outs and take the time to help your children find the best path for their future. Neither we nor Blake really made a point to look deeper into the pitfalls of certain loans over others. David and I were still recovering from our own financial mistakes and were not well equipped to advise him. We were not aware of the many ways to obtain money or the types of loans available to help pay for college, nor did we seek wise counsel. Blake was just thrust into that situation pretty much on his own. He had a student advisor at college, of course. However, the people employed as advisors at institutions of higher learning are not always the best source for financial advice. I am sure there are some individuals who give beneficial information to students, but remember, they are there primarily to earn the college money. Most student advisors will guide your child on the path of least resistance that will make their employer the most money.

As I said earlier, we learned a lot from the journey with our oldest child, Blake, so when Jessica and Joshua were ready to go to college, they both wanted to avoid debt as much as possible. Together, we all came to an agreement that as long as they were going to school and keeping their grades up, they could continue to live at home. They would not incur debt for or have to worry about their living expenses. They would only be responsible for paying for tuition, books, and fees. Both Jessica and Joshua found multiple ways to pay for their college expenses, and neither had to take out student loans.

As with every subject, your children will benefit most from the effort and preparation you put into their financial education. Along with your experience and instruction, as well as seeking sound financial advice, help and encourage your children to take responsibility and ownership of their finances as early as possible. Impress upon them the long-term implications of debt to be repaid for years to come, and the importance of addressing it sooner rather than later. If they have a mindset that unnecessary debt is unwise and to be avoided, they will look for paths to avoid debt as much as possible. And also, please teach your children about saving and investing for their future retirement. It is imperative they start now and continue for the rest of their lives so that when they are ready to retire, they will be able to do so. It is a very simple concept, but if they wait until they are retirement age, it will be too late. It doesn't matter how much money you have; if you manage it well, you will continue to reap benefits throughout life. If your child goes out into the world without this understanding, however, they will encounter many pitfalls, including much anxiety and sorrow from their ignorance and poor financial decisions.

David and I experienced many sorrows and much financial anxiety for the first ten to fifteen years of our marriage. Before leaving our parents' home, we did not have much, if any, financial education. The result was many years of incurring overdraft charges to our checking account, bill collectors incessantly hounding us, extra unnecessary penalties and late fees, and very low FICO scores. We struggled with handling our money, making mistake after mistake—and every mistake cost us more money. No one was there to provide us with sound financial advice for everyday living.

Eventually, our money problems led us to file for bankruptcy. I don't think I can relate to you what an extremely painful and humiliating experience the bankruptcy was for us. However awful it was, that bankruptcy was the beginning of our climb out of debt and the catalyst to begin obtaining an education in economics. It was good that we experienced all the monetary difficulties we did early on because it forced us to grow, and we have learned much about financial freedom over the years. An extremely important but simple takeaway we gained was to pay all our bills on time every month, without fail. One would think that concept is common sense, but it is not. You must teach this to your children long before their senior year. You must require that they have a good understanding of finances before leaving your care, and homeschooling provides parents with innumerable opportunities to do so.

EMPTY NEST

What about you, parents? Have you prepared yourselves for your child's senior year? You are going to be so busy during this year that it will pass in the blink of an eye. What have you done to prepare yourself for what comes after senior year? I (Terri) have had many conversations with other mothers about, as well as experiencing for myself, the very real condition of empty-nest syndrome. The conversation usually goes something like this: "I devoted all those years to my children, and now they are gone. What do I do now?" Or, "Why didn't anyone tell me this was going to happen?" Good question! However, after senior year is not the right time to ask it. The time to ask the question is before you even have children. Oh, wait—we already have them. So, ask it now. What are you going to do when your children have all left home? Begin to prepare now.

What is left? How do we prepare for something we have never experienced? We have invested a lot of time, energy, and heart, for years, into our kids. If we have done our job, they are prepared and able to move on from being a child and adjust to living life as an adult—but we are not prepared for them to leave. If your life revolves only around your children, you will feel adrift, disoriented. It may feel almost like someone died because all of a sudden, you feel alone. You feel lost.

When Blake went to college, I (Terri) felt very proud of him. He was very capable, and I felt confident in his ability to handle the next chapter in his life. I was not worried. He may have even felt abandoned by me because my attention quickly shifted to his younger sister and brother as we still had much to do. Having younger children made the transition easier because I was still busy. But when Jessica and Joshua completed their homeschool journey six and seven years later, I did feel lost. My job was done, and now I felt I had no purpose. I didn't know what to do with myself.

The mistake I made was allowing myself to put our children—mainly their activities and desires—as my top priority. I am not saying your children are not important and that you should put them at the bottom of the priority list, and I'm also not saying to cut out activities. Let's not be dramatic. What I am saying is you should find what is healthy for everyone in the family, including yourself. It is unhealthy to focus on only one person, whether that be yourself, your spouse, or your children. That is not good for anyone in the family or the family as a unit. We can never achieve perfection—that's not possible—but it is possible to seek balance. All family members are important and needed and necessary for the family unit to function. For me, if I could change the past, here's how I wish I could do it.

I would put my husband and our marriage before our children. Our love and partnership started before they were born. I would depend on him more rather than trying to do it all on my own. I would have had more respect for him and been more appreciative of his constant and abundant provision for us. He graciously gave his blessing for me to quit my job so that I could focus more on their school and activities. I would have given him more of my time to deliberately connect with him and cultivate our relationship. I would've actively continued the partnership we started when we said, "I do." I would've nourished respect, thankfulness, and high regard for David in our children—and then I would have given more of my time to connect with my kids to grow our relationship more. I would've been more present with them rather than focusing mostly on the daily activities and getting the "work" done by enjoying them, but not giving in and allowing them to have their way. Creating this kind of balance between the work that must be accomplished and the individual family members can be difficult, but it is 100 percent worth every ounce of effort it takes to improve and move toward that balance every single day. It is a continual quest. You will never regret the good that you do, but you will regret the good that you don't do. Especially when you look back and see that you could've, but you just didn't do it.

Although I would change those things mentioned previously, and I did experience a period of loss when I no longer was homeschooling our children, David and I have achieved some of the balance I mentioned. Part of that balance in the family that helps with the transition from parenting to an empty nest, is looking ahead and contemplating your future with your spouse. Think about what you would like to do with each other. Future projects, future travel, reclaiming old interests, or discovering new ones side by side with your life partner. Mutually planning ahead leads to looking forward to your life together after children and the things that had been put aside because you were too busy with your family and the daily grind of life. If you and your spouse anticipate having a great life together after your children leave home, you will be more excited for their new life and your own. David and I realized this concept before our children left home and began working toward our future together. We started enjoying life more and looking for ways to have fun together; it felt like we got to go back and pick up where we left off when we were having so much fun dating in high school.

I have a homeschool friend who was so excited when her children all left on their life's journeys because then she and her husband had the house to themselves. They could walk around naked if they pleased; they could do whatever they wanted, when they wanted, in their house. It was like when they were first married again. She giggled like a young newlywed. This couple had put continual work into their relationship. They both invested a lot into their children as well, but when the children left, they were not looking at a stranger. They had put each other first and were excited for the next chapter in their adventure. They had plans, together.

Are you so engrossed in the daily work of homeschooling and life that you are living with a stranger? Have you forgotten you are married to the love of your life because you are so bogged down with what must be accomplished? Wait, I hear you saying, "you said earlier in the book to be on a schedule and get everything done on time!" Yes, we did. But in all things, there must be balance. If you go off the side of the road into a ditch, regardless of how good that ditch may seem, it is still the ditch. You are not going to reach your goals because you will get stuck in that ditch eventually and go nowhere. If you move out of your lane into oncoming traffic, you will most likely get into a wreck or go off the road on the other side. Balance is staying on the path in the direction that leads to your goals. If you step back and realize you're experiencing the pitfalls of what I am talking about, that's okay! The good news is that you realize it—just start moving back toward the path and the right direction. Today is always a good day to change or to make improvements to something you recognize is not right, because there's always room for improvement. You and your spouse got in unison and sat down to create goals and map out a path, so stay in unison on the journey, even when the path changes. Not *if* the path changes—*when* it changes, because it will. Walking in partnership continuously will help you better handle the changes when they come.

CHAPTER 13

POST-HIGH SCHOOL AND EARLY COLLEGE: WHAT DOES SUCCESSFUL LAUNCHING LOOK LIKE?

I (David) graduated high school and was able to work full-time at one job instead of multiple. Finally! I worked for an electronics store called Radio Shack. Within a year, at the age of nineteen, I had supposedly become the youngest assistant manager our district ever had. Terri and I were still dirt poor, but despite everything, I graduated high school and quit what I thought were "lesser jobs," like bagging groceries or any number of other second and third jobs I carried during my senior year.

With Radio Shack, I had a name tag and wore office clothes to work. It felt like a "real" job. Once the dust of this transition settled, though, I realized that a "job," even at Radio Shack, wasn't much different than bagging groceries or making pizzas. Of course you know this—I didn't. A job was a bandage. For what, besides survival, I hadn't figured out yet.

I didn't know the monetary differentiation between being a fast-food manager or an accountant. The guy next door worked for a beer company as a driver, and he had a nice house and drove a nice car. Looked like he was living the dream. The neighbor across the street worked for the city and drove a crappy car; his lawn was overgrown all the time; and his angry wife was often wearing her robe and house shoes, yelling at him from the door. Was the beer delivery job really better than the city job? It had to be. At least that's how it looked from the outside.

These were the observation skills I was equipped with in my much younger days. What factors were at play that caused these neighbors to be so different? I did not know the distinction between a job and a career or profession. On this side of life, I can see that maybe the beer guy was tapped out on credit while the man with a city job was putting every penny into retirement and sucking it up for the time being.

I didn't have any idea of how to follow the money. The concept that an attorney could make tens of thousands a month or that a manager of a huge supermarket made $5,000 a month didn't exist in my mind. I couldn't comprehend making more in one month than I'd ever made in all my years combined. What I did know is that I needed a "real job," which I would later identify as a profession.

My parents only ever talked about jobs, never careers. What I believe today and taught our kids began to form in my mind at this time. What requires an education and is still hard to get? I began to identify rarity or uniqueness—the concept of developing an exclusive and uncommon skill set so that you stand out among your peers.

MY FAMILY DID NOT ENCOURAGE HIGHER EDUCATION

I (David) enrolled in college when I was nineteen and began a professional pilot program with aspirations of becoming an airline pilot. We lived near my grandparents on my dad's side and visited often—unless other relatives said they were coming into town and told us to stay away like the stray dogs they viewed us as. I've already said that my grandfather shared a lot with me. The following week, after being told to stay away on one occasion, I visited my grandfather and asked how the visit went. It turned out it was a few out-of-town relations, my parents, my brother and sister and their spouses. My grandfather oddly said, "You keep pushing, David. Don't let anyone turn you away. You can do it." I asked what he was talking about. He informed me there was quite the discussion at the house that I had started flying and intended to be an airline pilot. "He can't do that." "He'll give up." "He won't finish." It made more sense later when my parents angrily told me that I needed to quit college and "get a real job" and support my family. I thought that's what I was doing. Besides, I did have a job, Terri had a job, and we were supporting our family—we just happened to also be going to college at the same time.

To my family's satisfaction, finances forced me to place my flying aspirations on hold. I reenrolled in the aviation program at a vo-tech to become an aircraft mechanic. Yes, family gossip was relit, and they said I'd certainly "fail" again. Terri and I and our children were intentionally not included in every single one of these family get-togethers at my grandparents' because the entertainment of the night usually included gossip about us—the stray kid who didn't belong and his equally worthless family. Terri was in college and finished her course of study on the dean's honor roll. I finished my course of study near the top of my class and then continued my studies while working and going to school, earning licenses and certificates along the way. I never stopped working.

MY VEHICLE IS YOUR VEHICLE

When we were in our mid-twenties, Terri and I needed a place to stay for a few weeks while we moved from our apartment into a larger rental house. The apartment lease ended before the house could be ready, so we sucked it up and asked my parents if we could stay at their place for the two weeks because they had two empty bedrooms. Financially, we were fine, but we couldn't afford to stay in a hotel for half a month.

"You're not eating our food. You'll pay rent and you're going to do your share of work around here," they said. Not an open-ended "let's see what happens." Well, gee, what an odd way to say yes. It was only two weeks, family member Joe never got this speech.

Remember the car I bought with my own money that my parents would use anytime they pleased because I owed it to them? Terri and I had purchased a new truck when the beloved Camaro gave up the ghost. I came home from work one evening, and the truck was gone. "Where's the truck?" I asked Terri. Her eyes welled up. In tears, she told me that my mom angrily came into our room and demanded the keys. My dad followed with his "mean mug" act and physically stood behind Mom as she ranted. If we were living there, our truck was theirs to use.

Terri asked why they were treating us this way; my mom just yelled that we were adults now. I'm still not sure what that had to do with anything, but in the past, my parents had done everything they could to either block me or discourage me from obtaining a higher education. It seemed they were at it again. We needed both of our vehicles to get to work and school, and they knew it. They were down a car because they'd given a needy blood family member one of their two cars to drive, but instead of suffering the inconvenient consequences of their actions, they took our vehicle instead. Our work and school were in different places, each over twenty miles away. My mom's Cheetos supply and my dad's job were in the same location, two miles away.

We made other living arrangements and moved out of their house within the next two days. My parents knew I was hurt and angry. My mom pursed her lips and put her nose in the air with contempt, and Dad had a content, smug look on his face as they stood in the garage and watched us pack our truck in the driveway. My parents were treating Terri and me like we'd taken all *their* money and *their* car. Believe me, it's as weird as it sounds. They seemed pleased with themselves. I can't imagine why, especially with the information I knew.

What my parents weren't aware of was that I had been provided with the knowledge that they had wiped out my grandparents' savings and that my grandparents had also *given* my parents their extra car(s). Although my dad tried to sell some things to pay them back, I suspect it never happened because my grandparents ultimately had to take out a reverse mortgage on their property for money to live on. It literally cost my grandparents their house. More than once, I wanted to humiliate my parents with my knowledge. I'd done that before, though, when my parents would attack me over some perceived shortcoming, and I would respond with some coveted secret or information about someone that highlighted their hypocrisy against me. I don't know which made them more angry, that I knew or that I wouldn't explain *how* I knew.

The year before this, my parents had forced me to loan them a car I was working on for use by another family member. Our beloved Camaro that had issues. Demanding I let them use it in front of the person, my mom clawed my face and reached for my hair, pressing me for the keys. "It's not safe," I told them. It had a fuel and cooling issue. The car was in the process of being rebuilt. "That's why I'm not driving it." Because she would not stop nagging and against my better judgment, I handed over the keys and told them it wasn't insured and wasn't safe. "Use at your own risk," I warned.

I got a call the next day that my car was on the side of the interstate on fire. I wasn't surprised. There had been a fire in the engine bay that was ultimately extinguished by a passing motorist with a fire extinguisher. The call I received consisted of being yelled at about my "fucking car." When I finally retrieved my car at my own expense, every plastic piece under the hood was melted, including the hoses. The back seat had spilled drinks and dirty diapers with actual shit in them. Fast-food wrappers littered the floors and seats. The car I was so close to finishing was totaled, and we didn't even get an apology. "Too bad you didn't have insurance," the borrower said with a laugh. After they left, my mom reached back and swung at me with her fingernails—the dreaded claws. Thankfully, I caught her wrist in my hand. I told my mom that day that I wouldn't be around anymore. We finally had enough.

Terri and I had previously spent a few thousand dollars to build a new engine for our Camaro. We installed a new transmission and refurbished the interior with things like new carpet. After the fire, a car dealership advertised "push, pull, or drag" trade-ins. I loaded the burned and littered Camaro onto a trailer and towed it to the dealership. The car I bought at sixteen but somehow owed to my family fetched $500 as junk for a trade-in. The work accomplished on it represented the last of our extra money. We needed two cars.

That was the day we purchased our truck. Under my care, it was our transportation for over three hundred thousand miles. I gifted it to our oldest son, who had worked on it so much with me. He still uses it today to haul his dirt bikes. In the spirit of homeschooling, I was often accused of being "hard" on cars as well. We drove that truck for fifteen years. My son has had it since the early 2000s. It's never been wrecked and has nearly five hundred thousand miles on it, while the borrower and burner of the beloved Camaro so many years back has had an impressive array of destroyed vehicles since then. We just kept our heads down and kept pushing forward. I imagine that if there were an old-time family get-together today, people would still say the same things. Who knows why people can't look back and see their own paths of destruction; I'm just thankful that we've been able to reflect and make corrections for the future—we're thankful to have been able to give freely to people in need, even if they were only takers by nature.

TEACHING RESPECT FOR OTHER PEOPLE'S PROPERTY

I (David) just have to stress this over and over because it's part of the lesson: Whether my parents were right or wrong isn't really the point. Telling these stories is to illustrate that people close to you may not be able to even comprehend what you're trying to accomplish. Some people may not be a good source of advice. Like my parents, they could say, "Sonny boy, we've been there and done that. Don't you presume to know anything, you thankless shit."

What they and many people don't realize is that yes, people like my parents have been there and done that, and they're still doing it the same failing way. My parents kept losing and losing, and when they had nothing left to lose, they began to take from others and lose that. They literally never saw it. Furthermore, they showed absolute contempt, disregard, and disrespect for me and my property. I cannot stress this concept enough. If your child has earned money and bought something, it is theirs. Everyone in the family must respect the other's property. If anyone is allowed (either by force or by tacit consent) to take and use any other family member's property, it will breed anger, frustration, hurt, bitterness, and if allowed to continue, it will eventually tear apart relationships.

Just think about it this way. You have worked hard to pay for your home and your vehicles. You have saved and spent your hard-earned money. The next-door neighbor decides he or she needs to use your car or come into your house and raid your pantry because they are out of the food they need to make dinner. Somehow, they figure out how to do this without asking you—or they go to the police, who order you to allow this neighbor free access to and use of your home, belongings, and vehicle. How would you feel toward this person or toward the police? Personally, I would protest. No way, absolutely not!

I realize this scenario is a foreign concept to us in this day and age, but back in colonial times, British soldiers were allowed to force their way into the settler's homes, stay as long as they wanted, eat as much food as they liked, and even physically threaten the occupants by order of the king of England. This was a law called the Quartering Act and it was not fair. The people got so angry that this disregard for their personal rights was partly responsible for the colonists' Declaration of Independence from the king of England and the subsequent war against Great Britain, the American Revolution.

That was a long time ago and doesn't really apply to us, does it? We are family; it is different. We live together, we share everything. So where is the line? Can you take from your kids, threaten your kids, or force your kids to give up their property to another sibling just because you are family? Or must we share, in the name of family? What belongs to one belongs to all?

Where are your children supposed to learn respect for other people's property and rights? At home—from you, Dad and Mom. If you allow your little ones to have and do whatever they want whenever they want, don't be surprised when they show no restraint when it comes to wrecking your car or tearing up your home because it is just as much theirs as it is yours, and they can do as they please. Could attitudes like this be what directed my parents?

HIGHER AND CONTINUING EDUCATION HELP OPEN DOORS IN LIFE

I've never been able to understand what motivated my parents to treat me and my family this way. Trying to take education away from me didn't gain them anything. Obviously, they and other family members wanted to hurt us enough to push us away. What possesses a parent to emotionally or physically abuse their child (one child specifically) from five years old to twenty-five years old? Regardless of good or bad grades, they relentlessly punish the child for their school performance, and when that child breaks free and begins delivering academically in a real and monetary sense, then double down and try to sabotage their success? What in the hell is going on there? My parents literally never recognized any of my academic or career accomplishments, and I don't say that figuratively. They instead showered me with their excitement and admiration for the successes of others.

Some people, even my own wife, on occasion, think that I'm being selfish, self-centered, or spiteful when good things happen in other people's lives and my response isn't more enthusiastic. I'm unsettlingly indifferent—one could even think that I'm angry. I'm not anything. We would die without the sun—do we get excited to see the sun in the sky every day? We simply expect it. I've had to learn to be as outgoing and supportive as I am for the benefit of others. That's one that I accept and see as worthwhile. For lack of a better way to put it, I'm simply blind to certain things because I was taught to be blind.

I see the practical benefit to accomplishing big goals like graduating, and to that, I say, "Good job." Sincerely, it will make your life better than it would have otherwise been, but the whole sugary "let's party and make a big deal out of it," I don't get; I'm blind to it. I was taught to be blind to it in the stories you are reading throughout this book. I have very few memories of being that excited idiot kid just bursting with joy. The last time I recall not having to fabricate that emotion was as a young boy standing in our kitchen, conversing on the phone with a friend. It was evening and I was excitedly talking and laughing about whatever two grade school boys talk about. My dad appeared from the living room, pulled the phone out of my hand, and slammed it down to end the call. He backhanded my mouth and said, "Can't you just shut up?" I had to be in third or fourth grade. I shut up from that day forward. To this day, I speak quietly because if I spoke too loudly as a child, I would get punished. The die was cast. I'm not a good person to have at parties. Having me at a party is a bit like taking your deaf friend to the orchestra.

So, having climbed through this messy aspect of life, I connected what remained, blocked out the negativity, and pushed forward. I learned to observe the people around me and listened to their personal stories, trying to glean all the information that I could to make my own life better, as well as give some practical advice to others.

Over the years, I've had a handful of people express to me what they wanted to achieve and outright ask me what I would do if I were them to accomplish it. In each and every case, as a result of following my advice, these people attained something that appeared unrealistic, seemingly impossible. Each individual did exactly what I said to do, when I said to do it. Those who didn't follow my instructions to the letter failed. (That said, I have failed in advising someone on what to do once, and it was a biggie.)

So, what am I saying, that I'm an oracle? No, believe it or not, I don't want you to think I'm smarter than I actually am. What I do want to convey is that you can learn a lot by observing people around you. Not judging—that's useless. Where were they, what did they do, and where did they go after they did it? You'd be surprised by what you learn by watching and carefully considering the people you come into contact with.

For each person, I recommended that they acquire more education, unique skills and/or new knowledge. Maybe college, maybe tech school, maybe a certification—or usually, a combination of all three. Think about it: if you see a job opportunity and the interviewer says, "You need a degree," it would've been best if you already had a degree. At the point someone tells you that it's too late—you missed an opportunity. We told our kids to plan to go to college. We didn't care what degree they got as long as they did it. It's a professional rite of passage that almost always makes a beneficial difference; it opens doors otherwise closed to those who do not possess a degree.

To be competitive, your child needs a higher education. That ridiculously expensive piece of paper will multiply their earning ability over their lifetime. Homeschooling offers endless opportunities to cultivate that competitive edge and the qualities employers are looking for in future employees. I'll share something with you right away—I don't have a degree. I'm several credit hours short, about twenty, and as the years pass, that number increases. It used to be twelve. What I do have is somewhat unique; I have ratings and certificates and experience that I've leveraged to make me professionally valuable. Thankfully, some of my years of work experience included writing policies and procedures and technical writing. So, while writing isn't totally new to me, writing this book is certainly more fun!

I SHOULD HAVE GOTTEN A DEGREE

Looking back over the years, balancing providing for my family and creating opportunities for myself down the road, I (David) didn't prioritize higher education over the ridiculous amount of hours I was working for a significant rate of pay. "If I'm making $XXX, I really don't need a degree at this point, right?" You decide.

I worked for a large corporation as a senior field engineer. I was as high as I could go in my job category and had been a supervisor in this massive corporation; I held one of four coveted spots in a division. The job was unique, and I was good at it. I heard that my division was going to be gutted within the next year. *No biggie,* I thought. *It's a massive corporation; that's business.* Even though my career field was tumultuous, I was good at my job and hadn't been unemployed in the past twenty years. There was no reason for that to change. I perused the internal job listings of the company and looked at jobs at or above my level. I clicked into one, saw the job title, and as I was glancing at the page, I closed it. "Wait—did I just see what I think I saw?" I opened it back up. It was a senior manager position two levels above me. Experience requirements . . . I exceeded everything. Knowledge of systems, yes, verifiable. Ratings, bingo. I exceeded their requirements for ratings. Down the list I went, and I couldn't believe that I was competitive for this position. I exceeded the desired experience for this position. I was finally one of the "big boys." The low end of the starting salary was $470,000 a year. I'd negotiate an even half a million and get it. Being an employee already, I clicked the button to apply for the job. The link gave me the ability to write a note to the recruiting department, so I eloquently stated that my credentials were unquestionable and verifiable, I had a good history with the company, and I looked forward to an interview for the position.

I'd just gotten home from work, put on my flip-flops, and sat on the back deck of our boat with a beer. My phone rang. "Mr. Batts?" It was the company representative. She went on to tell me that she was a senior recruiter for the company and was excited to call me with information about the management job I'd applied for. She asked me about my unique talents and experience and discussed technical aspects related to performing the job. She talked about the required travel, and I was familiar and comfortable with what she was saying. She was getting excited.

"We discussed your résumé at length during our conference, and we're all excited." Believe me, I don't usually get too excited, but maintaining an even unemotional voice was difficult for me in that moment. "We have one question that we need to clarify . . ." I knew what was coming. "You seem to have omitted your college from your résumé." Just imagine a big bright balloon, and this woman had stuck a pin in it. "The listing said that it wasn't required." There was a pregnant pause. "You don't have a graduate degree?" she asked. "No, ma'am, I'm a few credit hours from my undergraduate degree. The reason I have all of the experience I do is because I've been working in this field and succeeding for a long time. It was one or the other."

The nice lady leveled with me. "I know it's not required; we have to say that. There is no way the board will sign off on this position for you or anyone else without a degree. You know we all have to report the education level of our management employees," she said. "Yes, ma'am, I do," I responded. "Otherwise, your résumé is amazing. Finish your degree, Mr. Batts." I don't know about you, but I think $500,000 a year would have been pretty great, and I missed it because I didn't have a piece of paper. It's the world we live in, not the world we think it should be.

DEVELOP UNIQUE SKILLS

You've read my story. I didn't come from money, my parents told me to get a job at a supermarket and "stick with it." Where could I have been if I'd had any idea about the value of having a degree and knowledge of the job market? You know and understand, so these are the things you will provide to your children.

I've made a career of being unique and rare in my industry. I continually worked toward getting more knowledge and as many certifications as I could to help me advance in my career. I am a certified aircraft mechanic and inspector, but I also possess other certificates and skills that seem unrelated but in fact make me uniquely qualified for specific kinds of jobs in aviation. For instance, does having my SCUBA certification or being a pilot figure into job possibilities? You would be surprised. Unique skill set, adaptable personality, and physically conscientious. I have the ability to arrange my qualifications to competently suit countless scenarios and succeed. I don't lie about my qualifications or abilities. I don't have to.

I'm not talking about getting the job; I'm talking about having a reputation for delivering. Being the total package. I'm one of countless certified aircraft mechanics, but how many of those mechanics could be dropped on a remote beach for a week to disassemble an airplane and recover the parts by helicopter and boats offshore? Not many, in my experience. Being a mechanic is crucial to the task but provides only a fraction of the skills necessary to accomplish the mission. In that spirit, I've made a career out of being unique. I encounter a lot of people who say, "Well, I could do that." To which I say, "Probably, but *have you*?" Right there is the difference—I have, over and over.

How can you cultivate the uniqueness in each of your children? It's there; you just need to search for it and then help them develop it. Use their interests as a springboard to expand and promote qualities and skills that will help your children stand out among the crowd. Homeschooling in and of itself is unique simply because it is not the norm. Academics are just the tip of the iceberg. As educators, we are able to use countless opportunities as they happen to give our children more than they could ever get in the traditional school setting. You are uniquely positioned to recognize and seize moments of learning, investigation, inquiry, and adventure that spark those gifts that are waiting to come to the surface within each of your children and be polished like a gem, year after year. That is what we are doing. Helping them to become who they were created to become.

SET THEM UP FOR SUCCESS

For the past thirty years, I've accomplished something rare or unique at every job I've had. In the position I held at the job I departed twenty years ago, I became the highest-paid person ever in that company, making more than many managers above me, yet I resigned to accept another job. In one year, I quickly rose to a division manager. Making twice as much as I had previously, I built a new division that earned the company $2 million to $4 million per month and I was being groomed by the chief executive officer for the president's chair.

I resigned from that position for a higher-paying job and quickly began rising again.

At any one of these jobs, most people would have settled in. Good pay, good benefits, and job security. Comfort. I delivered to each of these companies what they hired me for, and I left each company better than I found it. I was an asset who stood above the masses in some rare but beneficial way. Most of the people who were at these jobs when I arrived were still there and in their same positions when I left.

The thing is, what I've accomplished isn't because I'm so special. I'm just an average person trying to do better than average. I had to figure all this out on my own by trial and error. I've learned and applied everything that we talk about in this book. Extremely significant for me was not allowing the poisonous people in my life to define me. Some people just can't help themselves; that's why we talk about them over and over here. I would guess that certain people years back said, "About time he got his shit together." What these people will fail to realize—and what you and your children need to realize sooner rather than later—is that these kinds of people are the problem. Their gossip, their poison, their judgmental and nasty way of living life makes everything around them sick. Nothing good can be accomplished. When I was free of that, when *we* were free of that, I suddenly started "getting lucky" in my career and our marriage finally became happy and enjoyable.

There's advice that I've failed to mention anywhere else in this book up to this point: stay the hell out of other people's business. If you don't want others to opine about school or homeschool, don't bring it up; don't talk about it. If you don't want everyone's two cents about marriage and family, don't invite it by talking about it. Don't complain about your own, and don't give advice about theirs. We often have people tell us very personal information as a way of inviting our opinion. Nope. Marriage is tough, raising kids is tough, and having a job that sucks is tough. I have nothing else for you. I recently had a family member contact me about something like this. I told them that I was glad to listen but wouldn't take sides. Don't be a poisonous person.

What you'll notice about the people who typically give out advice is that their lives don't change. Everything will usually continue to be a struggle. In the world today, it is a rare person who can—and will—show up to work early enough to be ready to work at their scheduled start time and accomplish more than the job they were hired for. By the time you're done with your kids, this should be really easy for them. They should be a person who takes responsibility for their words and actions, someone who can function without complaining. I've said for decades that the bar just isn't that high to succeed. If you equip your children with the personal qualities and characteristics we cover in this book, success will be much easier for them to find compared with most of their public school counterparts.

WHAT IS MY JOB?

My (David's) job is to be a reliable, trustworthy, and knowledgeable employee with the desire and ability to be the solution.

To achieve the success I desired, I needed college. I still do. It's not too late to be of value. Again, it's the world we live in, not the world we think it should be. If a college degree and graduate school cost $200,000 for your children, does it matter, as long as it's in a field proven to provide quality opportunities?. If it was twice that, it'd still be worth it for the return on investment.

In my personal experience, the difference between no degree and having a degree, over a lifetime, can be millions of dollars. I'm not talking about becoming a doctor or any other time-intensive course of study, but if you want more of an opportunity to make money, it needs to be a course of study that is useful and applicable to industries, products, ideas, or skills that generate money. Nothing against women's studies or art history or any other incredibly specific course of study; history is important. Truly knowledgeable and insightful people are needed to keep our societies on a healthy path, but it's not a high-demand specialty. For example, consider a company with five hundred employees, but everyone applying for jobs has studied human resources (HR), and the company only has one HR position. I'm basically telling you to stay away from HR and get the degree that makes you HR's boss—or everyone's boss. That's my disclaimer, though. In the real world of delivering a product (unless you want to pursue an area of special interest), *you need a degree that companies making money can use to make **more** money through you*. It's really that simple.

Even if you are a citizen in a Communist country, who will the upper leaders choose to be near them? Someone with a lot of meaningful opinions or someone who competed academically and proved their intelligence and ability. It took me years to figure this out. If you do have a passion for women's studies or another specific degree that isn't directly related to the economic bottom line of a commercial business, that's not my expertise. What I do know is that every other personal quality still applies for success. Don't be an adult who needs to be babysat. Don't cry, don't complain; be a problem solver. Be an accomplisher. Be a leader in whatever you choose to do.

EVERYONE GETS A TROPHY

If the job is easier to obtain, the more competition there is. The easier a degree is to acquire, the more competition there is (and therefore generally fewer available jobs). Let's go to the future and then take this back to a couple who has just sent their toddler off to preschool. These parents and the public schools praised the child for nothing. The kid scribbled crap on a sheet of paper because they knew their parents and teachers would praise them. It wasn't illustrating their passion or ability to color; it didn't demonstrate any progress. It was the child manipulating others to give them praise, and they got that praise. Every kid got a trophy, whether they earned it or not—there was no meaning in accomplishment. The parents and the schools encouraged this meritless praise throughout the years, and now this child accomplishes nothing that literally seven billion other people on the planet haven't already accomplished, but this child expects everyone to give them brainless praise just like their parents and the public schools did.

We have been around parents like this, and we've been around their kids. Inherently, we respect the right of parents to raise their children the way they choose, or even schools to raise kids however they want because many parents don't want to do it themselves . . . but do not blame me (or anyone else) for your "lack of opportunities." I just die inside when parents tell us, "Those employers just don't know how good of a person/ worker/individual our child is. If they would just give them a chance!" I gave kids like these chances, and they blew it. I cannot and do not give preferential treatment because my job is to make money or provide a service. The outcome of that reflects directly on me and my professional reputation.

Before "diversity" was a buzzword, I was recognized for having the most diverse crew by my HR department, and they were happy I was setting an example. It never occurred to me what color or gender the members of my crew were. I had two women of different races, several Asian men of different heritage, a couple of men of African heritage, and two Caucasian males. Their ages ranged from twenties to fifties. You know how that happened? I hired the best applicant for the job at the time. Gender and race never occurred to me. I say this to frame in the following story, where I went against my usual standard of hiring.

Against my better judgment, I set up a "good ol' boy" hire. A parent called me to ask if I could please give their child a chance. "Let me get back to you," I said. I didn't operate that way. My own dad wouldn't give me a job in his private company. You make your own way on your own merit. I called the parents back and told them that I was highly regarded and that giving their little Scooter a chance would reflect directly upon me. I had a series of questions: Can he show up on time and follow instructions? Can he do the job without arguing or complaining? Can he, if unable to follow through on doing these things, resign without causing trouble and making himself and me look bad? "Oh, yes, yes, yes!" the mother replied. "Okay. Can he make it to an interview tomorrow?" I asked. "Well, he has plans tomorrow." Hmm. "So there are personal things more important than getting a job?" The parents did not think twice. They naturally expected *me* to accommodate their child like they did. *No wonder this loser is unemployed,* I thought. "Talk to me when being employed is the most important thing to them." I wasn't nasty or mean, just real. "No, no, no, I'm sorry!" the mother begged. I relented. "Tell you what, have him call me to set up the interview. I'll let you know how it goes."

Scooter called me, and we set up the interview for the next day. I explained that he wouldn't be working for me, but for someone who worked for someone who worked for me. The pay would be more than he'd ever made in his life (that just happened to be starting pay for the job), but he would be expected to work his ass off, if not for himself, then for my reputation. He thanked me profusely for the opportunity. I told him where to be and at what time. I told him what to wear. I told him the documents to bring, secured and organized in a yellow envelope.

Let's circle back—these are things a child in grade school should know. How to dress appropriately. Punctuality. I'm instructing an adult to do these things. He thanked me for my insight and help. It was painful that he was not equipped with even the basics of adulting. I called his enabling mother back and filled her in, and I stressed to her that he needed to be there ten minutes early. "Yes, yes, yes, and thank you so much!" she said. I informed HR of the appointment and scheduled his orientation for after the interview. The interview was just a formality. This was a "good ol' boy" hire; he would start work the next day.

While the mother was getting her son's things collected and assembled for his interview, he went out to celebrate his interview and new job. He drank; he did some drugs. He got picked up by the police for driving while intoxicated. Needless to say, he was in jail when it was time for his interview. The mom who was so quick to ask for my help just as quickly did not call to let me know her son wouldn't, in fact, be showing up. HR called to inform me that the appointment didn't show. *I called the mom.* Yes, I did. I was angry and offended. She told me what happened. I told her that a courtesy call would have been useful. A lot of people wasted their time planning and waiting for her son, I explained. "Yeah, I'm sorry . . ." she offered. "No, you're not. If you were, you would have called." Yes, I said that. I told her that my recommendation to HR was to never consider hiring this young man because he was apparently struggling with drugs and alcohol. I apologized to them myself and said that I didn't know this fact beforehand. This woman and her son used their one favor. That was a long time ago, and I've not spoken to them since. That opportunity was the only time I'm aware of that the young man had a chance at a career. Last I heard, he still works in fast food.

This is the best place I can find to make another point about the results of lack of initiative or laziness, whichever applies. People like this mom and her son are so ignorant that it now makes sense to them to push for increased minimum wages. She failed as a mom beyond making sure her baby lived to be an adult. Her son didn't have the initiative to better himself because his doting mother always told him how great he was, and now that life sucks for them, it's obviously someone else's fault. They say things like, "The system is broken," or "Minimum wage is too low!" What these people fail to realize is that it doesn't matter what minimum wage is. In my initial draft of this book, I created a scenario that put minimum wage at fifty dollars an hour. I was trying to be ridiculous. While writing this, California proposed a fifty-dollar hourly minimum wage. Honestly, if my estimated math is correct, they could make it almost $200. It still wouldn't change anything, but people like this son and his mom will never understand why. We just press on with accommodating the ignorant or ignorant *and* stupid people with no initiative whose parents failed to do the most basic level of parenting.

So, let's compensate burger flippers with $100 an hour and pass that increase on to the customers—$25 for a Whopper or Big Mac? I'd probably take a pass. So, to be able to sell burgers, the state requires restaurants to pay entry-level employees $100 an hour, but customers quit coming in because their pay hasn't caught up yet. The restaurant goes out of business, and now these masses of minimally educated people who "won the fight" are vying for even fewer available jobs. As a result, government handouts must increase, probably raising taxes and thus resulting in less recreational income for the people who used to buy burgers, but finally, their pay increases proportionally, so now they can enjoy burgers again. Whew! The cost of goods and services has risen across the board, and a $100-an-hour minimum-wage job has the same buying power that $3.32 did when I was sixteen years old and making minimum wage. You can either teach your child to be unique and excel, or they can get in line with billions of other people complaining and accept what the people with initiative are willing to give them.

Speaking to the example of people like the mom and her son, it seems to reason out that if you suck as a parent, you've definitely made the world worse off. A negative contribution. Did social media or alcohol or drugs or entertainment make the world bad? I mean, a volcano can't kill a person unless they choose to jump in or go near them. Nothing can have a negative effect on you unless you give yourself over to it. You will never be content until you are satisfied with the life you have achieved until you are living for what you have *worked* for. Living the life you have earned. There is no shortcut to overcome sucking at being an adult. It requires work, competition.

This takes me back to the dichotomy of the public school system. It espouses that everyone should be equal, or something like that. Equality, equity—one presents opportunities, and another uses a debit-and-credit system based on perceived entitlement. Contrast this against something else the school system is passionate about: Darwin's theory of evolution, or just plain old evolution. This is fact! Irrefutable! I have my take on the topic, but it doesn't matter. Public schools are social engineering. Don't get angry yet. No matter your political leaning, your race, or your gender, pick out a period in time, any period in our history, and you'll be able to find examples of any point of view, any political leaning in that government entity that counters survival of the fittest. This holds regardless of whether you have an all-white school, an all-black school, or a school like mine—(almost) all white, but treated the poor kids like shit and rolled out the carpet for the rich kids.

School policy goes against evolution, in my opinion. It's not survival of the fittest, but social engineering—none of the rich kids were beaten bloody or left alone in a parking lot at night or ridiculed in class. In my predominantly white school, the teachers and administrators devoted themselves to ensuring the rich kids continued in the family footsteps of being wealthy. At my school, if poor black kids were considered to be "ghetto," then poor white kids were deemed "trailer trash." Because these "trashy" kids had the audacity to stink up these entitled teachers' class-rooms, *obviously* they deserved nothing more than to go back to the trailer park. I expect it's the same for any poor kids. People—specifically, the teachers—use labels based on social class to make their nastiness more acceptable, so that they can show their disdain for a group publicly. As parents, we don't have to combat anything. The school system can profile children and be violent and racist; it will always be exactly what they make it and will never be what we (or you or our respective children) need it to be. That's why we chose homeschool—it'll be exactly what our children need to competitively enter the world, without labels placed on them in the system.

THE WORLD STAGE

I've been excited to touch on this topic since beginning this book. The United States ranks 125th out of 194 other countries in literacy rate.[33] Obviously, according to this statistic, Western secondary schools, specif-ically in the United States, aren't really competitive on the world stage. Our six-figure teachers cry about money while a teacher in India makes less than $200 a month—and that teacher's students outperform us.

Our culture can whine about opportunity and the cost of college and open nearly every government job to the uneducated, but here's the real-ity as I see it: we don't have enough jobs to replace welfare. We don't have enough jobs to provide for every person unwilling to invest in their education and their future, so our children need to be equipped to compete for the best jobs out there. San Fransisco can make people feel better by removing algebra from their school requirements, but the only people it helps is the workforce of other countries. Their citizens are learning and

---

33 - https://www.usareads.org/#:~:text=The%20US%20ranks%20125th%20out,who%20can%20read%20 and%20write.

will continue to learn algebra, so we homeschool because our children must be equipped to compete globally.

Take a flight outside the United States. You'll see "third-world" citizens who are multilingual. I've had conversations with "average people" who fluently speak multiple languages; they speak their native language and a couple of others, such as English, German, Spanish, Mandarin, Japanese, Arabic, Russian, or Swahili. They also possess at least a bachelor's degree, and these are just the flight attendants of airlines like Etihad or Emirates. In addition to this, they have college degrees in science, mathematics, engineering, or medicine. What do we think is so great about us in the United States anymore? The way we improve is by removing requirements and tests so that failure isn't an option? Is this really how we're going to make people equal? Just don't look at the kids from third-world nations who are begging for education funding . . . all while they're outperforming us in education.

Seriously, based on our education model, just send these countries and their children what they give us: gold stars and a diploma, "compliments of the US Department of Education." These children are now qualified to apply for 80 percent of the jobs within the US federal government. Supposedly, that's progress. It will look and sound great until the system begins failing more so than it already has, when the simple services required of our government cannot be obtained because the employees are incapable or unwilling to perform the jobs they were given—but weren't qualified for. Corporations will eventually need to choose between getting the job done or going bankrupt. Our government, just like the school system, has doubled down on blaming these shortcomings on anything but the real problem. So, the mentality of the school system is not only not going to be adjusted for a "better future," but it is going to grow to infect our entire system. You might think you have a good idea of where I'm going with this. You could think that I'm siding with one group or speaking ill of another, but when we said earlier that this book isn't about politics or worldview or a certain belief system, we meant it. So, what's the problem then?

Shit parents and laziness. In the United States, politically, we have the Red Team and the Blue Team. Both teams have shit parents who are lazy with lazy kids. I think the side that will prevail will be the side that takes their job as parents seriously and dedicates themselves to the task of raising their children.

In terms of beliefs, you might be a devout Muslim, Communist, Fascist, Socialist, Capitalist, conservative, liberal, LGBTQQIP2SA, Christian, member of the Church of Satan, Scientologist, or any other number of titles used to label the nuances of a particular set of beliefs or system of identity that is most important to you. The point that I'm trying to make is that there is a set of *skills* that must be a priority in the foundation of raising your child, no matter what. We don't care what belief system you identify with; that is between you, your children, and perhaps your government or your God(s). What we do care about is that your child is equipped to intelligently interact on a level that keeps our society and world functioning for everyone who inhabits it, so that your child can experience personal contentment through their success of their own personal achievements.

In the United States as a society, we've been skating by on the legacy of our innovation as a once great nation with a once unique and great education system, including primary, secondary, and post-secondary institutions. While other nations are working ever harder to raise the bar and achieve higher, groups like our teachers' unions are running around and kicking the bars of standards to the ground.

"USA! USA! USA!" we chant. We look like idiots; we sound like idiots—we are becoming a nation of idiots. I'll be on the side of my country for the rest of my life, but I hope to see us returning to our former glory and opportunities before I die. Not through bullying or intimidation, but through achievement and cohesion as a society. If your child exhibits the strength to be a leader and wants to build a comfortable life for themselves and their family one day, then college should be a nonnegotiable thing in your mind. A useful degree is an investment in their future. It's an investment in your family and in your country, because the information in this book doesn't only apply in the United States; it can work for any family within any country that allows parents to oversee their child's education. If your child isn't equipped for it, or just can't see the benefit of college, then maybe it's not for them.

Suggest unique trades like the computer industry, machining, welding, or tooling. They can also pursue careers in health care or public services. If they're exceptional, they could be the next stand-out artist, but at least make certain they have a good foundation of education to manage their craft.

There is something out there that is useful and rewarding for every child to learn and that will be of benefit to themselves and those around them, as well as provide a comfortable life. We didn't write this only for parents in the United States. If your children aren't equipped with basic social skills and some specialty knowledge they're good at, they will be one of tens of millions, billions of people vying for the same jobs but ultimately taking what someone is willing to give them. But hey, if all else fails, hopefully, they'll have attended state-sponsored public school and learned to socialize.

BE DIFFERENT

Education is important. I've seen it over and over in my career and in the careers of those around me. If you want your life to be different from those around you, you must be different from those around you. Not "better than" but more introspective and intentional in life. Terri and I never received welfare. We were eligible, but both of us felt like we would be giving up something of ourselves if we chose that path. We did go to the state office to look into it, though. Everyone in that waiting room was the same in some way that I can't quite put into words. Every face we looked at reflected part of us and our lives. It scared me. These people were going to be trapped as wards of the state. We didn't need welfare; we needed to do life differently. We needed to perceive life differently. We realized that welfare would not be our path to a better life and couldn't get out of that building quickly enough.

A doctor once told me, "Making money, being rich is easy." He didn't elaborate at the time, but bragging wasn't his point. Terri and I were working through the muck of years of struggle and were finally finding our way and our will to fight each other was waning. We desired peace in our lives together. The stress of life had put me into a funk, and so I went to visit with this guy. This doctor had economics and financial certificates on his wall, not psychology or sociology. He used to own a bank with a friend and partner. I kind of smiled and asked, "Why would you give up owning a bank? That has to make a lot more money than hearing people's bullshit all day." He allowed a tired smile; it was a look similar to the one my grandfather often gave me. "I made a lot of money, millions," he told me.

"And decided to go back to school? Isn't the point to make money?" I asked.

He told me it was my time and asked if I wanted to spend it hearing his story. Of course I did. The doctor went on to tell me that the psychiatrist who owned the clinic was his wife. She was a real medical doctor, a psychiatrist. He owned a bank with a partner and friend. He went on to tell me that he and his wife had been millionaires for longer than he could remember. They had the mansions, luxury cars, and anything else they wanted. That's just the way they lived and always had since their twenties. His partner and friend walked into the bank one day, sat in his office chair, put a gun in his mouth, and pulled the trigger. He'd rather be dead than own up to what he had been doing. The doctor said that with that event, he felt like his priorities had, all this time, been wrong. More than money, he wanted his friend. He couldn't bring his friend back, but maybe he could help others realize that the people around them wanted them to stick around—even if they had embezzled money. The doctor sold the bank and went back to college.

I understood why he would say making money is easy when compared to having special people in our lives. At an age older than I am now, this man went back to school and attained another degree. He changed the course of his life. Is it really that big of a deal to intentionally set a course in life and see it through? No; I was just raised to believe that it was.

GOTTA MAKE A LIVING

We need money to live, and the best way to get it is by being our unique selves. We need happiness, which comes from doing something that is rewarding to us and those we love. Get an education that will enhance your unique talents and abilities, something that you can build on for true fulfillment—something that also leaves room for someone to share your life with you and you with them.

During the time when I was seeing that doctor, life was hard for us. Money didn't come easy for us, but I desperately wanted to understand what he meant. I kept our crappy cars running by myself to save money. I can't count the number of engines and transmissions I either rebuilt or replaced in our garage or driveway over twenty years. Brake changes, CV joints, alternators, batteries, and belts. It was stressful, but I was blessed to be able to do the work that saved us thousands of dollars.

I also used these experiences to teach our children about maintenance. I continued to invest in my education while asking myself, "What's the point?" As a human being, I was exhausted. I had to have a silver lining just to get up and get through the next day, and then the next. I didn't care what I drove so long as it would just start in the morning and get me to and from work.

As I worked on our car once at a small house we rented, wondering, "What's the point?" a memory in the far back of my mind got my attention as though in response.

I remembered Terri and I were eating dinner in the little one-bedroom apartment we shared with our newborn son and cockroaches several years before this. We sat in folding chairs at a card table, eating pork and beans out of the can. We were smiling at each other, talking about the future. "Someday, we'll get a convertible sports car, and if something happens to it, we'll pay someone else to fix it . . . or buy another one. Won't that be great?"

We just smiled and nodded at each other in our quiet little apartment. It was a nice thought. We didn't even make enough money in a year for a down payment on a luxury car. With this memory in my head, I continued working on our car in the driveway. It would take me forever to get all of the grease and grime washed off my body so that I could get to bed and get a couple of hours of sleep before work. Sometimes all I could do was get up and make it through another day. As I write this, I sit and allow myself to think about things I'd sometimes rather forget. I remember working on that car outside so many years ago while remembering our hope as a young couple. These memories are still hard to think about.

At another point in time, this same pair of memories passed into my thoughts. Twenty years or so after pork and beans with the cockroaches, I was wrestling with these same memories for some reason. The hardest part of writing this book has been the sheer quantity of memories that I've had to sort through. Maybe I'm still trying to resolve myself to myself; my mind is always sifting through seemingly endless memories, and this random day in a hotel so many years later was no different.

Because I was supposed to be a failure, right? Well, we were in a nice hotel in another state and I looked in the mirror in the bathroom—it was just me, but the negative chatter in my head was there; it was usually there . . . but I'd noticed lately that it was getting less loud. I had acknowledged that I wouldn't be accepted by my family or Terri's. I wasn't and would never be part of the family legacy. Terri's mom once created a family genealogy book; it took years and was amazingly exhaustive. She even traveled to Europe multiple times and took rubbings of headstones from the 1600s.

What did the book contain from our generation? One woman—it included her two ex-husbands and the woman's stepchildren; each had significantly more written about them than I did, her daughter's husband of almost forty years. What did she write for me? That I'm her daughter's husband and that I was adopted. It said so much with so little information; she made it very clear who was important to her and who didn't matter.

I am the first in *my* family's line. That will have to do.

We were now different from who we were growing up; our kids were very different from us as children. I realized we had accomplished what I desperately wanted to achieve on that dark, hopeless night in our shitty apartment. Our kids were nothing like we were many years ago, and I was proud of that.

Back in the hotel, looking for that flash of a moment in the large bathroom mirror, *You're okay,* I thought. The memories swept away as if caught by a breeze. I was left remembering our conversation at that card table in our folding chairs, eating pork and beans, having nothing but naïve hope and each other.

I was going to make good on the dreams of that young hopeful couple. I opened the bathroom door and walked out. There was Terri's bright face smiling at me. "What do you want to do?" she asked. I smiled back at her. "We're going to the Porsche dealership."

I can offer even more emphasis on why your job as a parent relates to this story. The infant son with poor parents, who slept in his crib as we sat at our folding table that night, dreaming about better days, bought the beloved Porsche Boxster from us in his mid-twenties. As much as we enjoyed owning such a car, I'm honestly not sure which moment was better, buying the car in the first place or the day our son excitedly bought it from us. Over twenty years apart, they both represented personal achievements rooted in our determination to parent better than our parents did.

CHAPTER 14

POST-ACADEMICS AND WORKING A CAREER

We planned for our children to be successful but didn't know exactly what they would end up doing. Honestly, we thought our oldest son would end up being quasi-political in business, perhaps a subject-matter expert who was a lobbyist. He's an excellent communicator and very intelligent.

We secured a regular schedule for him to work in the state government as a volunteer page while he was in high school. He also worked for one of our House representatives at the state capitol and in his law office. Our young teenage son was accustomed to wearing a suit and tie to work, as he was interacting with House and Senate representatives and their staff, as well as other pages at the capitol, daily. He would also frequent the House floor when the representatives were in session. I (David) didn't know anything about these places; my school visited the capitol when the government was in session, but I was in grade school and it didn't mean much to me at that time. Our son seemed to like the idea and enjoyed working with our representative. It wouldn't surprise me if they've maintained their friendship all these years.

We did everything we could to expose him to the elected body of government and how political power flows in our state and country. We attended school with a boy who was now a police officer in our town, and through him, we were able to get our son a volunteer position at the police station. Apparently, they were quite surprised and happy with how well he could type at such a young age and were sad to see him leave. This was all before leaving home for college; we exposed our son to anything that had to do with "how things get done." If I had to look at how our oldest son's life has gone, I'd say it was a good thing to have him participate in these activities. He's comfortable rolling up his sleeves and doing dirty work, but equally comfortable in a suit and tie, speaking in front of rows of people. I secretly hope this book generates some public speaking engagements that he can attend with us, as we very much enjoy watching our children in their element.

Specific to each child, work to introduce them to the highest levels possible in their chosen area of interest. It will take research and a lot of phone calls if you are not already established in a specific discipline, but it is worth your effort. Our daughter worked with an assistant district attorney (ADA) and a partner of a law firm because she wanted to be a lawyer. Our youngest son accomplished the most before graduating high school, but he also had to face a major challenge his brother and sister had not faced in college. Regardless, he was able to achieve his goal of becoming a mechanical engineer. We supported our children in any way we could so that they could reach their goals. When it comes down to it, though, at this point in life, they are adults and are responsible for their decisions—all we parents can do is be there and provide emotional support, loan money for an electric bill or gas for the car, or just be a good listener.

IT'S TIME TO DO IT YOURSELF

The feeling I get when remembering our kids moving on after high school makes me think back to when they learned to ride a bicycle. "It's time to do it yourself." You give them a gentle push, and they're on their own. They wobble and sway, quit pedaling, and then remember to pedal, but momentarily quit steering. You're waiting to see if it clicks, or if they plop off the sidewalk into the grass. That's how this part of your child's life feels as a parent.

Did we do enough? Did we do well? Could we have done anything else? I hate to say it, but at this point, it doesn't matter; you either did the thing or you didn't. You can't redo it. Your child or children will show you if you did or not. Hopefully, it's not time to start cleaning out the basement. This is why, as you raised your children, you began giving them more and more freedom to make their own decisions. Now isn't the time to jump in and tell them everything that's wrong and take charge. They're doing exactly what you taught them to do in some way.

They're adults now, so work with them as peers. This is the only chance you get at additional lessons. When they come to you for help, they (hopefully) know they screwed up or at least, misjudged the situation. Respectfully bring attention to what they missed and the lesson learned, then move on. At this point, depending on the situation, we would loan our kids money. It wasn't that we cared about the money so much as them taking responsibility for their new adult lives. Banks and credit card companies can hurt them beyond their young understanding which we did not want. To us, we were protecting our kids.

When they were children at home, I didn't want money to get in the way of the bigger lessons, so we paid for anything that wasn't pure luxury. Sure, we paid for a lot of that, too, but if it was a big-ticket item, like a several-hundred-dollar game system when they already had a console, either they saved and paid for it, or we'd offer up a portion—at best, half—so that they could "feel" what it was like having a lot of money (to them) and instantly having little money. "Just how bad do you want that new console?" we'd ask. We secretly hoped something would come along right after the purchase that required money they no longer had, just to facilitate an understanding of what it means to spend money.

We tried to equip our children with adult experiences and nice things to unclutter the field as they moved to their new lives, a kind of "been there, done that" mentality. Unlike our humble beginnings, our children were able to experience nice things in moderation that gave them a realistic view of things to strive for in life.

What was a big deal, and what wasn't? What is worth your time and efforts, and what really isn't? Our children were able to go into the world confident of their place in it and confident of where they could go. Conversely, all Terri and I were ever told was that we weren't good enough. How many years did we lose trying to figure it out by ourselves? I'm telling you this now because we didn't have amazing experiences, but it seemed everyone else around us did.

We've said that we are writing the book we wished we would've had so many years ago, when we always felt "less than." I recall how Terri's mom, our biggest critic, began taking her other daughter on vacations; I specifically recall Disney World and a cruise to Alaska. She would come to our house and shower Terri with pictures of their adventures, as if to say, "You *could* have this, you know." Her sister was innocent and just excited to tell Terri the stories. It was obvious we were having a hard time. I think that's why my mother-in-law was so excited to share her stories . . . because it made Terri feel like shit. It was more of the same. Now that Terri has traveled to countless countries and more states than not, her mother isn't interested in hearing her stories. Terri will bring up yet another trip, and her mother will quickly change the topic. Our children started adult life having international travel stories and taking trips to other states. We tried to expose our children to an array of experiences hoping that no one could make them feel the way our extended family members worked so hard to make us feel. When your children are in this phase of their lives, they need to focus almost singularly on their education and careers and not be distracted by "shiny things." They need to understand that getting their careers in order will get them to the next place.

Respectfully keep up with your kids' lives. Be available. "Hey, we'd like to take you to dinner and catch up." Or, "What do you think about a trip? Can you fly and meet us in _____?" Or things that are gifts to encourage their relaxation. "Hey! We were shopping, and I saw Nutella and thought of you." Or, "I did some shopping. Can we drop off some groceries and have a coffee?" You know your children and are aware when they struggle. Be supportive and act as their biggest fan. For the child who is truly working their butt off to achieve their goal, recognize the need and give the help when they need it most without making them say it.

We've not spoken at all of Terri's dad or his sweet mother, Terri's grandma. Without these two, I'm not sure where we'd be. He was Blake's biggest fan, and I think Grandma was ours. Neither one was wealthy; Terri's dad was a judge in the juvenile justice system, working with the worst of the "bad kids" in the system. I recall him telling us about a boy who burned his parents to death in their bed while they slept. Grandma had grown up through the Great Depression. Grandma and Terri's dad were quiet and kind people, and these two seemed to know when our cupboards were empty. He would stop by our apartment each month and give Terri an envelope with money in it. When we were just starting out, I think he paid the rent on our first apartment for the first few months to help us get going. He would invite us out to dinner when we could not afford to eat out. Grandma would invite us to her house for a good home-cooked meal with an open invitation to come and eat any time—she just loved having visitors. Terri's dad tried to visit his mother every day, but I think he usually made it a few times a week as he lived completely across town from her.

Grandma would call Terri and ask if I could do some task for her, usually moving brush or mowing her lawn. Sometimes I think she looked for odd jobs for me to do, knowing I was too proud to accept a handout. We were poor, but we didn't want her money as a handout. Grandma would insist that she at least take us out to dinner. We would usually end up at Grandy's. Grandy's served everything that was chicken; fried chicken, chicken livers, and chicken fried steak.

Grandma had a bright-red clutch purse that looked like it was from the 1940s, and she'd ask little Blake, "Will you hold my million dollars, Blake?" Blake would gladly hang on to the purse while Grandma got into the car. I was aware of how far behind I was as a provider; they didn't have to point it out, and they knew nothing they could say could make me feel as bad as I did already. We needed to be encouraged. Grandma would say, "You two are gonna make it!" She would say it with sincerity and she said it every time she saw us. She would tell us that we were good parents and that we were good as a couple, and then she'd tell us stories of her life and living through the Great Depression.

It seemed impossible, but just like Grandma said, it all worked out just fine. I wondered at the time, but Grandma wasn't bullshitting us. What I came to realize was that Grandma was in the twilight of her life—she didn't have time for bullshit. She wasn't distracted by the noise of life. Grandma had a completely uncluttered view of what mattered and what didn't. What Grandma deemed as important, she saw in us. Sometimes I'd catch a look that said, "They'll make it, but they've got a long way to go."

Terri's dad was the same. I still miss that man. Terri's relationship with him wasn't great when I met her, but one time, our date plans conflicted with his "visitation" schedule. Terri said that she had a boyfriend and asked if he could go along, too. Her dad agreed. That was a really fun date. Terri just watched in shock as we talked and talked. We laughed and enjoyed an animated conversation that increasingly included Terri's participation. It didn't take long for Terri to get in on the fun, and from that day, she saw her dad in a completely different light, and their relationship was never the same again.

When we had been married for about three years, he got sick and never recovered. Terri was at his bedside every single day for six weeks. We took Grandma to the hospital; she was at his side the night he passed. The last thing he talked about with us was his grandson and us. To his mother, he said that he loved his daughters and her. We tried to fill his shoes after he passed and visited Grandma regularly. We knew that she wouldn't be far behind. Our two biggest supporters were going to be gone, but they gave us enough encouragement in those few years to last our lifetime.

This is my life's example and motivation for how to support your struggling children. Offer them love and sincere support. Your children will naturally wane in their belief that they can succeed. Sometimes we need to fill in with resources; sometimes we need to fill in with belief in them when they don't believe in themselves.

Terri and I were together when we had nothing. There was a lot more bad than good being directed at us, but the good made all the difference in the world. We had our moments of skidding out of control as a couple, but we always chose to stay together and get moving in the right direction again. It wasn't the easiest decision or the trouble-free option, but in our opinion, it was the best one.

Every destructive path we took and worked through made us stronger, but in no way am I saying to toughen up by making poor choices. I think if we could reveal our married souls, we'd be scarred and beaten, but we're a good match. Whether it's us you can see or our scarred souls, we belong together.

The next chapter is about a strong marriage, and we think this is one of the most important aspects of homeschooling. We know that homeschooling is hard, but why is it hard? What exactly is hard about it? We're talking about crayons and 1+1 here, right? We've had to talk about it a lot to nail down why we feel a certain way. We know it's based on our experiences, but time has a way of filtering individual events into a final idea or feeling. Writing this book has forced us to remember a lot of details we were more comfortable not remembering. Why is homeschooling hard? Because your marriage has to be on point, and when we started homeschooling, ours wasn't. You and your spouse need to function as one.

CHAPTER 15

A STRONG MARRIAGE

THE FOUNDATION A STRONG FAMILY IS BUILT UPON

STAYING MARRIED

What has our life together and marriage been like, and what is the dynamic like, now that we're more mature? First, what works for us may not be right for someone else. We can't say. Our experience is limited to a single marriage. Marriage blends the personalities, characteristics, wants, needs, desires, and dreams of two people. It is sacrifice and concession. Marriage is passion, desires, and goals. All of these things and countless more, shared.

Successful marriage exists in a sphere unto itself between two people. Within that place, no one else exists, not even your children. You and your spouse are yin and yang. Your differences are what make you, as a couple, unique and complete. Your strength is what you are together. You're stronger as a person because of your spouse. One is not over the other but each one compliments the other. To understand what a loving, lasting marriage is, read the short story "The Gift of the Magi" by O. Henry.[34] To me (David), it is a beautiful story of sacrifice and love.

---

34 - O. Henry, "The Gift of the Magi," U.S. Department of State American English, https://americanenglish. state.gov/files/ae/resource_files/1-the_gift_of_the_magi_0.pdf.

Our early years seemed like hell on Earth, and Terri agrees. In life, it can seem like everyone wants to chime in on your problems and offer hollow solutions just to hear themselves talk. Terri previously told a story about a young friend who instructed her on how to dress and talk to boys; this friend later told Terri that her life was being wasted, that Terri should leave me, share custody of our son, and party with her. She was insistent, but when Terri responded that she wasn't going to destroy her family to have random hookups, the friend disappeared. Today, she is still going it alone. To me, it seemed that she didn't actually want to be alone; she just didn't want to commit to anyone. Her choice, for sure, but was this a case of misery loves company? We'll likely never know.

Look at media personalities. If a couple stays together for more than ten years, it's celebrated, but you often hear about their divorce shortly after. The family and friends whispering or yelling in our ears about what Terri and I should do, often followed the same path as many of these divorced celebrity couples. Despite this, Terri and I have been together for almost forty years. It's not a competition, but forty years is a good amount of time to learn a few things along the way.

We have grown to cherish one another and any time we get to spend together. Our ultimate peace is when we are together, alone and quietly appreciating one another in each other's presence. I can't describe it any better than that. We're a team. We're partners. Depending on what we're doing, there's a word to describe us doing it together. If we're flying, we are copilots; if we're working, we are peers and coworkers; if we're writing a book, we are coauthors—you get the idea. We don't seek to spend time together as much as possible out of mistrust, jealousy, or fear; we want to hang out because we genuinely enjoy one another's company, because there's nowhere else we would rather be.

So, what's the point? Who cares how long you're with someone? Terri is a witness to my life; I'm a witness to hers. At the end of it all, will your existence even matter? Will anyone notice you're alive or miss you when you're dead? Aside from our youngest childhood years, Terri and I have an uninterrupted history together. We've been together and been married much longer than we were single. I get the distinct impression that in today's world, especially in Western culture, marriage is considered to be "overrated." Who cares if you stay with someone or not? Every time I hear people speaking about the negatives of marriage, what I hear is very distinctly selfish and self-centered. People increasingly treat marriage like the school system treats education. We're not willing to put the time in and do the work to succeed, so let's embrace failure, and anyone who succeeds is bad.

Marriage, at its very core, is selfless; it involves giving up oneself to create a partnership with the one person you wish to share your life with. This doesn't mean that what detractors of marriage say isn't true on some level, but it also doesn't mean that particular point of view is useful or healthy. How many articles can you find about the increasing loneliness people are experiencing in today's society? I've mentioned this regarding your children, but we are emphasizing that what you do in your marriage is also teaching your children. We've had times in our lives together when we could've divorced, and everyone would have supported us. That still doesn't make it right, it just makes it the popular choice.

One of our children believed that not divorcing was a financial decision for us. It's kind of shocking but makes me laugh. We never said that we were perfect—quite the contrary. Staying together is a choice, not for the sake of staying together, but to have a person in your life who's seen you at your best and at your worst—and vice versa. It's about traveling the journey that is your life with someone—that one special person who is your partner to enjoy all the good with, and to help shoulder the heavy loads.

I've been without money; I've had money. I've been a selfish asshole, and I've been gracious, loving, and caring. I've been absent; I've been attentive. Terri has seen the spectrum of where my personality and character can travel to, and she still chooses me. Likewise, I've seen the extremes of her personality and character. We choose each other every day. When I wake up and she's there, I know it's by choice. When she wakes up and I'm still there, she knows it's because I choose her.

Furthermore, before there were kids, there was us. Albeit not for very long, but we definitely had a great time together. Together, we made it through the ups and downs, successes and failures, celebrations and funerals. We never wonder if anyone will notice us in life. Will writing a book on homeschool make us famous authors? That's not the point, so we don't care—we have each other. Terri will celebrate with me, and she'll mourn with me. I will celebrate her successes and comfort her when she fails. The way you treat each other in your marriage will cast its light on how you treat and parent your children. Your children will learn what you teach them by example, and that is what they will be equipped with as adults in their own relationships in turn. If you truly work at it with a single-minded desire, almost as important as air itself, one day you will be in sync with your spouse. You will each wake up wanting the happiness of the other. Your life, your heartbeat, is for your spouse. To not be destructive, it needs to be a mutual effort.

How does that magic happen?

It took us more than ten years of marriage to begin to see it. We each slowly started to change. We began to focus on our life together gradually over time. We took part in accomplishing things in our life as a team. We didn't dictate to one another. Just like we are coauthors of this book, in life we are copartners in our endeavors. Do we agree on everything? No. Do we fight? Yes, but the way we fight now compared to years past is very different. We do our best to fight constructively. Do we go to bed angry? Sometimes. If you're striving for some fantasy, perfect relationship, it doesn't exist. If you look at the media or magazines and tabloids and think someone's life and relationship are perfect, they're not. If you have read our story and think that we have perfect lives, we don't. We have what we've worked for and look forward to the rest of our lives together, continually striving to make things better. The idea of perfection defeats the purpose of the relationship.

People ask us what in the world we still talk about after so many years. There's more every passing day. Marriage should be constant growth; we will grow together until we're gone from this Earth. Each year, we become better individuals and a better couple. What did we talk about when we were sixteen? School? It's not like someone has much to talk about at sixteen based on their life experience. Judging marriage falls into the same category as people judging homeschooling and saying your children won't learn to socialize. People assume that because we've been together for so long or that "we're so old," we have nothing left to talk about. If you're on the right track, you have more than ever to share together. We talk about everything—and I mean everything. If we can't share something without fear of rejection, then what are we doing here? We don't share for our spouse to judge. We share for our spouse to know us better. This is an advanced relationship that can take years, even decades to develop. At least in our case. What I do know is that my wife and I will not confide in anyone else over each other. If Terri wants or needs to share something with me, she will; that's our sphere of marriage. What she discusses with a close friend is her business. I don't want or need to know unless she wants to include me for reasons of her own, trust has to be watertight.

Years ago, I had a "friend's" wife call the house one day to tell Terri that I was cheating on her. They saw me at the bank with "another woman." Terri didn't freak out or accuse me of adultery; she simply asked me about it. I had to think back to the day and what in the world they could have seen—if they saw anything—because without a doubt, I wasn't cheating on her. "They saw me at the bank with my daughter," I said to Terri, who nodded knowingly. She remembered exactly what I was doing that day.

The wife who called was a stylist who had cut my hair in the past. After this incident, my thirteen-year-old daughter and I went by her shop to "see if I could get my hair cut." The shop was empty, yet the woman couldn't fit me in. I just smiled and told her, "By the way, this is my daughter; you may have seen us at the bank the other day . . ."

We never heard from that couple again. Your marriage has to be impenetrable, and that happens when you both work towards earning the other's trust and become worthy of that trust. If you betray it, you'll have to work very diligently to earn it back and may never recover all of it.

Through hard work and a singular desire, you'll have something few couples achieve. Do we agree on everything? No. Thank goodness we have differences. It's how we challenge each other. I admire and respect my wife's unique perspective on life. I'd be lost at sea without her and her viewpoint. I think she would say something similar, but you'd have to ask her. We don't keep score.

I think many people believe that their spouse has to agree with them on everything to truly love or accept them, but you don't have to wonder why people like this have relationships that fail or are less than happy. That know-it-all attitude defeats the purpose of marriage—either learn to be a part of a married team or go be alone and have a life that allows you to make every single decision yourself. Although we have known people in arranged marriages, it's a rare exception. No one is forcing you to endure another person. We often try to fit each other into our own neat little box. We want them to act or perform a certain way in order to be acceptable, to be loved. Does this come from what we were taught in school? To be accepted, everyone needs to walk in lockstep and agree on everything to conform and be worthy?

I feel like this entire book comes back to relationships. How are we supposed to boil down decades of lessons about children and marriage into a few hundred pages? Are you content? Is your spouse content? What about your children? If I really think about it, this is the main feature of a relationship. I think few people are content. You know, that feeling when you walk into your clean and quiet house, there's beautiful weather outside, and there is absolutely nothing that you need to do. Your world is momentarily at peace. That's the feeling I'm talking about.

Now add life back into this. Add your spouse into the kitchen, add your kitty standing by her bowl, add your child napping in the bedroom. Can you do this and still keep that content feeling? Add the dog barking out back and the possibility that it's going to wake the little one. We can keep doing this exercise, but you get the point. You imagine the last time you were content, at peace, and then start adding your life into it. Does your child stress you out because you know that every time they wake up, they're going to scream until you appear? Are you never able to relax in the moment because you're always waiting for that scream in the future? When an addition affects your "contentment," that's something to work on.

SPOUSE FIRST

Early in our marriage, I (Terri) was that person who was tired, dumpy, and angry at home, but when I would go to church, I would style my hair, put on makeup, and dress nicely. I would smile and give all my kindness and energy to strangers in the name of "ministry." By putting other people first, I was telling my family they were no good; they were less important than everybody else. And I was saying this to them "in the name of God," which turned them away from God. While I regret this now, then, I didn't see it at all. I just thought I was being a "good Christian." One day, my husband pointed out this disparity to me and asked me why I was dressing up only when I went to church. "Are you having an affair?" he asked. No, I wasn't having an affair (nor was I looking to have one), but I realized he was right—I was not giving my best self to him or our children. I would like to say I quickly changed, but I didn't. I got angry and was stubborn. It took a lot longer than it should have for me to choose my family over approval of others.

When you cherish your spouse and your children and you put all your energy into them, they will return that back to you. As you breathe life into them, they will in turn breathe life into you. I stole life from them, and they turned away from me. There was no joy at home, so I looked for it elsewhere, at church and in the presence of the people there. Even though I was not having an extramarital affair with another man, I was, for all practical purposes, having an affair with the church and the people I held in higher regard than my family.

The problem with this church—and many others—is that a good majority of the people there were doing the same thing with their families, and we all encouraged one another in this practice—that is not good. No one there encouraged me to put my family first. In fact, they were more gossip oriented and fed on any bad reports I had to offer in the form of "prayer requests." We all did it; it was like a bunch of cackling hens looking down their noses at us, at each other. It reminds me of those nasty little girls in grade school I told you about in Chapter 2. These women did not care. None of them ever reached out to be encouraging or helpful; they just clicked their tongues and said they would "pray for us." I fed their appetites for a long time and felt sorry for myself, which bred discontentment at home.

I grew increasingly unkind at home, but I never confessed to these women about how I acted at home. I never asked for prayer for myself—it was all directed at my family; they were the problem, not me. I had become a martyr. Once David confronted me, slowly, over time, I started realizing he was right. As much as I didn't want to admit it, I was destroying my own family with my words and actions. I finally decided that in order for me to truly refocus my attention on my marriage and family, I had to get away from these women; I had to leave this church. I am not advocating abandoning church or your specific religious ministry; I am just saying that for me, this was the step that I needed to take to get my priorities straight and my focus back on my family. When you see that something is not right, you must do whatever it takes to make it right for the sake of your marriage, your children, and your homeschool.

For me, it was primarily church, but it can be anything that we give more importance to that steals excessive time and life from us and them. Literally, anything can take our attention away from our spouse and children—work, church, friends, extended family, television, social media, the phone, school activities, even homeschooling. Church can (and should) be a place where you and your whole family can safely connect with like-minded people who encourage you in your marriage and with your children, and who are there to help with kindness and support when the need arises. There are churches like this out there, so if you find yourself in a church or any other group that is not life-giving, leave. Just leave. The same is true with friends; if you find yourself being drained of life by a "friend," just cut the ties immediately and move on.

Find people who will mentor you, who are the kind of people and spouses and parents you would like to emulate, people whom you admire. These are people who have a good relationship and mutual respect for each other, and whose older or grown children exhibit traits that you would like to see in your children; people who are successful and well-adjusted in their own lives, especially with their families; people who will walk alongside you, partner with you, encourage you, be honest and hold you accountable with kindness and love, and challenge you to become a better version of yourself, always looking for the success of your marriage and family. These are the kind of people who breathe life into you, your marriage, your family. No matter what group you choose to be involved with, these are the kind of people you should surround yourselves with outside of the home.

Homeschool is certainly not a cure-all, but it can be a great tool to pour life into your kids and connect with them for a lifetime. As you are teaching, it can be a vehicle used to focus on practicing thankfulness, joy, kindness, and encouragement. You can use it to smile, laugh and have fun, all while training and mentoring them; or it can become a weapon of anger, disgust, and contempt that teaches your children that they are not good enough and cannot succeed in life, so they won't. Or they will turn away and run from you to a place and people who will give them the encouragement and support they are looking for.

What kind of tool will your homeschool be? How will you use it? To build up and strengthen your family or to tear down and weaken your marriage and your children for the rest of their lives?

CHAPTER 16

BLENDED-FAMILY DYNAMICS

We are faced with choices every day, so is life. Some choices are on the relatively easy level of the clothes to wear or what to eat, while other choices are not so simple. This is your ultimate goal as parents: raising your children, teaching them how to distinguish what only matters a little, and understanding the implications for their lives when it matters a lot.

Toward the end of the seventh grade, I (David) met a girl on a church trip. We were both thirteen years old. She was from the rival school next to the town I lived in. She was a kind and cute girl. We liked talking and just hanging out. I think each of us felt like an afterthought, with each of our parents and families giving their attention to seemingly more important matters and so we quickly became inseparable.

The girl's mother was a cook at my school; she knew me as one of the popular students. The girl and I could easily pass notes to one another almost daily through her mother, and we also spent a lot of time on the phone after school each day. Soon, I would visit her house regularly, and she would visit mine. Our parents met each other, became friends, and would spend time playing cards as she and I spent time together visiting or playing the video games we each had. We were allowed, even encouraged, to spend time alone together. Not that we had to be told to, but we were accommodated in our desire to be together, often by ourselves, at her house or mine.

Her mom would occasionally give me the keys to her luxury car and let us drive to the store alone. Keep in mind my age—I was still only thirteen or fourteen years old. Suddenly, instead of being treated like a nuisance at home, I was being treated with respect, like an adult. We were adults. Everything was new to both of us, and it was only a matter of time before teen hormones would give way to opportunity. Less than two years into our relationship, she took a pregnancy test; it was positive. In total, we had dated off and on for about two years. Because of the pregnancy, I spent my freshman year of high school being less popular. I say that with heavy sarcasm—I was pretty popular before and was now a complete outcast. I no longer had sports and always looked over my shoulder for someone to follow through on the death threats I received on a regular basis, and I'm not exaggerating.

I knew her life was devastated. She and I were okay with one another, I think, but everyone else in our lives made sure to pass judgment, give their opinions, and gossip. Everything grew out of control very quickly. The situation caused so much stress that I started getting physically sick. Life was chaotic and no one was supportive or helpful.

She had always been a "good girl," but now she was "one of those girls." A lot of kids in school had sex, but she had to walk around as a freshman in high school, pregnant. She lost her friends, her school, and her respect in the church. She was pitied, and I was blamed. Our parents severed all ties between the two families and prohibited either of us from contacting the other. She eventually gave birth to a baby girl. I did everything I could think of to make contact with her, but both our families kept that from happening.

The last time I saw this girl's dad (I had successfully managed to get to her house to visit her and our daughter), he said he would shoot and kill me if he ever saw me again, and I believed him. Needless to say, I didn't get to see them. I understood it then and still understand it now. Everyone was stressed; everyone had a lot of secrets—everyone. It kills any of us to see our baby girls hurting.

Just imagine the DMZ between North and South Korea and the constant threat of war. That is what our lives felt like. My parents went as far as sending me out of state to stay with extended family when she gave birth, and ultimately, my dad and I moved across the state, one hundred miles away. The girl and I both knew we weren't really compatible beyond being two good-looking kids with raging hormones. The way we each viewed what adult life should be was just too different.

She never wanted to leave the town she grew up in; she was happy there. I couldn't get out and away quickly enough. Surely there was life beyond cowboy boots, rednecks, and four-by-fours, and my feelings weren't negated just because there was now a child involved. Even though I was able to see my daughter a few times throughout her childhood, for the most part, I would be blocked from having contact with her for years to come, while also being blamed for not being a part of her life. I mended the relationship with her mother's dad, though. He was someone I could sit and talk to for hours. As youngsters, we were probably a lot alike, and I'll always have nothing but respect for that man.

Worse than any pain the girl or I endured, I'm certain our daughter bears more than everyone combined, and there's nothing I can do to change that. I'll be aware of that fact as long as I live.

I HAVE A DAUGHTER

Terri always knew I had a daughter. I told her everything when it seemed that we might last longer as a couple than just a fun summer. I was now the weird outcast teenager at school, a popular has-been who swore off sex. Terri and I were great companions early on. We went to movies and out to eat at real restaurants; we went to theme parks and the city parks and the lake. We went swimming and hung out with our very few friends, but otherwise, it was just us.

Terri was the first person who didn't look at me the way everyone else did. Terri saw me for me. I could breathe for the first time in my life, it seemed. Would my daughter ever be a part of our lives? Terri never blinked. Even before Terri was a mother herself, she recognized that a precious little life could be a part of our lives, and she was welcome to it.

For all of our years apart, I was prepared for my daughter to knock on our door. Our children always knew they had a sister. That was part of being ready—no surprises for anyone.

The traumatic experience of being a teen father (but not a dad) to my little girl prepared me for many of the hard things I've faced in life. If I could endure having a child and being cut off from her, maybe I could endure just about anything. My first daughter grew up in challenging conditions that I had no control over. She experienced many of the same things I did as a child. Some worse. The difference between her life as a child and the life that Terri and I provided our children was night and day.

TIME TO MOVE ON

Terri and I as a couple were on solid ground. Our kids were getting older, and life was changing. I only had one thing still tying me to the past, unresolved. My daughter. My family could see it in my face over the years, aging me. I hadn't heard from her in almost fifteen years, so I finally told Terri that if it wasn't resolved by my daughter's next birthday, I would cut all ties with her for us, for our family. It was almost time to turn off the light and put that one to rest, so to speak.

Just over six months prior to that cutoff birthday, Terri walked into the room and looked at me. It was one of *those* looks that husbands never want to see. I let out a long breath. "What?" Terri paused and assembled the words in her mind before speaking.

"Your daughter messaged me. She understands if we say no, but she would like to know if she can at least talk to you and ask some questions." I looked at Terri through the absolute silence of the air.

"I can't say no, but I'll defer to you. You have to decide if you're ready for this, or you're not—it's okay if you're not." Terri slowly shook her head in thought. She was thinking of how she felt; she was considering my feelings; she was thinking of our own kids; she was thinking about our comfortable, stress-free marriage and a hundred other things. I could see her coming to a conclusion. "Don't say yes unless you really mean it. We can't turn back."

Terri nodded. "I'm good. If you think you're ready, I'm okay." I looked at her, shaking my head. "Okay—I don't know if I'm ready or not, but here we go." We were about to experience blended-family dynamics.

RESTORING FAMILY CONNECTIONS

My oldest daughter fled from her grandparents' home at the age of seventeen and married right away. Thankfully, she wasn't pregnant. It would take several more years after leaving home for her to find out (for the better) that the reputation she had been told about me and the actual man I was were two different people.

When my daughter came back into our lives, I couldn't comprehend the place that my wife was in. Terri was gracious and welcoming. I know she concealed her fears for my benefit. I took that as a cue to make sure our communication was on point and to reassure her. I would also use my actions to reassure her, choosing time with her over time with others. This would be a huge test for our whole family.

Jessica came to me early on, her eyes full of tears, her face red, and her hands shaking as she managed her anger fueled by fear. Our children had their place, their "earned" place, in our family. My older daughter, to them, was now an "outsider." "She didn't earn anything!" she yelled and cried. "She hasn't been here! I've been here the whole time!" Her fear broke my heart. I hugged Jessica. "This changes nothing, sweetheart. You and I are, and will always be, you and I." I told her that we all had our place in the family. That our family had always had a place for her older sister. That the relationship we'd always had would never change, and it didn't.

For my long-lost daughter, what did her "place in our family" really mean? We lost so many years; how much attention could I provide to her for her benefit and for a meaningful relationship? Could our relationship begin to heal the wounds that she'd had for so many years? Our children didn't know what it was like to not have a dad. All I expected was their understanding, in that I knew that they would respect this place in my life. I wouldn't place any expectations or demands on our children. Remember our sphere of marriage? The relationship between Terri and me absolutely had to come first. We had to confront this change in our family together and united as one.

We had to be brutally honest with one another, and we had to receive each other's truths with compassion and understanding. Terri and I knew the process had to begin with knowing that we each had our place with one another. We had to reassure our children by our actions that they still had, and would *always* have their place. Their importance to us and our love for and loyalty to them would not change. My daughter needed to know that she, as well, had her place in our family, with no caveats or exceptions. Her chair had always been at the table.

INSTANT GRANDCHILDREN

We also met my daughter's husband, and it turns out that we had three grandchildren, the youngest being two years old. We skipped the "Hey, Mom and Dad, we're pregnant," phase and went straight to three young grandchildren. As you've probably realized while reading this book, our family dynamic can be intense. We are focused, determined, and very set in the way we do "our family." To my oldest daughter and her family, we were different from anyone they knew. It didn't help, either, that her husband knew of me by my reputation and nothing else.

Our standard of how children are expected to behave was different from how they did family and kids. Not good or bad, just different, and we had to adjust. As parents, we needed to understand and respect their family. It wasn't just us adapting and making a place for my daughter in our family; we had to know our place in their family for there to be a relationship. They needed to decide if they wanted us in their family and make a place for us if they did. It wasn't easy for anyone. In the beginning, there was a bond between my daughter and me. She didn't know me well, but she did know me, and in her heart, she knew I was her dad.

Everyone else was along for an awkward ride, and I felt terrible about that. My wife and our three kids stood by me. They couldn't understand my perspective but were nonetheless there for me, always. They made themselves available for their half-sister to visit and ask questions.

I imagined my daughter asking her half-siblings questions to shed light on the bad reputation she had been told about me compared to the actual me. It makes me laugh to wonder if our kids would tell her that I was pretty cool but then warn her, "Don't piss him off." None of them ever told me what they talked about, and I'm glad. Those private conversations belong to them and are part of their unique relationship.

In this book, we've talked about the kind of relationships you should strive to build with your children; those relationships are based on the foundation of the relationship you have with your spouse. The outcome of every other major event in your lives as a couple and as a family will be determined by the health of your familial relationships. We, as individuals, make choices that complicate life, but I can't say that I made a mistake with my girlfriend so many decades back—not when we have a beautiful, successful daughter and new family that we've added to our family.

Considering homeschool and family, marriages or relationships do end for any number of reasons, from death to divorce; we carry on because we desire to live and hope for happiness tomorrow and every day after. There are endless combinations of struggles in life, created either by our own decisions or the decisions of those we love. The blended family, in my opinion, presents a significant challenge, at best, for homeschooling. In imagining a family that combines our children from our younger years with kids such as our grandchildren, it's two different groups of kids. There's no good or bad, but there is a lot of "different." I think about a scenario that involves a blended family with older children and stepparents. Kids thrive on routine, so who changes their routine? Whose normal life is sacrificed, and whose isn't? These are things you must determine constructively and continually work through. It's not impossible, but it seems the line between constructive and destructive is a thin one. This family must be on point with their commitment and devotion to one another's emotional health and success.

If I have learned anything in life, it's that if we want something bad enough, there is a way, a path to make it happen. An aspect of what we call sacrifice, is that the idea you see as perfect may not be shared by your spouse or children. This is where you should determine the "spirit" of your intent, consider and respect your significant other's point of view, and determine what serves the overall goal, positively and constructively. Sometimes we just need to sacrifice and let things go, because being healthy and happy is often better than being right. A decision that relies on aspects of each spouse is ultimately better than surrendering to the demands of one.

DON'T FORCE IT. MAKE ROOM FOR EACH PERSON. ALLOW TIME.

You can't force it; you can't expedite it. Like I said earlier about the kids at my Christian school versus those at my public school, you can make kids say anything you want and act any way you choose, but that doesn't mean that it's good, healthy, or sincere for anyone.

Does everyone else exist to make you feel like you're getting what you see as right? Does making your child or children think they're getting their way all the time serve their best interest in becoming a good adult? If there's bad blood because of a situation, we, as parents, try to fix the situation. To be bluntly honest, if your kid is being an asshole, then address manners and etiquette. Let's say Mom has an older son, and there's no common ground between him and the stepdad. In this scenario, both of them learning to be respectful to one another may be the best you'll achieve, and there's nothing wrong with that. Mom and Stepdad's connection is likely based on attraction and sex, if we're being honest, but your child has no reason to have a connection to this man. This man wasn't there in those bonding early years. In these types of situations, if they want to pursue a relationship with each other, that's up to them. If our children had not been able to accept their new sister, that would have had no bearing on the fact that I'm Dad. We, as parents, aren't here to create Norman Rockwell moments. We're here to nurture our children into their best selves, and maybe the best selves of our children just don't like each other.

During the holidays, my parents' house would be full of family, around twenty to thirty people. We hadn't seen each other in at least a year. Before dinner, my mom would adopt this almost childish smile and meekly, softly tell everyone to hold hands and say what they were thankful for. She wanted everyone to say how passionately thankful they were to be right here, right now with family.

Trust me, it was very cringey. You could see the same look cross everyone's faces—the electric turkey knife couldn't have cut the tension in the air. All of this family thankfulness just didn't exist. We weren't socially close; we were just a bunch of different families who only saw each other occasionally. We enjoyed seeing certain people and would catch up, and that was that. It was a family social until next year or whenever; everyone has a busy life. I imagine my mom saw us as some Norman Rockwell painting full of cheer and love in a cherished moment. But on the other 364 days in the year, my mom never worked to foster that closeness—she just expected it to appear because she wanted it.

We, as parents, have to teach our children the value of closeness and family. Contrary to what my mom would do, I might offer a toast and tell my family how grateful I am that they are there with me. This isn't something I've done much, however, because it gives me flashbacks to those awkward family kumbaya moments led by my mom. I do thank our children specifically for taking the time out of their lives to be with us and let them know how much we appreciate it and enjoy seeing them. I never ask them to tell me how they feel because if they want to, they will. My hope is that when they are in my shoes, someone will make a toast, and everyone else will want to jump in and convey how truly thankful they are to be there with their family. "Hear, hear!"

CHAPTER 17

STUFF HAPPENS

"*Woman, 21, Killed in Palm Bay Motorcycle Crash*"
Literally hours after police stood at our front door and told Terri our daughter was dead, this headline appeared in our morning newspaper. The story reported, "Jessica Nicole Batts, 21, of Melbourne was killed when a car turned into her Honda motorcycle's path . . ."

This would be our biggest test yet, as a couple and as a family. We all know or have heard of someone who has lost a child, and before losing Jessica, speaking for myself (David), I would think, "That's sad. I can't imagine."

I was traveling for work when I was woken up by a call from Joshua. "Daddy . . . Jessica is dead." I needed to get home, but the TSA agent in Atlanta took a certain amount of pride in telling me that I looked shifty and needed to have an interview with another officer. I picked up my bag and went to the expectant officer, who dismissively waved me to her station. "Where have you been, sir?" I handed her my passport, open to the page of where I'd left that morning.

"My daughter was killed in Florida less than twenty-four hours ago. How am I supposed to act for you guys to let me get home to my wife?" I showed her the news article on my phone. "That's my daughter." The woman teared up. The asshole who sent me there was mean-mugging me at a distance. She shook her head at him. I thanked her for her sympathy and said quietly, "That guy is an asshole." She nodded, and I passed through. It took everything for me just to hold myself together emotionally. It took me twenty hours to get home.

How right I was to say I couldn't imagine losing a child. It's a loss that can't be related to anything else life has to offer. We all have dead people; parents, grandparents, aunts, uncles, or maybe even cousins . . . but you're not designed to be their protector. You are designed to protect your children and their passing destroys a part of who you are as a human being. Each person in our family has a unique place, and to remove one leaves an unrepairable void for everyone. Our sons not only lost their sister, but they watched their parents emotionally crumble and seemingly grow old overnight, and they couldn't do anything to stop or fix it.

For the first time in my life, I thought, *I wouldn't wish this on my worst enemy.* For once, I couldn't describe my feelings—there were no words. The closest I can manage is the image of drowning, being held underwater with the surface in sight, but just out of reach. All you can do is scream underwater until you're suffocating and out of breath. That is the moment in which I was mentally suspended: suffocation. I could look around and see my wife and sons suffocating with me, and I couldn't do anything about it. I couldn't save my daughter, and I couldn't help my family. *I can't do this!* I thought. So, I got into my car and drove to the place where she was killed. By myself in the car, I screamed until I tasted blood from my throat. Somehow, I had to be strong for my family.

YOU WILL MISS THAT SOMEDAY

Terri: "Jessica, do you have my eyeliner?"

Jessica: "Yes, Mama."

Terri: "I don't mind if you use it, but would you put it back when you're finished, please?"

Jessica: "Yes, Mama."

Jessica and I (Terri) repeated this conversation every day. Sometimes there would be other items she had borrowed, my good sewing scissors, the tape, or our good Nikon digital camera. She never misused or damaged the items, but they usually didn't find their way back to their spot, either. I found myself getting irritated the longer this went on. When I felt irritated, a nagging voice in my head would say, *Someday you will wish she was still borrowing your eyeliner because she won't be with you anymore.* I dismissed the thought, *Yah, yah, I know. She is going to go off to college someday and have a life of her own and I will miss her, but right now, this is starting to get on my nerves.* I didn't know what else to do. I really didn't want it to become a point of contention or confrontation between us, so I did nothing—I just let it ride and repeated the conversation almost daily.

Recently, I have had conversations with different parents who complain about their children talking too much, seemingly nonstop. Just as our daily eyeliner ritual seemed quite the nuisance, Jessica used to talk nonstop. She would come home from work and start talking and talking and talking, telling me all about her day. I would sit and listen to her for about an hour until she had gotten everything out. These memories are something I treasure, something I miss with all my heart and wish I could have with her again.

Sometimes amid the constant daily grind, the seemingly endless barrage of tasks, appointments, and obligations that consume our lives, we lose sight of the truly important and precious moments with our children. What may seem like a bother or an interruption to us is actually opportunity after opportunity to make connections with our children, to learn about them as unique individuals. Take the chance to guide them, in the context of right where they are, at any given moment, to actually have conversations with them. This is your child inviting you into their world, into their unique mindset, and into their hearts. They are revealing the things that interest them and what they are thinking about, learning, and struggling with. They want to draw close to you and have you draw close to them, to know and see them apart from yourself and their siblings. To listen and to hear them. As a parent, these priceless moments when our children invite us into their thought processes are the greatest opportunities we will ever have to form and strengthen our bond with them. This is the time that can set up a great connection with them for the rest of their lives. Or, if we squander this time and let other things intrude upon us and steal away that time with them, we will find out (most likely when it is too late) that we no longer have these opportunities. When they don't find a safe and nurturing relationship with us, their parents, they look to others who will provide what they are looking for.

We sincerely hope that no one reading our book ever has to go through what we have gone through. Nothing could have prepared us for Jessica's death. It is absolutely not a good thing to dwell on the possibility of death or negative happenings at all, so do not try to prepare for that.. Keeping your focus on what might happen is a waste of precious time and energy. We all know that "bad" stuff does happen; it is part of life. We cannot foresee or possibly prepare for all life's challenges. But we can build up our marriage, our family, and each individual child so that when challenges arise, we meet them head-on, without fear and over-come them—together. When we learn to work together as a team, we gain strength individually and as a whole.

If you do focus on the negative and are judgmental; if you are con-stantly ignoring your child; if you are continuously telling them not now, to go away, or to stop talking; if you choose not to take advantage of when they are openly communicating with you, then do not be surprised when they stop talking to you. Do not be surprised when they do not include you and do not share with you; when they are distant and withdrawn or even angry, resentful, and combative toward you. Do not be surprised if they fall in with the wrong crowd, leading them down a destructive path. Do not be surprised if they leave and never look back, or if they simply do not share their lives or family with you, including your grandchildren.

We have seen this happen in a lot of homeschool families—just because you homeschool does not make you immune to hard times. It does not inoculate you from having rough family issues. Instead, use this time together to love and cherish your spouse and children in every moment possible.

As homeschool parents, we have so many more opportunities to create connections with our children than those parents who send their children away for six to eight hours a day, five days a week. This is a gift that we choose, and to waste that gift would be a travesty. Make a point to connect with your children. Let each of your children know he or she is the most special, your favorite, wanted, and needed. Cause them to feel seen and to feel heard. When you do this, you will create a beautiful bond with each of them and many wonderful memories that you both will trea-sure. You will never regret spending quality time with your children, but you will regret squandering your time worrying about negative things that may never happen. This becomes especially poignant when something bad does happen, and you realize you can never get that time back. On the contrary, homeschoolers learn to meet each challenge when it happens, not before.

I (Terri) look back with such sadness and regret. I missed so many openings to connect with our children, especially Jessica. I was too busy, too selfish, too lazy. I did not cherish and love them enough to put them at the top of my priorities. Jessica would ask me to walk on the beach with her late at night and she would ask me to take her to church—I would not for whatever I deemed a good reason at the time. She would invite me out to dinner, but I would procrastinate or get distracted and not complete my transcriptions early enough, like I had when they were younger. When she would get home from work, I would still be typing and unable to go out to eat with her. Every time I squandered precious moments with her, I was telling her that she was not important to me. Each time I did this to our children, I let them know that everything else was held in higher regard than them. I wish now that I would have made the time to be with her every single time she asked. My heart continues to break, and tears are running down my cheeks as I write this—she *wanted* to spend time with me.

Please learn from my mistakes. Your children want to spend time with you, too. I am paying the ultimate price—Jessica is gone, and I cannot change anything with her. I live with the regret of missed opportunities every day. Her death has brought this clearly into focus for me, something I missed while she was alive. Do you want to have a healthy, enjoyable relationship with each of your children throughout the time they are living with you and into adulthood? Do you want to be included in their lives after they leave your home? Do you want them to want to be with you while they are at home and seek to be with you later in life? Then connect with them now. Take advantage of every opportunity and make time to be with them. Listen to them and include them in your life every day. You will never regret making time for your children. You will be so happy to have earned their genuine respect, trust, love, admiration, and friendship as adults.

If you find that you have followed in my footsteps even a little bit, it is never too late to start changing. Change something—anything—and keep changing. Keep working and making it right with each of your children and never give up. We continue to work on this with our children because we never want to stop trying to work toward better relationships with them. They are great people. We truly enjoy visiting with them and being around them, and are blessed that they want to spend time with us. You should strive for this outcome and be better on every day of your children's lives.

HOW DID WE HANDLE THE NEWS OF JESSICA'S DEATH?

I (Terri) was drowning, but not underwater; suffocating, but still breathing. Your mind cannot process what you have been told. "Your daughter has been killed in a motor vehicle accident." What does that even mean? The first reaction is simply denial. "No, that cannot be." But they had proof. A picture of her driver's license. Her helmet. Her favorite hoodie. Her blood-soaked bra. Each thing was uniquely Jessica's. I knew it. There was no mistake. It was our baby girl. My first question that morning was to God. *Do you have her? Is she with you in heaven?*

It is my daily practice to read the "Bible in a Year." So, I sat down to read the readings for that day. The scripture for that day read: "And I am convinced that nothing can ever separate us from God's love. Neither death nor life, neither angels nor demons, nor our fears for today nor our worries about tomorrow—not even the powers of hell can separate us from God's love. No power in the sky above or in the earth below—indeed, nothing in all creation will ever be able to separate us from the love of God that is revealed in Christ Jesus our Lord" (Romans 8:38–39). I knew in my heart this was God's answer. She was with him in heaven. I knew that she was safe. I knew that she was no longer in pain. That she no longer had to deal with the worries of this world. She was at peace.

It took a while for reality to set in, but I knew that I could not avoid walking this path set before me. It was forced upon me against my will. There was nothing I could do that could change what happened; she was gone, and we were left behind to learn how to live our lives without her.

All I knew was that I could not see the blue sky anymore. All joy had been completely snuffed out of existence and there was only pain, sorrow, grief—never-ending grief. I willingly walked down the long tunnel of despair; I wanted to sink into the dark void and never resurface.

David was working overseas, so Josh and I had to call him to tell him his baby girl was dead. With the police still there and me sobbing, Josh placed the video call. "Daddy, Jessica is dead." David was halfway around the world and in shock, numb. His coworkers took over immediately and booked flights to get him home as quickly as humanly possible. Blake and David's older daughter, Cherity, were flying in as well, and by no effort of our own, the three of them ended up on the same flight to our home from Atlanta. Within twenty-four hours of our phone call, we were all together to grieve and mourn our loss as a family.

It would be accurate to say that each of us wished it would have been us who died instead of Jessica. I (David) don't think we've ever talked about it conversationally, but I've thought about it and said it. The world is darker without her in it.

Perhaps the family of my childhood and so many other people were right: the world would be even better *without* me in it. I wonder if that's a cop-out, wishing for my own death. For me, it's saying I'd rather die than live through this, but the result would be the same for the rest of the family. Jessica would have been just as devastated to lose any of us.

I had to climb out of the abyss I was in because I had a family that needed me. I had to circle the wagons and protect what was left of us. I've been fierce on poisonous family and friends a lot in this book because it has been such a big factor in our lives. It's one of those things that feels like you can never properly convey enough for someone else to understand, but you want people to understand because of how destructive it can be.

Looking out over the landscape of our lives and thinking that I seriously wouldn't wish the death of a child on my worst enemy, I was shocked at how some people responded to us. What causes people to act in such an ugly and inconsiderate way toward others? There are some people you expect it from and are prepared for, but others are truly a surprise. When we went to Jessica's employer to gather her things, a bitter old coworker actually caught Terri and said, "I told Jessica she was going to get killed riding that motorcycle!" as though she was proud to be vindicated. We still hadn't buried our daughter. The boss, an attorney, was shocked and apologized profusely.

How do you handle this? This goes back to our family and homeschool. We allocated only what was necessary to keep functioning after Jessica's death, and the rest of our energy (myself and our son's) went to rallying around Terri. She had just lost her baby girl.

To Jessica's dismay as an adult, she and her mom were often mistaken for sisters because Terri retained her youthfulness. They were buddies, friends, a happy mom and adult daughter who liked to be girly girls together. They borrowed each other's clothes and would go out for coffee and shop at the mall.

Terri lost the most important female in her life. Her daughter was taken from her before they were done. You realize how many things weren't said, how many plans would now simply pass on the calendar. She would never see her daughter's wedding or hold her newborn children. Our grief had to take a back seat to Terri's, and we didn't know if that would even be enough to keep her from falling into a pit of despair.

Cherity, my (David) older daughter, had reentered our lives a little over a year before Jessica passed. She loved and admired Jessica. She told me once that she felt like Jessica's *little* sister. My older daughter never had a place that was distinctively hers in a family, I think, until our family. To this day, Cherity will sometimes look at me with tears in her eyes and say that she feels responsible, that she misses her sister. Of course she wasn't responsible. Jessica was killed by a person who chose to run a red light, but she felt like somehow her presence had something to do with Jessica's passing—like she was a bad omen. Her existence has always been surrounded with scandal, anger, and hate. For everything I missed over the years, if I could only give her one thing besides the love of a dad, it would be for her to realize that it wasn't her fault. Not when she was born into this world or when her sister, Jessica, left it. From her childhood all the way to Jessica's death, none of it was her fault. It was obvious to her that Jessica and I were close, but that's what her specific attention was noticing; our whole family is that close.

It has taken years to develop, but now my older daughter has a distinct place within our family that is uniquely hers. We're proudly Stepmom and Dad, Grandma and Grandpa, and we cherish that she and her family are finally in our lives and a part of our family.

As a parent, we must be watchful and sensitive to our spouse and children and be there for their good. Our personal needs, wants, and desires should often come after theirs if at all possible, when "stuff happens." We must be strong for our children; when we can't manage that, that's when we get help. Hopefully, your spouse is the first stop, and then together, you can get professional help. I'm not saying spouses have to be the full support or that couples must attend professional help together, but do your best to make it happen as a couple. Be engaged. Terri has had things happen with family or friends that really upset her, and I just couldn't understand how it made her feel. It doesn't make me a bad person; I just wasn't equipped to provide the reasoning and emotional support she needed, but I could still be there, present with her.

Likewise, she can recognize when I'm dealing with something and she's not equipped to help me work through it. We support one another by positively supporting getting constructive help, because that emotional support isn't and should not be your minor or adult children.

WHAT DID YOU TALK ABOUT?

As a teenager, my mom demanded that I (David) see a psychiatrist to "get my thinking right." I agreed to go; there weren't any negative connotations in my mind about telling someone what was bothering me, so long as it wasn't any family members. From the beginning, the doctor reassured me that anything and everything I said would stay in that room.

I told him many of the things about my childhood you've read in this book. One day, I showed up at his office with a cut on my face. Teenage boys get cuts and scrapes. The doctor casually asked what happened. I asked him again if everything I said was truly confined to the office, and he reassured me that it was.

In the car, my mom (and later, back at home, my mom and dad) demanded to know everything I'd told the doctor. I reminded them that sharing kind of defeated the purpose of going to see someone who was sworn to keep my secrets. When I refused to tell them, my mom reached out to grab a handful of my hair, and her fingernail cut my face next to my eye. I told the doctor that I ended up telling my parents the main things I'd shared with him.

My mom tried to call the doctor and tell him that I was "overblowing" minor incidents. The doctor told her that he felt compelled to contact child services, but he took a pause because I'd asked specifically if what we discussed stayed in the office. He did not want to betray me, and the doctor refused to see me if they were going to force me to share everything we discussed. After my mom's call to the doctor, I never returned to see him. My parents weren't going to help me, and they essentially forbid me from seeking help with anyone else as well. Just to point out the obvious: I would get in trouble for *not* going to see a doctor because my mom wanted me to for some reason, but then when I agreed to go, I was in trouble for talking to the doctor. Obviously, my mom wanted me to see someone for her own reasons—it was never about my health and well-being.

What I walked away with as a teenager was to push everything down, don't feel. But certainly, if you do feel any emotions, don't let anyone know. People are going to do bad things. We are going to get hurt, and we need to push it down for the benefit of others. We need to act like nothing's wrong, act like everything is fine. That's just the way it was.

The problem is that it all adds up. When your children or your spouse need your support, you're resentful because your basket is full, and they want you to help shoulder their problems as well. We have to accept that stuff happens and process it as it happens. We must encourage and help our children to do the same to be healthy individuals.

In the case of our daughter's passing, I did have to stuff my feelings a lot. Terri was having trouble handling her emotions. I had good practice stuffing emotions and carrying extra baggage. This was a task I could handle for a while, and it gave me something to do. What we had to realize was that nothing would be resolved overnight. It was going to affect us for years to come, perhaps the rest of our lives. Just because our daughter died, though, it didn't stop the usual array of things in life that go wrong.

SELF-CONTROL, ESPECIALLY IN THE TOUGH TIMES

My human resources (HR) representative called me the day after our daughter died and demanded a date that I'd be back at work. She wanted it to be the following Monday. No kidding. Shockingly inappropriate for any job or employer. I responded to her as though it wasn't the single most tragic event in my life and our family. I politely informed her that when we knew when the funeral would be, I'd call her back. She acted as though I'd just been involved in a fender-bender and it was no big deal. According to her, I could possibly lose my job if I didn't get back to work ASAP.

I knew her boss's boss, and doing my best to manage my overwhelming stress, I calmly called him directly and relayed what had happened to us and the call I'd just received from his HR rep. He apologized and thanked me for the call. I can't say how big of a factor my call was, but the representative was terminated in the weeks before I returned to work. I had been told by the director to take all the time I needed.

Teach your children that 99.9 percent of the time, self-control and moderation will serve them well. If I would have acted out against this person the way I wanted to, the way I felt in the moment of her call, it would have diluted the offensiveness of her actions and possibly resulted in my termination. How often have you seen truly successful people "lose it" publicly? Contrast this against the people who brawl or shoot each other over a bad experience at a fast-food restaurant. Every kind of response has a time and place. Successful people are better at determining appropriate times and places—or is it because someone has good judgment that they are successful? I think that's a huge factor.

People who can maintain self-control when stuff happens will rise to the top. Teach your children why that is. Conversely, good stuff happens, too. How about the people who win the lottery and go into their jobs and tell everyone "what they really think." The very good times *and* the very bad times reveal who we really are. Grace and self-control reign supreme for successful people with a fulfilled life.

While some events include the whole family, life is full of much smaller lessons on self-control. The car has broken down; the washer flooded the kitchen; your spouse's car was wrecked. We know these things are going to happen in life. Is it necessary to cuss and yell and throw things or cuss at people to resolve it? Your children are watching you. Did all of the negative words and actions contribute to the solution, or did you just teach your children that they need to act out before accomplishing something? In the end, you're still going to do the thing you need to do, so just accept that stuff happens and get it done. Include your children as much as possible regarding what happened and what the solution is, and maybe one day they'll be a department supervisor, instead of shooting someone over french fries at a fast-food counter.

DAILY HURDLES

When you go to the supermarket for the first time after a life-altering event, it takes everything you have to hold it together in a public place. As soon as you step through the doors, a feeling of claustrophobia envelops you. Panic and anxiety well up, and your breath is somehow taken away. You encounter people getting angry over where your cart is, a snotty checkout clerk, people honking as you back out of a space. Everywhere you look, there are angry, nasty people for no reason. I don't know if these people were actually worse than normal or if it just seemed that way.

After the death of our daughter, Terri and I had a new language. It was, "I know you can tell I'm in a crisis, but my brain cannot process one more word." We couldn't even speak. We quietly allowed the other to have space and silence to process. We had days of total silence, together. The bigger an event is, the more insignificant everything else seems to be.

We can't respond with the extreme emotion that is inside us or let things fall through the cracks. I realized that I'd reverted back to stuffing and appearing fine. I stood in the living room with my family members who were falling to pieces. Jessica was gone. I was trying to focus on them and not my own grief because my family didn't need me to add my grief to theirs, I thought.

Then, I snapped. I don't recall doing it, but I do recall right after. The glass in my hand was launched across the living room into the wall, shattering into a thousand pieces. My drink and shards of glass sprayed across the wall and over the floor as I broke down in sobs of pain and rage and screamed. All I wanted to do was scream and keep screaming— something had to quell this raging turmoil inside me. I was suffocating and needed to breathe. Maybe Jessica could hear me if I screamed loud enough, maybe she would finally understand how much I loved her. My family breathed a sigh of relief. We have to share the worst of times, too.

The first days after getting the news of Jessica's death are like from a dream. We were all numb. We had no past experience to draw from. At points like this in life, you're overwhelmed with feeling the need to do something, but what can you do? So many people who had loved Jessica reached out to us and provided bits of comfort that helped to soothe our frazzled nerves, if only for a moment. We are very thankful for all the support we received.

One week after she died, a memorial motorcycle ride was held in Jessica's honor. At the Harley dealership, our son Blake had to give all of the speeches because my mind was mush. Along the route, we stopped for a few moments with Jessica's wadded-up motorcycle in the back of a pickup and blocked the intersection in the spot where she took her last breath. We all revved our bikes in honor of our lost angel. In our group, there was a Latin motorcycle club; a black sport-bike club; individual riders like me and Terri, Blake, and Cherity; my brother and sister-in-law; and our assorted friends and coworkers. We had friends and relatives following in cars and trucks in our tribute as well, and at some point, the police showed up to escort, basically telling the road-ragers to fuck off, we were allowed to have our moment.

Two weeks had passed, what seemed like an eternity, and finally, we were able to hold Jessica's funeral. The best I could do was interact one on one with people, walking away often to calm my mind and recompose myself. I hugged everyone who showed up, because that's what Jessica would have done. We're still not over it and at this point, nine years later, we accept that we will never be over her death, because to be over it would mean we've forgotten our daughter—and that's never going to happen.

LIFE MUST GO ON

I (Terri) was twenty-one years old when my dad died. He had been in the hospital for six weeks. David and I went to see him every day after school and work; we only missed one day each during that time. With his mother sitting by his bedside, my dad passed away early one morning. His nurse called us to come to the hospital, and when we went into his room, it felt as if all the life and joy had been sucked out of it. I remember looking out the window, down at the people walking around in the parking lot. Didn't they know my dad had just died? Why were they all walking around like nothing had happened? It was at that moment that I realized that for everyone else, life continued on, and it must go on for us, too.

We are always going to have things happen. Everyone does at one point or another. But you can't let it stop your life. We can't abandon our loved ones and close ourselves off as much as we might want to in the moment. In the homeschool dynamic, this especially holds true. Classes must remain on schedule. It's not that the classes are inherently that important, but your family continuity is. Remember, you're teaching your children by example. I (David) have seen children who cannot function because they lost their phone or broke up with their boyfriend or girlfriend. Mom or Dad shit-talks the new ex and tells their child they are better off without them, or they rush to replace the phone because that's the fix for the crisis— but is it, though? We've seen how that works when the kid is older and the parent gets a divorce and shit-talks the other parent. Whatever happens, someone else rushes in and tries to make it so that it never happens, and as a result, the kid doesn't have to learn to deal with it.

For the real life I've seen, that's not how it works. Is this how life works for you? Does someone swoop in and take care of everything so that you don't have to? Most likely not. Difficult events happen so that we may teach our children, by example, how to appropriately respond when stuff happens to them. Terri and I learned incrementally throughout our lives how to handle challenges and obstacles, but nothing had prepared us for the death of our child. Nobody knows how to get through such a major loss except those who have gone through it, and that's okay. As with many trials in life, this was a learn-as-you-go situation. I couldn't surrender myself to my grief because our daughter died. There are no exceptions, life had to go on and we had to persevere.

Ultimately, my career did suffer. As I worked personally to overcome the loss of our daughter, I needed to be there for my wife and kids to preserve the closeness of our family. I needed to preserve the relationship with my wife. There wasn't enough of me left to cover everything. Several years later, I ended up sacrificing my career to step into a position that was less demanding. At some point, life will make each of us decide what is most important. Like the doctor said, "Making money is easy." I decided that I may or may not recover my career, but regardless, I still have my family.

I wanted this chapter to be called "Shit Happens," but in the spirit of maintaining self-control, I thought dialing back the language for the chapter talking about self-control would emphasize the point. Not saying exactly what or how I feel is okay here, because the point is that an idea is conveyed clearly, not that I use vulgar language. I've told a lot of stories in this book. It's kind of like my life is "stuff happens." The stories I told between Chapter 10 and 11 bring us to what I've said in this chapter and into blended-family dynamics. If you are an aspiring homeschooler and the chapter on blended-family dynamics caught your attention, you've had your share of shit happen.

CHAPTER 18

LIFE AS ADULTS AND PEERS

As we are writing this book, geographically, our family is all over the world. It's a life that we couldn't have dreamed possible almost forty years ago. More to the point, most people we know can't comprehend the kind of life we live now. As with most things, it's more exciting to observe it than to live it, but it is our life, and we are content. Writing this book has forced us to look back over the years and the significant events that shaped who we are as individuals and as a couple. It has forced us to compare, side by side, our lives as children to the lives of our children, to see what worked and what didn't. My way of writing to you is just as raw as the way that I perceive the world and my place in it.

I (David) have been reticent to tell my stories because it will likely be mistaken that I'm publicly judging the people in my life throughout the years. How can we possibly convey a perspective without a reference point? I'm not here to give toxic people even more of a voice or to shame anyone who treated me as "less than." If that is the takeaway, then I've not accomplished my goal. The fact is, we are all going to have bad experiences in life. I am certainly not unique nor the worst case of parental abuse, either psychological or physical. That's why the stories need to be told—because most people in the world experience pain at the hands of someone else. You need to know that you're not alone. My genuine desire is to convey the idea of seeing events in life for what they are and using the knowledge gained from those bad experiences to find healing, while also providing something better and more constructive to your children and your marriage—not having your parents hand you a pile of shit and you simply passing it on to your kids.

If my life didn't begin the way it did; my birth mother abandoning me, my adoptive parents abusing me, some family members betraying me, and most certainly, the school system mostly failing me, then I wouldn't be writing to you right now. To be healthy, you need to work through and accept these struggles in life in a healthy way. Your goal isn't to shelter your children from adversity; the goal is to gradually expose them to it once they are capable of handling it in a healthy way with your wise guidance.

Another point of sharing my detailed stories is an attempt to capture the endless nuances between what my parents did and the effect it had on me in the moment, the way I perceived it later in life, what we did as parents, and the result it had on our children as adults and peers; then comparing the two extremes. What worked and what didn't? What did we expect, and what actually happened? Our children are adults now. We aren't "hoping" that our successful homeschooled kids will go on to accomplish something— they've already gone out and accomplished it. I've held back, believe it or not, with the stories about my parents, but enough is enough; it's a book on homeschooling, not a tell-all. We've interviewed our sons for this book and had some tough conversations. We are talking to them because they are our children, but we are also asking for their adult perspectives and opinions. I've asked our sons to give me their unadulterated feelings, opinions, and memories of significant events that stuck. For good or bad, they did. How cool is that? The fact that I still feel guilty or ashamed isn't their fault; they're just calling it like they remember it in much the same way I have.

We respect our children for the adults they've become and value their opinions. Never once did they express the feeling that they "missed out" on anything. To them, the question didn't make sense, but we had to ask it. We also had to ask about socialization, which also had them wondering why we asked the question. They had all the friends they wanted—must mean we were perfect! No. No and no. Based on what we were told, the hard relationship between Terri and me in the early years has negatively affected them for their entire lives. We weren't perfect, not even close.

Terri and I started to adjust our course on marriage about ten years in. Our two youngest weren't even kindergarten age. That would have made our oldest son between ten and eleven, and so his die was cast, just like my dad with his alcoholic father. Terri and I couldn't see beyond ourselves back then, and it hurt our son. Honestly, our fighting and anger were a form of emotional abuse to our son that we weren't aware of. It makes me sad and ashamed to know that we hurt him in a lasting way.

The second thing was how we pushed them. Terri and I were young and in panic mode, desperate for our children *not* to be like us. We pushed them in countless directions in an attempt to expose them to and accomplish as much as possible. They did do these things, and they did well, but it was too stressful for their ages. Those are the two big items in a list of things the boys shared. While we used the "wooden spoon" when appropriate, and our sons now want to get matching "I survived the spoon" T-shirts, the spoon wasn't part of their trauma.

I conducted myself in ways that I regret, but the son who mentioned my shouting and our fighting then relayed a story of an encounter he had as a young adult in which he remained totally calm while aggressively being yelled at by a superior. The superior noticed and commented on it. Our son replied that his dad had prepared him for this moment. So while he's not irreparably scarred by my outbursts, I could've done better.

What about happy memories? Never have our children's happy memories been about "stuff." We've spent a lot of money on our kids because we enjoy giving them things, but I'm also very glad that when I ask what their good memories are, they have nothing to do with money or buying them things. Are you ready for it? At the top of the list is time together. Every story they told is something we did together or they did with one of us or their siblings. Our kids were each other's best friends by choice. Our firstborn son would go with me any chance he got—to the store or to the Catholic school, racing bicycles or motorcycles, or building playthings in the yard. He remembers the games we would play in the car and funny things we would say. It's not all intentionally fun things they remember, though. He also remembers me cussing out other drivers. (I'm ashamed.) These are the things he recalls, but they're all fond memories.

Terri and I talk a lot; our conversations are often deep. We have mutual shame that we could have done better. Don't mistake that for more; we did enough for our kids. We are beyond proud of our children, but we both wish that we would have been better individuals and better as a couple for our kids. We cherish being a part of their lives and relating to them as adult peers while also being Mom and Dad. They recognize that we've experienced a lot in life and that they can still come to us both—or either of us individually—for insight or advice or just to vent.

I don't need to offer advice if all they need to do is share their incredible frustration or pain. Give it to me; I have room in my basket for it. We're safe. We don't offer platitudes or bumper-sticker logic. None of us has achieved perfection, but we have achieved happiness and success together. Each of us lives a fulfilled life and shares it. Our sons have a lot of unique adult experiences as well; I'm not beyond asking either of them for their opinion. Why wouldn't I seek their perspective on topics I know they're well versed in?

Our oldest son has a major and two minors from college in addition to the experience of managing multimillion-dollar companies, so when I casually interviewed him about the book, he asked what we were doing— in addition to writing a book. I kind of shrugged my shoulders.

"If you're going to give people all of this information, they might appreciate a follow-up with some resources," he offered. I smiled at him, replying "This isn't what I do for a living; this is my life, our lives." He began to ask me questions and offer ideas for if we were interested in providing more support than writing a book. How cool is that? Of course I listened to my son! International business and business development are his specialties. I asked if he wanted a job, and he smiled at me kindly. He already has goals in life, but when I floated the idea of having several in-person talks, he said he'd be willing to come speak if we wanted him to.

I'm giving you a deeper look behind the curtain to illustrate our relationship with our children as adults and peers. We don't know how much interest our memoir homeschool book will garner, if any. It's just our story about how we were equipped as children and ultimately, how it informed our approach to homeschooling. We hope our story will help others to make better, more informed decisions with parenting and home-schooling by observing our good and not-so-good decisions. Our sons think it's a good idea for their mom and dad to write a book—it's all very matter-of-fact to them.

As children get older and go into the world as adults themselves, we find ourselves with the parenting mindset burned into our identities. We have doctorate degrees in parenting earned by years of struggle and perseverance. You don't just toss it in the can on the way out. These years of your life have changed you as a person. With or without your children by your side, you are Mom or Dad, and always will be. You've modified your role to make room for your adult children and to respect them as peers—but that observant parent with an eagle eye for everything going on at home, who's ready to schedule four years of lessons for a child while cooking dinner, is still in there.

Hopefully, your children are going to make you a grandparent. Believe us when we say that when you see a young child you're asso-ciated with, like a grandchild, your impeccable skills as a parent and provider of education will want to kick in as surely as a lion wants an antelope. Pump the brakes and take a deep, relaxing breath. There's a new mama bear in town, and she knows as little as you did so many years ago. You have to let the mama bear find her way, and that can be hard. This is where women fail to see they're not too different from man-splaining men. A woman's mama instinct kicks in, and she wants to mom-splain every aspect, from breastfeeding up through the child's eventual college graduation.

Seriously, I love seeing Terri go back into her element of mom mode! She is Mama and wears the badge with a bursting pride. Being a parent is hard to begin with. Your kids were impossibly hard to raise, but now you miss it more than the glory days of football. You want a place at the table. Sniff-n-smoochin' on a little baby's head, watching a little boy's endless energy, listening to the four-year-old whose words never stop coming out of their little mouth unless you give them an ice cream (knowing they're eating the ice cream while thinking of what they want to talk about next). The little girl who isn't so little anymore, and Mom and Dad and Grandma and Grandpa aren't quite as cool. The things that drove you berserk as a parent, you cherish now, and you want to pick up some of the pieces you let fall away the first time, wondering why you didn't see it so many years back.

You're Grandma and Grandpa now. Or, you're not there yet—you're the parent and you've been blessed with grandparents for your children. Grandparent jealousy is a real thing; it can get tense. As if parents don't have enough to contend with, having new babies or young children, and now you have to deal with some jealousy from the older generation. It's that parental instinct. Grandma wants to be a part of this child's life, and the baby's mom keeps getting in the way! And now Grandma has to share the baby with "the other grandma?" Ghastly! We've already shared that our little family spent many years on a family island as persona non grata, but what we did get to witness was the dynamic of our siblings and their children's grandparents. We also have three grandchildren to whom we are Grandma and Grandpa, but we are not the only grandparents; there are multiple sets. So, of course we have to have a chapter titled "Grandparent Dynamics." Let's get ready to rumble!

CHAPTER 19

GRANDPARENT DYNAMICS

I (David) think of us as "the crazy grandparents." I've been considered a bad influence throughout my life in one way or another, and I'm proud to say that I've continued this tradition with our grandkids.

When I talk about the things I do, like riding motorcycles or flying, I do it with so much enthusiasm that it's contagious. The next thing I know, there's a coworker's angry wife telling her husband to stay away from me. "You are not getting a pilot's license!" she says to her husband. It's my personality more than anything; after seeing him drive a car, I *never said* he should fly an airplane.

I've been there too many times to count. This book represents my specific way of presentation. We've said that anyone can homeschool, but not everyone should homeschool. I'm certain that we've allowed you a glimpse of what is possible if you get yourself and your family together and accept the challenge. If so, you see the possibilities, and you're excited. That said, there are some spouses or family members who will counter that excitement or even read the book to list the countless things that "are wrong with it," for everyone—or just for you (in reference back to Chapter 3).

We have either seen or encountered the same thing with grandparenting—it's bonkers. We've seen an entrenched grandmother tell another grandparent everything that is "wrong" with the mother or her children in an attempt to keep other grandparents away. That's the nice version of that story. I raise a concerned eyebrow to things like this. It makes me think of *Lord of the Rings:* this is Grandma Sauron, one grandma to rule them all!

What I've noticed with some grandparents is that they can be much like children who go to one parent and don't get what they want, so they go to the other parent. We've seen grandparents do this, and if the marriage isn't on point . . . "Oh, oh, so we can't see my mother, but we have to spend every weekend with your parents? Is that it?" The instant this happens, you two need to work on you. This is one of those times we'd suggest going to a mutually agreed-on counselor. They can at least mediate a passionate topic. You don't want the issue to become worse.

BEYOND LABELS

You might recall from an earlier chapter that Terri and I had instant grandkids. While they are my biological grandkids, we're Grandma and Grandpa to them, without question. There are other grandparents involved who could view Terri as an outsider, even if my daughter sometimes chooses to call her mom. I don't know if Terri agrees with me, but I feel like she is in a tough spot; I have a direct biological connection and she doesn't. That can create feelings contrary to our sphere of marriage. We went to our counselor before anything could fester. "What do we need to look out for?" we asked. Terri and I have a lot of answers, but when you're in the middle of the forest, even for us, it's hard to see the forest for the trees. That said, Terri is the coolest grandma ever—just look at the kids' faces when they see her and scream "Grandma!" and run into her arms. All that happens before they even notice Grandpa is there. Terri adores the kids, and they love her. She has even read bedtime stories to them at night from across the country until they're fast asleep.

We've not tried to insert ourselves in any permanent place. My daughter and her family are busy. Not in the conventional "we're so busy" sense, but in the vein of coordinating dozens of kids traveling to other states for various competitions on a regular basis. Besides owning and running a successful business, my daughter organizes and handles the finances and arrangements for these groups as a volunteer (as if being a working mom isn't quite enough for her.) She is also a taxi service, as most moms are. Where do we fit in?

First and foremost, we're always just a phone call, FaceTime, or text away. Sometimes a relaxing escape can be provided by being a good listener and allowing your kids or grandkids to just vent while offering reassurance that you believe in them. Maybe you can offer a simple solution to something that seems overwhelming to them. Maybe we can offer to take the kids for a fun few days and let the grown-ups do whatever they want to do—take a getaway or just get the house clean.

It's not about us. It's about being there for your family, and when we're there for our grandkids, we have fun, and the parents know the kids are in good hands. My parents were going to do "whatever they wanted to do, by God!" Not us—we view ourselves as an extension of the intent and will of the parents. After that is ensured, we have fun within those boundaries. Gift buying? We check with the parents. Activities? We check with the parents. It's all in how you look at it. Yes, we've "been there and done that," and were decently successful at it. We're doing exactly what we wish our parents or others would have done with us—giving respect. The funny thing is, instead of creating a lifelong rift between parents and children, the grand kids know they can't bullshit us, their parents know their kids can't bullshit us, and therefore they don't have to worry "How are things going with the kids, I wonder?" The kids know we talk with their parents, we know the parents talk with their kids, and we're all on the same page. Unless it's for a surprise party, we don't condone going behind anyone's back and having secrets. If, on the off chance, we became aware of abuse, the kids or parents would know we're a safe place.

Do you see this coming full circle again? Did any of my family do anything when they saw my face bruised or lip busted open? Did I feel like I could show my bloody wounds to anyone when my mom pulled out my hair or dug her fingernails into my face to force me to look at her? Hell no. They'd have told my dad what I told them, and that cry for help would have been punished, too. For my dad "being such a nice guy," nobody risked pissing him off. It's just the uncomfortable truth.

Our parents and family helped us become cool grandparents. Our desire is to be a positive force in our children's and grandchildren's lives and relationships. Terri and I have our own lives to live and enjoy together, but we also have a lot of great life experiences that we can share when the opportunity arises to spend with our family. We don't feel the need to "control them all," because they're all doing just fine.

We have done our best to present and to convey that regardless of whether it's just your marriage and children or if your life also includes homeschooling, it all begins within your sphere of marriage. You and your spouse's relationship excludes everyone else and while we earlier specified your children, know that this includes meddling grandparents, too, and everyone else on the planet. Now you have a reference point on how to respect your children's marriages, too—don't allow anyone to crack the sphere.

We don't take sides in our kids' relationships. If they ask for direction, we try to give advice (not tell them what to do) within the bounds of a functioning, healthy relationship. "From what we know to be constructive, this is all the insight we have." If our children or their significant other is resistant to that course, we have nothing else to offer, and we've kept our mouths shut as we've watched various relationships disintegrate over the course of months or years. If it's your children, you usually have to resist using your superhuman powers of observation and let them experience life for themselves.

We had a conversation with one of our sons about a couple who split. He was surprised—we obviously weren't. He asked when we first noticed something. "Two years ago, maybe?" we said, and we shared the innocuous exchange we both caught that, to us, was like a flashing light with Klaxon horns. The more flashing lights you see, the more Klaxon horns you hear, and the more often you see them—the closer a relationship is to doom. There is a point of "not likely" return. I'm not getting off track. You'll see these things with your kids and their relationships. You can't run like it's a code red and start yelling, "Fire!" Yes, I am speaking to you, grandparent.

Remember, you're not taking sides. It could be your child who's being coarse. Gently, respectfully guide them and help them build a strong relationship. It is up to them whether to listen or not. If they're homeschoolers, remember that their relationship has a large impact on their children's—your grandchildren's—lives. It's important to be a force for good for the whole family.

Our families always took sides, and every answer was divorce. It's not surprising that most of them are alone, trudging through life with a trail of destroyed relationships behind them—simply because people wouldn't do what they wanted them to do, when it was none of their business in the first place. We look around us and see estranged families littering the landscape. Fathers and sons, mothers and daughters, families and grandparents, siblings against siblings. Most, for no good reason.

It's interesting to me that people who are the least successful in very specific areas of their life tend to give the most casual advice. I have a crude saying that is just a truth I noticed. "The fattest, most out-of-shape people have the most to say about proper fitness and diet." I had dropped seventy pounds after spending my thirties close to obesity, unhealthy, and in pain. At forty, I was literally in the best shape of my life, even compared to my teenage athlete years.

I couldn't keep count of the obese, fried-food-eating, zero-calorie-soft-drink-chugging men who suddenly came out of the woodwork to tell me "what I needed to do" now that I was healthy and in shape. It actually took a while for me to recognize the pattern because I just take people as people, rather than judging and then weighing their value. When I realized what was happening, I changed my response. "Cool. Do you have some pics? It's always neat seeing what people accomplish when they work out." Their response? "Nope."

"Oh, motherfucker, I'm fat, so I don't know anything about diet and exercise?" I wanted to say that, but I didn't.

What I did say was, "You seem really knowledgeable. I assumed you had some good pics. We all go through fitness cycles." Full circle again. I use this example because it's obvious.

People hear something and feel smart repeating it, but they can't go any deeper than repeating what they were told to say. This is exactly what people meddling in your relationship are doing. The people with the most to say about what to do or what not to do are the ones who are divorced and alone. Like me with fitness, it took a while to realize this fact—but they are one and the same. If you want to know how to be obese and out of shape, ask someone who is obese and out of shape. If you want to have an estranged family and end up divorced, listen to someone who is divorced and estranged from their family, and so on and so forth.

Once, we had a family member who sat us down with another pregnant teenage couple around our age. This family member was determined to get rid of our unborn child, Blake. It was a group effort. This equally young couple praised that they chose the right thing by giving up their baby. We told them we all have decisions to make and respected theirs, but we'd be keeping our baby, thank you very much.

Fast-forward a year. The couple got married when she graduated from high school. The boy was a year or two older. The girl couldn't resolve that she had given up her baby. She tried to commit suicide. Her husband dealt with his stress by using drugs. The girl resigned herself that her baby was gone, and last I heard, they both had been using (either crack or meth), were in separate rehabs, and were getting divorced. She blamed her boyfriend for convincing her to give up her child.

Our family member couldn't see the path of destruction for this couple that followed their decision. Not that she didn't know about it, but they had served their purpose to her, and she was done with them. This particular family member was divorced, estranged from their kids, and just couldn't see that their life was a path of destruction because of their selfishness and the sickness they pushed onto others. All our family saw was that we didn't do what they wanted, and they moved on.

This way of thinking and acting is within your capability as a parent or grandparent, so take it seriously. You have the power to lift up, and you have the power to destroy—which will you choose? Remember way back at the beginning of this book, we said that to undertake this lifelong journey, *you* would be forced to become a better person. Situations involving alcohol, drugs, and abuse can be exceptions, but otherwise, when two people have chosen each other; respect that choice and be a force for good. Don't try to undermine the commitment your child has made to someone.

We can always be ready to catch our children if they fall, but we shouldn't push them down. If you're the parent or parents, having open communication with the grandparents and with your spouse is necessary.

If you don't want to go to your spouse and tell them that your mother said they were pig-headed, then don't allow your mother to talk like a child. She can speak however she wants, but you don't have to listen. Maybe a spouse is pig-headed, but let's raise the bar and constructively make things better.

If you're the elder parent or grandparent to your adult child or their spouse, how about saying "Honey, if you two want to go talk to someone and work on some things, I'll gladly watch the kids each week." Or if you're not in a position to watch the kids, "Hey, if you two agree to see someone, we'll cover a sitter and pay for dinner." Just do something positive in your children's lives. They might be adults, but they're still your kids. You can provide positive reinforcement. Finally, stay out of their business. You don't need to know everything; you're just setting yourself up to meddle.

I've said it before: parenting is a thankless task, but to be a grandparent is divine because it's comparatively easy. Parents do the heavy lifting, and as a grandparent your job is to have fun. Any grandparents I knew had their favorite chair and favorite shows and enjoyed having visitors. We're more of a "we're going flying, motorcycle riding, or boating" kind of grandma and grandpa, "you can come if you want." Our backstory is the reason why. We want to stay active, but also, our teen years early in our marriage were spent taking care of business as a family. We missed a lot of our young adult life, by choice, accepting it as a necessary sacrifice. Taking care of our family and the really important things came first and getting our family and relationship on track and healthy while providing for our kids was the top priority. Now, we're empty nesters, not broke teenagers—I'll take this side of life any day.

Terri and I had a fun summer when we met. Now, we're picking up where we left off. Why can't we still do the things we used to do or wanted to do but never did? So that's what we do. Also, we're setting an example for our kids and grandkids. If most kids only see grandparents who are out of shape and not very active, then they'll most likely become accepting of being out of shape and not very active.

Our grandchildren can't comprehend what we've seen or been through in our lives, and it really doesn't matter right now. One day, after we're long gone, they'll have the life experience and knowledge to put things together and realize that we made a choice to live the life we did despite having every reason to tune it all out, sit down, and watch television. We want them to know us as knowledgeable and experienced people. We hope to be a positive influence in their lives when they're our age or older, and we also want them to have fond experiences with and memories of us for their benefit and for the benefit of their future children and grandchildren.

Life is precious, and it's an honor to contribute to their development and happiness in a real and constructive way. Should they ever be in a place where they're unsure of what to do, we want them to recognize us as a safe place, too. We want them to have trust in us that is similar to or better than the trust we built with our children.

Also, we want our children to see us as a safe place for their kids. We've heard a lot of people profess that they're going to give their kids everything they didn't have growing up, but it usually centers around money and things. My wife, children, and grandchildren have my loyalty. I didn't have trust in my parents and couldn't confide in my family without gossip. I didn't have many people to offer me wise advice with discretion when I badly needed it—these are the things I want to give our children and grandchildren. Our family starts with us and the example we set.

My parents wanted our young kids to stay overnight with them and hang out the next day. We were generally okay with that. We always traveled with extra clothes for the kids. "Yeah, that's fine . . ." Then we started telling them about limited candy, no candy after a certain time, no more than one soft drink, and so forth. My mom instantly became offended and defensive. "They are our grandkids! We will do what we want to do with them! You don't tell us how to raise kids." Whoopsies. "I'm sorry, but if you can't respect the rules that we've set in place for good reason, then it's best they don't stay over." My parents dug their heels in and would rather not see the kids because we didn't condone letting them run free and overindulge.

Years later when I told my mom some of the awful things that went on with the grandchildren they watched at her house, she said, "Oh! Well,

I had no idea *that* was going on here. If I would've known, I wouldn't have allowed it." Again, in retrospect, did we make the right choice? I'm going to say yes. I knew how my parents raised us, and I saw how they "took care of" their other grandkids. Mom sat in front of the television while the kids did whatever they could find to do—yikes. People often wrongly assumed that we thought our kids were "too good" to be around other children. That wasn't the case. These parents obviously weren't noticing what we were noticing. Not my dog, not my fight, but I will protect my children even if it offends people. Grandparents must respect your family. This book begins with your family being offended by your efforts, and now we've come full circle.

Terri and I had put our little roach-infested apartment together and were making our first home. Within a few months of having our son, we actually had an open evening for date night and an extra twenty dollars we could spend. We invited Terri's younger sister out to the movies if their mom, our son's grandmother, would watch our son. She reluctantly agreed. In her estimation, we deserved nothing but suffering and quite possibly, still do. We certainly didn't deserve to have an enjoyable evening after the past year of incredible struggle. "You better be back at nine-thirty!" she demanded. Terri's sister was glad to get out of the tense house, and we were just happy to feel like we could relax for a couple of hours.

We picked up fast food and drove to the theater for a movie, which one, I can't recall. On the way home, there was a wreck that blocked the entire four-lane highway. We looked at the clock. We didn't have time for a wreck. In my mind, we stood to lose babysitting resources if we were late. We stopped at a pay phone and called to tell her what happened, saying that although we'd be a little late, we'd be back sooner rather than later. "Okay," she said—but a meteor could have taken out the road and it still wouldn't have mattered. Really, what she should have said was, "I won't accept any excuses."

Before we even opened the door to the house, we heard our baby screaming. We discovered that his diaper was beyond full. She had placed him behind the couch in his baby carrier across the living room and then sat down on the other side of the living room to watch her television program. Terri essentially said, "What the fuck, Mama?" without the f-word, but the sentiment was there.

"I told you to be back by nine-thirty; it's now after ten. I quit taking care of him at nine-thirty. It's your fault."

Terri's sister came to her defense. "Mom, there was a wreck; traffic was backed up. David got us here as quickly as he could."

Her response? "You're grounded for the next week. Maybe you'll learn to be on time." She looked back at her television and then back at Terri and me. "You need to get your things and leave."

We never took Terri's sister out again after that. Yes, you guessed it, we didn't allow the kids to be alone with that grandmother, either. If a person would allow an infant to suffer as a way to lash out at their own child, what kind of cold hate is that, against your own blood, against an innocent child? Mix in her absolute contempt for me, and it was a recipe for disaster. We got the hint: you do not want to be a part of our children's lives. Many other members of Terri's family agreed with Grandma acting out against us and our children. My family could be mean; these people were malicious.

This was literally our first experience leaving our baby with someone else—his grandmother. When Terri refused to get an abortion, her mother angrily told us she would never love this child. The night our son was left to sit in his feces, I realized that it wasn't just angry rhetoric; she had become the bitter grandmother she knew from her own childhood. We didn't want to find out just how far she would go to hurt us.

WHAT KIND OF GRANDPARENT DO YOU WANT TO BE?

Being a grandparent can be one of the most rewarding roles in life you'll ever know. Just like being a parent, it is what you make it. My (Terri) mother told me stories primarily about one set of her grandparents. After her father died when she was five years old, her mother had to get a full-time job outside the home to provide for their family, which was uncommon in the 1940s. There were no daycare centers back then, so during the week, my mom and her younger brother would go to stay with their grandparents while her mother was working. These grandparents shaped her life significantly; her grandmother noticeably favored her younger brother while her grandfather very much favored her. From what I remember, my mom's grandmother seemed very strict and stern, perhaps even angry, especially toward my mother. This deeply hurt my mom and caused jealousy and resentment to form inside her—a resentment that persisted, which she later exhibited toward us and her grandchildren.

You can pass on to your children good or bad, positive or negative, life or death. Why so dramatic? Because it is the truth. It is so easy to pass down negative and damaging habits, attributes, beliefs, and attitudes—much easier than positive. Not only do children seem to quickly latch on to our negative ways, but they multiply them. It is a very vicious cycle that leads to hurt, anger, bitterness, and resentment, eventually causing the breakdown and eventual death of relationships and families. This is also equally true of the positive.

When we actively work toward beneficial, loving, and healthy habits, attributes, beliefs, and attitudes, we breathe life into our children, who then multiply those characteristics, bringing life and joy to all those around them. This has been true of all of our kids, especially Jessica. She would say to me, "Mama, every day, I try to go out of my way to show kindness to at least one person because you never know if just one word of kindness might make their day." Eventually, in turn, your children will breathe that life into their children and grandchildren, life which will continue to blossom for generations to come.

What we learned from our parents was more negative than positive. Not all negative; there was some positive in there for sure. The overarching message to both of us was that we were no good, we were not going to make it, and we were going to ruin our children. However, beneath all the negative voices, there were three people, my dad, my grandma, and David's grandpa, who very quietly but consistently encouraged us. "Keep pushing. Don't listen to the naysayers. You two are going to make it. You are going to be alright." We both knew that we wanted to be better parents for our children than what our parents had been for us. I would love to say we got it all right, but we didn't. We have both said as much several times throughout this book.

This book isn't about us being the perfect parents. Our book isn't about our perfect homeschool. It isn't about our perfect children and their perfect lives after homeschool, because they were homeschooled, not at all. This is a book about the experiences that shaped who we became as parents and our homeschool journey. It is about learning from the mistakes our parents made, and learning from the mistakes *we* made as parents and as homeschoolers. This memoir is a tool you can use to learn from us; a tool to help parents learn about the good, the bad, the ugly of our homeschool experience. Hopefully, it will help you to make more informed decisions about how you raise and homeschool your children.

We weren't perfect parents, and our homeschool was not without its challenges and difficulties. This is true for you, too—it is true for everyone. We are still learning from our mistakes. Despite all our faults and errors, we feel truly blessed to have children and grandchildren who want to be around us. We are so humbled and thankful when they want to spend their own time and money to travel across the country to be with us. We enjoy each of them and love them with all our hearts. It is our greatest joy and pleasure to be around our children and grandchildren—it's the most wonderful feeling in the world. I can promise you that you will not regret a moment of all your hard work as a homeschool parent when you reach this point in your life.

So, what kind of grandparent do you want to be? Do you want to enjoy your adult children and grandchildren? It starts now, when they are still in your home, under your diligent care and watchful eye. Become the person you want to be later in life and be that person for your children now, today. Forge a special connection with each of them, and continuously nurture that relationship so that they will want to be around you when they are adults. Be the kind of parents where your child *wants* the person they're dating to meet you, because it is so important to them that this person fits in well with everyone in your family. Be the grandparent your child and their spouse will *want* their children to have fun with and spend time with. This will become one of your greatest pleasures in life. For us, it is our greatest pleasure in life, second only to our love for and friendship with each other.

ONE MORE THING

David and I are among the older employees at our respective jobs. I was put in my place the other day. I said to a group of younger coworkers, "Getting old sucks. My advice to you—just don't do it." A little later that day, I was listening to a podcast, and the speaker said, "Getting old is a blessing, a gift." He was right. It is a gift. I am fifty-five years old. My dad passed away when he was fifty-four. Our daughter, Jessica, was killed right before her twenty-second birthday. No one knows how much time they have on this Earth, and none of us are guaranteed tomorrow. What are we going to do with the time we have? Time is more precious than money; we will never get any of it back once it is gone.

In order to continue living life to the fullest and enjoying the time we have left, we all must take care of our body, mind, emotions, and spirit. Being healthy in all of these areas enables us to keep on living life. If we don't continue to exercise, our muscles will atrophy, we will lose our balance, and our bones and joints will freeze. We will be unable to continue to do the fun physical activities we used to do; we cannot go and have adventures with our spouses, children, and grandchildren. We slowly lose the ability to move, and we become sedentary. If we do not continue to challenge our minds and acquire new knowledge and new skills, our brains will atrophy and lose pathways and synaptic connections, eventually leading to Alzheimer's disease and dementia. An active mind is a healthy mind. Just like an active body is a healthy body. We must also learn to process our emotions and not let them rule over us, as we are no longer children who are controlled by our emotions. Emotions actually create a physical response in our bodies. So, we can either create a river of healing as we allow them to flow through us as we process them, or they will build up and eventually cause physical damage and illnesses.

Finally, we must come to terms with our own spirituality, the question of God, and life after death. The spirit is what makes us who we are and ties everything together. If we are not spiritually healthy, the other elements that make us ourselves cannot be healthy. We must seek the truth of God and everlasting life. We must diligently search for the answers to these questions, and must learn to forgive and to accept forgiveness, because every single day that goes by brings us one day closer to our own death and the question of where we will spend eternity. We must use each day wisely, for it may be our last—it may be our spouse's last or our child's last. Make sure to make it count, make the most of each day, and live to love and enjoy your spouse, your children, and your grandchildren.

CHAPTER 20

REALIZATIONS

We've felt strongly about writing this book for years, but it just was never the right time. Our story was always going to be blunt and raw, not only because that's how life has been for us, but because it's also how we've successfully navigated through it. Remember when I (David) said that what I think matters, too? That has been my perspective in writing this book—telling the stories and saying the things I was supposed to bury for the comfort of others. Instead of doing that and simply allowing others to go through life to blindly figure it out, I could possibly save a lot of time (and possibly money on therapy) for you or your kids by pointing things out ahead of time. You're not alone, and none of this is new.

I can say from our perspective that we've been to the mountaintop, this is what we saw, and here's a map that may help as you travel this road. I fully expect to hear from someone trying to attack or shame me for some of the things I've said. What audacity must I possess to think for a second that I could say, for instance, anything negative about my dad? It doesn't change the man they knew, but they didn't know him the way I did.

However, the point was never to impugn my dad or mom—or anyone else, for that matter. Like the rest of us, they lived their lives the way they thought was best and did the best they were equipped to do, which is the point of this entire book: making thoughtful decisions.

My parents made choices; we made choices; you make choices. Do we make our way through life as narcissists, believing that we're beyond reproach; or do we make thoughtful decisions, reflect on our motivations when the outcome is revealed, and adjust course for the betterment of ourselves and those around us?

As far as my life goes, the concept of unending pain and torment is reserved for a place like hell; I didn't live in hell. Countless people on this planet have lived a truly tortuous life, and I'm not one of them. Is your goal just to not be the worst, or is your goal to strive to be your best and raise your children to do the same?

As my parents' child, my view is that my parents were just motivated as individuals and as a couple by reasons that were never clear to me. What was *their* point? I think that they wanted the *appearance* of the "American dream." How important were appearances? One of my worst offenses growing up was embarrassing my parents.

As couples often do, my parents once went to another couple's house on a Saturday evening to play cards. I didn't get a brief on the evening's activities and wasn't informed of my parents' expectations of me. We just showed up, and I was told to sit on the couch, which I did for several hours. All of the other kids, including my siblings, had activities, so I was the only kid present.

Looking back, there must have been something I missed. I really believe that, but I never saw it. While sitting on that couch, I was allowed to watch television. The couple didn't have cable TV because cable was not available outside the city, and VCRs were not found in homes yet. There were three television channels, and two of the main shows on television on Saturday nights were *The Love Boat* and *Fantasy Island.* One of the hosts, the husband, would not allow the channel to be changed because of his strict religious beliefs. It seems like I watched evening talk shows like *20/20*, but I can't recall.

What I *do* recall is when we were finally leaving, the couple smiled down at me with these forced smiles on their faces like we'd just gotten back from the amusement park. My parents were looking between them and me with their own weird smiles, and the man tousled my hair, exclaiming, "Did you have fun?" I don't recall my actual thoughts, but I remember my emotions. I wondered, why in the hell did he ask me that? It had felt like I was in a waiting room all night. I shrugged my shoulders slowly. "It was kind of boring, but that's okay." All the adults laughed and my mom tousled my hair. "Someone is just tired," she laughed, and everyone laughed more. Creepy, right?

It was unsettling, but I saw something this weird couple didn't—I'd fucked up big time. We lived ten minutes away, but I wouldn't be in bed for at least two hours, and only after I'd been physically injured. I had unintentionally embarrassed my parents—badly—with my response of saying I'd been bored.

Farewells were called out in the night air as we walked to the blue station wagon. *Fuck!* about covered my swirling thoughts—it was going to be a long ride home. Would we make it through the garage at home before the physical shit started? My parents entered their parked car in the driveway, closed their doors, looked towards this couple's house with one last smile, and waved. I thought to see if their friends were watching from the window—they weren't.

Without warning, my mom spun in the front seat and blasted me across the face. She grabbed a handful of my hair, her fingernails digging into my scalp, and she pulled my face hard against the back of the front bench seat (we weren't wearing seatbelts) so that my mouth and nose were pressed against it, only my eyes visible to look up at her. I could taste blood but didn't know if I was bleeding onto the seat and having my face rubbed through it or if she had hit me hard enough to bust open my lip or inside cheek.

My dad turned and clenched my face in his hand. It smelled like sweaty cigarettes. "Boring? You were bored?" I had answered truthfully and respectfully. My dad forcefully shoved me back like he was throwing something. My head hit the back seat so hard that the back of my skull bounced off the tube frame of the underlying seat structure, and I bounced forward again and doubled over. A knot rose on my head.

It was dark outside, but I could feel my vision and my head swirling. My vision felt weird. I felt what turned out to be blood dripping from my face into my hand. My mom grabbed a handful of my hair and craned my head back to face her. "You need to think about what you've done!" When she let go, I just sort of slumped onto my side and passed out. In the distance of my mind, I heard something slam. Then the car door nearest my head flew open so fast, there was a suction of air in the car. My dad grabbed the back of my shirt, pulled me out of the car, and stood me up. I fell down in the driveway. "Wake up! We're not done yet!" He held the back of my shirt and dragged me into the house while my mom ranted about my many shortcomings as a child. That's all I recall of that night.

A few years later when I received my first brain scan, the doctor pointed out multiple areas of previous damage, concussions. My mom clicked her tongue and blamed me and my motorcycle riding. From what I recall, two concussions I had were from football, and they were in the same location of my head and didn't happen until high school. One concussion I received while riding a motorcycle, I was thirty-five years old and racing arenacross. My bike landed on me and knocked me out. In the altercation with my parents just described, I was maybe in third or fourth grade.

Everything that the doctor saw the first time were injuries inflicted by my parents, and my mother fucking knew it. To her, I wasn't sleepy when we left their friends' house; I just was bored. No, actually, I couldn't stay awake or stand up because I was concussed. Tying back to my original point, though, my parents were going to have the *appearance* of the American dream without regard to the cost, and that meant the appearance of perfect kids, even if they had to injure them to accomplish it. That's my point, buried in these details.

I intentionally said "without regard to the cost" rather than "at any cost," because my parents never considered the cost. They never looked back at yesterday or last week or last year . . . They never looked back and said, "You know, this isn't good for any of us." They never once thought, *We just beat the shit out of our kid . . . for what?* In my lifetime, my parents' life together was focused on what others thought. I've always expected some negativity from putting our story out there, but I couldn't say why specifically until this chapter, in keeping with everything we've experienced, the following story captures the family dynamic.

My parents would host large family get-togethers. It seems everyone thought that because my dad was in the grocery business, he got groceries for free or something. I really don't know, but when milk was $1.19 a gallon or on sale for 79 cents, my parents would spend a couple hundred dollars on food, cook it, and serve it. People might show up, they might not, but if they did, they showed up embarrassingly late—always.

My parents just fawned on everyone outside of my family. My mom would do her "let's hold hands and say what we're thankful for" bullshit, and it worked. Everyone to this day believes the appearances, but even they know Mom's kooky kumbaya routine was an act.

It's as if my parents' get-togethers and feeding these people somehow negated what happened behind closed doors. My parents' children were not equipped to live a successful life. This further illustrates my point of looking back and reevaluating. None of the many people who came, ate, and left the mess—and who will forever defend their view of my parents—will ever notice or consider that my parents' kids all struggled.

It's because everyone outside of the immediate family bought the appearance act. They'll defend the appearance they know about my mom and dad, so my parents' investment obviously paid off. Regardless of our relationships, jobs, kids . . . doing everything across the board for their children does not reflect them as having been competent parents.

This fact is lost on people like this. Of my parents' three kids, one child's life is distinctly different from those of their siblings, the parents, and the family—mine, ours. Do not read this as "better than." I don't view myself as better than my siblings, or even my parents; I just chose to be different and do it away from the memories of my childhood home. While Terri's childhood story is quite a bit different than mine, it grants the same results: strife. Together, we chose to focus on something other than what our parents taught us to focus on, and so our lives have been dramatically different than theirs. Mainly, my parents and Terri's were consumed with appearances. I think we've made it obvious that we often march to the beat of our own drum; we're polar opposites, but here's one example of why . . .

As my dad withered from the effects of Alzheimer's, all the people they were so worried about impressing weren't there. They hadn't been there since my dad quit serving free food. My parents just couldn't see people for who they really were. After my dad passed, my mom was on her own. Where are all the "we're just thankful for our family," moochers? Yeah, it was all bullshit. Sitting in their chalets looking down on the world, I'd guess. They're certainly not concerned about my mom. "You have no right to talk about your parents that way!" some might say. To this, I would ask, "When was the last time you saw them? Since you're obviously so concerned." This response to abandonment is what my parents spent their energy on instead of their kids—this is what they earned by being so nice and giving. It's what was worth beating their children over, not spending time with their children.

My dad once hit me in the face in the kitchen because I'd made a sandwich and opened a bag of chips (we didn't usually have chips beyond my mom's Cheetos or cheese puffs, but what I opened were left over from a get-together). My dad grabbed the sandwich from my hand and slung it into the yellow enamel sink; he also poured the bag of chips out into the trash so that I couldn't possibly retrieve the bag and still eat it. Apparently, we had limited food for the week and he thought I was "eating it all."

So because they spent all the grocery money on appearances, my dad ripped the food from my hands and threw it away? In the moment, I just didn't want to get hit, but it didn't make sense to me, either—it still doesn't. There were no instructions not to eat it. I've said it more than once: the best thing I could do as a kid was avoid my parents if at all possible. I can still see the mountains of paper plates with food going into the large trash bag at the big get-together and my dad happily hauling the bag out to the garage. Somehow in the moment, throwing away my sandwich made from a small amount of leftovers made sense and satisfied my dad.

In my young adult years, my mom would ask if I was coming to an event, or why I didn't come to the last family event. Terri or I always let them know ahead of time that I wouldn't be there. When Mom questioned, "Seriously?" I would respond, "You don't want me there, Mom. Besides, I had to work." She would then say, "I don't think you're being truthful," so I'd respond along the lines of, "Make a note that you're calling me a liar about working on this date. I'm going to print out my timecard and show you that I was working. It won't make a difference, but you'll see it."

I would print it out and make a special trip to her house (before she could conveniently forget) to say, "You accused me of lying about working during the family get-together," which she would then deny, accusing me of lying. "Here is my time card so far this week, here is the date of the get-together, and here's the ten hours I worked." You'll recall that on the flip side: I would be admonished for not working enough to take care of my family—insanity.

I cannot recall, as an adult, ever attending the "birthday party" get-together. "Mom, my birthday came and went. I don't understand why you're asking me about my birthday," I'd say. "We had a party to celebrate you and your brother's birthdays," she'd respond. "So, you wanted me to come to *his* birthday party? My birthday has long passed. It was his birthday."

My mom received her birthday wishes on the actual date; my sister, my dad, and my brother did as well. "Well, where's David? We want to wish him a happy birthday, too." It's all about appearances. It's not like she couldn't have called *on* my birthday, no, she was at least a week too late.

My mom never heard me through my direct words to her or through my actions. It was the same thing every year. This played out year after year. My dad knew exactly what I was doing and why, and it was exactly why he wasn't going to budge—just on principle. All I was saying was that I'd recognize their happy wishes *on* my birthday, but clearly, I didn't deserve that.

What my dad failed to see was that I'd never gotten my own birthday, so I wasn't losing anything in this deal; Dad was doubling down on thin air. Be mad—I don't care. I just didn't give a fuck anymore. My parents were so focused on appearances that reality, including my reality that my birthday wasn't worth mentioning unless it was my brother's birthday, was invisible to them.

I'll let you in on a secret that I've never even shared with my wife. I laugh about it every year. Not in anticipation that anyone will wish me happy birthday but to watch the texts flood in each year *on my brother's birthday*. This speaks to another point regarding your children or people in your lives. If people don't progressively get better after the first couple times of having to apologize (like being late for birthday wishes or events), they just don't give a shit, so don't devalue yourself by listening to excuses. They don't give a shit, and they never will—your move.

My dad was a tough son of a bitch if he was facing a kid, but otherwise, not so much. My dad never retired, but he cut back on work to babysit. I had gone to their house one afternoon, and there were several screaming kids running around. I kind of laughed, looked at my dad, and asked, "Enjoying the retirement dream?" I thought my mom was busy with one of the kids and wouldn't hear my jab. She spun on her heel. "Your dad loves these kids! He wants to spend time with them!"

I couldn't help but laugh. I said, "Where most men dream of being on the lake, fishing, Dad dreamed of retirement consisting of screaming kids. I hope it's everything you hoped it'd be, Dad." The funny thing was, I *never* heard my dad say how much he was enjoying the follow-on rounds of raising kids. At least from my view, he hated it the first time—why would round two be any better? He never backed up what my mom said. Dad always sat back quietly while Mom answered for him. He literally worked his entire life for it to end without being able to do anything he wanted to do.

My dad and I often communicated without direct words. It worked better for us. He knew I was casting light on his shitty situation. He also knew I was intentionally poking my mom. He knew I was calling him a bitch, just *daring* him to toss the kids and go fishing. I wasn't doing it to be mean, I was trying to break them out of their routine that was literally draining the life from my dad.

I'd offered to buy him a boat, but he said he couldn't tow or launch a boat by himself anymore. Later when we had a yacht, I told him we would pay to fly them to us, and I'd buy a recliner to put on the back of the yacht by the wet bar. He could do the things he loved most: sit in a recliner, drink a beer, and fish. I wasn't joking. He started to cry on the phone.

The times when my dad was emotional with me throughout my life could be counted on one hand, even with some fingers missing. My mom took the phone from him, and for the last time, I was told why they couldn't make a trip to be with us. They had to watch the great grandkids and taxi them to ballgames. That was that. I saw my dad two more times before he passed away and then that chapter of my life was finished. It's in reflection of this span of decades that I have to ask, What was the point? What was the goal of all the screaming, the threats of violence, the acts of violence, the gossip, the judgment, the preferential treatment, the exclusion, the excuses, and the hypocrisy?

The way my parents, and so many other parents, raise their kids just ensures that their children will live the same exact life, or worse. It's insane to me. I don't recall how many years my parents were married, but it was over fifty years. We have to *give* life a point; we have to teach our children to have a point in their lives. From the time my parents moved into their big new house, they were trying to play catch-up and simply never did. Every time they got close, they used their resources on appearances and went back down the hole.

My mom and dad are the extremely rare case for me in which, I believe, divorce would have been in their best interest. It didn't matter what my dad did, my mom would destroy it. If he had an extra $100, she would spend $200. If their car situation was finally worked out, my mom would somehow wreck hers. My mom even squandered my dads retirement to babysit other people's kids. Back when my grades-for-a-race-bike story took place and my mom secretly visited my teacher, my parents sent me to stay with a friend one weekend while they took a trip, and I was home that Saturday when they returned. My mom was over-joyed and smiling like a kid—she'd bought a new camera. When she saw me, her smile vanished. How reassuring. That weekend, she unpacked and organized her new goodies. Like many things I've shared, I'm not proud of it, but I intentionally looked for the receipt and finally found it. They couldn't afford a dirt bike; what could they afford?

They'd spent almost $3,000. Mom's 35 mm SLR camera body was over $1,000. I believe she had three lenses; one, a 200 mm, was $800. There was the remote cord for night shots, fully articulating flash, the bag, the batteries, the strap, and so forth. That was a shitload of money and equipment in the 1980s. Comparatively, my race bike and full gear would have been $800 total—brand new.

It was their money to spend as they chose; I can't argue that. My mom arranged everything just so in her bag and took pictures for her new photography class (which was another few hundred dollars), and then put the camera away. She never used it. Apparently, she didn't consider the cost of developing the film before she spent all the extra money they had.

My mom did the same thing with art supplies. Endless money on expensive sable brushes and paints she would never use. I've never been a painter, yet she repeatedly accused me of stealing her art supplies, and eventually she accused others. I finally dismissed her protests of me "getting into her things" and started digging through the room—which she still hasn't cleaned decades later—and found all the items, some still new in the bags, that she'd accused people of stealing. She dismissed the accusations of theft as though they were of no consequence. I told my dad that I found everything Mom thought was stolen, buried in her hobby closet. She could start painting again.

My mom didn't *have* to work a day in her life. She had no purpose, no motivation. She had no reason to do anything except float along with the whims of her skewed reality, watch talk shows, eat cheese puffs, and smoke cigarettes. She had no point. She certainly wasn't a positive force in her husband or kids' lives.

If she and my dad had tapped out, my dad could have worked toward something and enjoyed the fruits of his decades of labor. My mom could have been held accountable for her decisions and been swayed to be productive for her own good. Like my mom's hoarder hobby room that's always "going to be cleaned" but never has been, my mom has allowed herself to believe that doing nothing until something is forced on you is the same as making the decision to do it. It was always "someday," that was never today. If she didn't always have my dad there enabling her, she would have been better for it. My grandmother would often say that my dad should make my mom get a job; my dad knew she was right. "She needs to get her butt out the door," my grandma would say. I can't think of too many times I'd say divorce is the best answer, but when I was sixteen and seemingly trying to end it all with drugs and alcohol, that would've been a good time for them to part ways and get their own lives on track and healthy.

When we lived away from Mom during my sophomore year, my dad would go other places instead of coming home from work. I think part of him hoped he'd find me dead. It sounds horrible, but in a world where mothers or fathers murder their family or children for a new lover, it's not that far-fetched. I'd caused a lot of stress on top of the existing issues in our family. I was not innocent by any means. My dad didn't actually want me in the first place, so many years before, but like a baby or cameras and paints, Dad gave my mom what she wanted to make her happy. I was obviously not in a good place as a person at this point, as attested by my drug use and drinking. My mom didn't have any solutions, only complaints, and my dad was drowning in debt. He should have said fuck it and punched out (whether bankruptcy or divorce, a life reset). One of the nights he did not come home after work, he was invited to a family dinner at a nearby relative's house. I was never invited to these dinners. He shared his frustration about me with them, and their advice to him was surprising—in a bad way. But first, a story to preface my opinion.

WHAT HAPPENED TO THE PUPPIES?

We always had an excess of animals around while I was growing up. For myself, in seventeen years, I had three pets that were mine. One was a runt pig from one of my brother's litters—I named it Rastus. The sow (mama) tried to kill it, so I cared for it. He thought he was a dog and stayed with the dogs. I had a goat named Billy that was attacked and killed by the neighbor's German shepherd, and then there was Floyd. Floyd was a collie mix dog that I got as a puppy. Terri and I eventually took him with us when we moved from our little apartment and had a yard. Floyd was the best; he was an amazing and loyal friend. He lived to be fourteen and died in our backyard under a tree near the balance beam.

My parents had a female Irish setter that had puppies. With two horses and countless dogs and cats to take care of, my dad stressed about the cost of feed. One night when I was a teenager, I was in bed and heard a specific kind of bark outside my window. The hair on my neck stood up. It was saying, "Danger," and then I heard a puppy yelp. When you live in the country, you learn the sounds; I know some of you reading this know exactly what I'm talking about.

I looked out my window; someone was out front. I didn't have a shotgun in my room, which was probably a good thing on this night. I ran out of my bedroom door to the living room and apprehensively told my mom that someone or something was out front. The ruckus continued, so I bolted for the front door. My mom shouted at me and said that I was supposed to be in bed. Her eyes bugged out, and she clenched her jaw and forcefully, angrily, pointed down the hall to my room. I paused. "Okay. . . whatever it is, is on you." I went back to my room, barking and puppies screaming—and then silence.

Earlier, to help my dad, I had dug a long trench out front for the replacement of a buried sewage line. The broken pipe was under the sidewalk and it had rained, so my dig-out was full of water. The morning after hearing dogs screaming and barking, I went out and looked at the ground all around the front door and sidewalk area. There were paw prints in the dirt. The mama dog wasn't there. Oddly, she was in the backyard.

I retrieved the rake used for breaking up the ground while digging and started fishing in the water. Squatting down and rotating the tines up, I scraped the underside of the sidewalk. Two dead puppies came out. In total, I retrieved six two-month-old puppies. All drowned.

My dad would wear old dress shoes to do yard work. It seemed like a generational thing because he wasn't alone. There were dress shoe prints in the mud next to where I had dug, and my dad distinctly was not in the living room when my mom was telling me to ignore the dogs' barking. Dad drowned the dogs and locked the mama in the backyard so that she wouldn't pull them out.

What scared me most was the anger toward me and the secrets they kept from me. It's not like I hadn't intentionally killed animals before due to injury or illness. That's part of living in the country. But this was different. These puppies could have been given new homes, taken to the pound, or even painlessly injected or shot. No, he drowned them one at a time, their last moments filled with painful terror. What the actual fuck? I laid them all out in a row and called to my mom from the front door. She finally appeared. I pointed to the dead dogs. "All that barking . . . they were drowning, or being drowned." My mom just paused and said, "That's too bad," and then she turned and walked away. I was stunned.

What Was The Surprising Advice Given To My Dad?

To leave me to my own outcome. As my dad enjoyed that family dinner I spoke of earlier (the one I wasn't ever included in or invited to, and wasn't even supposed to know about)—were those family members secretly hoping that in his absence, I'd just solve his problem for him by offing myself accidentally or intentionally? When essentially, their response was. "You can't watch him all the time. Let what's bound to happen, happen," there's no doubt in my mind. It is always sobering to discover brutal truths that conflict with the lies of love, loyalty, and close family ties we're taught to believe.

Secrets are exhilarating until they are no longer secret; my life was on display. What made me realize that my situation wasn't as bad as it seemed was that everyone was gossiping about and attacking me with things that were usually, only true *in part*. To paraphrase one of my favorite rock songs, they'd fired their six-shots into the wind.[35]

I've been writing this book for over a year. My first individual manuscript was well over a hundred thousand words. These memories don't live in the front of my mind, so I had to sit down and write in complete detail everything related to our story to ensure it was in order; determine whether details needed to be skewed to protect the innocent or guilty, whichever the case; and decide whether the story maintained the point of telling it.

The stark contrast between the contemptuous glares from relatives and the knowledge of their own questionable behaviors suddenly becomes humorous. From illegal drug use to a drunken escapade with a close relative, and the outspoken critic of the queer community who had their own past with those same activities—swingers, police assaults, and intent to distribute; these are just a glimpse into a family dynamic that could be described as chaotic. The countless jail visits are a testament to their escapades, which feel almost routine for some. Perhaps my visibility kept their misdeeds in the shadows. While I've never been involved in wrecks, theft, being arrested or the other misfortunes that have colored my family's past, I recall many incidents over the last 45 years. It's ironic that I've become the family's non-gossiping keeper of secrets. Reflecting on my life, I'm thankful I never turned to deflection or scapegoating. Such strategies lead nowhere, don't foster personal growth, and leave me wary of my own flaws being exposed.

---

35 - "18 and Life Lyrics," Genius, 2024, https://genius.com/Skid-row-18-and-life-lyrics.

With all these memories swimming around for my reflection, do I think my family discussed really hurting me or, by inaction, allowing me to be hurt? I do. Thankfully, I didn't allow their wish to come true. I'm glad my dad wasn't quite dark enough to encourage my demise beyond possibly ensuring he would be absent if I needed help. But yeah, this time period would have been perfect for my parents to get on a better path as individuals and have a healthier, more rewarding life until the end.

CARS

I've brought up the subject of cars several times throughout this book, which is something I hadn't thought much about until I began writing last year. When I offered to buy my dad a boat, I had also bought him a truck that he wasn't aware of yet. He had two work trucks that I recall, but Dad never had his own truck. The nice one he received from work was brand new. Unfortunately, Dad didn't have it long before one fateful night he was driving home late on a narrow, two-lane, blacktop road and crested a hill at forty-five miles per hour, and just over the top was a Hereford cow. The truck was totaled—dead truck, dead cow. Dad was shaken up but otherwise okay. He was again relegated to his old work truck.

I knew Dad always wanted a truck and I also knew he didn't have much time left to enjoy it. They needed another vehicle anyway, as Dad couldn't do anything himself with Mom holding the car keys in the name of endless babysitting. So, we bought him a Ram 1500. It was used, but I thought it was nicer than any vehicle he'd ever owned. I coordinated from out of state and went to Mom and Dad's to share the surprise.

My mom interrogated me. She wanted to know why I was there; it was unexpected, and my visit was for no apparent reason, which was odd. I worked out of state and wasn't around much. "I came to get Dad! I bought something for him," I said. "What? Where is it? Why can't you just bring it here?" she asked suspiciously. "It won't fit in my Porsche," I said. I thought that was funny. Dad heard the conversation and walked over. "Jeez, I hoped it'd be a surprise, but it doesn't matter. I bought you a truck, Dad. A white Dodge Ram with a blue interior and not too many miles—get dressed and we'll go get it. The guy is expecting us. It's paid for, and he'll sign the title over to you."

"What?" my mom exclaimed. "You can't do that. Who is this guy?" I responded, "What? What are you talking about, Mom? It's the guy who owned this truck; he got a new truck and kept this one because I told him I wanted to buy it for my dad." The guy, a good friend for years, sold it to me for what the dealer said they'd give for it. So, I sent him the money, and he kept the truck until I could get there; he even had it detailed for my dad.

"Your dad doesn't drive anymore," my mom said. "Yes, he does," I responded. "No," she insisted, "I need to be with him when he does and I'm not comfortable driving a truck." I looked at my dad. "Dad?" I said, as though to say, "Maybe you'd like to contribute to this conversation?" I could see the excitement on his face, and then I watched it die. "No, if your mom says I shouldn't, I better not." To which I replied, "So, we'll go get it and park it in the driveway. I'll fill it up and pay for the insurance just so you know, 'by God,' that you have a truck in the driveway," I said.

"No, we are not doing that," my mom interrupted. "Okay. Well, I tried," I said abruptly.

My mom wanted to know how I paid for it and what I was going to do now. "I wrote the guy a check. I'm going to get in my car, put the top down, and go tell the guy that my mom said that my dad doesn't want the truck and whatever. I have a truck; I don't need another one. I'll park it on a street corner with the keys in it." My dad was obviously upset and I was intentionally being an asshole at this point. My mom was confused, but it wasn't like I hadn't spent money on them before. Taking them to Europe could have paid for a brand-new truck.

Speaking to her opinion that my dad couldn't drive, years later my mom, on the other hand, drove into oncoming traffic for a mile with police cars behind her and still argues that she should be able to have her car and her independence. I know that's the disease talking. For my dad though, I'd just lived enough life to want him to have a small taste of someone giving to him for no reason other than it would make him happy.

Every time I'm on the water in our boat with Terri and we're skimming across the waves, jamming to our retro rock music, I literally think,

"We are living the dream." My dad didn't get that calm solitude in his life without having to think of ten other people first. I'm sad for him, but do you see the point(s) of the story? People will use or utilize you for their interests until the day you die. This is why you have to determine what's important. What are your priorities? Just because a person is drowning doesn't make them a bad person, but that won't stop them from drowning their rescuer, either. Sometimes, people need to endure bad things to make positive changes in their lives and quit expecting others to make up for their shortcomings; it's not easy for anyone.

You may be wondering why I've displayed acts of compassion toward my dad, considering everything I've shared. I understand why my dad was the way he was: because no one taught him how to constructively live life. My mom made it a perfect storm. Her husband existed to provide *to* her. As far as she was concerned, good kids should be grateful for being brought into this world; her children were indebted *to* her from day one. We all existed to serve her—we owed it to her.

Again, I don't know much about my mom's childhood. I do know her parents weren't rich, though. Essentially, my mom was still a child. She could call people names and judge them. She could accuse them of stealing or any other random thing, and when she realized her accusations were not true, oh well. She didn't blink an eye and there was never remorse. When she didn't get her way, she would fly into a rage and hurt people. She didn't care; she didn't even notice. My mom did not look back and see the path of absolute destruction left in her wake. Since she didn't develop these characteristics as an adult, I think my mom simply never grew up.

The day before our daughter's funeral, we had our closest family and friends join us for dinner at a restaurant. Ten years before, when her mother passed away, my mom had accused her own brother of stealing from her, which he hadn't—we had proof. The proof showed that to the contrary, my mom had taken from him. My mom would rehash the fabricated past offenses anytime the topic came up though, and never let it go. Toward the end of our daughter's memorial dinner, my mom finally exploded at her brother and sister-in-law in the restaurant and began to be verbally abusive, yelling and continuing her decade-long poisonous rant.

Mom's outburst in the middle of a restaurant full of grieving people began to make me understand. She is so self-absorbed, so narcissistic, and so self-centered that the context of why we were all there together never occurred to her. "Our daughter died! Your granddaughter died, and we are burying her tomorrow." On her end, it was "Yeah, but . . ." She wouldn't—couldn't—drop it because what she thought outweighed everything else, simply because she thought it.

Whenever my mom was gifted yet another car she needed it because she didn't take care of the car she had. The car I offered to buy from her was the brand-new, fully loaded car she bought after my dad passed; she actually took care of this one. To my knowledge, my dad never experienced buying a brand-new car for himself. He had a work truck, he borrowed his dad's van, and then bought a van very similar to it that was also twenty years old. You would think that my mom would have been ecstatic for my dad to get the truck he always talked about. No, because it wasn't for her, she couldn't have cared less.

No, my mom was a spoiled child her entire life. My dad never saw it and never quit trying to make her happy. Mom would never in her life be content and happy, though—her parents didn't do their job and gladly passed the responsibility of my mom to my dad. The seed for that realization for me was our daughter's death—about which my mom still says matter-of-factly, "Yeah, we really miss her a lot." I've never lost an infant child, and not to take anything away from her—nothing compares to a parent losing a child—but my mom will go on and on about her loss. Her son lived for three days; my daughter lived for almost twenty-two years. We had a mutual relationship; we had life and experiences together, and my mom thinks that, as her dad, I just miss her a lot?

I wish I would have realized this about my mom sooner. You know, if I knew then what I know now . . . I could have navigated my relationship with my mom with more success. My personality put her on a power trip. I gave her control because she was a mom, but she responded the way a child would respond. It was always, "Give me what I want first, and then I'll give you what you want," and then she wouldn't follow through because she didn't have to; she was in charge. As a kid, lying, for me, was beating her at her own game. I was *saying* that she was in charge. I was saying what she told me to say, and that's what she wanted to hear. After that, my mom's brain turned off because it wasn't about her. It was all about appearances, not anything of real value.

When I asked her about her car, it was during a phone conversation. She had called me, and when I answered, I said I could talk for as long as she wanted. Rather than calling me at work, which often happened, she'd actually caught me at the beginning of a long, boring drive. She wanted my approval so badly that she burst out with, "You can *have* my car if you want it!" Even after agreeing to me giving her money for it, she thought she had me. As long as she had her car, I'd be beholden to her. She refused to follow through, because she had gotten what she wanted. Her word and what I wanted meant nothing—they never had. That's an easy pill to swallow. What will happen to her car is what always happens with my mom; she won't make a decision, and the car will just disappear, given to someone "more deserving."

My mom created drama between the siblings because it made her the information clearinghouse. She would always have a kid coming to her to get the info about family. If she gossiped about me (which she did excessively at the family functions Terri and I weren't invited to), she was the center of attention. The problem is, for the first twenty-five years of my life, they didn't recognize it for what it was; my mom was willing to destroy anything to be needed and wanted. Not surprisingly, when I disappeared, that's when I started getting calls about the who, what, and where of Mom's latest antics—usually involving verbally attacking another family member the way she had attacked me for years.

We had changed our lives long before this realization, but it validated the change made so many years ago. It's like I'd thrown a basketball over my shoulder, started walking, and twenty-five years later—I heard the swoosh.

Okay, so shitty people are shitty, and you've been hurt and lied to—cry me a river, who cares?

Exactly.

No one cares. No one is *going* to care. It occurred to me that someone could be reading this with tears streaming down their face, though, and you're not alone. Whatever has happened to all of us in life does make us stronger and I'll tell you why, beyond a bumper-sticker saying like, "What doesn't kill you makes you stronger." If what our parents and family did to us caused so much pain, was there an alternative that would cause an equally positive result? Why do we have to continue to live in the bed of shit our families put us in? We don't. We have to choose to understand it and act in a way counter to the pain; we don't have to pass it on to our kids. I can remember my mom, eyes bugging out with contempt, screaming, "I can't wait until you have kids and they do this to you!"

Even as a kid, this statement seemed fucked up. My mom, and so many parents like her, couldn't wait to see their children in distress? Failing as adults? Seriously, let your mind absorb that line of thinking for a moment. How did we positively respond to this upbringing? Well, I never wanted our children to endure what we did. Sometimes as a parent, you see things coming, and it breaks your heart. We just wanted to be there for our kids when they needed to take a moment.

In what positive ways do you now do your lives differently? What can you do at home that really makes a difference in the health of your family?

Do thoughtful things for each other—send your spouse and kids cards in the mail! Include a note to say how much you love them, how proud you are of them, and how much they mean to you. Why do you have to wait for a holiday to give your spouse or kids a special gift or take them on a special outing?

Don't squander your kids' success. If they finish early, you still have scheduled time. "You guys are done already? Let's go to the park!" Or, "Let's go to the zoo!" Or, "Let's go to the museum—field trip!" How about the working spouse encouraging (and teaching) their children to show appreciation for everything their teacher (and parent) does for them? Let's buy a custom mug with special coffee to give our teacher. Let's give our teacher Saturday off with a trip to the spa, and clean the house while they're gone.

Every single one of these things says, "I see you and I notice you, and you make a difference in our lives. You matter." Let's teach our children how to interact with appreciation and handle giving and receiving with grace and gratitude. Or, "Here, Scooter, Daddy bought Mom a vacuum cleaner. Sign the card. It's from all of us."

Mom gets all excited and thanks her sweet baby for the vacuum cleaner and showers him with kisses. He just learned he didn't have to do shit to get high praise. He can give Mom pretty much anything, and she'll treat him like he's special. I hope Scooter can find a woman willing to be happy with that later in life. Something I've done for my wife for more years than I can recall is leaving her messages on the bathroom mirror. Guys, beware, we don't want to mess up their cosmetics—I use an old lipstick or eyeliner pencil to write directly on the mirror, and a cotton swab or tissue with isopropyl alcohol on it wipes it right off. Tell her you love her—you never know what encouragement she might need when she gets up in the morning.

GOOD STUFF!

What do I remember that was positive or even fun from my childhood? Well, we went to the lake for several years. We had a boat, and my aunt and uncle and cousins had a boat, so we went to the lake a few times a year. My dad and uncle would pull us all over the lake on water skis for most of the day, every day. The dads were in the seat all day, dragging at least six kids plus adults. I've gotta be honest, I don't know how they did it; I don't think I could.

Not everything about the lake trips was good, though. Our parents all smoked. They'd relax outside and drink beer and smoke and flick their cigarette butts into the yard. Eventually, there would be unsightly cigarette butts scattered everywhere.

My cousin and I were usually given the unsavory task of "policing" the stinky cigarette nubs. We'd scour the yard and driveway for the countless errant butts and bits of trash and throw them away, then go ask if we were done. Sometimes we got approval, and sometimes we didn't. I concluded that they didn't like seeing shameful evidence of the cigarettes everywhere, so my take was to clean where they could see, but otherwise, I did what I did at home—stay away from the adults. That's what they really wanted, a break from the kids. I can't speak for my cousins or aunt and uncle, but my staying away from my parents at home applied at the lake, too. The longer I was out of their sight, the happier Mom and Dad were. That's what I acted on, and it seemed to give positive results.

Waterskiing was absolutely my favorite part of going to the lake. My dad was limited in how fast he could pull us kids behind the boat. The limit was enforced by my mom and how she felt. "Oh no, no, this feels too fast!" my mom would say. We kids would make the best of it when my dad was at the helm. It was a completely different story, however, when my uncle was in control. Despite my mom's objections, my uncle would deliver. He knew I was a bit of an arrogant risk taker. To me, the best things in life were adrenaline-charged challenges. He'd let me get out on the water by myself, and he'd "floor it" with me on one ski behind the boat. *I know where this is going,* I'd think eagerly. Everyone in the boat would hang on at full power, and he'd cut the steering wheel hard left or right. I'd blast over the wake and pull against the rope. If I was doing 50 miles per hour when he cut it, I was doing 90 miles per hour now, possibly over 100? It depends on the rope length that day, but I can still remember my ski skipping across the water so fast that it hurt my feet. My rudder once came out of the water, my ski spun, and I went "down." Down to a water surface that at, the speed I was traveling, felt like concrete. My body skipped and flailed over the top of the water as though I'd crashed at high speed on a motorcycle. It just wasn't ending until I'd slowed down enough that part of my body caught the water and flipped me up into the air, and I, in my full life jacket, went completely underwater. As I bobbed back up to the surface, my ski that was skipping across the water skimmed right over my head. It felt like I was hit in the head with a baseball bat. I immediately saw blood drifting out through the water. My bell was rung. "Oh my God!" my aunt hollered. "You're gonna kill him!" When I looked up, there was a little concern on my uncle's face, but he was smiling. If I'd dared to say what I was thinking, I'd have said, "Fuck yes! That's what I'm talking about!" My uncle knew it, but my poor aunt had her limitations on damaging kids.

My aunt and uncle were hilarious as a couple then, and still are. My uncle would pour on the coals at my request. It was as much fun for him as it was for me. He would allow me to get what I asked for. While remaining a responsible adult, he'd let me take it as far as I dared. Those were fun lessons to learn. My dad only allowed me to do what Mom allowed *him* to allow me to do, and she lived in a constant state of fear. If my mom felt that way, it applied to everyone she had control over. If I had to pick up cigarette butts and beer cans in order to take part in whatever was going to happen at the lake, to me, it was a fair trade and my memories of our lake trips are good.

I enjoyed having fun and getting into trouble with my cousin. These trips offered me life experiences that were unique. I watched a boy jump off a cliff into the lake; he never came back up. They found his body six hours later. Supposedly, a large catfish was dining on the bone marrow of his snapped leg, but seeing the search teams come to the lake gave me an interest in SCUBA diving.

I can't count the number of teenage boys we helped who forgot their boat plugs and their boats were sinking. I learned to clean fish and what to watch out for when you're going to "swing a ski rope like a cowboy." Something as random as my uncle saying, "Waffle, waffle, waffle," in a silly voice will forever be seared into my brain from trips like this, along with a funny memory from when I was barely six years old and in the backseat of a station wagon outside of Dallas, Texas. All of my positive childhood memories of my dad are the few things we did together as a family, going to the lake or cutting firewood. These weren't really designed for him and me to spend time together, but parents and kids as a family still happened. Whether my dad intended it or not, I must give him credit for the positive memories and experiences of my young life.

The most positive memory I can come up with about my mom was that she helped me study for a school test once. This one time in particular, she kindly would not let me go to bed until I understood the material. I aced the test and couldn't have completed it faster with a cheat sheet— that was all her. Although they were rare for me, my mom had her lucid moments. I'm compelled to desperately search my memories for happy bonding moments shared with my parents and all I get back is condemnation. From being lost at an amusement park to a thousand other things afterward, the relationship between me and my parents was mostly without fondness, only tolerance through clenched teeth.

Mom always "knew" tomorrow would be better. My mom never allowed tomorrow to be *today*. She never proactively did anything positively different today to make tomorrow any better. I felt bad for her when I was old enough to see her as a person and not just as Mom. I feel sad for her now, in the twilight of her life, that with all of her interests and talents, she never embraced that today *is* the day.

My mom was a talented artist; she painted with oils and watercolors and sometimes even coffee grounds. My mom also drew with charcoal and pastels. Despite her skill, she always needed more training, more experience for it to mean anything to her. Rather than pursue it, she put her tools of art in the closet and lamented her lack of training. My mom was also into photography at a decently serious level for a short time. She was a gifted nature photographer, but she decided that she was never good enough to do anything with it; she needed something more, that she would inevitably get "later" and put her photography gear in the closet to never use again.

Because of these interests, she planted the interest in me. Through the years, I've enjoyed drawing and dabbled in photography. I have to give her credit for influencing those outlets in my life. I was good enough to be content, and when I would try to have conversations with her, simply to connect, my mom would say "I'm not that good. You keep trying, though, and one day you'll get there." She couldn't understand that I was content where I was and simply wanted to have a conversation. I would *tell* her this, and she literally didn't hear me.

If I had waited until I was a "real writer" to write this book, it wouldn't have happened. I had to accept myself for what I am today and put myself out there. Now, I'm a real writer. That doesn't mean I'm a great, or even good, writer, but I am proudly a coauthor of a book with my wife, and our voices have been released into the world, part of our life story has been told to the world. I'm honored by that. I'm honored that my peers of humanity have read my words and heard my voice, and maybe, possibly, we've played a part in positively effecting change in people's lives.

As I sit writing, I stare at the page with reels of memories tearing through my mind, unsure of what best applies to each topic—I have even heard the voice of our late daughter laughing and encouraging me. As my muse, Jessica often kept me on track: that it's about the kids. It's about your kids. It's about family connecting and nurturing one another—ours and yours. Jessica's family meant everything to her.

This project has given me more time with the daughter we lost years ago. Jessica was a month short of her twenty-second birthday when she died. Twenty-two years of life, eighteen of which were spent together, homeschooling. That's a lot of memories. Terri and I have talked about what we can do to honor her memory, and nothing seemed perfect enough. We couldn't let her life and influence end in the middle of an intersection, so this is the closest we've gotten. We've taught our children to take action in life. "Do it like you mean it," I like to say. So, we're going to tell the whole world how amazing our Jessica was.

Jessica didn't know a stranger, and was somehow attracted to people having a bad day. She would compliment the tired cashier about how pretty her fingernails were or the pretty hair-tie they wore. To the little kids she mentored, Jessica was a bright, smiling angel, always ready for a hug, or for the occasional brat, she'd make them do planks when they misbehaved . . . while doing the planks with them, encouraging and counting as she made it fun.

From the time she was a little girl, I could swear there was an aura of light around her. Jessica was just a "bright light." She had her own struggles and challenges in life, like anyone else, but they rarely deterred her outlook. This brings me to my final point about family and homeschooling. Homeschooling isn't a cure-all. Homeschooling won't make truly average children the next prodigy. Homeschooling done thoughtfully, with preparation, planning, and a lot of patience, is a tool to give your children the best chance to be their best selves. Homeschooling will give you and your family exponentially more time together and if you're a good homeschool parent, your children will have a chance to blossom, so don't let this time slip by. Live in each moment to your best ability and enjoy your family to the fullest extent.

We said that we don't measure success in money alone, because money is necessary. But if currency isn't king, then what is? When the lights go out, what was the point? We think the point is striving to give the best of us to ourselves and our family. As we learn and understand

and grow as individuals, sure, it benefits us, but it's for the betterment of our legacy—for our family and children and in turn, for our grandchildren and great-grandchildren. You have a chance to make an impact for generations.

Previously, I mentioned my great-grandfather Merle and my grandpa. These men changed my life for the better. My great-grandfather was born in the 1890s, and I'm thinking and talking about him in a book almost 130 years later. I knew him personally! When you are together as a family, don't let streams of meaningless media vie for your attention; put the electronics away. Honestly, if I'm talking with someone, and in the middle of what I'm saying, they pick up a phone and start looking at it and scrolling, I immediately stop what I'm saying and walk away. Not angry, just indifferent in the same way this person disregarded me, effectively saying to me, "What is on the phone is more important than you." I refuse to be less important than random media. Also if we are around people who can't put their phone away for more than a moment but then don't respond to texts or messages for days/weeks/months and in one case over a year, take the hint. Do you think they've suddenly given up their smart-phone? No? You're only marginally more important than a complete stranger and they're trying to tell you this, you're just not listening.

Do you ever see truly successful people zombie-scrolling their phones, or do they respectfully give their undivided attention to the person they're communicating with? Do you or your kids turn up your volume in a public space, as though everyone there wants to hear what you're so interested in? Putting technology into its appropriate place will enhance your family experience and perception of those around you. That said, we do own all the latest electronics, even a PlayStation. We used to play games online with our sons when we could, because they're interested in it and enjoy it.

I won't say never, but 99 percent of the time, don't compete with your kids. Enjoy them being good at something, or allow them to enjoy you being good at something. Especially for us men and boys. We like to trash-talk, but don't emasculate your sons or daughters. They already think the world of you. I learned this the hard way. To me, it was fun but self-serving, and to my sons, it's filled with bad memories. I ignorantly screwed up, and nothing can change the effect it has had. Maybe you're really good at baseball or a fearless motocross rider; it doesn't matter—let your kids discover their own love and talent for a new activity. You can still be good at it, but don't judge them based on your ability. Encourage them on their effort and their ability. Just like learning to walk, they'll automatically want to be just like you and make you proud. Allow them to try to be as good as you . . . or better.

CHAPTER 21

AM I QUALIFIED TO HOMESCHOOL MY CHILDREN?

This entire book has been painting a picture of what homeschooling looks like and your role as a parent administering your child or children's education. In true homeschooling fashion though, let's get into the weeds of the vocabulary that defines what it means to be capable and prepared to provide an education to your children.

Let's begin by considering the word *qualified*. What is the definition of qualified?

1. Oxford Languages definition: "officially recognized as being trained to perform a particular job; certified."[36]
2. *Merriam-Webster* definition: "fitted (as by training or experience) for a given purpose: competent."[37]

Now let's break these two definitions down. Regarding the first definition, I can see there are a few words or phrases that I need to define in addition to the word *qualified*:

---

36 - Oxford Languages app, s.v. "Qualified."

37 - *Merriam-Webster*, s.v. "Qualified," last updated July 8, 2024, https://www.merriam-webster.com/dictionary/qualified.

- *Officially recognized:* given official approval after meeting certain standards. Adjective. Traditionally, or generally, recognized and accepted.
- *Trained:* having been taught a particular skill or type of behavior through practice and instruction over a period of time.
- *Certified:* officially recognized as possessing certain qualifications or meeting certain standards. (There is the phrase "officially recognized" again.)
- *Official:* relating to an authority or public body and its duties, actions, and responsibilities.
- *Officially:* with the authority of the government or some other organization.
- *Recognized:* acknowledge the existence, validity, or legality of.

Doing the same for *Merriam-Webster*'s definition of *qualified,* let's define a few of the words for better clarity and understanding: [38]

- *Fitted:* having the appropriate qualities or skills to do something.
- *Purpose: noun,* the reason for which something is done or created or for which something exists; *verb,* to have as one's intention or objective.

So how do we know which definition of *purpose* to choose? We ask the question: Is the word *purpose* used as a noun or verb in this definition?

It is a noun because it is the object of the prepositional phrase "for a given purpose." How do we know that? We go back to our definitions of the parts of speech to help us determine the use of the word *purpose* in this sentence. The word *for* is a preposition, *a* is an article, and *given* is an adjective that describes the word *purpose*—adjectives modify or describe nouns. The definition of the object of a preposition is either a noun or a pronoun that comes after a preposition. We know by definition, that a pronoun takes the place of a noun, so this is not a pronoun; therefore, in this sentence, the word *purpose* is used as a noun. Now that we know what part of speech the word *purpose* is used as in the definition, we know which definition of *purpose* to use, the noun definition—the reason for

---

38 - https://www.google.com/search?q=definition+for+fitted

which something is done or created or for which something exists. But how is it done?

Here are our options:

- *Competent*—having requisite or adequate ability or qualities; having the necessary ability, knowledge, or skill to do something successfully.
- *Adequate*—satisfactory or acceptable in quality or quantity.

Using our defined words, let's rewrite our definitions of the word *qualified*, in regard to homeschooling:

1. Given official approval after having met certain standards and having been taught to homeschool through practice and instruction over a time period to perform the job of teacher with the authority of the government or some other organization that acknowledges the existence, validity, or legality of our possessing certain qualifications and meeting certain standards to homeschool our children.

2. Having the appropriate qualities or skills to homeschool; having the requisite or adequate (satisfactory or acceptable) ability, knowledge, or skill to homeschool successfully.

If, when we were deciding to homeschool, we had chosen to follow the first definition of *qualified*—"officially recognized as being trained to perform a particular job; certified"—then according to this definition, no, we were not qualified. And that is exactly what everyone around us said. "You are *not qualified* to teach your children. You are going to ruin them." We would have stopped right there and not continued to move forward with our homeschool.

So then, back to the question: Am I qualified to homeschool my children?

This is unequivocally the wrong question. By rephrasing *Merriam-Webster*'s definition of *qualified*, we come up with a better question: Do I have the requisite or adequate ability, knowledge, or skill to homeschool my children successfully? Let me ask you further, did you go to school? Do you know how to read and do basic math? Yes? Then 100 percent you have acceptable ability, knowledge, and skill to homeschool your children successfully!

We chose not to listen to the people asking the first question and instead chose to use the second definition of *qualified*. When we first started our homeschool journey, did we have adequate ability, knowledge, and skill to teach our three children from birth through high school? No. But we did have adequate ability, knowledge, and skill to teach our fourth grader and our babies. We probably could have figured high school out if we had to, but that's not what is required at the beginning. It is not required that you be able to teach every single subject from birth to graduation immediately when you start—you grow as they grow, you learn as they learn. You increase your knowledge and skills in order to teach the next year, one year at a time. That's it. That is exactly what we did, and so can you.

ABOUT THE AUTHORS

David Batts was a married high school teenager with no resources and nowhere to go. David leveraged lessons learned from his personal history and each new piece of knowledge he gained to successfully build and navigate his own life. In his many accomplishments, being a husband and dad always came first. Through David's process of growth and development, he realized the true concept of homeschooling and, with his wife, successfully developed that idea into motion to fully prepare their three children for college and life ahead. David's professional career has been in aerospace, ranging from an aircraft mechanic to inspector, technical and policy writer, and department management. He enjoys time with his wife of thirty-eight years—working together, traveling, flying, riding motorcycles, and boating. They also immensely enjoy spending time with their kids and grandkids.

 Terri Batts is a passionate, successful first-generation homeschool parent. Even though she was married as a teenager, Terri refused to accept that she was powerless when faced with being forced to send her children to a failing public school system. Terri, an excellent student herself with a special penchant for English and grammar, not only thrived in high school and college but also has continued as an adult to seek out new challenges, from flying to book writing. Terri diligently worked with her husband to develop the foundation of her children's formal studies and undertake the task of administering each child's personal growth and education. Before committing herself to being a home educator, Terri's work outside the home was in the medical industry as an emergency room medical transcriptionist and as a medical assistant performing autopsies. She enjoys continuing her adventures with her high school sweetheart and husband of thirty-eight years, as well as spending time with her children and grandchildren.